Child Growth and Development 10/11
Seventeenth Edition

EDITORS

Ellen N. Junn
California State University, Fresno

Ellen Junn is a professor of psychology and associate provost at California State University, Fresno. She received her BS with distinction in psychology and with high honors from the University of Michigan and her MA and PhD in cognitive and developmental psychology from Princeton University. Dr. Junn's areas of research include college teaching effectiveness, educational equity, faculty development, and public policy as it affects children and families.

Chris J. Boyatzis
Bucknell University

Chris Boyatzis is a professor of psychology at Bucknell University. He received a BA with distinction in psychology from Boston University and his MA and PhD in developmental psychology from Brandeis University. His primary research focus is religion and spiritual development across the lifespan, but especially during childhood, adolescence, and the college years. He is on the editorial boards of several psychology journals.

The McGraw·Hill Companies

Connect
Learn
Succeed™

ANNUAL EDITIONS: CHILD GROWTH AND DEVELOPMENT, SEVENTEENTH EDITION

1 2 3 4 5 6 7 8 9 0 QWD/QWD 0 9

ISBN 978–0–07–812784–7
MHID 0–07–812784–X
ISSN 1075–5217

Managing Editor: *Larry Loeppke*
Senior Managing Editor: *Faye Schilling*
Developmental Editor: *David Welsh*
Editorial Coordinator: *Mary Foust*
Editorial Assistant: *Cindy Hedley*
Production Service Assistant: *Rita Hingtgen*
Permissions Coordinator: *DeAnna Dausener*
Senior Marketing Manager: *Julie Keck*
Marketing Communications Specialist: *Mary Klein*
Marketing Coordinator: *Alice Link*
Project Manager: *Joyce Watters*
Design Specialist: *Tara McDermott*
Senior Production Supervisor: *Laura Fuller*
Cover Graphics: *Kristine Jubeck*

Compositor: Laserwords Private Limited
Cover Image: © Brand X Pictures/Punchstock/RF (inset); © Lars Niki (background)

Library in Congress Cataloging-in-Publication Data
Main entry under title: Annual Editions: Child Growth and Development. 2010/2011.
  1. Child Growth and Development—Periodicals. I. Junn, Ellen N., *comp*. II. Title: Child Growth
and Development.
658'.05

www.mhhe.com

Editors/Academic Advisory Board

Members of the Academic Advisory Board are instrumental in the final selection of articles for each edition of ANNUAL EDITIONS. Their review of articles for content, level, and appropriateness provides critical direction to the editors and staff. We think that you will find their careful consideration well reflected in this volume.

ANNUAL EDITIONS: Child Growth and Development 10/11
17th Edition

EDITORS

Ellen N. Junn
California State University, Fresno

Chris J. Boyatzis
Bucknell University

ACADEMIC ADVISORY BOARD MEMBERS

Preface

In publishing ANNUAL EDITIONS we recognize the enormous role played by the magazines, newspapers, and journals of the public press in providing current, first-rate educational information in a broad spectrum of interest areas. Many of these articles are appropriate for students, researchers, and professionals seeking accurate, current material to help bridge the gap between principles and theories and the real world. These articles, however, become more useful for study when those of lasting value are carefully collected, organized, indexed, and reproduced in a low-cost format, which provides easy and permanent access when the material is needed. That is the role played by ANNUAL EDITIONS.

We are delighted to welcome you to this seventeenth volume of *Annual Editions: Child Growth and Development 10/11.* The amazing sequence of events of prenatal development that lead to the birth of a baby is an awe-inspiring process. Perhaps more intriguing is the question of what the future may hold for this newly arrived baby. For instance, will this child become a doctor, a lawyer, an artist, a beggar, or a thief? Although philosophers and prominent thinkers such as Charles Darwin and Sigmund Freud have long speculated about the importance of infancy on subsequent development, not until the 1960s did the scientific study of infants and young children flourish. Since then, research and theory in infancy and childhood have exploded, resulting in a wealth of new knowledge about child development.

Past accounts of infants and young children as passive, homogeneous organisms have been replaced with investigations aimed at studying infants and young children at a "microlevel"—as active individuals with many inborn competencies who are capable of shaping their own environment—as well as at a "macrolevel"—by considering the larger context surrounding the child. In short, children are not "blank slates," and development does not take place in a vacuum; children arrive with many skills and grow up in a complex web of social, historical, political, economic, and cultural spheres.

As was the case for previous editions, we hope to achieve at least four major goals with this volume. First, we hope to present you with the latest research and thinking to help you better appreciate the complex interactions that characterize human development in infancy and childhood. Second, in light of the feedback we received on previous editions, we have placed greater emphasis on important contemporary issues and challenges, exploring topics such as understanding development in the context of current societal and cultural influences. Third, attention is given to articles that also discuss effective, practical applications. Finally, we hope that this anthology will serve as a catalyst to help students become more effective future professionals and parents.

To achieve these objectives, we carefully selected articles from a variety of sources, including scholarly research journals and texts as well as semi-professional journals and popular publications. Every selection was scrutinized for readability, interest level, relevance, and currency. In addition, we listened to the valuable input and advice from members of our board, consisting of faculty from a range of institutions of higher education, including community and liberal arts colleges as well as research and teaching universities. We are most grateful to the advisory board as well as to the excellent editorial staff of McGraw-Hill/Contemporary Learning Series.

Annual Editions: Child Growth and Development is organized into five major units. Unit 1 includes articles regarding some exciting advances in fertility technology and premature babies. Unit 2 presents information regarding brain development, perception, memory, and language in infants and young children, as well as information on schooling. Unit 3 focuses on social and emotional development, including peers, gender socialization and play, aggression, and bullying, as well as issues of institutional deprivation, antisocial behavior, and resiliency. Unit 4 is devoted to parenting and family issues such as discipline, effects of divorce, sibling interactions, adoption, and gay and lesbian parents. Finally, Unit 5 focuses on larger cultural and societal influences such as media and marketing, and on special challenges (e.g., obesity, autism, and abhorrent conditions such as child sex exploitation and trafficking).

Instructors for large lecture courses may wish to adopt this anthology as a supplement to a basic text, whereas instructors for smaller sections might also find the readings effective for promoting student presentations or for stimulating discussions and applications. Whatever format is utilized, it is our hope that the instructor and the students will find the readings interesting, illuminating, and provocative.

As the title indicates, *Annual Editions: Child Growth and Development* is by definition a volume that undergoes continual review and revision. Thus, we welcome and encourage your comments and suggestions for future editions of this volume. Simply fill out and return the *article rating form* found at the end of this book. Best wishes, and we look forward to hearing from you!

Ellen N. Junn
Editor

Chris J. Boyatzis
Editor

Contents

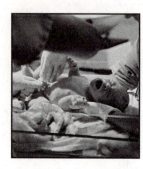

UNIT 1
Conception to Birth

UNIT 2
Cognition, Language, and Learning

The concepts in bold italics are developed in the article. For further expansion, please refer to the Topic Guide.

UNIT 3
Social and Emotional Development

The concepts in bold italics are developed in the article. For further expansion, please refer to the Topic Guide.

UNIT 4
Parenting and Family Issues

The concepts in bold italics are developed in the article. For further expansion, please refer to the Topic Guide.

UNIT 5
Cultural and Societal Influences

The concepts in bold italics are developed in the article. For further expansion, please refer to the Topic Guide.

The concepts in bold italics are developed in the article. For further expansion, please refer to the Topic Guide.

The concepts in bold italics are developed in the article. For further expansion, please refer to the Topic Guide.

Correlation Guide

The *Annual Editions* series provides students with convenient, inexpensive access to current, carefully selected articles from the public press. **Annual Editions: Child Growth and Development 10/11** is an easy-to-use reader that presents articles on important topics such as *fertility technology, prenatal development, brain development,* and many more. For more information on *Annual Editions* and other *McGraw-Hill Contemporary Learning Series* titles, visit www.mhhe.com/cls.

This convenient guide matches the units in **Annual Editions: Child Growth and Development 10/11** with the corresponding chapters in two of our best-selling McGraw-Hill Child Development textbooks by Santrock.

Annual Editions: Child Growth and Development 10/11	Children, 11/e by Santrock	Child Development: An Introduction, 12/e by Santrock
Unit 1: Conception to Birth	**Chapter 2:** Biological Beginnings **Chapter 4:** Birth	**Chapter 2:** Biological Beginnings **Chapter 3:** Prenatal Development and Birth
Unit 2: Cognition, Language, and Learning	**Chapter 6:** Cognitive Development in Infancy **Chapter 9:** Cognitive Development in Early Childhood **Chapter 12:** Cognitive Development in Middle and Late Childhood **Chapter 15:** Cognitive Development in Adolescence	**Chapter 6:** Cognitive Developmental Approaches **Chapter 7:** Information Processing **Chapter 8:** Intelligence **Chapter 9:** Language Development
Unit 3: Social and Emotional Development	**Chapter 7:** Socioemotional Development in Infancy **Chapter 10:** Socioemotional Development in Early Childhood **Chapter 13:** Socioemotional Development in Middle and Late Childhood **Chapter 16:** Socioemotional Development in Adolescence	**Chapter 10:** Emotional Development **Chapter 11:** The Self and Identity **Chapter 12:** Gender **Chapter 13:** Moral Development
Unit 4: Parenting and Family Issues	**Chapter 3:** Prenatal Development **Chapter 7:** Socioemotional Development in Infancy **Chapter 10:** Socioemotional Development in Early Childhood **Chapter 13:** Socioemotional Development in Middle and Late Childhood **Chapter 16:** Socioemotional Development in Adolescence	**Chapter 10:** Emotional Development **Chapter 13:** Moral Development **Chapter 14:** Families
Unit 5: Cultural and Societal Influences	**Chapter 4:** Birth **Chapter 6:** Cognitive Development in Infancy **Chapter 8:** Physical Development in Early Childhood **Chapter 9:** Cognitive Development in Early Childhood **Chapter 10:** Socioemotional Development in Early Childhood **Chapter 11:** Physical Development in Middle and Late Childhood **Chapter 12:** Cognitive Development in Middle and Late Childhood **Chapter 13:** Socioemotional Development in Middle and Late Childhood **Chapter 14:** Physical Development in Adolescence **Chapter 15:** Cognitive Development in Adolescence **Chapter 16:** Socioemotional Development in Adolescence	**Chapter 9:** Language Development **Chapter 11:** The Self and Identity **Chapter 13:** Moral Development **Chapter 15:** Peers **Chapter 16:** Schools and Achievement **Chapter 17:** Culture and Diversity

Topic Guide

This topic guide suggests how the selections in this book relate to the subjects covered in your course. You may want to use the topics listed on these pages to search the Web more easily.

On the following pages a number of websites have been gathered specifically for this book. They are arranged to reflect the units of this Annual Editions reader. You can link to these sites by going to *http://www.mhcls.com*.

All the articles that relate to each topic are listed below the bold-faced term.

Aggression
18. Girls Just Want to Be Mean
19. The Role of Neurobiological Deficits in Childhood Antisocial Behavior

Attachment
5. New Advances in Understanding Sensitive Periods in Brain Development
12. A Neurobiological Perspective on Early Human Deprivation
20. Children of Lesbian and Gay Parents
21. Evidence of Infants' Internal Working Models of Attachment

Autism
33. Three Reasons Not to Believe in an Autism Epidemic

Birth and birth defects
1. New Calculator Factors Chances for Very Premature Infants
2. Success at Last
22. Children of Alcoholics

Brain development
5. New Advances in Understanding Sensitive Periods in Brain Development
12. A Neurobiological Perspective on Early Human Deprivation
19. The Role of Neurobiological Deficits in Childhood Antisocial Behavior

Child abuse
12. A Neurobiological Perspective on Early Human Deprivation
27. Trials for Parents Who Chose Faith Over Medicine
32. The Epidemic That Wasn't

Classroom management
11. When Should a Kid Start Kindergarten?
31. How to Win the Weight Battle

Cognitive development
3. Infants' Differential Processing of Female and Male Faces
4. The Other-Race Effect Develops during Infancy
5. New Advances in Understanding Sensitive Periods in Brain Development
6. Contributions of Neuroscience to Our Understanding of Cognitive Development
8. Language and Children's Understanding of Mental States
9. Children's Biased Evaluations of Lucky versus Unlucky People and Their Social Groups
10. Future Thinking in Young Children
15. Children's Social and Moral Reasoning about Exclusion
21. Evidence of Infants' Internal Working Models of Attachment
24. Adoption Is a Successful Natural Intervention Enhancing Adopted Children's IQ and School Performance
25. The Case against Breast-Feeding
35. What Causes Specific Language Impairment in Children?

Cross-cultural issues
4. The Other-Race Effect Develops during Infancy
9. Children's Biased Evaluations of Lucky versus Unlucky People and Their Social Groups
24. Adoption Is a Successful Natural Intervention Enhancing Adopted Children's IQ and School Performance

Culture
7. It's Fun, but Does It Make You Smarter?
20. Children of Lesbian and Gay Parents
22. Children of Alcoholics
25. The Case against Breast-Feeding
26. Goodbye to Girlhood
31. How to Win the Weight Battle
34. Getting Back to the Great Outdoors

Development
1. New Calculator Factors Chances for Very Premature Infants
2. Success at Last
5. New Advances in Understanding Sensitive Periods in Brain Development
11. When Should a Kid Start Kindergarten?
15. Children's Social and Moral Reasoning about Exclusion
20. Children of Lesbian and Gay Parents
21. Evidence of Infants' Internal Working Models of Attachment
24. Adoption Is a Successful Natural Intervention Enhancing Adopted Children's IQ and School Performance

Developmental disabilities
12. A Neurobiological Perspective on Early Human Deprivation
34. Getting Back to the Great Outdoors
35. What Causes Specific Language Impairment in Children?

Discipline
23. Within-Family Differences in Parent–Child Relations across the Life Course

Drug use/abuse
22. Children of Alcoholics
32. The Epidemic That Wasn't

Economic issues
9. Children's Biased Evaluations of Lucky versus Unlucky People and Their Social Groups
24. Adoption Is a Successful Natural Intervention Enhancing Adopted Children's IQ and School Performance

Education
7. It's Fun, but Does It Make You Smarter?
11. When Should a Kid Start Kindergarten?
22. Children of Alcoholics
24. Adoption Is a Successful Natural Intervention Enhancing Adopted Children's IQ and School Performance
31. How to Win the Weight Battle
34. Getting Back to the Great Outdoors

Internet References

The following Internet sites have been selected to support the articles found in this reader. These sites were available at the time of publication. However, because websites often change their structure and content, the information listed may no longer be available. We invite you to visit *http://www.mhcls.com* for easy access to these sites.

Annual Editions: Child Growth and Development 10/11

General Sources

American Academy of Pediatrics
http://www.aap.org

This organization provides data for optimal physical, mental, and social health for all children.

CYFERNet
http://www.cyfernet.mes.umn.edu

The Children, Youth, and Families Education Research Network is sponsored by the Cooperative Extension Service and USDA's Cooperative State Research Education and Extension Service. This site provides practical research-based information in areas including health, child care, family strengths, science, and technology.

KidsHealth
http://kidshealth.org

This site was developed to help parents find reliable children's health information. Enter the Parents site to find such topics as General Health, Nutrition and Fitness, First Aid and Safety, Growth and Development, Positive Parenting, and more.

National Institute of Child Health and Human Development
http://www.nichd.nih.gov

The NICHD conducts and supports research on the reproductive, neurobiological, developmental, and behavioral processes that determine and maintain the health of children, adults, families, and populations.

UNIT 1: Conception to Birth

Babyworld
http://www.babyworld.com

Extensive information on caring for infants can be found at this site. There are also links to numerous other related sites.

Children's Nutrition Research Center (CNRC)
http://www.bcm.tmc.edu/cnrc/

CNRC, one of six USDA/ARS (Agricultural Research Service) facilities, is dedicated to defining the nutrient needs of healthy children, from conception through adolescence, and pregnant and nursing mothers. The *Nutrition and Your Child* newsletter is of general interest and can be accessed from this site.

Zero to Three: National Center for Infants, Toddlers, and Families
http://www.zerotothree.org

This national organization is dedicated solely to infants, toddlers, and their families. It is headed by recognized experts in the field and provides technical assistance to communities, states, and the federal government. The site provides information that the organization gathers and disseminates through its publications.

UNIT 2: Cognition, Language, and Learning

Educational Resources Information Center (ERIC)
http://www.ed.gov/about/pubs/intro/pubdb.html

This website is sponsored by the U.S. Department of Education and will lead to numerous documents related to elementary and early childhood education, as well as other curriculum topics and issues.

Parent's Action for Children
http://store.parentsactionstore.org/prostores/servlet/StoreFront

Information regarding early childhood development is provided on the video series, *I Am Your Child*, that's available on this site. Resources for parents and caregivers are available.

National Association for the Education of Young Children (NAEYC)
http://www.naeyc.org

The National Association for the Education of Young Children provides a useful link from its home page to a site that provides resources for "Parents."

Project Zero
http://pzweb.harvard.edu

Harvard Project Zero, a research group at the Harvard Graduate School of Education, has investigated the development of learning processes in children and adults for 30 years. Today, Project Zero is building on this research to help create communities of reflective, independent learners, to enhance deep understanding within disciplines, and to promote critical and creative thinking. Project Zero's mission is to understand and enhance learning, thinking, and creativity in the arts and other disciplines for individuals and institutions.

Vandergrift's Children's Literature Page
http://www.scils.rutgers.edu/special/kay/sharelit.html

This site provides information about children's literature and links to a variety of resources related to literacy for children.

UNIT 3: Social and Emotional Development

Max Planck Institute for Psychological Research
http://www.mpg.de/english/institutesProjectsFacilities/instituteChoice/psychologische_forschung/

Results from several behavioral and cognitive development research projects are available on this site.

National Child Care Information Center (NCCIC)
http://www.nccic.org

Information about a variety of topics related to child care and development is available on this site. Links to the *Child Care Bulletin*, which can be read online, and to the ERIC database of online and library-based resources are available.

Internet References

Serendip
http://serendip.brynmawr.edu/serendip/

Organized into five subject areas (brain and behavior, complex systems, genes and behavior, science and culture, and science education), Serendip contains interactive exhibits, articles, links to other resources, and a forum area for comments and discussion.

UNIT 4: Parenting and Family Issues

The National Association for Child Development (NACD)
http://www.nacd.org

This international organization is dedicated to helping children and adults reach their full potential. Its home page presents links to various programs, research, and resources in topics related to the family and society.

National Council on Family Relations
http://www.ncfr.com

This NCFR home page will lead you to articles, research, and a lot of other resources on important issues in family relations, such as stepfamilies, couples, and divorce.

Parenting and Families
http://www.cyfc.umn.edu

The University of Minnesota's Children, Youth, and Family Consortium site will lead you to many organizations and other resources related to divorce, single parenting, and stepfamilies, as well as information about other topics of interest in the study of children's development and the family.

Parentsplace.com: Single Parenting
http://www.parentsplace.com/family/archive/0,10693,239458,00.html

This resource focuses on issues concerning single parents and their children. Although the articles range from parenting children from infancy through adolescence, most of the articles deal with middle childhood.

National Stepfamily Resource Center
http://www.stepfam.org

This website is dedicated to educating and supporting stepfamilies and to creating a positive family image.

UNIT 5: Cultural and Societal Influences

Association to Benefit Children (ABC)
http://www.a-b-c.org

ABC presents a network of programs that includes child advocacy, education for disabled children, care for HIV-positive children, employment, housing, foster care, and day care.

Children's Defense Fund
http://www.childrensdefense.org/

CDF is a national proponent and advocate of policies and programs that safeguard children's needs in the areas of amelioration of poverty, protection from abuse and neglect, and increased access to health care and quality education.

Children Now
http://www.childrennow.org

Children Now uses research and mass communications to make the well-being of children a top priority across the nation. Current articles include information on the influence of media on children, working families, and health.

Council for Exceptional Children
http://www.cec.sped.org

This is the home page for the Council for Exceptional Children, a large professional organization that is dedicated to improving education for children with exceptionalities, students with disabilities, and/or the gifted child. It leads to the ERIC Clearinghouse on disabilities and gifted education and the National Clearinghouse for Professions in Special Education.

Prevent Child Abuse America
http://www.preventchildabuse.org

Dedicated to their child abuse prevention efforts, PCAA's site provides fact sheets and reports that include statistics, a public opinion poll, a 50-state survey, and other resource materials.

UNIT 1

Conception to Birth

Unit Selections

1. **New Calculator Factors Chances for Very Premature Infants,** Denise Grady
2. **Success at Last,** Deborah Kotz

Key Points to Consider

- New research points to multiple factors such as diet, exercise, obesity, alcohol and drug use, and stress as having significant effects on women, as well as men, in influencing fertility and the likelihood of conception. If you and your spouse wanted to have a baby, what lifestyle adjustments in diet, exercise, and other areas would you be willing to make in order to try and conceive? Explain. What if your spouse did not want to make these adjustments; how would you deal with their resistance to making some of these lifestyle changes?

- The data regarding very premature babies (less than 2.2 pounds and born as early as 22 weeks) show that the overwhelming number of these babies will die and of those few who do survive, virtually all will have neurological impairments, with half of the impairments being severe. Given these sobering odds, not to mention the significant medical costs of intensive care even after a hospital discharge, if you were parents of a very premature baby, would you still advocate for utilizing any and all medical interventions possible? Why or why not?

Student Website
www.mhcls.com

Internet References

Babyworld
  http://www.babyworld.com
Children's Nutrition Research Center (CNRC)
  http://www.bcm.tmc.edu/cnrc/
Zero to Three: National Center for Infants, Toddlers, and Families
  http://www.zerotothree.org

Gone are the carefree ideas of starting a family as exemplified by the nursery rhyme, *"First comes love. Then comes marriage. Then comes baby in a baby carriage,"* With more and more women and men delaying marriage and childbirth to pursue education, forge professional careers, or enjoy the single life, trying to conceive a child later in life is proving more challenging. Today, however, couples are well aware of the complexities of the biology of reproduction and now have a host of options available to them.

For example, recent research points to the importance of considering many other factors such as body weight, diet, exercise, alcohol and drug use, and stress as important factors determining both female and male fertility. "Success at Last" discusses some of these factors and provides important advice for both men and women who hope to conceive a child and become future parents.

Similarly, our scientific understanding of conception and prenatal development has expanded tremendously in the last several decades. For example, we are now witnesses to dramatic changes in reproductive technologies and surgical options. Advances in this new "prenatal science" include fertility treatments for couples who have difficulty conceiving and a host of prenatal diagnostic tests, such as amniocentesis and alpha-fetoprotein testing, which assess the well-being of the fetus as well as detect genetic or chromosomal problems, not to mention in utero surgery.

In spite of the recent explosion of knowledge about prenatal development, knowledge about how to sustain and promote development in fetuses who are born prematurely still lags behind. Babies born prematurely or very prematurely face crushing challenges once outside of the protection and nurturance of

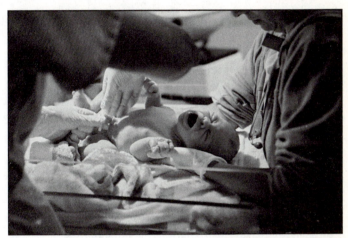

© Punchstock/BananaStock

the mother's womb. The author of the article, "New Calculator Factors Chances for Very Premature Infants" discusses a new method of statistically assessing the chances of a very premature baby's survival and likelihood of disabilities now available online with the National Institute of Child Health and Human Development. Since the vast majority of very premature babies will die and of those who do survive, roughly half will sustain permanent and debilitating disabilities necessitating significant hospital and ongoing future medical costs that continue well beyond the intensive care provided by hospitals. This new online calculator helps physicians and parents understand the odds when making difficult life decisions regarding their premature baby.

New Calculator Factors Chances for Very Premature Infants

DENISE GRADY

Researchers are reporting that they have developed a new way to help doctors and parents make some of the most agonizing decisions in medicine, about how much treatment to give tiny, extremely premature infants.

These are infants at the edge of viability, weighing less than 2.2 pounds and born after 22 to 25 weeks of pregnancy, far ahead of the normal 40 weeks. About 40,000 babies a year are born at this very early stage in the United States.

The new method uses an online calculator developed for such cases factoring in traits like birth weight and sex and generating statistics on chances of the baby's survival and the likelihood of disabilities (www.nichd.nih.gov/neonatalestimates).

The statistics are not a personal prediction. They estimate risk based on data from similar infants in a large study being published on Thursday in *The New England Journal of Medicine.*

Certain factors gave babies an advantage. At any given gestational age, they were more likely to survive and escape serious disability if they weighed more than others, if they were singletons rather than twins or multiples or if their mothers had been given steroids before birth to help the fetal lungs to mature.

Girls also fared better than boys of the same age, a factor doctors have known a long time without being able to explain.

Any of those factors was about as good as being a week older, which makes an enormous difference in development from 22 to 25 weeks' pregnancy, the researchers said. The finding means that a girl at 23 weeks could be as strong as a boy at 24.

"If you could take what the girls have and give it to the boys, we'd be one step ahead of the game," said Dr. Rosemary D. Higgins, an author of the study and a program scientist at the Neonatal Research Network of the National Institute of Child Health and Human Development.

Although some extremely premature infants do well, many die, sometimes after weeks or months of painful invasive procedures in the intensive care unit. Survivors often suffer brain damage, behavior problems, vision and hearing loss and other disabilities.

Outcomes are nearly impossible to predict at birth. Doctors and parents struggle to decide when aggressive treatment seems reasonable—and when death or severe disability seems so likely, even with treatment, that it would be kinder to avoid painful procedures and provide just "comfort care," letting nature take its course and letting the child die.

These decisions, made every day in hospitals around the country, are "heart wrenching and passionate," Dr. Higgins said. "No one ever thinks they're going to be in this situation, and it's difficult, for families and also for physicians."

Dr. Higgins said the study and the calculator were part of an effort to give doctors and parents more solid evidence to make decisions. She said people might be misled by occasional reports of tiny "miracle babies" who beat the odds and wrongly imagined high rates of survival and good health.

Dr. Higgins said she had no idea what overall effect the study and calculator might have on medical practice or whether they would lead to more or less treatment of extremely premature infants. Two families in the exact same situation could easily make opposite decisions about whether to pursue treatment.

Currently, decisions about using respirators, intravenous feeding and other forms of intensive care are mostly based on estimates of a baby's gestational age—how far along the pregnancy was. Intensive care is often given to infants born in the 25th week, but not the 22nd. The hardest judgment calls are for babies in the 23rd and 24th weeks.

Plugging numbers into the calculator shows that two infants with the same gestational age, the usual criterion to decide treatment, can have quite different odds of survival and disability.

For instance, a 24-week-old two-pound male twin whose mother did not receive steroids has survival odds of 69 percent and a 50 percent chance of having a severe impairment. A female twin the same age and weight has survival odds of 86 percent and a 23 percent chance of severe impairment.

In theory, at least, the calculator would seem to favor treating girls, because, all else being equal, their odds for survival are better.

The study included 4,446 infants born at 22 to 25 weeks at 19 hospitals in the Neonatal Research Network; 744, generally the smallest and most premature, did not receive intensive care, and all died. The babies were assessed at birth, and the survivors were examined again shortly before turning 2.

Over all, half the infants died, half the survivors had neurological impairments, and half the impairments were severe.

Many survivors spent months in the hospital, at a typical cost of $3,400 a day. The researchers estimated that if all babies born at 22 to 23 weeks received intensive care, for every 100 infants treated there would be 1,749 extra hospital days and zero to nine additional survivors, with zero to three having no impairment.

Dr. Eric C. Eichenwald, medical director of the newborn center at Texas Children's Hospital in Houston, said that the study was important and that its most striking finding was how large the benefits of the various factors could be.

Dr. Eichenwald said the calculator was "a way in which we can provide more accurate information to the process of counseling parents as to what the burdens of intensive care might be." Dr. Nehal A. Parikh, another author of the study, from the University of Texas Medical School at Houston, said he thought the statistics would help doctors in advising families.

"We lay out the facts, rather than our own opinions," Dr. Parikh said, "because we're not the ones taking these babies home."

Success at Last

Deborah Kotz

Tracy Ryan had given up hope of having a second child. Two years of trying to conceive, including three failed artificial inseminations, had finally culminated in a successful in vitro fertilization—and 2-year-old Christopher. But further attempts at in vitro had left Ryan, 35, disappointed and exhausted. Desperate to feel better, the stay-at-home mom from Fair Haven, N.J., decided to try acupuncture, kick her six-can-a-day Diet Pepsi habit, and eat more fish, fruits, and vegetables. Eight weeks later and slimmer by 7 pounds, Ryan was shocked to discover that she was pregnant. "I was literally shaking when I saw the pregnancy test," she says. "My husband made me buy a different brand to verify it."

Ryan can't know whether to thank coincidence or her lifestyle changes for 9-month-old Brendan. But a growing body of evidence suggests that controllable factors (and not just a delay in childbearing) may be a reason 1 in 8 couples can't conceive. Success depends on the delicately timed release of four reproductive hormones, and all sorts of factors—too little iron in the blood, too much or too little body fat, too much exercise—can throw the sequence out of whack. "We're finding that everything matters—and moderation in terms of stress, body weight, diet, and physical activity is what's important," says Joel Evans, assistant clinical professor of obstetrics, gynecology, and women's health at the Albert Einstein College of Medicine and author of *The Whole Pregnancy Handbook.*

No one is talking about magic bullets. Some women will do everything right and still get the maddening diagnosis of "unexplained infertility." But institutions as well regarded as Duke University and Beth Israel Medical Center in New York are so convinced of the possibilities that they've recently opened "holistic fertility care" centers that offer women trying to conceive acupuncture, nutrition counseling, and relaxation classes. And a growing number of IVF clinics now host on-site yoga classes. At the very least, making healthful changes in the hope of improving your odds of a baby is bound to pay off in other ways.

Get ready. Sometimes, the body's refusal to get pregnant can be a sign of its wisdom, says Tracy Gaudet, an obstetrician-gynecologist and executive director of Duke Integrative Medicine. Being overweight, for instance, puts a woman at risk of such pregnancy complications as high blood pressure, diabetes, and an abnormally large baby. So it may be no accident that excess estrogen produced by body fat interferes with ovulation.

The body also may be saying "whoa" when a woman carries too little fat to sustain a growing baby: In underweight women, the pituitary gland releases less of the ovulation hormones FSH and LH.

Research from Harvard Medical School suggests that being at either end of the weight spectrum accounts for nearly 40 percent of failures to ovulate. Gaudet advises aiming for a body fat percentage in the range of 20 to 25 percent and a body mass index—a measure relating weight to height—of 20 to 25. That would equal about 117 to 145 pounds for someone 5 feet, 4 inches tall.

It's smart to quit smoking well before trying to get pregnant, too. A number of studies have shown that tobacco use can stretch the time it takes to conceive by a year or more, possibly because toxins in cigarette smoke accelerate the aging of a woman's eggs and damage the fallopian tubes. In fact, a 2006 study by Columbia University researchers found that women who smoked 14 cigarettes a day entered menopause an average of three years earlier than those who never smoked.

If you haven't ditched trans fats for other reasons already, this is a good time. A recent finding from the Harvard Nurses Health Study suggests that eating as little as 4.5 grams per day—the amount in one glazed Krispy Kreme cruller—could disrupt ovulation. Study author Jorge Chavarro, a research fellow in the department of nutrition at Harvard School of Public Health, notes that the results need to be replicated before firm conclusions can be drawn but speculates that trans fats could indirectly lead to a rise in testosterone, which suppresses the function of the ovaries. "Check for the trans fat content on food labels, and avoid any foods with partially hydrogenated oils in the ingredients list," he advises. His research group also found a link between low levels of dietary iron and a failure to ovulate, possibly because iron is important for the maturation of the egg.

There isn't one ideal preconception diet, but emphasizing nonprocessed foods like whole grains, fruits, and vegetables will steer you away from trans fats. It's also wise to limit your intake of large fish such as tuna and swordfish, since the mercury they contain has been shown in animal studies to affect fertility. In terms of alcohol consumption, the consensus is that a glass of wine on occasion is probably fine. But how much alcohol is safe isn't known.

On the flip side, it's possible to be too fit. Women who work out intensely can have trouble getting pregnant, possibly because reproductive hormones are suppressed when the body interprets excessive calorie burning or physical stress as danger. A study published last fall in the journal *Obstetrics & Gynecology* found that those who regularly exercised four or more hours per week were 40 percent less likely to conceive after their first IVF treatment than sedentary women. "Walking is fine, but spinning classes are out," says Alice Domar, an assistant professor of obstetrics, gynecology, and reproductive biology at Harvard Medical School and author of *Conquering Infertility.* "I generally recommend that my patients keep their heart rate below 110."

Couples who are actively trying to conceive need to understand some biology: Several hours before ovulation, the pituitary gland normally sends out a surge of LH, which causes the ovary's follicle to release an egg. But say you have a fender bender before the surge happens or suddenly discover you need a $10,000 roof repair. Such stresses can signal the pituitary gland that the body is in trouble, which slows the release of LH. If you have perfectionist tendencies, a single tear-your-hair-out day could be enough to disrupt ovulation that month, says infertility researcher Sarah Berga, a professor of obstetrics and gynecology at Emory University School of Medicine. Even if ovulation occurs, a shortage of LH could mean a shortage of progesterone, which is necessary to nourish and sustain a fertilized egg.

Skipping meals or taking a long run when you're feeling frantic might make matters worse. In a study of monkeys published last month, Berga and her colleagues created mild stress for one group by moving the monkeys to a new cage and found that 12 percent developed abnormal menstrual cycles. In the second group, which was moved plus given less food and a daily one-hour session on a treadmill, 70 percent experienced irregular menstruation.

Overcoming the level of stress associated with chronic infertility may require more formal interventions. On their first visit, about 40 percent of women seeking infertility treatments exhibit the same range and severity of symptoms—irritability, difficulty concentrating, sleep disturbances—as people diagnosed with an anxiety disorder, says Harvard's Domar. She developed a 10-week workshop for infertile women now in use around the country that includes group therapy, nutrition counseling, and relaxation techniques such as deep breathing, meditation, and yoga. In two studies, Domar and her colleagues found that 55 percent of women who took the workshop while getting fertility treatment wound up giving birth to a healthy baby compared with 20 percent of women who had treatment alone. "The women who took the class were also less anxious and depressed and had a much easier time coping with the medical procedures," Domar says.

Heidi Fallon, 36, of Ayer, Mass., found this to be true when she took Domar's workshop at Boston IVF 15 months ago after going through three unsuccessful rounds of treatment and a miscarriage. The class taught Fallon focused breathing techniques that she used while stuck in rush-hour traffic and provided comforting connections with other infertile women. "They knew exactly what I was going through—how hard it was when a friend or relative got pregnant," she says. An IVF cycle during the 10-week session produced Fallon's 9-month-old triplets.

For some infertile couples, a phone call to a travel agent seems to do the job. "My friends raise their eyebrows whenever I take a vacation," says Meredith Collins, 35, of Portsmouth, R.I. After three failed tries at artificial insemination, Collins took a much-needed break from her busy paint-your-own-pottery store and infertility treatments and headed to a beach in the Dominican Republic, where she promptly became pregnant with her now 19-month-old son. Her 6-month-old son was also conceived naturally on a 2006 family getaway to a quiet bed-and-breakfast.

Since the point is a healthy baby, success at getting pregnant doesn't mean it's OK to relax back into old habits. About 10 to 15 percent of pregnancies end in miscarriage, and lifestyle factors linked to infertility are probably responsible for some of them. In a study published last year, Danish researchers found that smokers had a higher risk of miscarrying during the first few weeks of pregnancy than nonsmokers. Stress, caffeine, and alcohol might also be associated with miscarriages, though the data have been conflicting.

Longer term, evidence is mounting that a pregnant woman's lifestyle and diet can affect her baby well into adulthood. Children born to mothers battling depression or anxiety during pregnancy appear to be smaller and to weigh less as they grow, for example. The American College of Obstetricians and Gynecologists now recommends that clinically depressed women consider staying on their antidepressant medication while pregnant (with the exception of Paxil, which has been tied to birth defects). One recent study suggested that expectant mothers who eat more than three servings of fish a week deliver babies with higher IQs, while gaining too much weight during pregnancy seems to raise a child's risk of developing obesity or diabetes as an adult.

And too little vitamin D puts babies at risk of asthma, type 1 diabetes, and bone deformities, says Lisa Bodnar, an assistant professor of epidemiology at the University of Pittsburgh whose research shows that, even with prenatal vitamins, most pregnant women aren't getting enough. She recommends at least 1,000 international units of vitamin D a day; most prenatal supplements contain 400 IUs. Clearly, there's good reason to make choices that go beyond standard practice. But most are common sense.

UNIT 2
Cognition, Language, and Learning

Unit Selections

Key Points to Consider

- Recently, researchers have shown the importance of supporting early interactions and experiences during infancy and preschool to support brain development. How has this information changed or not changed your perceptions and interactions with babies as a result?

- Given that infants experience very limited visual stimuli in the womb, at what point in infancy might they exhibit preferences for human faces? Do you think babies might distinguish and/or prefer female vs. male faces and if so, when and why? What are infants' responses to faces of people of difference racial or ethnic groups?

- It seems that the pressure to raise bright, high-achieving kids continues to increase. Do you think exposing kids to computers and the Internet will make kids smarter? Suppose your child fails at a math task. As a parent, should you emphasize the importance of math ability or effort? Since much of what is on the Internet is text-based, how do you think this might improve children's reading and language skills?

- Do you speak another language other than English? If so, how fluent are you and when did you first learn a second language? Do you think it is a "sensitive period" when it is easier to learn a second language as a child or as an adult? Explain why.

- In years past, mothers-in-law often scolded new mothers for picking up a crying baby due to fears of raising spoiled children. Research shows, however, that infants not only thrive when touched, but it may be critical to the formation of attachment bonds as well as promoting physical and cognitive growth and reducing stress. Explain how you would use this information to parent your baby.

- When do children first understand other people's feelings and mental states or how to evaluate other people's abilities? Do you think parents and teachers help teach children to promote this awareness and assessment of others? Why do you think people like lucky rather than unlucky individuals? Do you think this bias makes it more difficult for people to help or take care of disadvantaged or unlucky people? Explain why and discuss some of the fundamental assumptions about lucky and unlucky people.

Student Website
www.mhcls.com

Internet References

Educational Resources Information Center (ERIC)
  http://www.ed.gov/about/pubs/intro/pubdb.html
Parent's Action for Children
  http://store.parentsactionstore.org/prostores/servlet/StoreFront
National Association for the Education of Young Children (NAEYC)
  http://www.naeyc.org

Project Zero
  http://pzweb.harvard.edu
Vandergrift's Children's Literature Page
  http://www.scils.rutgers.edu/special/kay/sharelit.html

We have come a long way from the days when the characterization of cognition of infants and young children included phrases like "tabula rasa" and "booming, buzzing confusion." Infants and young children are no longer viewed by researchers as blank slates, passively waiting to be filled up with knowledge. Today, experts in child development are calling for a reformulation of assumptions about children's cognitive abilities, as well as calling for reforms in the ways we teach children in our schools. Hence, the articles in the first subsection highlight some of the new knowledge of the cognitive abilities of infants and young children, while the second subsection focuses on schooling and learning.

Researchers today continue to discover that babies are developing an impressive array of early social, emotional, and cognitive skills during infancy. In "Infants Differential Processing of Female and Male Faces," and "The Other-Race Effect Develops during Infancy," the authors describe new findings showing that infants' and young children's earliest interactions and experiences are critical in helping them develop normal social-emotional milestones and other linguistic, perceptual, and cognitive skills. From this perspective, babies are not as passive as once thought, and parents and teachers can provide environments that nurture and support their babies' developing abilities.

Researchers describe the complex interplay between brain maturational development and external experience in determining the emergence of abilities such as language acquisition, neonate imitation, and factors related to stress reactivity in "New Advances in Understanding Sensitive Periods in Brain Development" and "Contributions of Neuroscience to Our Understanding of Cognitive Development." For example, nurturing touch during infancy has been shown to be a very important factor in promoting growth, reducing stress and reducing depression and other cognitive deficits later in life.

We learn from research in "Language and Children's Understanding of Mental States" that maternal conversation and language interventions play a key role in helping children develop a theory of mind or the ability to understand other people's points of view and emotional states. Children advance in their understanding of mental states—a critical ingredient for building appropriate social skills—when their parents and teachers engage in rich conversations with them about others who

© BananaStock/PunchStock

have varying points of view and different emotions. Similarly, researchers in "Children's Biased Evaluations of Lucky versus Unlucky People and Their Social Groups" show that young children like lucky rather than unlucky peers and therefore prefer to socialize with peers of the lucky child.

In "Future Thinking in Young Children" researcher Cristina Atance reviews data showing that preschoolers begin to develop concepts about the future that permit them to begin to mentally project to plan and act now in anticipation of future events. The data indicate that this ability to think and prepare for the future begins to develop and increase in efficiency by the ages of four and five years.

In "It's Fun, but Does it Make You Smarter?" the author discusses the merits and pitfalls of exposing children to computers and the internet as well as the dangers of over-focusing on intelligence and talent in children.

With increasing pressures for children to do well in school, parents are asking questions such as, "Should I hold my child back from kindergarten for a year?" The author of "When Should a Kid Start Kindergarten?" addresses this question head on.

Infants' Differential Processing of Female and Male Faces

Infants show an interesting asymmetry in face processing: They are more fluent in processing female faces than they are at processing male faces. We hypothesize that such processing asymmetry results from greater experience with female faces than with male faces early in development. Asymmetrical face processing may have long-lasting implications for development of face recognition, development of knowledge structures regarding females and males, and social-information processing. We encourage researchers to use both female and male faces in their face-perception research and to conduct separate analyses for female and male faces.

JENNIFER L. RAMSEY-RENNELS AND JUDITH H. LANGLOIS

Categorization is a fundamental information-processing capability that allows reliable recognition and response to novel examples of familiar category members. For example, if Ariana walks into an unfamiliar room containing a telephone, she knows she can use the phone to talk to someone even though she has never before seen this particular telephone. Categorization of objects enables people to allocate cognitive resources efficiently—Ariana will expend more energy in figuring out what to say on the phone than in determining how it works.

Because of the adaptive nature of categorization, it is not surprising that categorization abilities emerge early in infancy (e.g., Quinn, 2002). Such abilities facilitate infants' early and rapid learning about the many different objects in the world. But what about categorization of people? Like categorizing objects, categorizing people has important benefits. For example, categorizing age allows one to interact with infants and children in a developmentally appropriate manner. Categorizing gender allows one to determine if a person would be an appropriate mate. There are, however, problems related to categorization of people—these categories could become linked to positive and negative attributions that might not be accurate characterizations of a particular member of that group. Thus, one byproduct of this otherwise adaptive process of categorization is the formation of stereotypes (e.g., Bargh & Chartrand, 1999).

Our work has focused on infants and the early origins of stereotypes, particularly on how infants recognize, evaluate, and categorize the facial appearance of adults. Our research in this area has led us to conclude that there is a potentially important asymmetry in how infants process male and female faces. Most of our research successes involved infants' responses to female faces (e.g., Rubenstein, Kalakanis, & Langlois, 1999). Yet, our research failures were equally illuminating because they almost always involved infants' responses to male faces (see Ramsey, Langlois, & Marti, 2005, for an overview).

Asymmetries in Infant Processing of Faces

Two different types of studies illustrate the asymmetry we observed. First, as part of our research program to understand the cognitive mechanisms underlying infants' preferences for attractive faces, we examined infants' ability to abstract an averaged (summary) representation, or prototype, of sets of female or male faces. Abstracting a facial prototype from category examples is important because a prototype (a) can facilitate processing of new exemplar faces from that category; and (b) may guide interest toward faces, as infants visually prefer faces most similar to their prototype (Rubenstein et al., 1999). Although we found that infants formed prototypes of female faces (Rubenstein et al., 1999), we could not find evidence that they formed prototypes of male faces. This asymmetry suggests that infants' initial prototype or representation of faces may be more female-like than male-like (Ramsey et al., 2005).

A second type of study, in which infants view male and female faces when they are paired together, shows another asymmetry: Infants look longer at female faces than they do at male faces (Quinn, Yahr, Kuhn, Slater, & Pascalis, 2002). We posit that infants visually prefer female faces to male faces because female faces are more similar than male faces are to the infant's facial prototype. Interestingly, however, when infants view female faces only or male faces only, they spend more time looking at male faces than they do at female faces, particularly when the task is complex (Ramsey et al., 2005). Because female faces are not available to "compete" for infants' attention in studies presenting male faces, longer looking times may reflect infants' lack of expertise and lack of efficiency in processing male faces. Longer looking at male faces in the absence of female faces is particularly evident when the task requires recognition or categorical abstraction, perhaps because infants do not yet have a fully developed male face prototype to facilitate processing (Ramsey et al., 2005).

These asymmetries in our work and that of Quinn et al. (2002) prompted us to explore the infant face-perception literature further for asymmetries in other areas of face processing. We discovered that most studies use only female faces to evaluate infants' reactions to faces. The lack of male-face studies caused us to question whether conclusions about infants' face recognition, interest in faces, understanding of emotion, and development of social expectancies from the existing infant face-perception literature really generalized to all faces, male and female, as is typically assumed.

When we examined the few studies that included male stimulus faces, we found further evidence of differences in infants' processing of female and male faces. First, 3- to 4-month-olds have more difficulty discriminating among male faces and subsequently recognizing them than they do female faces (Quinn et al., 2002). Second, older infants are more skilled at categorizing female faces than they are at categorizing male faces: Whereas 10-month-olds easily recognize that a sex-ambiguous female face does not belong with a group of sex-typical female faces, they have more difficulty excluding a sex-ambiguous male face from a group of sex-typical male faces (data interpretation of Younger & Fearing, 1999, by Ramsey et al., 2005). In addition, there is a lag between when infants recognize that female voices are associated with female faces and when male voices are associated with male faces; infants reliably match female faces and voices at 9 months (Poulin-Dubois, Serbin, Kenyon, & Derbyshire, 1994) but do not reliably match male faces and voices until 18 months. Even at 18 months; infants are more accurate at matching female faces and voices than they are at matching male faces and voices (Poulin-Dubois, Serbin, & Derbyshire, 1998).

Thus, the infant perception literature shows that (a) infants have more difficulty processing male faces than female faces, (b) infants prefer female to male faces, and (c) differential processing of male and female faces is related to the fluency with which infants form categories of male versus female faces. Why?

The Role of Experience with Faces

Early visual experience with faces appears to be very important for specialized processing of upright relative to inverted faces and within-species face recognition (e.g., Nelson, 2001; Pascalis, de Haan, & Nelson, 2002). In most instances, infants have significantly more exposure to adult female faces than they have to adult male faces. For example, the primary caregiver is female for the majority of infants, and infants spend approximately 50% of their personal interactions with her during the first year. Also, parents of 2-, 5-, 8-, and 11-month-olds report twice as many interactions between their infant and female strangers than between their infant and male strangers during a typical week (Ramsey & Simmons, 2005). There are also qualitative differences in how adults interact with infants (e.g., females play more visual games than males), which may cause females to elicit more attention from infants during social interactions than males do (Ramsey et al., 2005). Therefore, we posit that infants' typical experience with female faces early in development facilitates expert processing (discrimination, recognition, and categorization) of female faces. Greater experience with female faces than with male faces should result in more fluent processing of female faces.

An alternate hypothesis is that experience with faces is not formative; rather, evolution has predisposed infants to attend to female faces because mothers were generally the primary caregivers. Research, however, shows that experience is important for face processing: Babies who have fathers as their primary caregivers show more interest in male faces than in female faces (Quinn et al., 2002). Moreover, 3-month-olds more easily recognize faces from the race with which they are most familiar than they recognize faces from a different race (Sangrigoli & de Schonen, 2004). Thus, it seems unlikely that experience is irrelevant. Rather, predominant experience with faces from a particular sex, race, species, orientation, etc. should result in more fluent processing of the commonly experienced faces.

Once infants become more expert at processing female faces than male faces, the asymmetry may cascade because ease of processing is linked to affective preferences (Winkielman & Cacioppo, 2001). Increased positive affect toward female faces increases the likelihood that infants will look at female faces, further skewing experience and expertise with female faces. Infants' lack of experience with male faces may be compounded by an additional complexity: Male faces are more variable and less perceptually similar than female faces (Ramsey et al., 2005). Measurements of male faces show greater deviation from the mean than measurements of female faces do. This greater deviation means male faces are less prototypical (i.e., less representative of their sex category on average) than female faces are. Thus, infants not only have less experience with male faces than with female faces, but their experience with male faces is less productive because categories with more variable members can be difficult for infants to learn (e.g., Quinn, 2002). Such impediments may cause developmental delays in the attainment of coherent prototype formation for male faces (Ramsey et al., 2005).

Much as how early language input causes specialized processing of the native language, abundant experience with certain faces (e.g., female) during infancy results in expert processing of those faces (Nelson, 2001). Indeed, 9-month-olds perform almost like adults in being better able to recognize human faces than monkey faces, whereas 6-month-olds perform equally well in their recognition of human and monkey faces (Pascalis et al., 2002). The similarities between 9-month-olds and adults in their poorer recognition of monkey faces, as compared to 6-month-olds, is likely due to their greater experience with and specialization in processing human faces over monkey faces.

Unlike infants' experience with the native language relative to other languages and with human faces relative to monkey faces, the disparity between infants' experience with female faces and their experience with male faces is not as large, making this a unique type of problem regarding discrepancies in experience. We suggest, therefore, that differences in early experience with faces can have qualitative, long-lasting impact on how male and female faces are processed, but that these processing disparities may be subtle.

Implications of Early Differential Processing

What might be the enduring implications of differential processing of female and male faces? The fluency or ease with which infants more expertly discriminate, recognize, and categorize female faces relative to male faces has the potential to contribute to later face-recognition abilities, knowledge acquisition of the sex categories, and social-information processing.

Early fluency in processing female faces during infancy should contribute to a later advantage in adults' recognition of female faces. Indeed, adult females are better at recognizing female faces than they are at recognizing male faces, and they perform better than males do at recognizing female faces (e.g., Lewin & Herlitz, 2002). Why should the advantage seen in both female and male infants' recognition of female faces be sustained only in female adults? An important developmental task for young children is to learn about their gender. Because preschoolers typically learn about their own gender before they learn about the other gender (Martin & Halverson, 1981), girls may maintain or enhance their processing of female faces whereas boys may "lose" some of their expertise in processing female faces as male faces begin to compete for their attention. Obviously this proposed developmental pathway requires investigation and there are other mediating variables, but in a legal system that places great reliance on eyewitness testimony, a clear understanding of why females may possess an advantage in recognizing female faces relative to male faces is needed (e.g., Lewin & Herlitz, 2002).

Fluent processing of female faces should allow infants to more easily structure the female face category than the male face category, which should enable infants and young children to more readily learn about females than males because it is less effortful to make associations to the female face category (e.g., Quinn, 2002). Lack of experience with male faces will make it difficult to attain conceptual knowledge about the male face category, suggesting that knowledge structures associated with females should emerge earlier and be more elaborate than those associated with males, at least early in development. Furthermore, the variability of the male face category should make it difficult to associate and organize the conceptual knowledge that is attained. These proposed differences in knowledge structures for females and males would suggest that linking, organizing, and retrieving information should occur with greater ease when processing social information about female targets, relative to male targets.

Future Directions

Infants' differential experience with female and male faces influences their discrimination, recognition, and categorization of faces, although more work is needed to understand the full extent and origins of those differences. We suggest that particular attention be paid to experience with faces and to when interactions with males increase during development. Examining when (or if) the visual preference for female faces over male faces subsides or reverses should provide insight into face-processing changes due to experience and will likely require testing older children and perhaps even adults. Because categorization is inherently linked to knowledge acquisition, it is also important to investigate how the category structure for female and male faces develops, evolves, and reorganizes over time, with attention to both perceptual and conceptual components of the categories.

Unlike other research assessing the role of experience when there is overwhelming exposure to the commonly experienced category (e.g., native language) and minimal experience with alternate categories (e.g., foreign languages), the difference between infants' experience with female and male faces is more subtle. Understanding how subtleties in early exposure subsequently impact later face processing could be informative for researchers interested in sensitive periods in development. One question concerns whether limited early exposure to male faces extends the window for expert processing of male faces to develop or if fluency of processing male faces never develops to the same level that it does for female faces. Testing older children and adults, who should have more experience with male faces, is necessary for addressing this issue, but methods assessing reaction time or psychophysiological responses may be necessary to capture subtle differences in fluency of processing female and male faces.

Regardless of the age group being studied, we urge face-perception researchers to use both female and male faces in their studies, to make a priori hypotheses about potential differences in processing, and to conduct separate analyses for female and male faces in order to carefully examine the nature of any disparities in processing female and male faces (quantitative or qualitative divergence). Because aspects of adult face processing have roots in infancy, we suggest that researchers check the developmental literature for clues when they cannot identify why face-processing discrepancies occur among adult participants.

References

Bargh, J.A., & Chartrand, T.L. (1999). The unbearable automaticity of being. *American Psychologist, 54,* 462–479.

Lewin, C., & Herlitz, A. (2002). Sex differences in face recognition—women's faces make the difference. *Brain & Cognition, 50,* 121–128.

Martin, C.L., & Halverson, C.F., Jr. (1981). A schematic processing model of sex-typing and stereotyping in children. *Child Development, 52,* 1119–1134.

Nelson, C.A. (2001). The development and neural bases of face recognition. *Infant & Child Development, 10,* 3–18.

Pascalis, O., de Haan, M., & Nelson, C.A. (2002). Is face processing species-specific during the first year of life? *Science, 296,* 1321–1323.

Poulin-Dubois, D., Serbin, L.A., & Derbyshire, A. (1998). Toddlers' intermodal and verbal knowledge about gender. *Merrill-Palmer Quarterly, 44,* 338–354.

Poulin-Dubois, D., Serbin, L.A., Kenyon, B., & Derbyshire, A. (1994). Infants' intermodal knowledge about gender. *Developmental Psychology, 30,* 436–442.

Quinn, P.C. (2002). Beyond prototypes: Asymmetries in infant categorization and what they teach us about the mechanisms guiding knowledge acquisition. In R. Kail & H. Reese (Eds.), *Advances in child development and behavior: Vol. 29* (pp. 161–193). San Diego: Academic Press.

Quinn, P.C., Yahr, J., Kuhn, A., Slater, A.M., & Pascalis, O. (2002). Representation of the gender of human faces by infants: A preference for female. *Perception, 31,* 1109–1121.

Ramsey, J.L., Langlois, J.H., & Marti, C.N. (2005). Infant categorization of faces: Ladies first. *Developmental Review, 25,* 212–246.

Ramsey, J.L., & Simmons, R.E. (2005). [Two, 5, 8, and 11 month olds' interactions with familiar and unfamiliar individuals during a typical week]. Unpublished raw data.

Rubenstein, A.J., Kalakanis, L., & Langlois, J.H. (1999). Infant preferences for attractive faces: A cognitive explanation. *Developmental Psychology, 35,* 848–855.

Sangrigoli, S., & de Schonen, S. (2004). Recognition of own-race and other-race faces by three-month-old infants. *Journal of Child Psychology and Psychiatry, 45,* 1219–1227.

Winkielman, P., & Cacioppo, J.T. (2001). Mind at ease puts smile on the face: Psychophysiological evidence that processing facilitation elicits positive affect. *Journal of Personality and Social Psychology, 81,* 989–1000.

Younger, B.A., & Fearing, D.D. (1999). Parsing items into separate categories: Developmental change in infant categorization. *Child Development, 70,* 291–303.

Address correspondence to Jennifer L. Ramsey-Rennels, Department of Psychology, University of Nevada, Las Vegas, 4505 Maryland Parkway Box 455030, Las Vegas, NV 89154-5030; e-mail: ramseyj2@unlv.nevada.edu.

Acknowledgments—Preparation of this manuscript was supported by two grants from the National Institute of Child Health and Human Development, one to Jennifer Ramsey-Rennels (HD48467) and one to Judith Langlois (HD21332).

The Other-Race Effect Develops during Infancy
Evidence of Perceptual Narrowing

Experience plays a crucial role in the development of face processing. In the study reported here, we investigated how faces observed within the visual environment affect the development of the face-processing system during the 1st year of life. We assessed 3-, 6-, and 9-month-old Caucasian infants' ability to discriminate faces within their own racial group and within three other-race groups (African, Middle Eastern, and Chinese). The 3-month-old infants demonstrated recognition in all conditions, the 6-month-old infants were able to recognize Caucasian and Chinese faces only, and the 9-month-old infants' recognition was restricted to own-race faces. The pattern of preferences indicates that the other-race effect is emerging by 6 months of age and is present at 9 months of age. The findings suggest that facial input from the infant's visual environment is crucial for shaping the face-processing system early in infancy, resulting in differential recognition accuracy for faces of different races in adulthood.

DAVID J. KELLY ET AL.

Human adults are experts at recognizing faces of conspecifics and appear to perform this task effortlessly. Despite this impressive ability, however, adults are more susceptible to recognition errors when a target face is from an unfamiliar racial group, rather than their own racial group. This phenomenon is known as the *other-race effect* (ORE; see Meissner & Brigham, 2001, for a review). Although the ORE has been widely reported, the exact mechanisms that underlie reduced recognition accuracy for other-race faces, and precisely when this effect emerges during development, remain unclear.

The ORE can be explained in terms of a modifiable face representation. The concept of a multidimensional *face-space* architecture, first proposed by Valentine (1991), has received much empirical support. According to the norm-based coding model, individual face exemplars are represented as vectors within face-space according to their deviation from a prototypical average. The prototype held by each person represents the average of all faces that person has ever encoded and is therefore unique. Although it is unclear which dimensions are most salient and used for recognition, it is likely that dimensions vary between individuals and possibly within each person over time. The prototype (and therefore the entire face-space) continually adapts and is updated as more faces are observed within the environment. Consequently, individuating face-space dimensions of a person living in China are expected to be optimal for recognition of other Chinese persons, but not, for example, for recognition of African individuals.

Other authors have hypothesized that the dimensions of the face prototype present at birth are broad and develop according to the type of facial input received (Nelson, 2001). According to this account, predominant exposure to faces from a single racial category tunes face-space dimensions toward that category. Such tuning might be manifested at a behavioral level in differential responding to own- versus other-race faces, for example, in spontaneous visual preference and a recognition advantage for own-race faces.

Recent findings regarding spontaneous preference have confirmed the impact of differential face input on the tuning of the face prototype during early infancy. It has been demonstrated that selectivity based on ethnic facial differences emerges very early in life, with 3-month-old infants preferring to look at faces from their own group, as opposed to faces from other ethnic groups (Bar-Haim, Ziv, Lamy, & Hodes, 2006; Kelly et al., 2005, 2007). We (Kelly et al., 2005) have shown that this preference is not present at birth, which strongly suggests that own-group preferences result from differential exposure to faces from one's particular ethnic group. In addition, Bar-Haim et al. (2006) tested a population of Ethiopian infants who had been raised in an absorption center while their families awaited housing in Israel. These infants were frequently exposed to both Ethiopian and Israeli adults and subsequently demonstrated no preference for either African or Caucasian faces when presented simultaneously.

Collectively, these results provide strong evidence that faces observed in the visual environment have a highly influential role in eliciting face preferences during infancy. Additional evidence supporting this conclusion comes from a study concerning gender preference (Quinn, Yahr, Kuhn, Slater, & Pascalis, 2002), which showed that 3- to 4-month-old infants raised primarily by a female caregiver demonstrate a visual preference for female over male faces, whereas infants raised primarily by a male caregiver prefer to look at male rather than female faces.

Although the literature on differential face recognition contains discrepancies regarding the onset of the ORE, evidence points toward an early inception. Some of the initial investigations reported onset at 8 (Feinman & Entwhistle, 1976) and 6 (Chance, Turner, & Goldstein, 1982) years of age. More recent studies have found the ORE to be present in 5-year-olds (Pezdek, Blandon-Gitlin, & Moore, 2003) and 3-year-olds (Sangrigoli & de Schonen, 2004a). In addition, Sangrigoli and de Schonen (2004b) showed that 3-month-old Caucasian infants were able to recognize an own-race face, but not an Asian face, as measured by the visual paired-comparison (VPC) task. However, the effect disappeared if infants were habituated to three, as opposed to one, other-race face exemplars. Thus, although the ORE may be present at 3 months of age, it is weak enough to be eliminated after only a few instances of exposure within an experimental session.

Additional lines of evidence indicate that the face representation undergoes change throughout development. At 6 months of age, infants are able to individuate human and monkey faces, and although the ability to individuate human faces is maintained in later development, the ability to individuate monkey faces is absent in 9-month-old infants and in adults (Pascalis, de Haan, & Nelson, 2002). Although the face-processing system appears to adapt toward own-species faces, it still retains flexibility for within-species categories of faces (i.e., other-race faces). Korean adults adopted by French families during childhood (ages 3–9 years) demonstrated a recognition deficit for Korean faces relative to their ability to recognize European faces (Sangrigoli, Pallier, Argenti, Ventureyra, & de Schonen, 2005). Their pattern of performance was comparable to that of the native French people who were tested in the same study.

The purpose of the study reported here was to clarify the developmental origins of the ORE during the first months of life. Using the VPC task, we assessed the ability of 3-, 6-, and 9-month-old Caucasian infants to discriminate within own-race (Caucasian) faces and within three categories of other-race faces (African, Middle Eastern, and Chinese). This task measures relative interest in the members of pairs of stimuli, each consisting of a novel stimulus and a familiar stimulus observed during a prior habituation period. Recognition of the familiar stimulus is inferred from the participant's tendency to fixate on the novel stimulus. Previous studies have found that 3-month-old infants can perform this task even when they are exposed to different views of faces (e.g., full view vs. 3/4 profile) during the habituation period and the recognition test (Pascalis, de Haan, Nelson, & de Schonen, 1998). We also varied face views between familiarization and testing, a procedure that is preferable to using identical pictures in the habituation and testing

phases because it ensures that face recognition—as opposed to picture recognition (i.e., image matching)—is tested. Our selection of which age groups to test was based on previous research demonstrating that the ORE is found in infancy (3-month-olds; Sangrigoli & de Schonen, 2004b) and that the face-processing system appears to undergo a period of tuning between 6 and 9 months of age (Pascalis et al., 2002).

Method
Participants

In total, 192 Caucasian infants were included in the final analysis. There were 64 subjects in each of three age groups: 3-month-olds (age range = 86–102 days; 33 females, 31 males), 6-month-olds (age range = 178–196 days; 31 females, 33 males), and 9-month-olds (age range = 268–289 days; 30 females, 34 males). All participants were healthy, full-term infants. Within each age group, the infants were assigned in equal numbers ($n = 16$) to the four testing conditions (Caucasian, African, Middle Eastern, and Chinese). The infants were recruited from the maternity wing of the Royal Hallamshire Hospital, Sheffield, United Kingdom. In each age group, we tested additional infants who were excluded from the final analysis. Twenty-two 3-month-old infants were excluded because of failure to habituate ($n = 4$), side bias during testing (> 95% looking time to one side; $n = 15$), or fussiness ($n = 3$); sixteen 6-month-old infants were excluded because of failure to habituate ($n = 7$), side bias during testing ($n = 3$), parental interference ($n = 2$), or fussiness ($n = 4$); and eleven 9-month-old infants were excluded because of a failure to habituate ($n = 3$) or fussiness ($n = 8$).

Stimuli

The stimuli were 24 color images of male and female adult faces (age range = 23–27 years) from four different ethnic groups (African, Asian, Middle Eastern, and Caucasian). All faces had dark hair and dark eyes so that the infants would be unable to demonstrate recognition on the basis of these features. The images were photos of students. The Africans were members of the African and Caribbean Society at the University of Sheffield; the Asians were Han Chinese students from Zhejiang Sci-Tech University, Hangzhou, China; the Middle Easterners were members of the Pakistan Society at the University of Sheffield; and the Caucasians were psychology students at the University of Sheffield.

For each ethnic group, we tested male and female faces in separate conditions. The images for each combination of ethnic group and gender consisted of a habituation face and two test faces, a novel face and the familiar face in a new orientation. The two faces in the test phase were always in the same orientation, and this orientation differed from the orientation of the face seen during habituation. In one orientation condition, infants were habituated to full-view faces and saw test faces in 3/4-profile views; in the other orientation condition, the views were reversed. Equal numbers of infants were assigned to the two orientation conditions.

All photos were taken with a Canon S50 digital camera and subsequently cropped using Adobe Photoshop to remove the neck and background details. All individual pictures were then mounted on a uniform dark-gray background, and the stimuli were resized to the same dimensions to ensure uniformity. Sixteen independent observers rated a pool of 32 faces for attractiveness and distinctiveness, using a scale from 1 to 10, and the final set of 24 faces was selected so as to match gender, attractiveness, and distinctiveness within each face pair.

Procedure

All infants were tested in a quiet room at the department of psychology at the University of Sheffield. They were seated on their mother's lap, approximately 60 cm from a screen onto which the images were projected. Each infant was randomly assigned to one of the four ethnic-group conditions (African, Asian, Middle Eastern, or Caucasian). Within each of these four conditions, infants were tested with either male or female faces; testing was counterbalanced appropriately, with half the infants assigned to the male-faces condition and half the infants assigned to the female-faces condition. Equal numbers of infants were tested in the male and female conditions. Before the session started, all mothers were instructed to fixate centrally above the screen and to remain as quiet as possible during testing.

Habituation Phase

Each infant was first presented with a single face projected onto a screen measuring 45 cm × 30 cm. The face measured 18 cm × 18 cm (14° visual angle). The experimenter observed the infant's eye movements on a control monitor from a black-and-white closed-circuit television camera (specialized for low-light conditions) that was positioned above the screen. Time was recorded and displayed on the control monitor using a Horita (Mission Viejo, CA) II TG-50 time coder; video was recorded at 25 frames per second.

The experimenter recorded the infant's attention to the face by holding down the "z" key on a keyboard whenever the infant fixated on the image. When the infant looked away from the image, the experimenter released the key. If the infant's attention was averted for more than 2 s, the image disappeared from the screen. The experimenter then presented the image again and repeated the procedure. The habituation phase ended when the infant's looking time on a presentation was equal to or less than 50% of the average looking time from the infant's first two presentations. Thus, our measure of looking time was the sum of looking time across all presentations until the habituation criterion was reached.

Test Phase

The test phase consisted of two trials. First, two face images (novel and familiar), each measuring 18 cm × 18 cm (14° visual angle), were presented on the screen. The images were separated by a 9-cm gap and appeared in the bottom left and bottom right corners of the screen. When the infant first looked at the images, the experimenter pressed a key to begin a 5-s countdown. At the end of the 5 s, the images disappeared from the screen. The faces then appeared with their left/right position on the screen reversed.

As soon as the infant looked at the images, another 5-s countdown was initiated. Eye movements were recorded throughout, and the film was digitized for frame-by-frame analysis by two independent observers who used specialized computer software to code looking time to each of the two faces. The observers were blind to both gender and ethnic-group condition and to the screen positions of the faces being viewed by the infants. The average level of interobserver agreement was high (Pearson $r = .93$). Recognition was inferred from a preference for the novel face stimulus across the two 5-s test trials.

Results
Habituation Trials

A preliminary analysis revealed no significant gender differences for stimuli or participants, so data were collapsed across stimulus gender and participant's gender in subsequent analyses. Habituation time (total looking time across trials) was analyzed in a 3 (age: 3, 6, or 9 months) × 4 (face ethnicity: African, Middle Eastern, Chinese, or Caucasian) × 2 (face orientation: full face or 3/4 profile) between-subjects analysis of variance (ANOVA). The ANOVA yielded only a significant effect of age, $F(2, 189) = 73.193$, $p < .0001$, $\eta^2 = .535$. Post hoc Tukey's honestly significant difference (HSD) tests revealed that the habituation times of 6- and 9-month-old infants did not differ significantly, but both 6-month-old ($M = 42.67$ s) and 9-month-old ($M = 38.88$ s) infants habituated significantly more quickly ($p < .0001$) than 3-month-old infants ($M = 70.74$ s). There were no main effects of face ethnicity or face orientation, nor were there any interactions.

Test Trials

Again, a preliminary analysis yielded no significant gender differences for stimuli or participants, so data were collapsed across stimulus gender and participant's gender in subsequent analyses. Percentage of time spent looking at the novel stimulus, combined from both trials of the test phase, was analyzed in a 3 (age: 3, 6, or 9 months) × 4 (face ethnicity: African, Middle Eastern, Chinese, or Caucasian) × 2 (face orientation: full face or 3/4 view) between-subjects ANOVA. The ANOVA yielded a significant effect of age, $F(2, 189) = 5.133$, $p < .007$, $\eta^2 = .058$. Post hoc Tukey's HSD tests revealed that 3-month-olds ($M = 60.15\%$) showed significantly greater preference for the novel face ($p < .003$) than did 9-month-olds ($M = 53.19\%$). There were no main effects of face ethnicity or face orientation.

To investigate novelty preferences within each age group, we conducted one-way between-groups ANOVAs on the percentage of time spent looking at the novel stimuli in the four face-ethnicity conditions. A significant effect of face ethnicity was found for 9-month-old infants, $F(3, 60) = 3.105$, $p < .033$, $\eta^2 = .134$, but not for 3- or 6-month-old infants. These results suggest that novelty preferences differed between face-ethnicity conditions only within the group of 9-month-old infants.

To further investigate novelty preferences within each age group, we conducted a series of two-tailed t tests to determine whether the time spent looking at novel stimuli differed from

TABLE 1 Results of the Novelty-Preference Test, by Age Group and Face Ethnicity

Age and Face Ethnicity	Mean Time Looking at the Novel Face (%)	t(15)	p	p_{rep}
3 months				
African	60.88 (16.52)	2.635	.019*	.942
Middle Eastern	57.31 (11.37)	2.572	.021*	.937
Chinese	58.72 (14.07)	2.479	.026*	.929
Caucasian	63.71 (13.47)	4.072	.001*	.988
6 months				
African	55.35 (11.40)	1.880	> .05	.840
Middle Eastern	56.70 (12.89)	2.079	> .05	.871
Chinese	56.42 (7.79)	3.295	.005*	.965
Caucasian	58.27 (8.88)	3.725	.002*	.979
9 months				
African	51.33 (10.53)	0.505	> .05	.414
Middle Eastern	53.51 (8.47)	1.658	> .05	.799
Chinese	48.23 (13.31)	0.530	> .05	.642
Caucasian	59.70 (11.16)	3.476	.003*	.971

Note. Standard deviations are given in parentheses. Asterisks highlight conditions in which the infants viewed novel faces significantly more often than predicted by chance.

the chance level of 50% (see Table 1). The results showed that 3-month-old infants demonstrated significant novelty preferences in all four face-ethnicity conditions, 6-month-old infants demonstrated significant novelty preferences in two of the four conditions (Chinese and Caucasian), and 9-month-old infants demonstrated a novelty preference for Caucasian faces only.

Discussion

The aim of the current study was to investigate the onset of the ORE during the first months of life, following up on previous findings that 3-month-olds already show a preference for own-race faces (Bar-Haim et al., 2006; Kelly et al., 2005, 2007). The results reported here do not provide evidence for the ORE (as measured by differential recognition capabilities for own- and other-race faces) in 3-month-old infants, but they do indicate that the ORE emerges at age 6 months and is fully present at age 9 months.

Our results are consistent with the notion of general perceptual narrowing during infancy (e.g., Nelson, 2001). Our findings are also consistent with those of Pascalis et al. (2002), further demonstrating that the face-processing system undergoes a period of refinement within the 1st year of life. Collectively, these findings lend weight to the concept of a tuning period between 6 and 9 months of age. However, differences between the present study and the work by Pascalis et al. should be noted. For example, there is the obvious difference that Pascalis et al. found between-species effects, and our study focused on within-species effects. It should not be assumed that identical mechanisms necessarily underlie the reductions in recognition accuracy observed in the two cases. In addition, once the ability to discriminate between nonhuman primate faces has

diminished, it apparently cannot be recovered easily (Dufour, Coleman, Campbell, Petit, & Pascalis, 2004; Pascalis et al., 2002), whereas the ORE is evidently modifiable through exposure to other-race populations (Sangrigoli et al., 2005) or simple training with other-race faces (Elliott, Wills, & Goldstein, 1973; Goldstein & Chance, 1985; Lavrakas, Buri, & Mayzner, 1976). Furthermore, event-related potential (ERP) studies have shown that in 6-month-olds, the putative infant N170 (a face-selective ERP component elicited in occipital regions) is sensitive to inversion for both human and monkey faces, whereas the N170 recorded in adults is sensitive to inversion only for human faces (de Haan, Pascalis, & Johnson, 2002). An adult-like N170 response is not observed in subjects until they are 12 months of age (Halit, de Haan, & Johnson, 2003). The ERP response for other-race faces has not yet been investigated during infancy, but studies with adults have revealed no differences in the N170 response to own- and other-race faces (Caldara et al., 2003; Caldara, Rossion, Bovet, & Hauert, 2004).

Our findings differ from those reported by Sangrigoli and de Schonen (2004b) in the only other study to have investigated the emergence of the ORE during infancy. In their initial experiment, Sangrigoli and de Schonen found that 3-month-old infants discriminated own-race faces, but not other-race faces, as measured by the VPC task. However, numerous methodological differences between our study and theirs (e.g., color stimuli in our study vs. gray-scale stimuli in theirs) could have contributed to these contrasting results. Furthermore, Sangrigoli and de Schonen were able to eliminate the ORE with only a few trials of exposure to multiple exemplars, which suggests that even if the ORE is already present in 3-month-olds, it is weak and reversible. Between Sangrigoli and de Schonen's work and our own, there are now three VPC experiments (one here, two in Sangrigoli & de Schonen)[1] that have been conducted with 3-month-old infants, yet only one has yielded evidence for the ORE. The weight of the evidence thus suggests that a strong and sustainable ORE may not be present at 3 months of age, but rather develops later.

One might ask whether the ORE arises from differences in the variability of faces from different ethnic groups. However, the available evidence indicates that no category of faces has greater homogeneity than any other (Goldstein, 1979a, 1979b). More-over, the data suggest that the ORE does not exclusively reflect a deficit for non-Caucasian faces: Individuals from many ethnic groups demonstrate poorer recognition of other-race than own-race faces (Meissner & Brigham, 2001). Evidently, a full account of the ORE will involve factors other than heterogeneity.

We have argued elsewhere (Kelly et al., 2007) that the ORE may develop through the following processes: First, predominant exposure to faces from one's own racial group induces familiarity with and a visual preference for such faces. Second, a preference for faces within one's racial group produces greater visual atten-tion to such faces, even when faces from other racial groups are present in the visual environment. Third, superior recognition abilities develop for faces within one's racial group, but not for faces from groups that are infrequently encountered. Although supporting evidence for the first two processes has been obtained previously (Bar-Haim et al., 2006; Kelly et al., 2005, 2007), the data reported here provide the first direct evidence for the third. According to our account, the ORE can be explained by a modifi-able face prototype (Valentine, 1991). If each person's face pro-totype is an average of all faces that person has encoded during his or her lifetime, then one may assume that it will resemble the race of the faces most commonly encountered. Furthermore, one would expect that individuating dimensions will be optimized for recognition of own-race faces, but not other-race faces.

An alternative to the single-prototype account is that people may possess multiple face-spaces that represent different face categories (e.g., gender, race) separately within a global space. In this contrasting scheme, rather than individuating dimensions being unsuitable for recognition of other-race faces, a face-space for other-race faces (e.g., Chinese faces) either does not exist or is insufficiently formed because of a general lack of exposure to those face categories. In both accounts, recognition capabilities improve through exposure to other-race faces. In the case of the single-prototype account, individuating dimensions acquire prop-erties of newly encountered other-race faces that facilitate recogni-tion. Alternatively, in the multiple-face-spaces account, a relevant space for other-race faces develops through similar exposure.

In summary, this is the first study to investigate the emergence of the ORE during infancy by comparing three different age groups' ability to recognize faces from their own race and a range of other races. The data reported here support the idea that very young infants have a broad face-processing system that is capa-ble of processing faces from different ethnic groups. Between 3 and 9 months of age, this system gradually becomes more sensi-tive to faces from an infant's own ethnic group as a consequence of greater exposure to such faces than to faces from other racial groups. This shift in sensitivity is reflected in the emergence of a deficit in recognition accuracy for faces from unfamiliar groups.

Future research should address whether the pattern of results we obtained with Caucasian infants is universal, or whether the ORE emerges at different ages in other populations.

Note

1. But note that in a recent study using morphed stimuli, Hayden, Bhatt, Joseph, and Tanaka (2007) demonstrated that 3.5-month-old infants showed greater sensitivity to structural changes in own-race faces than in other-race faces.

References

Bar-Haim, Y., Ziv, T., Lamy, D., & Hodes, R.M. (2006). Nature and nurture in own-race face processing. *Psychological Science, 17,* 159–163.

Caldara, R., Rossion, B., Bovet, P., & Hauert, C.A. (2004). Event-related potentials and time course of the 'other-race' face classification advantage. *Cognitive Neuroscience and Neuropsychology, 15,* 905–910.

Caldara, R., Thut, G., Servoir, P., Michel, C.M., Bovet, P., & Renault, B. (2003). Faces versus non-face object perception and the 'other-race' effect: A spatio-temporal event-related potential study. *Clinical Neurophysiology, 114,* 515–528.

Chance, J.E., Turner, A.L., & Goldstein, A.G. (1982). Development of differential recognition for own- and other-race faces. *Journal of Psychology, 112,* 29–37.

de Haan, M., Pascalis, O., & Johnson, M.H. (2002). Specialization of neural mechanisms underlying face recognition in human infants. *Journal of Cognitive Neuroscience, 14,* 199–209.

Dufour, V., Coleman, M., Campbell, R., Petit, O., & Pascalis, O. (2004). On the species-specificity of face recognition in human adults. *Current Psychology of Cognition, 22,* 315–333.

Elliott, E.S., Wills, E.J., & Goldstein, A.G. (1973). The effects of discrimination training on the recognition of White and Oriental faces. *Bulletin of the Psychonomic Society, 2,* 71–73.

Feinman, S., & Entwhistle, D.R. (1976). Children's ability to recognize other children's faces. *Child Development, 47,* 506–510.

Goldstein, A.G. (1979a). Race-related variation of facial features: Anthropometric data I. *Bulletin of the Psychonomic Society, 13,* 187–190.

Goldstein, A.G. (1979b). Facial feature variation: Anthropometric data II. *Bulletin of the Psychonomic Society, 13,* 191–193.

Goldstein, A.G., & Chance, J.E. (1985). Effects of training on Japanese face recognition: Reduction of the other-race effect. *Bulletin of the Psychonomic Society, 23,* 211–214.

Halit, H., de Haan, M., & Johnson, M.H. (2003). Cortical specialisation for face processing: Face-sensitive event-related potential components in 3- and 12-month-old infants. *NeuroImage, 19,* 1180–1193.

Hayden, A., Bhatt, R.S., Joseph, J.E., & Tanaka, J.W. (2007). The other-race effect in infancy: Evidence using a morphing technique. *Infancy, 12,* 95–104.

Kelly, D.J., Ge, L., Liu, S., Quinn, P.C., Slater, A.M., Lee, K., et al. (2007). Cross-race preferences for same-race faces extend beyond the African versus Caucasian contrast in 3-month-old infants. *Infancy, 11,* 87–95.

Kelly, D.J., Quinn, P.C., Slater, A.M., Lee, K., Gibson, A., Smith, M., et al. (2005). Three-month-olds, but not newborns, prefer own-race faces. *Developmental Science, 8,* F31–F36.

Lavrakas, P.J., Buri, J.R., & Mayzner, M.S. (1976). A perspective on the recognition of other-race faces. *Perception & Psychophysics, 20,* 475–481.

Meissner, C.A., & Brigham, J.C. (2001). Thirty years of investigating the own-race bias in memory for faces: A meta-analytic review. *Psychology, Public Policy, and Law, 7,* 3–35.

Nelson, C.A. (2001). The development and neural bases of face recognition. *Infant and Child Development, 10,* 3–18.

Pascalis, O., de Haan, M., & Nelson, C.A. (2002). Is face processing species-specific during the first year of life? *Science, 296,* 1321–1323.

Pascalis, O., de Haan, M., Nelson, C.A., & de Schonen, S. (1998). Long-term recognition assessed by visual paired comparison in 3- and 6-month-old infants. *Journal of Experimental Psychology: Learning, Memory, and Cognition, 24,* 249–260.

Pezdek, K., Blandon-Gitlin, I., & Moore, C. (2003). Children's face recognition memory: More evidence for the cross-race effect. *Journal of Applied Psychology, 88,* 760–763.

Quinn, P.C., Yahr, J., Kuhn, A., Slater, A.M., & Pascalis, O. (2002). Representation of the gender of human faces by infants: A preference for female. *Perception, 31,* 1109–1121.

Sangrigoli, S., & de Schonen, S. (2004a). Effect of visual experience on face processing: A developmental study of inversion and non-native effects. *Developmental Science, 7,* 74–87.

Sangrigoli, S., & de Schonen, S. (2004b). Recognition of own-race and other-race faces by three-month-old infants. *Journal of Child Psychology and Psychiatry and Allied Disciplines, 45,* 1219–1227.

Sangrigoli, S., Pallier, C., Argenti, A.M., Ventureyra, V.A.G., & de Schonen, S. (2005). Reversibility of the other-race effect in face recognition during childhood. *Psychological Science, 16,* 440–444.

Valentine, T. (1991). A unified account of the effects of distinctiveness, inversion, and race in face recognition. *The Quarterly Journal of Experimental Psychology, 43A,* 161–204.

DAVID J. KELLY: University of Sheffield, Sheffield, United Kingdom; **PAUL C. QUINN:** University of Delaware; **ALAN M. SLATER:** University of Exeter, Exeter, United Kingdom; **KANG LEE:** University of Toronto, Toronto, Ontario, Canada; **LIEZHONG GE:** Zeijiang Sci-Tech University, Hangzhou, People's Republic of China; and **OLIVER PASCALIS:** University of Sheffield, Sheffield, United Kingdom

Address correspondence to David J. Kelly, University of Sheffield, Psychology Department, Western Bank, Sheffield, South Yorkshire S10 2TP, United Kingdom, e-mail: david.kelly@sheffield.ac.uk

Acknowledgments—This work was supported by National Institutes of Health Grants HD-46526 and HD-42451 and by an Economic and Social Research Council studentship awarded to David J. Kelly.

New Advances in Understanding Sensitive Periods in Brain Development

MICHAEL S. C. THOMAS AND MARK H. JOHNSON

T he idea that there are "critical" or sensitive periods in neural, cognitive, and behavioral development has a long history. It first became widely known with the phenomenon of *filial imprinting* as famously described by Konrad Lorenz: After a relatively brief exposure to a particular stimulus early in life, many birds and mammals form a strong and exclusive attachment to that stimulus. According to Lorenz, a critical period in development has several features, including the following: Learning or plasticity is confined to a short and sharply defined period of the life cycle, and this learning is subsequently irreversible in the face of later experience. Following the paradigmatic example of filial imprinting in birds, more recent studies on cats, dogs, and monkeys, as well as investigations of bird song and human language development, have confirmed that critical periods are major phenomena in brain and behavioral development (see Michel & Tyler, 2005, for review). However, it rapidly became evident that, even in the prototypical case of imprinting, critical periods were not as sharply timed and irreversible as first thought. For example, the critical period for imprinting in domestic chicks was shown to be extendable in time in the absence of appropriate stimulation, and the learning is reversible under certain circumstances (for review, see Bolhuis, 1991). These and other modifications of Lorenz's original views have led most current researchers to adopt the alternative term *sensitive periods* to describe these widespread developmental phenomena.

A fundamental debate that continues to the present is whether specific mechanisms underlie sensitive periods or whether such periods are a natural consequence of functional brain development. Support for the latter view has come from a recent perspective on developing brain functions. Relating evidence on the neuroanatomical development of the brain to the remarkable changes in motor, perceptual, and cognitive abilities during the first decade or so of a human life presents a formidable challenge. A recent theory, termed *interactive specialization*, holds that post-natal functional brain development, at least within the cerebral cortex, involves a process of increasing specialization, or fine-tuning, of response properties (Johnson, 2001, 2005). According to this view, during postnatal development, the response properties of cortical regions change as they interact and compete with each other to acquire their roles in new computational abilities. That is, some cortical regions begin with poorly defined functions and consequently are partially activated in a wide range of different contexts and tasks. During development, activity-dependent interactions between regions sharpen up their functions, such that a region's activity becomes restricted to a narrower set of stimuli or task demands. For example, a region originally activated by a wide variety of visual objects may come to confine its response to upright human faces. The termination of sensitive periods is then a natural consequence of the mechanisms by which cortical regions become increasingly specialized and finely tuned. Once regions have become specialized for their adult functions, these commitments are difficult to reverse. If this view is correct, sensitive periods in human cognitive development are intrinsic to the process that produces the functional structure of the adult brain.

In order to better understand how sensitive periods relate to the broader picture of vertebrate functional brain development, researchers have addressed a number of specific questions. In any given species are there multiple sensitive periods or just a few (e.g., one per sensory modality)? If there are multiple sensitive periods, do they share common underlying mechanisms? What are the processes that underlie the end of sensitive periods and the corresponding reduction in plasticity?

Varieties of Sensitive Period

Recent work indicates that there are multiple sensitive periods in the sensory systems that have been studied. For example, within the auditory domain in humans, there are different sensitive periods for different facets of speech processing and other sensitive periods, having different timing, related to basic aspects of music perception. Similarly, in nonhuman-primate visual systems there are, at a minimum, different sensitive periods related to amblyopia (a condition found in early childhood in which one eye develops good vision but the other does not), visual acuity, motion perception, and face processing (see Johnson, 2005, for review).

How these different and varied sensitive periods relate to each other is still poorly understood. But high-level skills like human language involve the integration of many lower-level systems, and plasticity in language acquisition is therefore likely to be the combinatorial result of the relative plasticity of underlying auditory, phonological, semantic, syntactic, and motor systems, along with the developmental interactions among these components. The literature currently available suggests that plasticity tends to reduce in low-level sensory systems before it reduces in high-level cognitive systems (Huttenlocher, 2002).

While it is now agreed that there are multiple sensitive periods even within one sensory modality in a given species, there is still considerable debate as to whether these different sensitive periods reflect common underlying mechanisms or whether different mechanisms and principles operate in each case.

Mechanisms Underlying Sensitive Periods

A major feature of sensitive periods is that plasticity appears to be markedly reduced at the end of the period. There are three general classes of explanation for this: (a) termination of plasticity due to maturation, (b) self-termination of learning, and (c) stabilization of constraints on plasticity (without a reduction in the underlying level of plasticity).

According to the first view, endogenous changes in the neurochemistry of the brain region in question could increase the rate of pruning of synapses, resulting in the "fossilization" of existing patterns of functional connectivity. Thus, the termination of sensitive periods would be due to endogenous factors, would have a fixed time course, and could be specific to individual regions of the cortex. Empirical evidence on neuro-chemical changes associated with plasticity (such as expression of glutamatergic and GABA receptors in the human visual cortex) indicate that the periods of neurochemical change can occur around the age of functional sensitive periods. However, this does not rule out the possibility that these neurochemical changes are a consequence of the differences in functional activity due to termination of plasticity for some other reason, rather than its primary cause (Murphy, Betson, Boley, & Jones, 2005).

The second class of mechanism implies that sensitive periods involve self-terminating learning processes. By this, we mean that the process of learning itself could produce changes that reduce the system's plasticity. These types of mechanisms are most consistent with the view of sensitive periods as a natural consequence of typical functional brain development. An important way to describe and understand self-terminating learning comes from the use of computer-simulated neural networks (Thomas & Johnson, 2006). These models demonstrate mechanistically how processes of learning can lead to neurobiological changes that reduce plasticity, rather than plasticity changing according to a purely maturational timetable. Such computer models have revealed that, even where a reduction in plasticity emerges with increasing experience, a range of different specific mechanisms may be responsible for this reduction (see Thomas & Johnson, 2006). For example, it may be that the neural system's computational resources, which are critical for future learning, have been claimed or used up by existing learning, so that any

new learning must compete to capture these resources. Unless earlier-learned abilities are neglected or lost, new learning may always be limited by this competition. Another mechanism discovered through modeling is called entrenchment. In this case, prior experience places the system into a state that is nonoptimal for learning the new skill. It takes time to reconfigure the system for the new task and learning correspondingly takes longer than it would have done had the system been in an uncommitted state. A third mechanism is assimilation, whereby initial learning reduces the system's ability to detect changes in the environment that might trigger further learning.

Evidence from humans relevant to self-terminating sensitive periods is reported by Lewis and Maurer (2005), who have studied the outcome of cases of human infants born with dense bilateral cataracts in both eyes. Such dense bilateral cataracts restrict these infants to near blindness, but fortunately the condition can be rectified with surgery. Despite variation in the age of treatment from 1 to 9 months, infants were found to have the visual acuity of a newborn immediately following surgery to remove the cataracts. However, after only 1 hour of patterned vision, acuity had improved to the level of a typical 6-week-old; and after a further month of visual experience, the gap to age-matched controls was very considerably reduced. These findings correspond well with experiments showing that rearing animals in the dark appears to delay the end of the normal sensitive period. Thus, in at least some cases, plasticity seems to wait for the appropriate type of sensory stimulation. This is consistent with the idea that changes in plasticity can be driven by the learning processes associated with typical development.

Returning to the paradigmatic example of filial imprinting in birds, O'Reilly and Johnson (1994) constructed a computer model of the neural network known to support imprinting in the relevant region of the chick brain. This computer model successfully simulated a range of phenomena associated with imprinting behavior in the chick. Importantly, in both the model and the chick, the extent to which an imprinted preference for one object can be "reversed" by exposure to a second object depends on a combination of the length of exposure to the first object and the length of exposure to the second object (for review, see Bolhuis, 1991). In other words, in the model, the sensitive period was dependent on the respective levels of learning and was self-terminating. Additionally, like the chick, the network generalised from a training object to one that shared some of its features such as color or shape. By gradually changing the features of the object to which the chick was exposed, the chick's preference could be shifted even after the "sensitive period" had supposedly closed. The simulation work demonstrated the sufficiency of simple learning mechanisms to explain the observed behavioral data (McClelland, 2005).

The third class of explanation for the end of sensitive periods is that it represents the onset of stability in constraining factors rather than a reduction in the underlying plasticity. For example, while an infant is growing, the distance between her eyes increases, thereby creating instability in the information to visual cortical areas. However, once the inter-eye distance is fixed in development, the visual input becomes stable. Thus, brain plasticity may be "hidden" until it is revealed by some perturbation to another constraining factor that disrupts vision.

This mechanism offers an attractive explanation of the surprising degree of plasticity sometimes observed in adults, for instance after even brief visual deprivation. Sathian (2005) reported activity in the visual cortex during tactile perception in sighted human adults after brief visual deprivation—activity similar to that observed in those who have suffered long-term visual deprivation. While this line of research initially appears consistent with life-long plasticity, it is important to note that this tactile-induced visual-cortex activity is much greater if vision is lost early in life or was never present. Thus, although there appears to be residual connectivity between sensory systems that can be uncovered by blocking vision in sighted people, there is also a sensitive period during which these connections can be more drastically altered.

Sensitive Periods in Second Language Acquisition

Given the variety of mechanisms that may underlie sensitive periods, it would be interesting to know how such periods affect the acquisition of higher cognitive abilities in humans. Recent research on learning a second language illustrates one attempt to answer this question. If you want to master a second language, how important is the age at which you start to learn it? If you start to learn a second language as an adult, does your brain process it in a different way from how it processes your first language?

It is often claimed that unless individuals acquire a second language (L2) before mid-childhood (or perhaps before puberty), then they will never reach native-like levels of proficiency in the second language in pronunciation or grammatical knowledge. This claim is supported by deprivation studies showing that the acquisition of a first language (L1) is itself less successful when begun after a certain age. Further, functional brain-imaging studies initially indicated that in L2 acquisition, different areas of the cortex were activated by the L2 than by the L1; only in individuals who had acquired two languages simultaneously were common areas activated (e.g., Kim, Relkin, Lee, & Hirsch, 1997).

However, subsequent research has painted a more complex picture. First, claims for sensitive periods have tended to rely on assessing final level of attainment rather than speed of learning. This is because there is evidence that adults can learn a second language more quickly than children can, even if their final level of attainment is not as high. Indeed adults and children appear to learn a new language in different ways. Children are relatively insensitive to feedback and extract regularities from exposure to large amounts of input, whereas adults adopt explicit strategies and remain responsive to feedback (see, e.g., Hudson Kam & Newport, 2005).

Second, even when the final level of L2 attainment is considered, it has proved hard to find an age after which prospective attainment levels off. That is, there is no strong evidence for a point at which a sensitive period completely closes (see, e.g.,

Birdsong, 2006). Instead, L2 attainment shows a linear decline with age: The later you start, the lower your final level is likely to be (Birdsong, 2006).

Third, recent functional imaging research has indicated that at least three factors are important in determining the relative brain-activation patterns produced by L1 and L2 during comprehension and production. These are the age of acquisition, the level of usage/exposure to each language, and the level of proficiency attained in L2. Overall, three broad themes have emerged (Abutalebi, Cappa, & Perani, 2005; Stowe & Sabourin, 2005): (a) The same network of left-hemisphere brain regions is involved in processing both languages; (b) a weak L2 is associated with more widespread neural activity compared to L1 in production (perhaps because the L2 is more effortful to produce) but less activation in comprehension (perhaps because the L2 is less well understood); and (c) the level of proficiency in L2 is more important than age of acquisition in determining whether L1 and L2 activate common or separate areas. In brief, the better you are at your L2, the more similar the activated regions become to those activated by your L1. This finding fits with the idea that certain brain areas have become optimized for processing language (perhaps during the acquisition of L1) and that, in order to become very good at L2, you have to engage these brain areas. The idea that later plasticity is tempered by the processing structures created by earlier learning fits with the interactive-specialization explanation for the closing of sensitive periods.

Finally, in line with idea that language requires integration across multiple subskills, increasing evidence indicates that sensitive periods differ across the components of language (Neville, 2006; Wartenburger et al., 2003; Werker & Tees, 2005). Plasticity may show greater or earlier reductions for phonology and morphosyntax than it does for lexical-semantics, in which there may indeed be no age-related change at all. In other words, for the late language learner, new vocabulary is easier to acquire than new sounds or new grammar.

Conclusion

It is important to understand the mechanisms underlying sensitive periods for practical reasons. Age-of-acquisition effects may shape educational policy and the time at which children are exposed to different skills. The reversibility of effects of deprivation on development has important implications for interventions for children with congenital sensory impairments or children exposed to impoverished physical and social environments. And there are clinical implications for understanding the mechanisms that drive recovery from brain damage at different ages.

Exciting vistas for the future include the possibility of using genetic and brain-imaging data to identify the best developmental times for training new skills in individual children, and the possibility that a deeper understanding of the neurocomputational principles that underlie self-terminating plasticity will allow the design of more efficient training procedures (McClelland 2005).

Recommended Reading

Birdsong, D. (2006). (See References). Discusses recent research on sensitive periods and second-language acquisition.

Huttenlocher, P.R. (2002). (See References). An overview of neural plasticity.

Johnson, M.H. (2005). *Developmental cognitive neuroscience* (2nd ed.). Oxford, UK: Blackwell. An introduction to the relationship between brain development and cognitive development.

Knusden, E.I. (2004). Sensitive periods in the development of brain and behavior. *Journal of Cognitive Neuroscience, 16,* 1412–1425. A discussion of mechanisms of plasticity and sensitive periods at the level of neural circuits.

References

Abutalebi, J., Cappa, S.F., & Perani, D. (2005). What can functional neuroimaging tell us about the bilingual brain? In J.F. Kroll & A.M.B. de Groot (Eds.), *Handbook of bilingualism* (p. 497–515). Oxford, UK: Oxford University Press.

Birdsong, D. (2006). Age and second language acquisition and processing: A selective overview. *Language Learning, 56,* 9–49.

Bolhuis, J.J. (1991). Mechanisms of avian imprinting: A review. *Biological Reviews, 66,* 303–345.

Hudson Kam, C.L., & Newport, E.L. (2005). Regularizing unpredictable variation: The roles of adult and child learners in language formation and change. *Language Learning and Development, 1,* 151–195.

Huttenlocher, P.R. (2002). *Neural plasticity: The effects of the environment on the development of the cerebral cortex.* Cambridge, MA: Harvard University Press.

Huttenlocher, P.R., & Dabholkar, A.S. (1997). Regional differences in synaptogenesis in human cerebral cortex. *Journal of Comparative Neurology, 387,* 167–187.

Johnson, M.H. (2001). Functional brain development in humans. *Nature Reviews Neuroscience, 2,* 475–483.

Johnson, M.H. (2005). Sensitive periods in functional brain development: Problems and prospects. *Developmental Psychobiology, 46,* 287–292.

Kim, K.H.S., Relkin, N.R., Lee, K.M., & Hirsch, J. (1997). Distinct cortical areas associated with native and second languages. *Nature, 388,* 171–174.

Lewis, T.L., & Maurer, D. (2005). Multiple sensitive periods in human visual development: Evidence from visually deprived children. *Developmental Psychobiology, 46,* 163–183.

McClelland, J.L. (2005). How far can you go with Hebbian learning and when does it lead you astray? In Y. Munakata & M.H. Johnson (Eds.), *Attention and Performance XXI: Processes of change in brain and cognitive development* (pp. 33–59). Oxford, UK: Oxford University Press.

Michel, G.F., & Tyler, A.N. (2005). Critical period: A history of the transition from questions of when, to what, to how. *Developmental Psychobiology, 46,* 156–162.

Murphy, K.M., Betson, B.R., Boley, P.M., & Jones, D.G. (2005). Balance between excitatory and inhibitory plasticity mechanisms. *Developmental Psychobiology, 46,* 209–221.

Neville, H.J. (2006). Different profiles of plasticity within human cognition. In Y. Munakata & M.H. Johnson (Eds.), *Attention and Performance XXI: Processes of change in brain and cognitive development* (pp. 287–314). Oxford, UK: Oxford University Press.

O'Reilly, R., & Johnson, M.H. (1994). Object recognition and sensitive periods: A computational analysis of visual imprinting. *Neural Computation, 6,* 357–390.

Sathian, K. (2005). Visual cortical activity during tactile perception in the sighted and the visually deprived. *Developmental Psychobiology, 46,* 279–286.

Stowe, L.A., & Sabourin, L. (2005). Imaging the processing of a second language: Effects of maturation and proficiency on the neural processes involved. *International Review of Applied Linguistics in Language Teaching, 43,* 329–353.

Thomas, M.S.C., & Johnson, M.H. (2006). The computational modelling of sensitive periods. *Developmental Psychobiology, 48,* 337–344.

Wartenburger, I., Heekeren, H.R., Abutalebi, J., Cappa, S.F., Villringer, A., & Perani, D. (2003). Early setting of grammatical processing in the bilingual brain. *Neuron, 37,* 159–170.

Werker, J.F., & Tees, R.C. (2005). Speech perception as a window for understanding plasticity and commitment in language systems of the brain. *Developmental Psychobiology, 46,* 233–251.

Address correspondence to **Michael S. C. Thomas,** Developmental Neurocognition Laboratory, School of Psychology, Birkbeck College, University of London, Malet Street, Bloomsbury, London WC1E 7HX, United Kingdom; e-mail: m.thomas@bbk.ac.uk.

Acknowledgments—This research was supported by Medical Research Council (MRC) Career Establishment Grant G0300188 to Michael S.C. Thomas, and MRC Grant G9715587 to Mark H. Johnson.

Contributions of Neuroscience to Our Understanding of Cognitive Development

ADELE DIAMOND AND DIMA AMSO

Neuroscience research has made its greatest contributions to the study of cognitive development by illuminating mechanisms (providing a "how") that underlie behavioral observations made earlier by psychologists. It has also made important contributions to our understanding of cognitive development by demonstrating that the brain is far more plastic at all ages than previously thought—and thus that the speed and extent by which experience and behavior can shape the brain is greater than almost anyone imagined. In other words, rather than showing that biology is destiny, neuroscience research has been at the forefront of demonstrating the powerful role of experience throughout life. Besides the surprising evidence of the remarkable extent of experience-induced plasticity, rarely has neuroscience given us previously unknown insights into cognitive development, but neuroscience does offer promise of being able to detect some problems before they are behaviorally observable.

Providing Mechanisms That Can Account for Behavioral Results Reported by Psychologists

Here we describe two examples of behavioral findings by psychologists that were largely ignored or extremely controversial until underlying biological mechanisms capable of accounting for them were provided by neuroscience research. One such example concerns cognitive deficits documented in children treated early and continuously for phenylketonuria (PKU). The second example involves neonatal imitation observed by psychologists and mirror neurons discovered by neuroscientists.

Prefrontal Dopamine System and PKU Cognitive Deficits

Since at least the mid-1980s, psychologists were reporting cognitive deficits in children with PKU that resembled those associated with frontal cortex dysfunction (e.g., Pennington, VanDoornick, McCabe, & McCabe, 1985). Those reports did not impact medical care, however. Doctors were skeptical. No one could imagine a mechanism capable of producing what psychologists claimed to be observing.

PKU is a disorder in the gene that codes for phenylalanine hydroxylase, an enzyme essential for the conversion of phenylalanine (Phe) to tyrosine (Tyr). In those with PKU, that enzyme is absent or inactive. Without treatment, Phe levels skyrocket, resulting in gross brain damage and mental retardation. Phe is an amino acid and a component of all dietary protein. PKU treatment consists primarily of reducing dietary intake of protein to keep Phe levels down, but that has to be balanced against the need for protein. For years, children with PKU were considered adequately treated if their blood Phe levels were below 600 micromoles per liter (μmol/L; normal levels in the general public being 60–120 μmol/L). Such children did not have mental retardation and showed no gross brain damage, although no one disputed that their blood Phe levels were somewhat elevated and their blood Tyr levels were somewhat reduced (Tyr levels were not grossly reduced because even though the hydroxylation of Phe into Tyr was largely inoperative, Tyr is also available in protein). Since Phe and Tyr compete to cross into the brain, a modest increase in the ratio of Phe to Tyr in the bloodstream results in a modest decrease in how much Tyr can reach the brain. Note that this is a global effect—the entire brain receives somewhat too little Tyr. How was it possible to make sense of psychologists' claims that the resulting cognitive deficits were not global but limited to the cognitive functions dependent on prefrontal cortex?

Neuroscience provided a mechanism by which psychologists' findings made sense. Research in neuropharmacology had shown that the dopamine system in prefrontal cortex has unusual properties not shared by the dopamine systems in other brain regions such as the striatum. The dopamine neurons that project to pre-frontal cortex have higher rates of firing and dopamine turnover. This makes prefrontal cortex sensitive to modest reductions in Tyr (the precursor of dopamine) that are too small to affect the rest of the brain (Tam, Elsworth, Bradberry, & Roth, 1990). Those unusual properties of the prefrontal dopamine system provide a mechanism by which children treated for PKU could show selective deficits limited to prefrontal cortex. The moderate imbalance in the bloodstream between Phe and Tyr causes a reduction in the amount of Tyr reaching the brain that is large enough to impair the functioning of the prefrontal dopamine system but not large enough to affect the rest of the brain. Diamond and colleagues provided evidence for this mechanism in animal models of PKU and longitudinal study of children (Diamond, 2001). That work, presenting a mechanistic explanation and providing convincing evidence to support it, resulted in a change in the medical guidelines for the treatment of PKU (blood Phe levels should be kept between 120 and 360 µmol/L) that has improved children's lives (e.g., Stemerdink et al., 2000). Also, by shedding light on the role of dopamine in the prefrontal cortex early in development, such work offers insights on the development of cognitive control (executive function) abilities that are relevant to all children.

Mirror Neurons and Neonate Imitation

In 1977, Meltzoff and Moore created a sensation by reporting that human infants just 12 to 21 days old imitated facial expressions they observed adults making. That was followed by a second demonstration of such imitation in infants as young as 42 minutes (Meltzoff & Moore, 1983). For years, those reports met strong resistance. Such imitation was thought to be far too sophisticated an accomplishment for a neonate. After all, infants can feel but not see their own mouth and tongue movements, and they can see but not feel the mouth and tongue movements of others. To equate their own motor movements with the perception of those same movements by others would seem to involve high-level cross-modal matching.

The discovery of mirror neurons by Rizzolatti and his colleagues, Fadiga, Fogassi, and Gallese (for review, see Rizzolatti & Craighero, 2004) provided a mechanism that could conceivably underlie newborns' ability to show such imitation rather automatically. Mirror neurons fire when an individual executes an action or when an individual observes someone else executing that action. The cross-modal association occurs at the neuronal, single-cell level. It has since been demonstrated that 3-day-old rhesus monkeys also imitate the facial movements of adult humans (Ferrari et al., 2006) and that the close link between perception and action is not limited to vision; hearing a sound associated with an action activates mirror neurons associated with that action just as does the sight of that action (Kohler et al., 2002).

Whereas the preceding examples are of neuroscience elucidating possible neurobiological bases for observed psychological phenomena, we move on to describe phenomena—concerning plasticity and environmental influences—that neuroscientists have brought to the attention of developmentalists.

Powerful Effects of Early Experience on Brain, Body, Mind, Behavior, and Gene Expression

Ironically, one of the most important findings to emerge from neurobiology is that biology is not destiny. Neuroscience research has shown that experience plays a far larger role in shaping the mind, brain, and even gene expression than was ever imagined. This insight is particularly important in advancing theory in cognitive development, where debates have raged about the importance of nature versus nurture.

Examples of striking experience-induced plasticity abound—for example, the groundbreaking work of Greenough, Merzenich, Maurer, Neville, Pascual-Leone, Taub, Sur, and Kral. Here we highlight work by Schanberg and Meaney, in part because that work emphasizes a sensory system that has received far less attention by psychologists than have vision and audition: the sense of touch.

Nurturing Touch and its Importance for Growth

Two independent, elegant lines of work have demonstrated the powerful effects of touch. Schanberg and colleagues have shown that the licking behavior of rat mothers is essential for the growth of rat pups. If rat pups are deprived of this touch for even just 1 hour, DNA synthesis is reduced, growth-hormone secretion is inhibited, and bodily organs lose their capacity to respond to exogenously administered growth hormone (Butler, Suskind, & Schanberg, 1978; Kuhn, Butler, & Schanberg, 1978). Schanberg and colleagues have identified molecular mechanisms through which deprivation of the very specific kind of touch rat mothers administer to their pups produces these effects (e.g., Schanberg, Ingledue, Lee, Hannun, & Bartolome, 2003).

Nurturing Touch and its Importance for Reducing Stress Reactivity and for Cognitive Development

Meaney and colleagues have demonstrated that rat moms who more frequently lick and groom their pups produce offspring who, throughout their lives, explore more, are less fearful, show milder reactions to stress, perform better cognitively as adults, and preserve their cognitive skills better into old age (Liu, Diorio, Day, Francis, & Meaney, 2000). It is the mother's behavior that produces these effects rather than a particular genetic profile that produces both a particular mothering style and particular offspring characteristics. Pups of high-licking-and-grooming moms raised by low-licking-and-grooming moms do not show these characteristics, and pups of low-touch moms raised by high-touch moms do show this constellation of attributes (Francis, Diorio, Liu, & Meaney, 1999).

Furthermore, rats tend to raise their offspring the way they themselves were raised, so these effects are transmitted intergenerationally, not through the genome but through behavior. Biological offspring of low-touch moms who are cross-fostered to high-touch moms lick and groom their offspring a lot; in this way the diminished stress response and cognitive enhancement is passed down through the generations (Francis et al., 1999).

Meaney and colleagues have elegantly demonstrated that maternal behavior produces these behavioral consequences through several mechanisms that alter gene expression. Not all genes in an individual are expressed—many are never expressed. Experience can affect which genes are turned on and off, in which cells, and when. For example, methylation (attaching a methyl group to a gene's promoter) stably silences a gene; demethylation reverses that process, typically leading to the gene being expressed. High licking by rat mothers causes demethylation (i.e., activation) of the glucocorticoid receptor gene, hence lowering circulating glucocorticoid (stress hormone) levels as receptors for the stress hormone remove it from circulation.

Nurturing Touch and Human Cognitive and Emotional Development

Unlike newborn rats, human newborns can see, hear, and smell, as well as feel touch. Yet despite the additional sensory information available to them, touch is still crucial. Human infants who receive little touching grow more slowly, release less growth hormone, and are less responsive to growth hormone that is exogenously administered (Frasier & Rallison, 1972). Throughout life, they show larger reactions to stress, are more prone to depression, and are vulnerable to deficits in cognitive functions commonly seen in depression or during stress (Lupien, King, Meaney, McEwen, 2000).

Touch plays a powerful role for human infants in promoting optimal development and in counteracting stressors. Massaging babies lowers their cortisol levels and helps them gain weight (Field et al., 2004). The improved weight gain from neonatal massage has been replicated cross-culturally, and cognitive benefits are evident even a year later. It is not that infants sleep or eat more; rather, stimulating their body through massage increases vagal (parasympathetic nervous system) activity, which prompts release of food-absorption hormones. Such improved vagal tone also indicates better ability to modulate arousal and to attend to subtle environmental cues important for cognitive development. Passive bodily contact also has substantial stress-reducing, calming, and analgesic effects for infants and adults (e.g., Gray, Watt, & Blass, 2000). Thus, besides "simple touch" being able to calm our jitters and lift our spirits, the right kind of touch regularly enough early in life can improve cognitive development, brain development, bodily health throughout life, and gene expression.

Future Directions

Neuroscience may be able to make extremely important contributions to child development by building on repeated demonstrations that differences in neural activity patterns precede and predict differences in cognitive performance. Often, when the brain is not functioning properly, people can compensate so their performance does not suffer until the neural system becomes too dysfunctional or until performance demands become too great. Thus, an underlying problem may exist but not show up behaviorally until, for example, the academic demands of more advanced schooling exceed a child's ability to compensate.

So far, differences in neural activity patterns have been demonstrated to precede and predict differences in cognitive performance only in adults. For example, Bookheimer and colleagues tested older adults (ranging in age from 47 to 82 years) with a genetic predisposition for Alzheimer's disease, selected because they performed fully comparably to controls across diverse cognitive tasks. Nevertheless, functional neuroimaging revealed that the brains of several of the genetically predisposed individuals already showed predicted differences. Two years later, those individuals showed the cognitive impairments predicted by their earlier neural-activity patterns (Bookheimer et al., 2000). Similarly, adults in the early stages of other disorders may show no behavioral evidence of a cognitive deficit while neuroimaging shows their brains are compensating or working harder to achieve that behavioral equivalence. As the disease progresses, the compensation is no longer sufficient and the cognitive deficit becomes evident (e.g., Audoin et al., 2006).

What this suggests is that functional neuroimaging in developing children may perhaps be able to detect evidence of learning disorders—such as attentional, sensory-processing, language, or math deficits—before there is behavioral evidence of a problem. Already, research is being undertaken to see if infants' neural responses to auditory stimuli might be predictive of later linguistic problems (e.g., Benasich et al., 2006). The earlier a problem can be detected, the better the hope of correcting it or of putting environmental compensations in place.

Recommended Reading

Diamond, A. (2001). (See References). Summarizes studies with young children and animals showing the role of maturation of prefrontal cortex in the early emergence of executive function abilities and the importance of dopamine for this.

Grossman, A.W., Churchill, J.D., Bates, K.E., Kleim, J.A., & Greenough, W.T. (2002). A brain adaptation view of plasticity: Is synaptic plasticity an overly limited concept? *Progress in Brain Research, 138,* 91–108. Argues that synaptic, even neuronal, plasticity is but a small fraction of the range of brain changes that occur in response to experience, and that there are multiple forms of brain plasticity governed by mechanisms that are at least partially independent, including non-neuronal changes.

Meaney, M.J. (2001). Maternal care, gene expression, and the transmission of individual differences in stress reactivity across generations. *Annual Review of Neuroscience, 24,* 1161–1192. Provides an overview of research demonstrating that naturally occurring variations in maternal care modify the expression of genes affecting offspring's cognitive development as well as their ability to cope with stress throughout life, and that these changes are passed down intergenerationally (epigenetic inheritance).

Meltzoff, A.N., & Decety, J. (2003). What imitation tells us about social cognition: A rapprochement between developmental psychology and cognitive neuroscience. *Philosophical Transactions of the Royal Society of London – B: Biological Sciences, 358,* 491–500. Reviews the psychological evidence concerning imitation in human neonates and the neurophysiological evidence of a common coding at the single cell level (in mirror neurons) between perceived and generated actions.

Neville, H.J., & Bavelier, D. (2002). Human brain plasticity: Evidence from sensory deprivation and altered language experience. *Progress in Brain Research, 138,* 177–188. Summarizes research, using behavioral measures and neuroimaging, on individuals with altered visual, auditory, and/or language experience, showing ways in which brain development can, and cannot, be modified by environmental input, and how that varies by the timing of the altered input and by specific subfunctions within language or vision.

References

Audoin, B., Au Duong, M.V., Malikova, I., Confort-Gouny, S., Ibarrola, D., Cozzone, P.J., et al. (2006). Functional magnetic resonance imaging and cognition at the very early stage of MS. *Journal of the Neurological Sciences, 245,* 87–91.

Benasich, A.A., Choudhury, N., Friedman, J.T., Realpe Bonilla, T., Chojnowska, C., & Gou, Z. (2006). Infants as a prelinguistic model for language learning impairments: Predicting from event-related potentials to behavior. *Neuropsychologia, 44,* 396–441.

Bookheimer, S.Y., Strojwas, M.H., Cohen, M.S., Saunders, A.M., Pericak-Vance, M.A., Mazziota, J.C., et al. (2000). Patterns of brain activation in people at risk for Alzheimer's disease. *New England Journal of Medicine, 343,* 450–456.

Butler, S.R., Suskind, M.R., & Schanberg, S.M. (1978). Maternal behavior as a regulator of polyamine biosynthesis in brain and heart of the developing rat pup. *Science, 199,* 445–447.

Diamond, A. (2001). A model system for studying the role of dopamine in prefrontal cortex during early development in humans. In C. Nelson & M. Luciana (eds.), *Handbook of developmental cognitive neuroscience* (pp. 433–472). Cambridge, MA: MIT Press.

Field, T., Hernandez-Reif, M., Diego, M., Feijo, L., Vera, Y., & Gil, K. (2004). Massage therapy by parents improves early growth and development. *Infant Behavior & Development, 27,* 435–442.

Ferrari, P.F., Visalberghi, E., Paukner, A., Fogassi, L., Ruggiero, A., & Suomi, S. (2006). Neonatal imitation in rhesus macaques. *PLoS Biology, 4,* 1501–1508.

Francis, D., Diorio, J., Liu, D., & Meaney, MJ. (1999). Nongenomic transmission across generations of maternal behavior and stress responses in the rat. *Science, 286,* 1155–1158.

Frasier, S.D., & Rallison, M.L. (1972). Growth retardation and emotional deprivation: Relative resistance to treatment with human growth hormone. *Journal of Pediatrics, 80,* 603–609.

Gray, L., Watt, L., & Blass, E.M. (2000). Skin-to-skin contact is analgesic in healthy newborns. *Pediatrics, 105,* 1–6.

Kohler, E., Keysers, C., Umiltà, MA., Fogassi, L., Gallese, V., & Rizzolatti, G. (2002). Hearing sounds, understanding actions: Action representation in mirror neurons. *Science, 297,* 846–848.

Kuhn, C.M., Butler, S.R., & Schanberg, S.M. (1978). Selective depression of serum growth hormone during maternal deprivation in rat pups. *Science, 201,* 1034–1036.

Liu, D., Diorio, J., Day, J.C., Francis, D.D., & Meaney, M.J. (2000). Maternal care, hippocampal synaptogenesis and cognitive development in rats. *Nature Neuroscience, 3,* 799–806.

Lupien, S.J., King, S., Meaney, M.J., & McEwen, B.S. (2000). Child's stress hormone levels correlate with mother's socioeconomic status and depressive state. *Biological Psychiatry, 48,* 976–980.

Meltzoff, A.N., & Moore, M.K. (1977). Imitation of facial and manual gestures by human neonates. *Science, 198,* 75–78.

Meltzoff, A.N., & Moore, M.K. (1983). Newborn infants imitate adult facial gestures. *Child Development, 54,* 702–709.

Pennington, B.F., VanDoornick, W.J., McCabe, L.L., & McCabe, E.R.B. (1985). Neuropsychological deficits in early treated phenylketonuric children. *American Journal of Mental Deficiency, 89,* 467–474.

Rizzolatti, G., & Craighero, L. (2004). The mirror-neuron system. *Annual Review of Neuroscience, 27,* 169–192.

Schanberg, S.M., Ingledue, V.F., Lee, J.Y., Hannun, Y.A., & Bartolome, J.V. (2003). PKC mediates maternal touch regulation of growth-related gene expression in infant rats. *Neuropsychopharmacology, 28,* 1026–1030.

Stemerdink, B.A., Kalverboer, A.F., van der Meere, J.J., van der Molen, M.W., Huisman, J., de Jong, L.W., et al. (2000). Behaviour and school achievement in patients with early and continuously treated phenylketonuria. *Journal of Inherited Metabolic Disorders, 23,* 548–562.

Tam, S.Y., Elsworth, J.D., Bradberry, C.W., & Roth, R.H. (1990). Mesocortical dopamine neurons: High basal firing frequency predicts tyrosine dependence of dopamine synthesis. *Journal of Neural Transmission, 81,* 97–110.

Address correspondence to **ADELE DIAMOND,** Canada Research Chair Professor of Developmental Cognitive Neuroscience, Department of Psychiatry, University of British Columbia, 2255 Wesbrook Mall, Vancouver, British Columbia, V6T 2A1, Canada; e-mail: adele.diamond @ubc.ca.

Acknowledgments—AD gratefully acknowledges grant support from the National Institute on Drug Abuse (R01 #DA19685) during the writing of this paper.

It's Fun, but Does It Make You Smarter?

Researchers find a relationship between children's Internet use and academic performance.

Erika Packard

For most children and teenagers, using the Internet has joined watching television and talking on the phone in the repertoire of typical behavior. In fact, 87 percent of 12- to 17-year-olds are now online, according to a 2005 Pew Research Center report. That's a 24 percent increase over the previous four years, leading parents and policy-makers to worry about the effect access to worlds of information—and misinformation—has on children.

Psychologists are only beginning to answer that question, but a study led by Michigan State University psychologist Linda Jackson, PhD, showed that home Internet use improved standardized reading test scores. Other researchers have found that having the Internet at home encourages children to be more self-directed learners.

"We had the same question for television decades ago, but I think the Internet is more important than television because it's interactive," says Jackson. "It's 24/7 and it's ubiquitous in young people's lives."

The positive effects of Internet use appear especially pronounced among poor children, say researchers. Unfortunately, these children are also the least likely to have home computers, which some experts say may put them at a disadvantage.

"The interesting twist here is that the very children who are most likely to benefit from home Internet access are the ones least likely to have it," says Jackson. "It's a classic digital divide issue."

Point, Click and Read

In her research, published in a 2006 *Developmental Psychology* (Vol. 42, No. 3, pages 429–435) special section on Internet use, Jackson studied 140 urban children as part of HomeNetToo, a longitudinal field study designed to assess the effects of Internet use in low-income families. Most of the child participants were African American and around 13 years old; 75 percent lived in single-parent households with an average annual income of $15,000 or less. The children were also underperforming in school, scoring in the 30th percentile on standardized reading tests at the beginning of the study.

Jackson and her colleagues provided each family with a home computer and free Internet access. The researchers automatically and continuously recorded the children's Internet use, and participants completed periodic surveys and participated in home visits.

They found that children who used the Internet more had higher scores on standardized reading tests after six months, and higher grade point averages one year and 16 months after the start of the study than did children who used it less. More time spent reading, given the heavily text-based nature of Web pages, may account for the improvement. Jackson also suggests that there may be yet-undiscovered differences between reading online and reading offline that may make online reading particularly attractive to children and teenagers.

"What's unique about the Internet as compared with traditional ways of developing academic performance skills is that it's more of a fun environment," she says. "It's a play tool. You can learn without any pain. Beneficial academic outcomes may just be a coincidental effect of having a good time."

> **"The interesting twist here is that the very children who are most likely to benefit from home Internet access are the ones least likely to have it. It's a classic digital divide issue."**
>
> Linda Jackson
> Michigan State University

What's more, online reading may enhance skills that traditional book reading doesn't tap, says Donald Leu, PhD, the John and Maria NeagEndowed Chair in Literacy and Technology at the University of Connecticut and director of the New Literacies Research Lab. He's found no substantial association between online reading comprehension performance and performance on state reading assessments, as described in a 2005 report submitted to the North Central Regional Educational Laboratory/Learning Point Associates (available online at www.newliteracies.uconn.edu/ncrel_files/FinalNCRELReport.pdf). That's because online reading takes different skills than traditional book reading, he says. Online reading relies heavily on information-location skills, including how to use search engines, as well as information-synthesis and critical evaluation skills.

"The studies that just look at learning fail to recognize that you have to have these online reading comprehension strategies in place before you can really learn very much with Internet information," says Leu.

Leu is looking for ways to improve adolescents' Internet reading comprehension through a three-year, U.S. Department of Education-funded research project, co-led by reading education expert David Reinking, PhD, Eugene T. Moore Professor of Teacher Education at Clemson University.

About half of the children the team studies don't use search engines, Leu says, preferring to use an ineffective "dot com strategy." For example, if they are searching for information on the Iraq War, they will enter the URL "iraqwar.com." This often leads to ad-filled trap sites that provide incorrect or irrelevant information, says Leu. And, the 50 percent of children who do use search engines use a "click and look strategy" of opening each returned site instead of reading the search engine synopsis. If a site appears as the children imagine it should, they believe it's reliable, he says.

Leu and colleagues asked 50 top-reading seventh-graders from school districts in rural South Carolina and urban Connecticut to assess the reliability of a slickly designed Web site on the mythical "endangered Pacific Northwest Tree Octopus." Though the site is a known hoax, all but one child claimed it was scientifically valid. And even after the researchers informed the participants that the site was a joke, about half of the children were adamant that it was indeed truthful, says Leu.

Self-Directed Learners

To help children winnow the tree octopus sites from legitimate information, they must develop online reading comprehension skills. These skills are particularly crucial because other researchers have found that children go online to clarify what they're being taught in school.

"Instead of waiting for a tutor or someone to help them, they are very proactive in seeking help for themselves," says Kallen Tsikalas, director of research and learning services for Computers for Youth (CFY), a national educational nonprofit organization.

Home Internet use during the middle-school years appears to empower students and re-engage them in learning at an age when their academic achievement traditionally drops, adds Tsikalas.

Indeed, 70 percent of students in CFY's program consistently say that having a home computer helps them become more curious and feel more confident, and nearly two-thirds of students report working harder in school because they have a home computer, the organization reports.

Though researchers have found encouraging evidence that Internet use can help children stay interested in school and develop reading skills, it's not an easy area to study, say experts.

"A big challenge to researchers here is that we are dealing with a major generational gap—we are still struggling to catch up with evolving technology and how young people are using it," says Elisheva Gross, PhD, of the Children's Digital Media Center at the University of California, Los Angeles.

The publication lag of scholarly research is also at odds with a technology that's changing and expanding by the day.

"Especially when you talk about books published on this topic, they are historical documents at this point," says Gross.

Is America Lagging?

Although the challenges of studying Internet use abound, Leu argues that America needs to catch up with other countries that are harnessing the Internet for educational purposes. In Finland, for example, teachers take five weeks of paid leave to complete professional development training on teaching online reading comprehension and Internet-use skills. In Japan, the government provides 98 percent of its households with broadband access for only $22 a month.

"The government knows that kids read more out of school than they do in school, and they want to make certain that kids are reading online when they are at home," says Leu. "Most developed nations . . . know their kids will have to compete in a global information environment and they are trying to prepare them for that."

By contrast, America's "report card," the National Assessment of Educational Progress, just defined its framework for the 2009–19 assessment and chose not to include a measure of online reading skills.

"This is supposed to be the gold standard of our performance on reading, and until 2019 we are not going to have a handle on how our kids are doing on the most important information resource we have available," says Leu.

Language and Children's Understanding of Mental States

Children progress through various landmarks in their understanding of mind and emotion. They eventually understand that people's actions, utterances, and emotions are determined by their beliefs. Although these insights emerge in all normal children, individual children vary in their rates of progress. Four lines of research indicate that language and conversation play a role in individual development: (a) Children with advanced language skills are better at mental-state understanding than those without advanced language skills, (b) deaf children born into nonsigning families lag in mental-state understanding, and (c) exposure to maternal conversation rich in references to mental states promotes mental-state understanding, as do (d) experimental language-based interventions. Debate centers on the mechanism by which language and conversation help children's understanding of mental states. Three competing interpretations are evaluated here: lexical enrichment (the child gains from acquiring a rich mental-state vocabulary), syntactic enrichment (the child gains from acquiring syntactic tools for embedding one thought in another), and pragmatic enrichment (the child gains from conversations in which varying perspectives on a given topic are articulated). Pragmatic enrichment emerges as the most promising candidate.

PAUL L. HARRIS, MARC DE ROSNAY, AND FRANCISCO PONS

In the past 20 years, a large body of research has shown that normal children progress through a series of landmarks in their understanding of mental states. At around 4 years of age, children understand that people's actions and utterances are guided by their beliefs, whether those beliefs are true or false. At around 5 to 6 years of age, they come to realize that people's emotions are also influenced by their beliefs (Pons, Harris, & de Rosnay, 2003). This gradual acquisition of what is now routinely known as a *theory of mind* can be illustrated with the classic fairy tale of Little Red Riding Hood. When 3-year-olds are told that the wolf is waiting for Little Red Riding Hood, they typically fail to realize that she mistakenly expects to be greeted by her grandmother as she knocks at the cottage door. By contrast, 4- and 5-year-olds understand Little Red Riding Hood's false belief. Yet many 4-year-olds and some 5-year-olds say that when she knocks, she must be afraid of the wolf—the very wolf that she does not know about! By the age of 6 years, however, most children fully grasp Little Red Riding Hood's naiveté. They understand not only that she fails to realize that a wolf is waiting to eat her, but also that she feels no fear.

Children's acquisition of a theory of mind emerges in orderly steps (Wellman & Liu, 2004; Pons et al., 2003), but individual children vary markedly in their rate of progress. In this article, we review four lines of evidence indicating that language and conversation play a key role in helping children develop an understanding of mental states. We then ask about the causal mechanism involved.

Children's Language Skill and Mental-State Understanding

Among normal children and children with autism, accuracy in the attribution of beliefs and emotions has been correlated with language skill (Happe, 1995; Pons, Lawson, Harris, & de Rosnay, 2003). It could be argued that this correlation shows that a theory of mind facilitates language acquisition. However, longitudinal research has offered little support for such an interpretation. Astington and Jenkins (1999) found that preschoolers' theory-of-mind performance was not a predictor of subsequent gains in language. Rather, the reverse was true: Language ability was a good predictor of improvement in theory-of-mind performance. Children with superior language skills—particularly in the domain of syntax—made greater progress over the next 7 months than other children did in their conceptualization of mental states.

Restricted Access to Language: The Case of Deafness

Does a child's access to language, as well as a child's own language skill, affect his or her theory of mind? When children are born deaf, they are often delayed in their access to language, including sign language. Late signers are particularly common among deaf children born to hearing parents because the parents themselves rarely master sign language. Late signers—like children with autism—are markedly delayed in their understanding of mental states. By contrast, deaf children who learn to sign in a home with native signers are comparable to normal children in their performance on theory-of-mind tasks (Peterson & Siegal, 2000).

Even when efforts are made to bypass problems that late signers might have in grasping the language of such tasks—for example, by substituting a nonverbal (Figueras-Costa & Harris, 2001) or pictorial (Woolfe, Want, & Siegal, 2002) test of mental-state understanding—late signers still have marked difficulties. By implication, late-signing children are genuinely delayed in their conceptualization of mental states; it is not simply that they have difficulty in conveying their understanding when the test is given in sign language.

Maternal Conversation and Mental-State Understanding

Two recent studies show that, even when children have normal access to language, mothers vary in their language style and this style appears to affect children's mental-state understanding. Ruffman, Slade, and Crowe (2002) studied mother-child pairs on three occasions when the children ranged from 3 to 4 years of age. On each occasion, they recorded a conversation between mother and child about a picture book and measured the child's theory-of-mind performance and linguistic ability. Mothers' use or nonuse of mental-state language-terms such as *think, know, want,* and *hope*—at earlier time points predicted children's later theory-of-mind performance. Moreover, the reverse pattern did not hold.

The experimental design used in this study allowed the role of maternal conversation to be clarified in important ways. First, it was specifically mental-state references that predicted children's theory-of-mind performance; other aspects of maternal discourse, such as descriptive comments (e.g., "She's riding a bicycle") or causal comments (e.g., "They have no clothes on because they're in the water"), had no impact on children's theory-of-mind performance over and above the effect of mental-state utterances. Second, children's earlier language abilities also predicted their later theory-of-mind performance independently of their mothers' mental-state discourse.

The study by Ruffman et al. (2002) focused on false-belief tasks mastered somewhere between 3 and 4 years of age. We investigated whether mothers' mental-state discourse is linked to children's performance on a more demanding task typically mastered at around 5 or 6 years of age. Recall the story of Little Red Riding Hood: Only around the age of 5 or 6 years do many children realize that Little Red Riding Hood feels no fear of the wolf when she knocks at the door of grandmother's cottage. In a study of children ranging from 4½ to 6 years (de Rosnay, Pons, Harris, & Morrell, 2004), we found that mothers' use of mentalistic terms when describing their children (i.e., references to their children's psychological attributes as opposed to their behavior or physical attributes) and their children's own verbal ability were positively associated not only with correct false-belief attributions, but also with correct emotion attributions in tasks utilizing stories akin to that of Little Red Riding Hood. Moreover, mothers' mentalistic descriptions predicted children's correct emotion attributions

even when the sample was restricted to children who had mastered the simpler false-belief task. So, even after children have mastered the false-belief task, there is still scope for maternal discourse to help the child make further progress in understanding mental states.

Four important conclusions emerge from these studies. First, mothers who talk about psychological themes promote their children's mental-state understanding. Second, it is unlikely that psychologically precocious children prompt more mental-state language in their mothers; rather, the direction of causation is from mother to child. Third, mere talkativeness on the part of a mother does not promote mental-state understanding—it is the mother's psychological language that is critical. Fourth, mothers' psychological orientation has sustained influence: This influence is evident among 3-year-olds and 6-year-olds alike. The effect of maternal language is not restricted to false-belief understanding. It also applies to the later understanding of belief-based emotions.

Language-Based Interventions

So far, we have summarized correlational findings demonstrating a link between language and mental-state understanding. However, experimental language interventions also produce gains in mental-state understanding. In one study, Lohmann and Tomasello (2003) pretested a large group of 3-year-olds. Those who failed a standard test of false-belief received various types of intervention and were then retested using other false-belief tasks. The most effective intervention for improving children's understanding of false belief combined two factors: (a) the presentation of a series of objects, some of which had a misleading appearance (e.g., an object that looked initially like a flower but turned out to be a pen); and (b) verbal comments on what people would say, think, and know about the perceptible properties and actual identity of these objects. Hale and Tager-Flusberg (2003) also found that language-based interventions were effective in improving children's false-belief understanding. In one intervention, children discussed story protagonists who held false beliefs. In a second intervention, they discussed story protagonists who made false claims. In each case, the children were given corrective verbal feedback if they misstated what the protagonists thought or said. Both interventions proved very effective in promoting 3-year-olds' grasp of false belief.

These intervention studies confirm that conversation about people's thoughts or statements has a powerful effect on children's understanding of belief. One additional finding underscores the critical role of conversation. When Lohmann and Tomasello (2003) presented children with various misleading objects but offered minimal verbal comment—other than a request to look at the objects—the impact on children's mental-state understanding was negligible.

How Does Language Help?

Given the converging evidence just described, the claim that language makes a difference for children's developing theory of mind is convincing. Not only do children's own language abilities predict their rate of progress in understanding the mind, but their access to conversation, especially conversation rich in mentalistic words and concepts, is an equally potent and independent predictor.

Despite this solid evidence for the role of language, there is disagreement over how exactly it helps. Consider the type of comments that a mother might make as she and her preschool child look at a picture book—"I think it's a cat" or "I don't know whether it's a dog" (Ruffman et al., 2002, p. 740). It could be argued that such comments help the child develop an understanding of mental states because the words think and know draw the child's attention to mental processes. But there are other possible explanations. For example, such comments are also syntactically distinctive: They embed a proposition (". . . it's a cat" or ". . . whether it's a dog") in another clause containing a mental verb ("I think . . ." or "I don't know . . ."). Mastery of the way propositions can be embedded in other clauses might help children to conceptualize mental states that take particular states of affairs as their target. Mental-state understanding often calls for an appreciation of the way in which a mental state such as a thought, a belief, or a hope is targeted at a particular state of affairs. But also, such comments play a role in the pragmatics of conversation. More specifically, they set out a claim (e.g., ". . . it's a cat") and they convey the particular perspective of the speaker toward that claim. Accordingly, such comments might underline the way people can vary in the mental stance or perspective they adopt toward a given claim. In short, mentalistic comments contain distinctive words (e.g., think and know), grammatical constructions (e.g., embedded propositions), and pragmatic features (e.g., the enunciation of individual perspectives). Which factor is critical? It is too early to draw firm conclusions, but the evidence increasingly points to the importance of pragmatic features.

First, two recent studies with children speaking languages other than English suggest that the syntax of embedded propositions is not the reason why language skill correlates with theory-of-mind understanding. In German, want sentences such as "Mother wants George to go to bed" must be rendered with a that proposition—"Mutter will, dass George ins Bett geht" (literally, "Mother wants that George into the bed goes"). Perner, Sprung, Zauner, and Haider (2003) studied whether early exposure to, and understanding of, the want–that structure is associated with good performance on standard theory-of-mind tasks, but they found no evidence supporting such a relationship. Similarly, a study of Cantonese-speaking children failed to uncover any link between mastery of verbs that can serve to embed another proposition and theory-of-mind understanding, once general language competence had been taken into account (Cheung et al., 2004).

Second, our findings (de Rosnay et al., 2004) make both the lexical and the syntactic explanations problematic. Maternal usage of terms like think and know together with their embedded propositions might plausibly help children to understand false beliefs because when they attribute a false belief to someone, children will need to use the same linguistic constructions. For example, to describe Little Red Riding Hood's mistaken belief, it is appropriate to say: "She thinks that it's her grandmother" or "She doesn't know that it's a wolf." However, the

attribution of emotion, including belief-based emotion, does not call for the use of mental-state terms with embedded propositions. It simply calls for appropriate use of particular emotion terms. "Little Red Riding Hood felt happy as she knocked at the cottage." Yet we found that mothers' mental discourse not only helped children understand false beliefs, but also helped them move on to understand belief-based emotions. An emphasis on pragmatics can readily explain this twofold impact: Mothers disposed to talk about varying individual beliefs regarding a given situation will probably also articulate the feelings that flow from those individual beliefs.

Conclusions

People often observe other people's facial expressions and bodily postures for clues to their mental life. Indeed, a great deal of research on the early development of a theory of mind has focused on infants' skill at interpreting these nonverbal clues. However, in contrast to any other species, human beings are also able to talk to each other about their mental lives. They can talk about their feelings, compare their beliefs, and share their plans and intentions.

The research reviewed here shows that such conversations play a key role in helping children to make sense of mental states. We are on the brink of designing longitudinal and intervention studies that will help us determine just how conversation helps children in this endeavor. So far, research on children's mental-state understanding has mainly focused on the milestone of understanding false beliefs. We have shown here, however, that maternal discourse is also linked with how well children attribute belief-based emotions to other people, and specifically that this link holds true even among children who have already mastered false beliefs.

In the future, it will be important to study various other milestones in children's mental-state understanding. For example, only around age 5 or 6 do children understand that the emotions people actually feel may not correspond to the emotions that they express. Also, it is not until middle childhood that children fully understand self-conscious emotions such as guilt—or understand that it is possible to feel conflicting emotions about the same situation. In the future, researchers can focus on these developmental advances to better understand the influence of parents' conversation on children's mental-state understanding. If it is found that the same type of parental conversation style (e.g., coherent psychological discourse) has a pervasive influence across different aspects of mental-state understanding, then it will become less likely that specific lexical or semantic features of discourse are the crucial factor. Instead, as we have noted, it will be more plausible to assume that some parents elucidate a variety of mental states in conversation with their children. That elucidation is not tied to particular lexical terms or syntactic constructions. Instead, it reflects a wide-ranging sensitivity to individual perspectives and nurtures that same sensitivity in children.

Researchers may also consider the implications of mental-state understanding for children's behavior and social relationships. An increasing body of evidence indicates that good performance on theory-of-mind tasks is correlated with the ability to form relationships with peers (Pons, Harris, & Doudin, 2002). A plausible—but as yet untested—interpretation is that children's mental-state understanding helps them both to initiate and to maintain friendships. This hypothesis can be tested by assessing the impact of a discourse-based intervention not just on children's mental-state understanding, but also on their relationships with peers.

Finally, researchers may look forward to an important bridge between developmental and clinical psychology. The mother who is alert to her child's mental states, who accurately puts thoughts and feelings into words, and who nurtures her child's sensitivity to different mental perspectives may have an effect on her child that is not unlike that of a clinician or therapist who fosters a reflective stance in his or her patients.

References

Astington, J.W., & Jenkins, J.M. (1999). A longitudinal study of the relation between language and theory-of-mind development. *Developmental Psychology, 35,* 1311–1320.

Cheung, H., Hsuan-Chih, C., Creed, N., Ng, L., Wang, S.P., & Mo, L. (2004). Relative roles of general and complementation language in theory-of-mind development: Evidence from Cantonese and English. *Child Development, 75,* 1155–1170.

de Rosnay, M., Pons, F., Harris, P.L., & Morrell, J. (2004). A lag between understanding false belief and emotion attribution in young children: Relationships with linguistic ability and mothers' mental state language. *British Journal of Developmental Psychology, 22,* 197–218.

Figueras-Costa, B., & Harris, P.L. (2001). Theory of mind in deaf children: A non-verbal test of false belief understanding. *Journal of Deaf Studies and Deaf Education, 6,* 92–102.

Hale, C.M., & Tager-Flusberg, H. (2003). The influence of language on theory of mind: A training study. *Developmental Science, 6,* 346–359.

Happé, F.G.E. (1995). The role of age and verbal ability in the theory of mind task performance of subjects with autism. *Child Development, 66,* 843–855.

Lohmann, H., & Tomasello, M. (2003). The role of language in the development of false belief understanding: A training study. *Child Development, 74,* 1130–1144.

Perner, J., Sprung, M., Zauner, P., & Haider, H. (2003). Want that is understood well before say that, think that, and false belief: A test of de Villiers's linguistic determinism on German-speaking children. *Child Development, 74,* 179–188.

Peterson, C.C., & Siegal, M. (2000). Insights into theory of mind from deafness and autism. *Mind and Language, 15,* 123–145.

Pons, F., Harris, P.L., & de Rosnay, M. (2003). Emotion comprehension between 3 and 11 years: Developmental periods and hierarchical organization. *European Journal of Developmental Psychology, 2,* 127–152.

Pons, F., Harris, P.L., & Doudin, P.-A. (2002). Teaching emotion understanding. *European Journal of Psychology of Education, 17,* 293–304.

Pons, F., Lawson, J., Harris, P.L., & de Rosnay, M. (2003). Individual differences in children's emotion understanding: Effects of age and language. *Scandinavian Journal of Psychology, 44,* 347–353.

Ruffman, T., Slade, L., & Crowe, E. (2002). The relation between children's and mothers' mental state language and theory-of-mind understanding. *Child Development, 73,* 734–751.

Wellman, H.M., & Liu, D. (2004). Scaling of theory of mind tasks. *Child Development, 75,* 523–541.

Woolfe, T., Want, S.C., & Siegal, M. (2002). Signposts to development: Theory-of-mind in deaf children. *Child Development, 73,* 768–778.

PAUL L. HARRIS Harvard University, **MARC DE ROSNAY** Cambridge University, and **FRANCISCO PONS** University of Aalborg, Denmark.

Children's Biased Evaluations of Lucky versus Unlucky People and Their Social Groups

KRISTINA R. OLSON ET AL.

Hurricanes strike some houses and spare others, lotteries are won and lost, and children are born into wealthy and poor families. Rationally, there is no reason to prefer people who are lucky to those who are unlucky. In fact, the explicit codes of ethics by which modern societies govern themselves emphasize neutrality or even a favoring of the least advantaged (Rawls, 1971). But rationality is not always a quality of human minds (Simon, 1957; Tversky & Kahneman, 1974), and this is so even when decisions involve the dimension of right versus wrong (Banaji & Bhaskar, 2000).

Understanding how children think about other people who experience luck or misfortune can provide a window into the origins of attitudes and preferences toward social groups that vary in privilege. Accordingly, we tested children's preferences for lucky versus unlucky individuals. Then we pushed further to test the generalization of such preferences beyond the individuals themselves to others who shared a group marker (same-colored T-shirt).

Study 1

Do children show a preference for those peers who experience randomly occurring (uncontrollable) positive rather than negative events? In Study 1, we compared evaluations of lucky versus unlucky individuals with evaluations of individuals performing purposeful (intentional) positive versus negative actions. Thirty-two 5- to 7-year-old children[1] (18 female, M = 6 years) heard four types of scenarios involving another child: intentional and positive (e.g., the child helped the teacher), intentional and negative (e.g., the child told a lie to his or her mother), uncontrollable and positive (e.g., the child found $5 on the sidewalk), and uncontrollable and negative (e.g., the child's soccer game was rained out).

The participants were read two-line vignettes about fictitious target children, one at a time. After each one, they were asked, "How much do you like [name]?" Responses were made on a 6-point smile-to-frown scale anchored by a large frowning face

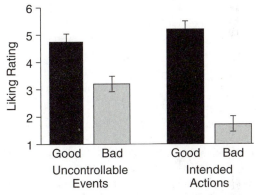

Figure 1 Results from Study 1: children's rated liking of people who were targets of uncontrollable good or bad events, or perpetrators of intentional good or bad actions. Error bars indicate standard error of the mean.

(*really don't like*) and a large smiling face (*really like*). Each child responded to 10 scenarios (out of 40 total), including at least 1 of each type. A mean preference rating was computed for each of the four types of scenarios for each subject.

The mean ratings differed across the types of scenarios, as demonstrated in a one-way repeated measures analysis of variance, $F(3, 93)$ = 49.18, $p < .001$ (see Figure 1). Not surprisingly, the children showed a preference for intentionally good peers over intentionally bad peers, $t(31)$ = 11.76, $p_{rep} > .99$, d = 3.04 (Imamoglu, 1975). But they also showed a similar preference for beneficiaries of uncontrollable good events over victims of uncontrollable bad events, $t(31)$ = 3.87, p_{rep} = .99, d = 1.07. As one might expect, the children also distinguished between intentional and uncontrollable events, showing a preference for victims of uncontrollable bad events over children who intentionally performed bad actions, $t(31)$ = 4.53, $p_{rep} > .99$, d = 1.01, but only a marginal preference for children who intentionally performed good actions over beneficiaries of uncontrollable good events, $t(31)$ = 1.84, p_{rep} = .84, d = 0.40.

Study 2

In a second experiment, we investigated whether this preference for the lucky over the unlucky spreads to new members of groups associated with good versus bad fortune. On each of two trials, forty-three 5- to 7-year-old children[2] (21 female, $M = 6$ years) were introduced to members of two groups (five members each) distinguished by their T-shirt color and location on the computer screen (right or left side). Three members of one group were described as beneficiaries of uncontrollable positive events, whereas three members of the other group were described as victims of uncontrollable negative events. The remaining two members of each group were described neutrally (e.g., "Charlie likes oatmeal"). Thus, although group membership was never explicitly mentioned, the descriptions created a systematic yet imperfect association between group and luck. Subjects were then introduced to two new people, one belonging to each group, and were asked, "Who do you like more?" A similar procedure was followed to introduce the children to groups associated with intentional good versus bad actions and then to assess the children's liking for new people wearing T-shirts of the colors associated with these groups.

We calculated the proportion of trials on which the children preferred the member of the lucky or good group. We then conducted separate chi-square goodness-of-fit tests for the uncontrollable-events and intentional-actions scenarios to determine whether the children had a significant preference for people who appeared to belong to the good and lucky groups.[3] The children preferred new individuals who belonged to the mostly lucky group to those who belonged to the mostly unlucky group, $x^2(2, N = 38) = 7.68$, $p_{rep} = .92$, $w = .45$. In other words, the children preferred individuals who belonged to groups with lucky members despite the fact that (a) the group distinctions were arbitrary (T-shirt color and screen location), (b) the groups were never labeled as groups (e.g., "This is the blue-shirt group"), and (c) the children had no knowledge of the new members besides their group membership. Most remarkably, the effect was obtained even though group membership was not perfectly correlated with event type. Not surprisingly, children also preferred new individuals who belonged to the intentionally good group to those who belonged to the intentionally bad group, $x^2(2, N = 40) = 27.8$, $p_{rep} > .99$, $w = .83$.

Conclusion

Every society is marked by social inequalities. Recognition of the source of inequalities (often luck) might suggest favoring the disadvantaged, as evinced by messages in holy books, theories of justice, and the values expressed on surveys. But such abstract principles of justice are less often seen in the actions of individuals (e.g., Lerner, 1980). The two experiments reported here show the difficulty that confronts young humans as they make interpersonal decisions about how much they like individuals who benefit from sheer luck or experience misfortune. Young children (a) express stronger liking for people who are the beneficiaries of good luck compared with people who are the victims of bad luck and (b) generalize this preference beyond the individuals themselves to those who belong to the same group. Because people who begin life with disadvantage are also more likely than others to experience negative events that are beyond their control (e.g., those most affected by hurricanes are often the people who are the poorest), this preference for people with privilege may further increase negativity toward the disadvantaged. Such preferences may, in turn, help explain the persistence of social inequality.

Notes

1. One additional child was excluded because of inattentiveness.
2. Two additional participants were excluded because of parental interference or limited English comprehension.
3. A trial was dropped from analysis if the participant announced that his or her choice was based on the child's name or T-shirt color (4.4% of trials).

References

Banaji, M.R., & Bhaskar, R. (2000). Implicit stereotypes and memory: The bounded rationality of social beliefs. In D.L. Schacter & E. Scarry (Eds.), *Memory, brain and belief* (pp. 139–175). Cambridge, MA: Harvard University Press.

Imamoglu, E.O. (1975). Children's awareness and usage of intention cues. *Child Development, 46,* 39–45.

Lerner, M. (1980). *The belief in a just world: A fundamental delusion.* New York: Plenum.

Rawls, J. (1971). *A theory of justice.* Cambridge, MA: Harvard University Press.

Simon, H. (1957). *Models of man.* New York: Wiley.

Tversky, A., & Kahneman, D. (1974). Judgment under uncertainty: Heuristics and biases. *Science, 185,* 1124–1131.

Address correspondence to Kristina Olson, 33 Kirkland St., Cambridge, MA 02138, e-mail: krolson@wjh.harvard.edu.

Acknowledgments—We thank A. Reynolds for drawings used in Study 2, Harvard Museum of Natural History for research space, and A. Russell, C. Borras, R. Rau-Murthy, R. Ruhling, M. Mahone, V. Loehr, P. Hayden, and R. Montana for data collection. This research was supported by the Beinecke Scholarship, National Science Foundation, National Institutes of Health, and Third Millennium Foundation.

From *Psychological Science*, October 2006, pp. 845–846. Copyright © 2006 by the Association for Psychological Science. Reprinted by permission of Wiley-Blackwell.

Future Thinking in Young Children

CRISTINA M. ATANCE

Humans spend a great deal of time anticipating, planning for, and contemplating the future. Our future thinking is directed toward such ordinary events as what to wear the next day or where to go for lunch, but also toward more significant choices that will potentially impact our long-term happiness and success, such as accepting a job or getting married. The fact that we think (and often ruminate) about these and numerous other aspects of our personal futures is argued to be a reflection of our cognitive capacity for mental time travel (e.g., Atance & Meltzoff, 2005; Suddendorf & Corballis, 2007; Tulving, 2005).

Mental Time Travel

Tulving's (1984) distinction between "semantic" and "episodic" memory has deeply influenced theory and research in human cognition. Semantic memory is described as an early-developing system that allows one to retrieve facts about the world (e.g., knowing that Paris is the capital of France). It is often contrasted with episodic memory, which is described as a later-developing system that mediates one's memory for personally experienced events (e.g., remembering the first time I strolled down the Champs-Elysées). Episodic memory is argued to be unique to humans and critical to mental time travel (Tulving, 2005). Although research and theory have focused almost exclusively on mental time travel into the past, the adaptive significance of the episodic system may be that it allows humans to mentally travel into the future and thus anticipate and plan for needs not currently experienced (e.g., imagining a state of hunger when currently satiated; Suddendorf & Corballis, 2007; Tulving, 2005).

Although other animal species engage in future-oriented behaviors (e.g., food hoarding, nest building, and planning), there is substantial debate about whether these behaviors are carried out with the future in mind. For example, food hoarding may be driven by genetically programmed, species-specific behavioral tendencies (Roberts, 2002), whereas planning (e.g., a chimpanzee preparing a stick for retrieving termites) may be driven largely by the animal's current motivational state rather than by an anticipated future one (e.g., Roberts, 2002; but see Mulcahy & Call, 2006; and Raby, Alexis, Dickinson, & Clayton, 2007). Debates about mental time travel in nonhuman animals have led to the interesting question of when this capacity emerges in human development.

The Development of Mental Time Travel

Busby and Suddendorf (2005) tested preschoolers' ability to mentally project into the future by asking them to verbally report something that they would do "tomorrow." Whereas 4- and 5-year-olds were quite successful in providing reports that their parents judged as plausible (69% and 63% of total reports, respectively), 3-year-olds were not (31%). Meltzoff and I (Atance & Meltzoff, 2005) adopted a different approach requiring verbal and nonverbal responses. Preschoolers were asked to pretend that they would make an outing to various locations (e.g., mountains, desert) and were asked to choose one item from a set of three to bring with them. Only one of these could be used to address a future physiological state. For example, in the mountain scenario, a lunch—which could address the future state of hunger—was the correct choice, whereas a bowl and a comb were incorrect. Scenarios were designed to be ones for which children would have little direct experience, thus reducing the likelihood that children could succeed based on semantic knowledge alone. Across scenarios, 3-year-olds chose the correct item significantly more often than would be expected by chance, with the performance of the older children being nearly perfect. Moreover, to explicitly test whether children recognized that the correct item could be used to address a future state, they were asked to verbally explain their choices. Four- and 5-year-olds were significantly more likely (62% and 71% respectively) than 3-year-olds (35%) to reference a future state of the self (e.g., "I might get hungry").

These two studies suggest that 4- and 5-year-olds are able to mentally travel into the future to consider what they may do the next day and to anticipate a variety of states that could arise across different situations. In contrast, 3-year-olds only show the rudiments of these abilities.

Mental Time Travel and Verbal Ability

Might limitations in verbal ability mask young children's understanding of the future? Comprehension of temporal terms such as *tomorrow* and *yesterday* emerges only gradually during the preschool and early school years. *Tomorrow,* in particular, is understood by most 3-year-olds to refer to the future, but not necessarily the next day (Harner, 1975). Asking a young child to report an event that will occur "tomorrow" may result in the child stating an anticipated event, but not necessarily one that falls within the conceptual boundaries of this term. At the other end of the spectrum is debate about whether a child who *can* talk about the future should be credited with mental time travel into the future (e.g., Suddendorf & Busby, 2005). Children as young as 2 years of age talk about the future, but such talk may reflect preexisting knowledge (or "scripts") of how routine activities such as "bedtime" unfold, rather than a true projection into the future (Atance & O'Neill, 2001). To guard against under- or over-estimating children's future thinking ability, researchers have strived to create tasks that rely as little as possible on verbal ability and that are structured to test when children's *behavior* evidences the anticipation of a state that they are not currently experiencing—the litmus test of mental time travel into the future.

Acting Now *in Anticipation of* Later

Suddendorf and Busby (2005) tested preschoolers' ability to act in the present to avoid a future state of boredom. Children in the experimental group were led to an empty room (Room A) containing only a puzzle board, whereas children in the control group were also led to Room A, but with no puzzle board present. After a brief stay in Room A, children were led to Room B. Several minutes later, they were told that they would return to Room A and were asked to select an item to bring with them— one of these being puzzle pieces. Whereas 4- and 5-year-olds in the experimental group chose puzzle pieces significantly more often than those in the control group, 3-year-olds' choices did not differ across groups, suggesting that only the older children were able to act in the present (i.e., choose puzzle pieces) in anticipation of a future state (i.e., play/avoid boredom).

Using a different behavioral paradigm, Meltzoff and I (Atance & Meltzoff, 2006) manipulated preschoolers' current state to observe how this would impact their choices for the future. Three-, 4-, and 5-year-olds were assigned either to intervention groups, in which they were given pretzels to snack on, or baseline groups, in which they were not. After a delay (which allowed children in the intervention groups to eat the thirst-inducing pretzels), one group of intervention children and one group of baseline children were asked to choose between pretzels and water. Most intervention children, who were presumably thirsty, chose water, whereas most baseline children chose pretzels. More importantly, the remaining two groups of children (one intervention and one baseline) were asked to choose for *tomorrow*. Again, most baseline children chose pretzels, showing that when they were not in a state of thirst they preferred pretzels. In contrast, the intervention children were unable to override their current desire for water to anticipate that pretzels would be desirable the next day (see Figure 1). This was true of all three age groups, despite the fact that most 4- and 5-year-olds correctly responded to comprehension questions about *tomorrow*, which suggests that their difficulty did not lie in an inability to comprehend the temporal reference of the test question.

Rather, the 4- and 5-year-olds' difficulty may involve what social psychologists (e.g., Loewenstein & Schkade, 1999) refer to as "empathy gaps." This term captures the difficulty that people experience when trying to imagine themselves in a

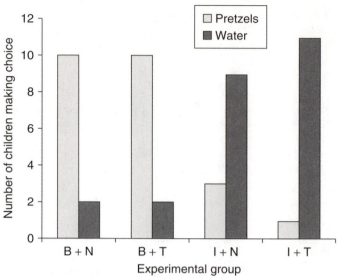

Figure 1 Number of children choosing pretzels or water as a function of whether they had been given pretzels to snack on (intervention groups) or not (baseline groups), and whether they had been asked to choose for *now* or *tomorrow*. B + N = Baseline + Choice for Now; B + T = Baseline + Choice for *Tomorrow;* I + N = Intervention + Choice for *Now;* I + T = Intervention + Choice for *Tomorrow*.

different state than their current one. Most notably, people in a "hot" state (e.g., hunger or thirst) tend to have difficulty imagining that they will eventually "cool off" (i.e., become satiated or quenched). Consequently, predictions, or choices, for the future are biased in the direction of current states. Buying more groceries when hungry than when satiated is a common consequence of empathy gaps. It is likely that the children in our study (Atance & Meltzoff, 2006) were falling prey to this very phenomenon (i.e., they could not imagine a future desire for pretzels while in a state of thirst). Arguably, the children in Suddendorf and Busby's (2005) "two rooms" study did not need to bridge as wide an empathy gap because imagining playing with the puzzle (or avoiding boredom) was not directly conflicting with their current state, nor was their current state one as salient as thirst or hunger. Our (Atance & Meltzoff, 2006) findings do not contradict the claim that mental time travel emerges in the preschool years, but they identify conditions in which the capacity to do so is compromised.

Mental Time Travel and Future-Oriented Behaviors
Planning

Studies examining the development of planning rarely discuss how it is affected by children's growing knowledge about the future (cf. Haith, 1997). Because components of planning, including goal representation and the envisioning of actions necessary to achieve a goal, require thought about the future, planning capacity should shift qualitatively at ages 4 or 5, mirroring episodic-memory development and the emergence of mental time travel. Reinterpretation of data from Hudson, Shapiro, and

Sosa (1995) is consistent with this claim. One group of 3- to 5-year-olds was asked to provide scripts for going to the beach and going grocery shopping (e.g., "Can you tell me what happens when you go to the beach?"), whereas another group was asked to formulate plans (e.g., "Can you tell me a plan for going to the beach?"). Because plans are more future-oriented than scripts, and arguably rely more heavily on the episodic system, a prediction is that they should show more development than scripts during the preschool years.

Results are consistent with this prediction: Children's scripts did not improve significantly with age, whereas their plans did. Moreover, by age 5, children's plans and scripts for the same event were noticeably different. According to Hudson et al., this difference reflected the awareness that planning an event entails more than simply recounting "what happens." Indeed, the older children's plans included more mention of advance preparations than did their scripts, suggesting foresight. Their planning behavior was also more flexible, as evidenced by the capacity to state both how they could remedy an occurrence (e.g., forgetting to bring food to the beach) and prevent its recurrence. This suggests that older children were not merely drawing on their knowledge of how an event typically unfolds (semantic system) but rather were able to imagine different outcomes and how these could be addressed. The foresight and flexibility of the older preschoolers' plans are characteristic of the episodic system and may signal that it, and the mental time travel that it supports, are in place. In contrast, in the absence of a well-developed episodic system, the younger children may have been drawing largely on the semantic system for both script and plan construction.

Delay of Gratification

Future thinking may also be crucial for an important aspect of self-control: delaying gratification. In a delay of gratification paradigm, children are asked to choose between a smaller (e.g., one mini-marshmallow) or a larger (e.g., 10 mini-marshmallows) reward. They are then told that the larger reward can only be obtained after a delay. Although children's ability to delay for the larger, more desirable reward improves with age (e.g., Mischel, Shoda, & Rodriguez, 1989; Moore, Barresi, & Thompson, 1998), there is also individual variability due to self-regulatory strategies (e.g., not looking directly at the reward), for example (Mischel, Shoda, & Rodriguez, 1989). Might an additional source of variability stem from differences in mental time travel capacity? Mischel, Shoda, and Peake (1988) report that 4-year-olds who were good at delaying gratification became adolescents whose parents rated them as being, among other characteristics, better at planning and thinking ahead than the adolescents who were less able to delay gratification. Although these results do not address whether these adolescents also planned more and were future-oriented as preschoolers (an interesting issue for future research), they suggest a mutual interdependence between future thinking and delaying gratification. Indeed, were an organism not able to conceptualize a time other than the present, then delaying would make little sense. These findings also raise the interesting issue of individual differences in mental time travel capacity in both children and adults.

Future Directions

An intriguing issue to consider is the overlap between adopting the perspective of one's future self and the perspective of another person. Research suggests that people experience not only "intrapersonal" empathy gaps but also "interpersonal" ones, such that judgments about the emotional states of others are influenced by one's own (Van Boven & Loewenstein, 2003). Our (Atance & Meltzoff, 2006) state-manipulation paradigm offers a potential means of addressing this issue from a developmental perspective. For instance, do children's current states (e.g., thirst) affect judgments about not only their own future desires but also those of others (both current and future)? A related issue is how thinking about, or planning, one's own future may differ from planning someone else's (e.g., that of one's child or elderly parent). Both processes likely draw on mental time travel but may draw differentially on theory of mind (i.e., mental state attribution).

Because research on the development of future thinking is in its early phases, a primary goal has been to devise methods to assess what young children know about the future. However, in addition to refining existing methodologies, it is important to explore how this knowledge develops. According to Suddendorf and Corballis (2007), mental time travel is not an encapsulated capacity but relies on a host of cognitive processes such as theory of mind, inhibitory control, and working memory. By this view, an organism that lacks some (or all) of these processes will have impaired mental time-travel ability. Exploring whether children's mental time-travel ability is related to individual differences in such skills as theory of mind and inhibitory control will be useful in evaluating this claim.

There is also growing consensus from neurophysiological (e.g., Addis, Wong, & Schacter, 2007) and behavioral (e.g., Busby & Suddendorf, 2005) data that thinking about the future and thinking about the past are intricately entwined; our memories form the basis from which we construct possible futures. Young children (and arguably nonhuman animals) who are limited in their sense of the past will likely also show limitations with respect to the future. Despite this proposed overlap, research findings also suggest neural differentiation between thinking about the past and imagining the future, which may be due to the fact that future events involve some novelty (Addis, Wong, & Schacter, 2007). This view echoes that of Haith (1997), who noted that humans do not just base their future thinking on past events but can also "imagine and create things and events that have never occurred before" (p. 34). Future research efforts will undoubtedly result in significant increases in our knowledge about how the human brain is capable of such a feat, when it becomes attainable in development, and why it may be unattainable for nonhuman animals.

Recommended Reading

Atance, C.M., & Meltzoff, A.N. (2006). (See References). This paper introduces a paradigm to test how children's current states affect their reasoning about the future.
Atance, C.M., & O'Neill, D.K. (2001). (See References). This paper discusses the role of future thinking in different areas of human cognition and behavior.

Haith, M.M., Benson, J.B., Roberts, R.J., Jr., & Pennington, B.F. (Eds.). (1994). *The development of future-oriented processes.* Chicago, IL: University of Chicago Press. A comprehensive volume outlining different aspects of future orientation.

Suddendorf, T., & Corballis, M.C. (2007). (See References). A thorough, highly accessible overview of mental time travel.

Tulving, E. (2005). (See References). A recent, comprehensive review of episodic memory.

References

Addis, D.R., Wong, A.T., & Schacter, D.L. (2007). Remembering the past and imagining the future: Common and distinct neural substrates during event construction and elaboration. *Neuropsychologia, 45,* 1363–1377.

Atance, C.M., & Meltzoff, A.N. (2005). My future self: Young children's ability to anticipate and explain future states. *Cognitive Development, 20,* 341–361.

Atance, C.M., & Meltzoff, A.N. (2006). Preschoolers' current desires warp their choices for the future. *Psychological Science, 17,* 583–587.

Atance, C.M., & O'Neill, D.K. (2001). Episodic future thinking. *Trends in Cognitive Sciences, 5,* 533–539.

Busby, J., & Suddendorf, T. (2005). Recalling yesterday and predicting tomorrow. *Cognitive Development, 20,* 362–372.

Haith, M.M. (1997). The development of future thinking as essential for the emergence of skill in planning. In S.L. Friedman & E. Kofsky Scholnick (Eds.), *The developmental psychology of planning: Why, how, and when do we plan?* (pp. 25–42). Mahwah, NJ: Erlbaum.

Harner, L. (1975). Yesterday and tomorrow: Development of early understanding of the terms. *Developmental Psychology, 11,* 864–865.

Hudson, J.A., Shapiro, L.R., & Sosa, B.B. (1995). Planning in the real world: Preschool children's scripts and plans for familiar events. *Child Development, 66,* 984–998.

Loewenstein, G., & Schkade, D. (1999). Wouldn't it be nice? Predicting future feelings. In D. Kahneman, E. Diener, & N. Schwarz (Eds.), *Well-being: The foundations of hedonic psychology* (pp. 85–105). New York, NY: Russell Sage Foundation.

Mischel, W., Shoda, Y., & Peake, P.K. (1988). The nature of adolescent competencies predicted by preschool delay of gratification. *Journal of Personality and Social Psychology, 54,* 687–696.

Mischel, W., Shoda, Y., & Rodriguez, M.L. (1989). Delay of gratification in children. *Science, 244,* 933–938.

Moore, C., Barresi, J., & Thompson, C. (1998). The cognitive basis of future-oriented prosocial behavior. *Social Development, 7,* 198–218.

Mulcahy, N.J., & Call, J. (2006). Apes save tools for future use. *Science, 312,* 1038–1040.

Raby, C.R., Alexis, D.M., Dickinson, A., & Clayton, N.R. (2007). Planning for the future by western scrub jays. *Nature, 445,* 919–921.

Roberts, W.A. (2002). Are animals stuck in time? *Psychological Bulletin, 128,* 473–489.

Suddendorf, T., & Busby, J. (2005). Making decisions with the future in mind: Developmental and comparative identification of mental time travel. *Learning and Motivation, 36,* 110–125.

Suddendorf, T., & Corballis, M.C. (2007). The evolution of foresight: What is mental time travel and is it unique to humans? *Behavioral and Brain Sciences, 30,* 299–351.

Tulving, E. (1984). Précis of elements of episodic memory. *Behavioral and Brain Sciences, 7,* 223–268.

Tulving, E. (2005). Episodic memory and autonoesis: Uniquely human? In H.S. Terrace & J. Metcalfe (Eds.), *The missing link in cognition: Origins of self-reflective consciousness* (pp. 3–56). New York, NY: Oxford University Press.

Van Boven, L., & Loewenstein, G. (2003). Social projection of transient drive states. *Personality and Social Psychology Bulletin, 29,* 1159–1168.

Address correspondence to CRISTINA M. ATANCE, School of Psychology, University of Ottawa, 120 University, Room 407, Ottawa, Ontario, Canada KIN 6N5; e-mail: atance@uottawa.ca.

Acknowledgments—The writing of this article was supported in part by a Discovery Grant from the Natural Sciences and Engineering Research Council of Canada. I thank Daniel Bernstein, Christopher Fennell, Andrew Meltzoff, Julie Scott, and two anonymous reviewers for their comments.

When Should a Kid Start Kindergarten?

Elizabeth Weil

According to the apple-or-coin test, used in the Middle Ages, children should start school when they are mature enough for the delayed gratification and abstract reasoning involved in choosing money over fruit. In 15th- and 16th-century Germany, parents were told to send their children to school when the children started to act "rational." And in contemporary America, children are deemed eligible to enter kindergarten according to an arbitrary date on the calendar known as the birthday cutoff—that is, when the state, or in some instances the school district, determines they are old enough. The birthday cutoffs span six months, from Indiana, where a child must turn 5 by July 1 of the year he enters kindergarten, to Connecticut, where he must turn 5 by Jan. 1 of his kindergarten year. Children can start school a year late, but in general they cannot start a year early. As a result, when the 22 kindergartners entered Jane Andersen's class at the Glen Arden Elementary School near Asheville, N.C., one warm April morning, each brought with her or him a snack and a unique set of gifts and challenges, which included for some what's referred to in education circles as "the gift of time."

After the morning announcements and the Pledge of Allegiance, Andersen's kindergartners sat down on a blue rug. Two, one boy and one girl, had been redshirted—the term, borrowed from sports, describes students held out for a year by their parents so that they will be older, or larger, or more mature, and thus better prepared to handle the increased pressures of kindergarten today. Six of Andersen's pupils, on the other hand, were quite young, so young that they would not be enrolled in kindergarten at all if North Carolina succeeds in pushing back its birthday cutoff from Oct. 16 to Aug. 31.

Andersen is a willowy 11-year teaching veteran who offered up a lot of education in the first hour of class. First she read Leo Lionni's classic children's book "An Extraordinary Egg," and directed a conversation about it. Next she guided the students through: writing a letter; singing a song; solving an addition problem; two more songs; and a math game involving counting by ones, fives and tens using coins. Finally, Andersen read them another Lionni book. Labor economists who study what's called the accumulation of human capital—how we acquire the knowledge and skills that make us valuable members of society—have found that children learn vastly different amounts from the same classroom experiences and that those with certain advantages at the outset are able to learn more,

more quickly, causing the gap between students to increase over time. Gaps in achievement have many causes, but a major one in any kindergarten room is age. Almost all kindergarten classrooms have children with birthdays that span 12 months. But because of redshirting, the oldest student in Andersen's class is not just 12 but 15 months older than the youngest, a difference in age of 25 percent.

After rug time, Andersen's kindergartners walked single-file to P.E. class, where the children sat on the curb alongside the parking circle, taking turns running laps for the Presidential Fitness Test. By far the fastest runner was the girl in class who had been redshirted. She strode confidently, with great form, while many of the smaller kids could barely run straight. One of the younger girls pointed out the best artist in the class, a freckly redhead. I'd already noted his beautiful penmanship. He had been redshirted as well.

States, too, are trying to embrace the advantages of redshirting. Since 1975, nearly half of all states have pushed back their birthday cutoffs and four—California, Michigan, North Carolina and Tennessee—have active legislation in state assemblies to do so right now. (Arkansas passed legislation earlier this spring; New Jersey, which historically has let local districts establish their birthday cutoffs, has legislation pending to make Sept. 1 the cutoff throughout the state.) This is due, in part, to the accountability movement—the high-stakes testing now pervasive in the American educational system. In response to this testing, kindergartens across the country have become more demanding: if kids must be performing on standardized tests in third grade, then they must be prepping for those tests in second and first grades, and even at the end of kindergarten, or so the thinking goes. The testing also means that states, like students, now get report cards, and they want their children to do well, both because they want them to be educated and because they want them to stack up favorably against their peers.

Indeed, increasing the average age of the children in a kindergarten class is a cheap and easy way to get a small bump in test scores, because older children perform better, and states' desires for relative advantage is written into their policy briefs. The California Performance Review, commissioned by Gov. Arnold Schwarzenegger in 2004, suggested moving California's birthday cutoff three months earlier, to Sept. 1 from Dec. 2, noting that "38 states, including Florida and Texas, have kindergarten entry dates prior to California's." Maryland's proposal to move its date mentioned that "the change . . . will align the 'cutoff' date with most of the other states in the country."

All involved in increasing the age of kindergartners—parents, legislatures and some teachers—say they have the best interests of children in mind. "If I had just one goal with this piece of legislation it would be to not humiliate a child," Dale Folwell, the Republican North Carolina state representative who sponsored the birthday-cutoff bill, told me. "Our kids are younger when they're taking the SAT, and they're applying to the same colleges as the kids from Florida and Georgia." Fair enough—governors and state legislators have competitive impulses, too. Still, the question remains: Is it better for children to start kindergarten later? And even if it's better for a given child, is it good for children in general? Time out of school may not be a gift to all kids. For some it may be a burden, a financial stress on their parents and a chance, before they ever reach a classroom, to fall even further behind.

Redshirting is not a new phenomenon—in fact, the percentage of redshirted children has held relatively steady since education scholars started tracking the practice in the 1980s. Studies by the National Center for Education Statistics in the 1990s show that delayed-entry children made up somewhere between 6 and 9 percent of all kindergartners; a new study is due out in six months. As states roll back birthday cutoffs, there are more older kindergartners in general—and more redshirted kindergartners who are even older than the oldest kindergartners in previous years. Recently, redshirting has become a particular concern, because in certain affluent communities the numbers of kindergartners coming to school a year later are three or four times the national average. "Do you know what the number is in my district?" Representative Folwell, from a middle-class part of Winston-Salem, N.C., asked me. "Twenty-six percent." In one kindergarten I visited in Los Altos, Calif.—average home price, $1 million—about one-quarter of the kids had been electively held back as well. Fred Morrison, a developmental psychologist at the University of Michigan who has studied the impact of falling on one side or the other of the birthday cutoff, sees the endless "graying of kindergarten," as it's sometimes called, as coming from a parental obsession not with their children's academic accomplishment but with their social maturity. "You couldn't find a kid who skips a grade these days," Morrison told me. "We used to revere individual accomplishment. Now we revere self-esteem, and the reverence has snowballed in unconscious ways—into parents always wanting their children to feel good, wanting everything to be pleasant." So parents wait an extra year in the hope that when their children enter school their age or maturity will shield them from social and emotional hurt. Elizabeth Levett Fortier, a kindergarten teacher in the George Peabody Elementary School in San Francisco, notices the impact on her incoming students. "I've had children come into my classroom, and they've never even lost at Candy Land."

For years, education scholars have pointed out that most studies have found that the benefits of being relatively older than one's classmates disappear after the first few years of school. In a literature review published in 2002, Deborah Stipek, dean of the Stanford school of education, found studies in which children who are older than their classmates not only do not learn more per grade but also tend to have more behavior problems. However, more recent research by labor economists takes advantage of new, very large data sets and has produced different results. A few labor economists do concur with the education scholarship, but most have found that while absolute age (how many days a child has been alive) is not so important, relative age (how old that child is in comparison to his classmates) shapes performance long after those few months of maturity should have ceased to matter. The relative-age effect has been found in schools around the world and also in sports. In one study published in the June 2005 Journal of Sport Sciences, researchers from Leuven, Belgium, and Liverpool, England, found that a disproportionate number of World Cup soccer players are born in January, February and March, meaning they were old relative to peers on youth soccer teams.

Before the school year started, Andersen, who is 54, taped up on the wall behind her desk a poster of a dog holding a bouquet of 12 balloons. In each balloon Andersen wrote the name of a month; under each month, the birthdays of the children in her class. Like most teachers, she understands that the small fluctuations among birth dates aren't nearly as important as the vast range in children's experiences at preschool and at home. But one day as we sat in her classroom, Andersen told me, "Every year I have two or three young ones in that August-to-October range, and they just struggle a little." She used to encourage parents to send their children to kindergarten as soon as they were eligible, but she is now a strong proponent of older kindergartners, after teaching one child with a birthday just a few days before the cutoff. "She was always a step behind. It wasn't effort and it wasn't ability. She worked hard, her mom worked with her and she still was behind." Andersen followed the girl's progress through second grade (after that, she moved to a different school) and noticed that she didn't catch up. Other teachers at Glen Arden Elementary and elsewhere have noticed a similar phenomenon: not always, but too often, the little ones stay behind.

The parents of the redshirted girl in Andersen's class told a similar story. Five years ago, their older daughter had just made the kindergarten birthday cutoff by a few days, and they enrolled her. "She's now a struggling fourth grader: only by the skin of her teeth has she been able to pass each year," the girl's mother, Stephanie Gandert, told me. "I kick myself every year now that we sent her ahead." By contrast, their current kindergartner is doing just fine. "I always tell parents, 'If you can wait, wait.' If my kindergartner were in first grade right now, she'd be in trouble, too." (The parents of the redshirted boy in Andersen's class declined to be interviewed for this article but may very well have held him back because he's small—even though he's now one of the oldest, he's still one of the shortest.)

Kelly Bedard, a labor economist at the University of California, Santa Barbara, published a paper with Elizabeth Dhuey called "The Persistence of Early Childhood Maturity: International Evidence of Long-Run Age Effects" in *The Quarterly Journal of Economics* in November 2006 that looked at this phenomenon. "Obviously, when you're 5, being a year older is a lot, and so we should expect kids who are the oldest in kindergarten to do better than the kids who are the youngest in kindergarten," Bedard says. But what if relatively older kids keep doing better after the maturity gains of a few months should have ceased to matter? What if kids who are older relative to their classmates still have higher test scores in fourth grade, or eighth grade?

After crunching the math and science test scores for nearly a quarter-million students across 19 countries, Bedard found that relatively younger students perform 4 to 12 percentiles less well in third and fourth grade and 2 to 9 percentiles worse in seventh and eighth; and, as she notes, "by eighth grade it's fairly safe to say we're looking at long-term effects." In British Columbia, she found that the relatively oldest students are about 10 percent more likely to be "university bound" than the relatively youngest ones. In the United States, she found that the relatively oldest students are 7.7 percent more likely to take the SAT or ACT, and are 11.6 percent more likely to enroll in four-year colleges or universities. (No one has yet published a study on age effects and SAT scores.) "One reason you could imagine age effects persist is that almost all of our education systems have ability-groupings built into them," Bedard says. "Many claim they don't, but they do. Everybody gets put into reading groups and math groups from very early ages." Younger children are more likely to be assigned behind grade level, older children more likely to be assigned ahead. Younger children are more likely to receive diagnoses of attention-deficit disorder, too. "When I was in school the reading books all had colors," Bedard told me. "They never said which was the high, the middle and the low, but everybody knew. Kids in the highest reading group one year are much more likely to be in the highest reading group the next. So you can imagine how that could propagate itself."

Bedard found that different education systems produce varying age effects. For instance, Finland, whose students recently came out on top in an Organization for Economic Cooperation and Development study of math, reading and science skills, experiences smaller age effects; Finnish children also start school later, at age 7, and even then the first few years are largely devoted to social development and play. Denmark, too, produces little difference between relatively older and younger kids; the Danish education system prohibits differentiating by ability until students are 16. Those two exceptions notwithstanding, Bedard notes that she found age effects everywhere, from "the Japanese system of automatic promotion, to the accomplishment-oriented French system, to the supposedly more flexible skill-based program models used in Canada and the United States."

The relative value of being older for one's grade is a particularly open secret in those sectors of the American schooling system that treat education like a competitive sport. Many private-school birthday cutoffs are set earlier than public-school dates; and children, particularly boys, who make the cutoff but have summer and sometimes spring birthdays are often placed in junior kindergarten—also called "transitional kindergarten," a sort of holding tank for kids too old for more preschool—or are encouraged to wait a year to apply. Erika O'Brien, a SoHo mother who has two redshirted children at Grace Church, a pre-K-through-8 private school in Manhattan, told me about a conversation she had with a friend whose daughter was placed in junior kindergarten because she had a summer birthday. "I told her that it's really a great thing. Her daughter is going to have a better chance of being at the top of her class, she'll more likely be a leader, she'll have a better chance of succeeding at sports. She's got nothing to worry about for the next nine years. Plus, if you're making a financial investment in school, it's a less risky investment."

Robert Fulghum listed life lessons in his 1986 best seller "All I Really Need to Know I Learned in Kindergarten." Among them were:

Clean up your own mess.
Don't take things that aren't yours.
Wash your hands before you eat.
Take a nap every afternoon.
Flush.

Were he to update the book to reflect the experience of today's children, he'd need to call it "All I Really Need to Know I Learned in Preschool," as kindergarten has changed. The half day devoted to fair play and nice manners officially began its demise in 1983, when the National Commission on Excellence in Education published "A Nation at Risk," warning that the country faced a "rising tide of mediocrity" unless we increased school achievement and expectations. No Child Left Behind, in 2002, exacerbated the trend, pushing phonics and pattern-recognition worksheets even further down the learning chain. As a result, many parents, legislatures and teachers find the current curriculum too challenging for many older 4- and young 5-year-olds, which makes sense, because it's largely the same curriculum taught to first graders less than a generation ago. Andersen's kindergartners are supposed to be able to not just read but also write two sentences by the time they graduate from her classroom. It's no wonder that nationwide, teachers now report that 48 percent of incoming kindergartners have difficulty handling the demands of school.

Friedrich Froebel, the romantic motherless son who started the first kindergarten in Germany in 1840, would be horrified by what's called kindergarten today. He conceived the early learning experience as a homage to Jean-Jacques Rousseau, who believed that "reading is the plague of childhood. . . . Books are good only for learning to babble about what one does not know." Letters and numbers were officially banned from Froebel's kindergartens; the teaching materials consisted of handmade blocks and games that he referred to as "gifts." By the late 1800s, kindergarten had jumped to the United States, with Boston transcendentalists like Elizabeth Peabody popularizing the concept. Fairly quickly, letters and numbers appeared on the wooden blocks, yet Peabody cautioned that a "genuine" kindergarten is "a company of children under 7 years old, who do not learn to read, write and cipher" and a "false" kindergarten is one that accommodates parents who want their children studying academics instead of just playing.

That the social skills and exploration of one's immediate world have been squeezed out of kindergarten is less the result of a pedagogical shift than of the accountability movement and the literal-minded reverse-engineering process it has brought to the schools. Curriculum planners no longer ask, What does a 5-year-old need? Instead they ask, If a student is to pass reading and math tests in third grade, what does that student need to be doing in the prior grades? Whether kindergarten students actually need to be older is a question of readiness, a concept that itself raises the question: Ready for what? The skill set required to succeed in Fulgham's kindergarten—openness, creativity—is well matched to the capabilities of most 5-year-olds but also substantially different from what Andersen's students need. In early 2000, the National Center for Education Statistics assessed 22,000 kindergartners individually and found, in general, that yes, the older children are better prepared to start an academic kindergarten than the younger ones. The older kids are four times as likely to be reading, and two to three times as likely to be able to decipher two-digit numerals. Twice as many older kids have the advanced fine motor skills necessary for writing. The older kids also have important noncognitive advantages, like being more persistent and more socially adept. Nonetheless, child advocacy groups say it's the schools' responsibility to be ready for the children, no matter their age, not the children's to be prepared for the advanced curriculum. In a report on kindergarten, the National Association of Early Childhood Specialists in State Departments of Education wrote, "Most of the questionable entry and placement practices that have emerged in recent years have their genesis in concerns over children's capacities to cope with the increasingly inappropriate curriculum in kindergarten."

Furthermore, as Elizabeth Graue, a former kindergarten teacher who now studies school-readiness and redshirting at the University of Wisconsin, Madison, points out, "Readiness is a relative issue." Studies of early-childhood teachers show they always complain about the youngest students, no matter their absolute age. "In Illinois it will be the March-April-May kids; in California, it will be October-November-December," Graue says. "It's really natural as a teacher to gravitate toward the kids who are easy to teach, especially when there's academic pressure and the younger kids are rolling around the floor and sticking pencils in their ears."

But perhaps those kids with the pencils in their ears—at least the less-affluent ones—don't need "the gift of time" but rather to be brought into the schools. Forty-two years after Lyndon Johnson inaugurated Head Start, access to quality early education still highly correlates with class; and one serious side effect of pushing back the cutoffs is that while well-off kids with delayed enrollment will spend another year in preschool, probably doing what kindergartners did a generation ago, less-well-off children may, as the literacy specialist Katie Eller put it, spend "another year watching TV in the basement with Grandma." What's more, given the socioeconomics of redshirting—and the luxury involved in delaying for a year the free day care that is public school—the oldest child in any given class is more likely to be well off and the youngest child is more likely to be poor. "You almost have a double advantage coming to the well-off kids," says Samuel J. Meisels, president of Erikson Institute, a graduate school in child development in Chicago. "From a public-policy point of view I find this very distressing."

Nobody has exact numbers on what percentage of the children eligible for publicly financed preschool are actually enrolled—the individual programs are legion, and the eligibility requirements are complicated and varied—but the best guess from the National Institute for Early Education Research puts the proportion at only 25 percent. In California, for instance, 76 percent of publicly financed preschool programs have waiting lists, which include over 30,000 children. In Pennsylvania, 35 percent of children eligible for Head Start are not served. A few states do have universal preschool, and among Hillary Clinton's first broad domestic policy proposals as a Democratic presidential candidate was to call for universal pre-kindergarten classes. But at the moment, free high-quality preschool for less-well-to-do children is spotty, and what exists often is aimed at extremely low-income parents, leaving out the children of the merely strapped working or lower-middle class. Nor, as a rule, do publicly financed programs take kids who are old enough to be eligible for kindergarten, meaning redshirting is not a realistic option for many.

One morning, when I was sitting in Elizabeth Levett Fortier's kindergarten classroom in the Peabody School in San Francisco—among a group of students that included some children who had never been to preschool, some who were just learning English and some who were already reading—a father dropped by to discuss whether or not to enroll his fall-birthday daughter or give her one more year at her private preschool. Demographically speaking, any child with a father willing to call on a teacher to discuss if it's best for that child to spend a third year at a $10,000-a-year preschool is going to be fine. Andersen told me, "I've had parents tell me that the preschool did not recommend sending their children on to kindergarten yet, but they had no choice," as they couldn't afford not to. In 49 out of 50 states, the average annual cost of day care for a 4-year-old in an urban area is more than the average annual public college tuition. A RAND Corporation position paper suggests policy makers may need to view "entrance-age policies and child-care polices as a package."

Labor economists, too, make a strong case that resources should be directed at disadvantaged children as early as possible, both for the sake of improving each child's life and because of economic return. Among the leaders in this field is James Heckman, a University of Chicago economist who won the Nobel in economic science in 2000. In many papers and lectures on poor kids, he now includes a simple graph that plots the return on investment in human capital across age. You can think of the accumulation of human capital much like the accumulation of financial capital in an account bearing compound interest: if you add your resources as soon as possible, they'll be worth more down the line. Heckman's graph looks like a skateboard quarter-pipe, sloping precipitously from a high point during the preschool years, when the return on investment in human capital is very high, down the ramp and into the flat line after a person is no longer in school, when the return on investment is minimal. According to Heckman's analysis, if you have limited funds to spend it makes the most economic sense to spend them early. The implication is that if poor children aren't in adequate preschool programs, rolling back the age of kindergarten is a bad idea economically, as it pushes farther down the ramp the point at which we start investing funds and thus how productive those funds will be.

Bedard and other economists cite Heckman's theories of how people acquire skills to help explain the persistence of relative age on school performance. Heckman writes: "Skill begets skill; motivation begets motivation. Early failure begets later failure." Reading experts know that it's easier for a child to learn the meaning of a new word if he knows the meaning of a related word and that a good vocabulary at age 3 predicts a child's reading well in third grade. Skills like persistence snowball, too. One can easily see how the skill-begets-skill, motivation-begets-motivation dynamic plays out in a kindergarten setting: a child who comes in with a good vocabulary listens to a story, learns more words, feels great about himself and has an even better vocabulary at the end of the day. Another child arrives with a poor vocabulary, listens to the story, has a hard time following, picks up fewer words, retreats into insecurity and leaves the classroom even further behind.

How to address the influence of age effects is unclear. After all, being on the older or younger side of one's classmates is mostly the luck of the birthday draw, and no single birthday cutoff can prevent a 12-month gap in age. States could try to prevent parents from gaming the age effects by outlawing redshirting—specifically by closing the yearlong window that now exists in most states between the birthday cutoffs and compulsory schooling. But forcing families to enroll children in kindergarten as soon as they are eligible seems too authoritarian for America's tastes. States could also decide to learn from Finland—start children in school at age 7 and devote the first year to play—but that would require a major reversal, making second grade the old kindergarten, instead of kindergarten the new first grade. States could also emulate Denmark, forbidding ability groupings until late in high school, but unless very serious efforts are made to close the achievement gap before children arrive at kindergarten, that seems unlikely, too.

Of course there's also the reality that individual children will always mature at different rates, and back in Andersen's classroom, on a Thursday when this year's kindergartners stayed home and next year's kindergartners came in for pre-enrollment assessments, the developmental differences between one future student and the next were readily apparent. To gauge kindergarten readiness, Andersen and another kindergarten teacher each sat the children down one by one for a 20-minute test. The teachers asked the children, among other things, to: skip; jump; walk backward; cut out a diamond on a dotted line; copy the word cat;

draw a person; listen to a story; and answer simple vocabulary questions like what melts, what explodes and what flies. Some of the kids were dynamos. When asked to explain the person he had drawn, one boy said: "That's Miss Maple. She's my preschool teacher, and she's crying because she's going to miss me so much next year." Another girl said at one point, "Oh, you want me to write the word cat?" Midmorning, however, a little boy who will not turn 5 until this summer arrived. His little feet dangled off the kindergarten chair, as his legs were not long enough to reach the floor. The teacher asked him to draw a person. To pass that portion of the test, his figure needed seven different body parts.

"Is that all he needs?" she asked a few minutes later.

The boy said, "Oh, I forgot the head."

A minute later the boy submitted his drawing again. "Are you sure he doesn't need anything else?" the teacher asked.

The boy stared at his work. "I forgot the legs. Those are important, aren't they?"

The most difficult portion of the test for many of the children was a paper-folding exercise. "Watch how I fold my paper," the teacher told the little boy. She first folded her 8 1/2-by-11-inch paper in half the long way, to create a narrow rectangle, and then she folded the rectangle in thirds, to make something close to a square.

"Can you do it?" she asked the boy.

He took the paper eagerly, but folded it in half the wrong way. Depending on the boy's family's finances, circumstances and mind-set, his parents may decide to hold him out a year so he'll be one of the oldest and, presumably, most confident. Or they may decide to enroll him in school as planned. He may go to college or he may not. He may be a leader or a follower. Those things will ultimately depend more on the education level achieved by his mother, whether he lives in a two-parent household and the other assets and obstacles he brings with him to school each day. Still, the last thing any child needs is to be outmaneuvered by other kids' parents as they cut to the back of the birthday line to manipulate age effects. Eventually, the boy put his head down on the table. His first fold had set a course, and even after trying gamely to fold the paper again in thirds, he couldn't create the right shape.

Elizabeth Weil is a contributing writer for the magazine. Her most recent article was about lethal injection.

UNIT 3

Social and Emotional Development

Unit Selections

Key Points to Consider

- Adopted children from other countries who were institutionalized as infants often show permanent negative effects. Why would institutionalization cause these deficits? Do you know anyone who has chosen to adopt a previously institutionalized baby? Would you consider adopting such a baby from another country and why or why not?

- Imagine growing up in a single-parent, homeless family where hunger, violence, drug abuse, and neglect were everyday occurrences. Then imagine trying to walk to school in the same poor, deprived, crime-ridden neighborhood and trying to learn in an inadequate, underfunded school. Most children are permanently scathed by such conditions, but a few prove resilient to even the direst of conditions. How and why does this happen? What factors might help offset these effects? What public policy implications would this have? What could you do to help more children become resilient?

- Who were the most and least popular children growing up? What made them so popular or so shunned? Were you a lonely child? Think of someone who appeared to be lonely. What can be done to assist lonely children? What about your adult friendships today? Do you see any parallels with your childhood friends? Explain. Do you think your childhood friendships helped you to develop improved social skills? Explain? If you have children, how will you help your children develop friends and build their social skills?

- What factors contribute toward making some children bullies and what can be done to defuse these potentially volatile situations? When you were growing up, what did you or your schoolmates do when confronted with a bully? Did you involve a teacher or a parent to help yourself or others out of the situation? Why or why not? What if you have a child who becomes a bully? What, as a parent, could you do to help your child?

- Look at almost any elementary school playground at recess or junior high lunchroom and you will see boys and girls playing. Most people think play is wasted energy and does not promote learning. Explain how playing can facilitate physical, language, and social development. Describe how boys and girls play differently and how this leads to different skill sets. As a teacher or parent, how might you introduce different kinds of play for children as a result of the research?

- Do you remember girls having special cliques when you were in school? As the movie title goes, do you think girls want to be mean? Explain why girls' aggression appears so different from boys' aggression. What factors contribute to these gender differences in aggression? Explain how you think these types of aggressive behaviors might continue into adulthood for men and women.

Student Website
www.mhcls.com

Internet References

Max Planck Institute for Psychological Research
http://www.mpg.de/english/institutesProjectsFacilities/instituteChoice/ psychologische_forschung/

National Child Care Information Center (NCCIC)
http://www.nccic.org
Serendip
http://serendip.brynmawr.edu/serendip/

One of the truisms about our species is that we are social animals. From birth, each person's life is a constellation of relationships, from family at home to friends in the neighborhood and school. This unit addresses how children's social and emotional development is influenced by important relationships with parents, peers, and teachers.

When John Donne in 1623 wrote, "No man is an island, entire of itself . . . any man's death diminishes me, because I am involved in mankind," he implied that all humans are connected to each other and that these connections make us who we are. Early in this century, sociologist C. H. Cooley highlighted the importance of relationships with the phrase "looking-glass self" to describe how people tend to see themselves as a function of how others perceive them. Personality theorist Alfred Adler, also writing in the early twentieth century, claimed that personal strength derived from the quality of one's connectedness to others: The stronger the relationships, the stronger the person. The notion that a person's self-concept arises from relations with others also has roots in developmental psychology. As Jean Piaget once wrote, "There is no such thing as isolated individuals; there are only relations." The articles in this unit respect these traditions by emphasizing the theme that a child's development occurs within the context of relationships.

Today's society is more complex than ever and children from at-risk families face growing challenges such as acute poverty, homelessness, foster care, illness, alcohol and substance abuse, abandonment, deprivation, death, and violence in families. Amazingly, in spite of these terrible odds, unlike most children, there are a lucky few who somehow manage to transcend these crushing effects and rise up to bounce back and develop normally. The author of "Children's Capacity to Develop Resiliency" describe how certain key factors such as an understanding of one's strengths and accomplishments, humor, and high, positive expectations can protect children and keep them on the path of normal development.

Unfortunately, infants who suffer severe and sustained early human deprivation and institutionalization will sustain enduring and permanent neurological damage that may result in later developmental problems. Researcher Charles Nelson describes some of these lasting negative effects in "A Neurobiological Perspective on Early Human Deprivation." In "Emotions and the Development of Childhood Depression: Bridging the Gap" researchers discuss childhood depression and identify risk factors that contribute to this condition in early childhood.

A significant milestone of early childhood involves a child's ability to socialize, communicate and play effectively with peers. The articles, "Cooperation and Communication in the Second Year of Life," "A 'Multitude' of Solitude: A Closer Look at Social Withdrawal and Nonsocial Play in Early Childhood," and "When Girls and Boys Play: What Research Tells Us" all focus on the critical importance of play as promoting neurological growth, enhancing cooperation and communication, and strengthening social and language development in children.

© Digital Vision/Getty Images

While boys may be more likely to resort to physical aggression, girls are more likely to engage in relational verbal and interpersonal aggression. In a related vein, with the increasing concerns about bullying, more schools are developing and implementing intervention programs to assist both the bullies and their potential victims. In "A Profile of Bullying at School," researcher Dan Olweus discusses the process of bullying. Given the detrimental effects of bullying on children's development and adjustment, the author advocates strongly for successful school bullying prevention programs both in the United States and in countries such as Norway.

Another major influence in the landscape of childhood is friendship. When do childhood friendships begin? Friends become increasingly important during the elementary school years. If forming strong, secure attachments with family members is an important task of early childhood, then one of the major psychological achievements of middle childhood is a move toward the peer group. Researchers for "Children's Social and Moral Reasoning about Exclusion" present new data on how prosocial or aggressive behavior as well as prejudice and stereotypes contribute to children's popularity standing and social and moral reasoning. Similarly, in "The Role of Neurobiological Deficits in Childhood Antisocial Behavior" researchers describe specific neurobiological deficits that combined with early adverse environments can lead to some children engaging in problematic antisocial behavior.

Finally, in "Girls Just Want to Be Mean," author Margaret Talbot describes differences between aggression found among girls versus boys.

A Neurobiological Perspective on Early Human Deprivation

The number of children who are abandoned or orphaned around the world is rapidly increasing owing to war, AIDS, and poverty. Many of these children are placed in institutional settings for lack of individual or societal resources or because of long-standing cultural traditions. It has been known for over half a century that rearing children in institutional care characterized by profound sensory, cognitive, linguistic, and psychosocial deprivation can be deleterious to their development. This article examines the neural mechanisms that likely underlie the maldevelopment many institutionalized children experience.

CHARLES A. NELSON

An extraordinary number of children throughout the world begin their lives in psychologically adverse circumstances. In some cases, these children live with their parents in profound poverty; in others, they either do not have parents (such as those orphaned by war or AIDS) or they are abandoned by their parents. Vast numbers of abandoned or orphaned children living in Eastern Europe, China, and Latin America live in institutional settings. This article describes the effects of profound early deprivation (common in many institutional settings) on brain and behavioral development.

The Nature of the Problem

UNICEF estimates that approximately 1.5 million children in Central and Eastern Europe live in public care (orphanages, group homes, psychiatric units). These include children who have been abandoned by their parents, whose parents have died, who live in hospitals because of chronic illness (e.g., AIDS), and who live in penal institutions. The European Commission for Social Cohesion estimates that 10–20 per 1,000 children birth to age 18 in Bulgaria, Russia, and Romania and 5–10 per 1,000 in Poland, Hungary, Moldova, Lithuania, Latvia, and Estonia live in orphanages, group homes, or psychiatric units.[1] In Sweden, Finland, Ireland, Belgium, The Netherlands, Italy, and Spain, 1.5–3.0 per 1,000 children younger than 3 years are institutionalized (Browne, Hamilton-Giachritsis, Johnson, Leth, & Ostergren, 2004).

Collectively, institutionalizing young children is a common practice throughout many parts of the world. The majority of these children will remain in such settings for many years, whereas a relatively small minority will be adopted, most internationally.[2] Indeed, in 2004, nearly 23,000 international adoptions took place in the United States. Not surprisingly given the figures cited above, the vast majority of these children were from Eastern Europe and Asia (Russia and China in particular).

As it does in families, the quality of care varies among institutions; there is also variability in the nature and degree of deprivation. For example, in some model institutions in Russia, the caregiver-to-child ratio is reasonable and the degree of sensory, cognitive, and linguistic deprivation not severe. At the other end of the spectrum, institutional life can be characterized by profound global deprivation. The ratio of children to caregivers can exceed 15:1; caregivers are generally poorly trained and, in many cases, uncommitted to the welfare of children and unresponsive and insensitive to children's needs. Nutrition can be substandard, cognitive stimulation can be inadequate, and exposure to mature language is frequently lacking owing to a paucity of adult caregivers. Basic sensory stimulation can be lacking across multiple modalities, leading to perceptual deficits (e.g., lack of patterned light stimulation because walls and ceilings are painted white and infants are left in their cribs for long periods of time; infants are not held or touched, leading to tactile deprivation). Finally, institutional care is frequently characterized by strict adherence to conformity (e.g., children are dressed alike) and regimen (e.g., children all eat at the same time, use the toilet at the same time). It would not be unreasonable to suggest that life in institutions that globally deprive young children resembles peer-rearing common in some nonhuman primate studies (e.g., Suomi, 1997). Of course, even this is misleading because nonhuman primates typically huddle together when left without caregivers, whereas human children typically do not.

Effects of Early Institutionalization on Development

For most of the 20th century, clinicians and researchers noted the deleterious effects of institutional rearing on the development of young children. Initially, many of these studies were uncontrolled or poorly controlled, but more rigorous, recent investigations have confirmed earlier findings that institutional care is often associated with a variety of deleterious outcomes (for recent review, see Maclean, 2003).

Contemporary research has documented many problems in young children adopted out of institutions in Eastern Europe and Russia. Abnormalities include a variety of serious medical problems (Johnson,

1997; Johnson et al., 1992), physical and brain growth deficiencies (Benoit, Jocelyn, Moddemann, & Embree, 1996; Johnson, 2000), cognitive problems (Morison, Ames, & Chisholm, 1995; Rutter & The English and Romanian Adoptees Study Team, 1998), speech and language delays (Albers, Johnson, Hostetter, Iverson, & Miller, 1997; Dubrovina et al., 1991; Groze & Ileana, 1996), sensory integration difficulties and stereotypies (Cermak & Daunhauer, 1997; Chisholm & Savoie, 1992), and social and behavioral abnormalities (Fisher, Ames, Chisholm, & Savoie, 1997; O'Connor, Bredenkamp, Rutter, & The English and Romanian Adoption Study Team, 1999). The latter include difficulties with inattention and hyperactivity (Rutter, 1999), disturbances of attachment (Chisholm, 1998; Chisholm, Carter, Ames, & Morison, 1995; O'Connor & Rutter, 2000; O'Connor et al., 1999), and a syndrome that mimics autism (Federici, 1998; Rutter et al., 1999). Some of these abnormalities are associated with risk factors that precede placement in the institutions (e.g., prenatal alcohol exposure), but quality of care is often appalling in these institutions, and many problems seem related to the ecology of institutional life (e.g., Ames, 1997).

Several longitudinal studies have examined the effects of institutionalization on children's development. Tizard and her colleagues compared four groups of young children who had been reared in institutions in the United Kingdom for the first 2–4 years of life: (a) a group that was adopted between ages 2 and 4, (b) a group returned to their biological families between ages 2 and 4, (c) a group that remained institutionalized, and (d) a group of never-institutionalized children of the same age (see, e.g., Tizard, 1977; Tizard & Hodges, 1978; Tizard & Reese, 1974, 1975). Across all domains, the adopted children fared better than the institutionalized children. Unfortunately, as is the case with virtually all studies of institutionalized children, they were not randomly assigned to the groups, and selection factors may have influenced the findings (i.e., more developmentally advanced children may have been the first adopted).

Two longitudinal studies have been conducted recently with children adopted from Romanian institutions. Ames, Chisholm, and colleagues (as cited in Maclean, 2003) included three groups of children adopted by Canadian parents: (a) children adopted after having spent at least 8 months in a Romanian institution, (b) children adopted from Romanian institutions at less than 4 months of age, and (c) a Canadian-born (but not adopted) comparison group matched on age and sex to the first group. They found more behavior problems, disturbances of attachment, and lower IQs in the group of children who had spent 8 months or more in Romanian institutions (Maclean, 2003).

O'Connor and Rutter (2000) compared young children adopted from Romania with those adopted within the United Kingdom (see also Rutter, O'Connor, & The English and Romanian Adoptees Study Team, 2004). They found that at both age 4 and again at age 6, the duration of deprivation was linearly related to the number of signs of attachment disorders. Children exhibiting indiscriminate sociability at age 6 had experienced deprivation for twice as long as those exhibiting no attachment disorder signs ($M = 22$ vs. 11 months). Cognitive recovery was inversely related to age of adoption, although social and emotional problems were less clearly related to timing.

Taken together, these findings suggest that although psychosocial deprivation may be associated with impairment across a range of developmental domains, the degree of impairment and trajectories of recovery may vary. These tentative conclusions must be tempered by the lack of randomization and potential selection bias in who is adopted, as well as by lack of data on individual differences in institutional experiences and lack of adequate comparison groups (i.e., native children who have never been institutionalized).

Recently, Zeanah et al. (2003) launched the Bucharest Early Intervention Project (BEIP), in which they examined three cohorts of children: (a) those abandoned at birth, placed in institutions, and who continue to reside in institutions; (b) those abandoned at birth, placed in institutions, and then randomly assigned to foster care; and (c) a sample of children living with their biological parents in the greater Bucharest community. Randomization and the use of an in-country comparison sample circumvent many of the shortcomings of previous studies. Early findings (Nelson, Zeanah, & Fox, 2007) suggest that institutional care has a profoundly negative effect on physical growth, language, cognitive, social–emotional development, and brain development, and that children placed in foster care show improvements in many (although not all) of the domains that are deleteriously affected by institutional life.

The Effects of Early Institutionalization on Brain Development

Given the dramatic behavioral abnormalities observed in institutionalized and formerly institutionalized children, it seems reasonable to consider the neural systems that might be associated with these behavioral abnormalities. Previous research on institutionalized children has not included measures of brain functioning, although some assessments have been conducted with children adopted from institutions. For example, Chugani et al. (2001) used positron emission tomography (PET) in 10 children (average age was 8 years) who had been adopted from a Romanian institution. PET employs a radioactive isotope to examine brain metabolism, for example, the brain's use of glucose, a form of energy. Nearly all children had been placed in the institution before age 18 months and had lived in the institution for an average of 38 months before being adopted. Compared with a control group of healthy adults and a group of 10-year-old children with medically refractory epilepsy (i.e., who were still experiencing seizures), the adoptees showed significantly reduced brain metabolism in select regions of the prefrontal cortex and the temporal lobe and regions associated with higher cognitive functions, memory, and emotion (e.g., the orbital frontal gyrus, the amygdala, and the hippocampus were all affected). Behaviorally, the adopted children suffered from mild neurocognitive impairments, impulsivity, attention, and social deficits—behaviors that are consistent with the patterns of brain findings.

More recently, this same group of researchers examined the connectivity of brain regions that are myelinated (the so-called white matter) in this same sample of previously institutionalized children (Eluvathingal et al., 2006). The authors found that white matter connectivity was diminished in the *uncinate fasciculus* region of the brain in the early deprivation group compared with the controls. Because this structure provides a major pathway of communication between brain areas involved in higher cognitive and emotional function (e.g., amygdala and frontal lobe), the authors concluded that connectivity between brain regions is negatively affected by early institutionalization. It is important to note, however, that these children all tested in the normal range of IQ (although their verbal IQ was lower than their performance IQ), and they suffered only mild impairments in a variety of neuropsychological domains (e.g., sustained attention), as they did in the PET study. How the functional anisotropy (FA; an index of myelination) and behavioral data relate to one another is unclear.

Collectively, results from these two studies point to the neurobiological sequelae of early and prolonged institutionalization. In particular, these children suffered from metabolic deficits in the areas of the brain believed to be involved in higher cognition, emotion, and emotion regulation. Unfortunately, because this sample was small and because this study suffers from the same methodological shortcomings as other post-adoption studies noted earlier, the generalizability of these findings may be limited.

Pollak and colleagues (as cited in Wismer Fries, Ziegler, Kurian, Jacoris, & Pollak, 2005) have also examined the effects of early institutionalization on neurobiological systems, although not the brain per se. This group examined oxytocin and vasopressin, two hormones long associated with affiliative and positive social behavior, in a sample of previously institutionalized children. The previously institutionalized children showed lower overall levels of vasopressin than controls. In addition, they showed lower levels of oxytocin after interacting with their caregiver compared with controls. Collectively, the authors suggest that "a failure to receive species-typical care disrupts the normal development of the [oxytocin and vasopressin] systems in young children" (p. 00). Unfortunately, because these data were collected several years after adoption and because no current data on children's social behavior (such as attachment) were reported, it is difficult to know if the early experiences caused these hormonal changes.

As noted earlier, the BEIP is designed to examine the effects on brain development of early institutionalization that is characterized by profound sensory, cognitive, linguistic, and psychosocial deprivation.[3] Because of the age of the children and limitations in the neuroimaging tools available for use in this project, we were limited to recording the electroencephalogram (EEG) and the event-related potential (ERP). The EEG assesses general cortical activity, whereas the ERP reflects the functioning of populations of neurons acting synchronously during a cognitive task, such as face processing, memory.

In prior work, we (Marshall, Fox, & The BEIP Core Group, 2004) have reported that the institutionalized group had increased levels of low-frequency power and decreased levels of high-frequency power in the EEG compared with the never-institutionalized group. That is, the institutionalized group had less cortical brain activity than the control group (whether subcortical activity is similarly affected is unknown). Similarly, Parker, Nelson, and The BEIP Core Group (2005a, 2005b) performed two cognitive manipulations while recording ERPs. In one manipulation, researchers presented children with images of different facial expressions. In another, they alternated images of the caregiver's face and the face of a stranger. In both cases, the institutionalized population showed reduced amplitude in several ERP components compared with the never-institutionalized group. In all three studies, then, the institutionalized group showed reduced brain activity, a finding that may be consistent with Chugani et al.'s (2001) PET data.

Collectively, it appears that early institutionalization in severe situations has a profoundly negative effect on brain development—although there is still a paucity of data. Specifically, institutionalization appears to lead to a reduction in cortical brain activity (both metabolically and electrophysiologically) and to dysregulation of neuroendocrine systems that mediate social behavior.

Why Is Institutional Rearing Bad for the Brain?

The initial evidence is compelling that early institutionalization (when characterized by profound sensory, cognitive, linguistic, and psychosocial deprivation) has a negative impact on behavioral development. It is also increasingly clear that some of the deficits and developmental delays that result from such institutional rearing have their origins in compromised brain development. The question I seek to address in this final section is why? To address this question requires that I first summarize what drives brain development.

In brief, postnatal brain development is driven by an interaction of genes and experience. Genes provide for the early specification of structures and circuits, whereas experience provides the specialization and fine-tuning needed to lead to mature function. As has been discussed in a variety of forums (e.g., Nelson et al., 2006), brain development reflects a combination of experience-expectant and -dependent mechanisms. The former refers to features of the environment that are (or at least, should be) common to all members of the species, whereas the latter refers to features of the environment that are unique to the individual. Thus, having access to patterned light information or a caregiver is a feature of the environment common to the species, whereas individual differences in environmental challenges (e.g., quality and quantity of stimulation) are unique to the individual.

A short list of experience-expectant features of the environment might include access to a caregiver, adequate nutrition, sensory stimulation (e.g., visual, auditory, tactile), and linguistic input. It likely also includes an environment that is low in the so-called toxic stress, or it provides the building blocks to cope with stress. Of course, if mental and language development is to occur, the environment requires cognitive and linguistic challenges. This list is far from exhaustive, but by inference, it illustrates a key point: many forms of institutional rearing lack most elements of a mental-health-promoting environment. As a result, the young nervous system, which actively awaits and seeks out environmental input, is robbed of such input. This lack of input leads to underspecification of circuits and the miswiring of circuits. Because children living in institutions lack input (stimulation) on a grand scale, we should not be surprised that they experience a range of problems due to "errors" in brain development.

There is also another potential consequence of early institutional rearing. Typical brain development is characterized by an initial overproduction of both neurons and synapses, followed by a retraction to adult numbers (which varies by area; for elaboration, see Nelson et al., 2006). It is believed that the process of overproducing neurons and synapses is guided by a genetic program, whereas the retraction process may depend more heavily on experience. If true, then it may be that living in a deprived environment can lead to errors in apoptosis (programmed cell death). In the BEIP study, we have observed two findings consistent with this hypothesis: smaller head size (even among children placed in foster care) and reduced brain activity. These findings may reflect apoptosis gone awry, specifically, that too many neurons or synapses, or both, were retracted. Because most regions of the brain do not make new neurons postnatally, it is possible that early institutional rearing may have a permanent effect on cell and synapse numbers.

Of course, institutional environments vary in the quality and quantity of deprivation. In my experience in Romanian institutions, I have seen considerable variability in quality of caregiving and the quality of sensory, linguistic, and cognitive stimulation. This leads to an important qualifier in modeling the neurobiology of early institutionalization: Some domains of function are more experience dependent than others, and domains vary in *when* experience is required to facilitate a typical developmental trajectory. Thus, the long-term development of children with histories of early institutionalization will depend on (a) at what age they were institutionalized, (b) how long they were institutionalized, and (c) the exact features of the environment. Moreover, these three dimensions must be set against a backdrop of a child's genetic makeup and his or her prenatal experience (e.g., Was the mother adequately nourished? Was the fetus exposed to alcohol or other teratogens?). Unfortunately, these last two dimensions are rarely known in most studies of post-institutionalized children because genetic information was not obtained and because no reports exist about prenatal development. However, the combination of these three factors—prenatal experience, postnatal experience, and genetic makeup—likely lead to developmental programming effects that may well set the stage for years to come (see Rutter et al., 2004, for elaboration).

Implications

There are many implications of this research. For example, many children living throughout the world (including North America) experience deprivation owing to neglectful parents. Although perhaps not quite as severe as the conditions in many institutions, these children still experience profound neglect. There is an urgent need for societies to respond to the needs of such children, and doing so may be informed by the results of this research.

A second implication of this work applies to the child protection systems in much of this world. We know that the longer a child lives under adversity, the more that child is at risk and the more difficult it will be to redirect that child's development along a typical trajectory. Most child protection systems, however, pay little heed to this clear evidence and fail to move children into permanent homes more quickly or remove them from abusive homes sooner.

Finally, the lessons learned from the BEIP should be noted by the many countries engaged in war or ravaged by disease. Thus, how the world will handle the thousands of children currently being orphaned in Africa, Afghanistan, and Iraq is unclear, although it is frequently the impulse of such countries (motivated by financial, cultural, or practical forces) to place such children in institutional settings rather than to develop a high-quality foster care or adoption system. Wasil Noor, Deputy Minister of Social Welfare in Afghanistan, estimates that of the 1.6 million orphaned Afghani children, more than 10,000 are living in institutional care. Approximately 85% of these children, he estimates, have surviving parents (often both). The government has recently launched a deinstitutionalization program, reunifying children with their families and providing income generating support.[4]

Overall, we have known for more than half a century that children reared in awful institutions are at great risk for atypical development. Most of this work has been descriptive in nature, with little elucidation of the biological mechanisms responsible for maldevelopment. Advances in neuroscience now make it possible to elucidate why, from a neurobiological perspective, children reared in certain institutions are at risk. Having laid the groundwork for a more mechanistic approach to understanding the effects of such early adversity on development, the next step will be to develop interventions targeted at the neural circuits that have been altered by institutional life, with the ultimate goal to use the science of early development to change the policies countries adopt to address their abandoned or neglected children.

Notes

1. Although Romania has made great strides in reducing the number of children living in institutions—from more than 100,000 a decade ago to 30,000 today—the number of children being abandoned has actually held steady at approximately 8,000 per year.

2. Again, using Romania as an example, because there is a moratorium on international adoption and because domestic adoption remains uncommon, abandoned children typically remain in institutions or, more recently, are placed in state-run foster care or are reunited with their biological parents (although the child protection system in Romania generally does an inadequate job of supporting foster care or policing reunification).

3. It is worth noting that in the data reported to date, an intent to treat design was adopted; thus, not all children relegated to the institutionalized group are currently living in institutions— some have been reunited with their biological families and

others have been placed in state-run foster care. Thus, our findings should be considered conservative.

4. A. L. Greenberg (personal communication, May 15, 2007).

References

1. Albers, L. H., Johnson, D. E., Hostetter, M. K., Iverson, S., & Miller, L. C. (1997). Health of children adopted from the former Soviet Union and Eastern Europe: Comparison with preadoptive medical records. *Journal of the American Medical Association, 278,* 922–924.

2. Ames, E. W. (1997). *The development of Romanian orphanage children adopted into Canada.* Final report to human resources development, Canada. Burnaby, Canada: Simon Fraser University.

3. Benoit, T. C., Jocelyn, L. J., Moddemann, D. M., & Embree, J. E., (1996). Romanian adoption: The Manitoba experience. *Archives of Pediatrics & Adolescent Medicine, 150,* 1278–1282.

4. Browne, K., Hamilton-Giachritsis, C., Johnson, R., Leth, L., & Ostergren, M. (2004). *Harm to young children through early institutionalisation/residential care: A survey of 32 European countries.* Paper presented to the EU/WHO Conference on Young Children in European Residential Care; March 19, 2004. Copenhagen, Denmark: World Health Organisation Regional Office for Europe.

5. Cermak, S. A., & Daunhauer, L. A. (1997). Sensory processing in the post-institutionalized child. *American Journal of Occupational Therapy, 51,* 500–507.

6. Chisholm, K. (1998). A three year follow-up of attachment and indiscriminate friendliness in children adopted from Romanian orphanages. *Child Development, 69,* 1092–1106.

7. Chisholm, K., Carter, M. C., Ames, E. W., & Morison, S. J. (1995). Attachment security and indiscriminately friendly behavior in children adopted from Romanian orphanages. *Development and Psychopathology, 7,* 283–294.

8. Chisholm, K., & Savoie, L. (1992, June). *Behavior and attachment problems of Romanian orphanage children adopted to Canada.* Paper presented at the Canada Symposium on Development of Romanian orphanage children adopted (E. W. Ames, Chair). Quebec City, Canada: Canadian Psychological Association.

9. Chugani, H. T., Behen, M. E., Muzik, O., Juhasz, C., Nagy, F., & Chugani, D. C. (2001). Local brain functional activity following early deprivation: A study of postinstitutionalized Romanian orphans. *Neuroimage, 14,* 1290–1301.

10. Dubrovina, I. et al. (1991). *Psychological development of children in orphanages* [Psichologicheskoe razvitie vospitanikov v detskom dome]. Moscow, Russia: Prosveschenie Press.

11. Eluvathingal, T. J., Chugani, H. T., Behen, M. E., Juhász, C., Muzik, O., Maqbool, M., et al. (2006). Abnormal brain connectivity in children after early severe socioemotional deprivation: A diffusion tensor imaging study. *Pediatrics, 117,* 2093–2100.

12. Federici, R. S. (1998). *Help for the hopeless child: A guide for families.* Alexandria, VA: Author.

13. Fisher, L., Ames, E. W., Chisholm, K., & Savoie, L. (1997). Problems reported by parents of Romanian orphans adopted to British Columbia. *International Journal of Behavioral Development, 20,* 67–82.

14. Groze, V., & Ileana, D. (1996). A follow-up study of adopted children from Romania. *Child and Adolescent Social Work Journal, 13,* 541–565.

15. Johnson, D. E. (1997). Medical issues in international adoption: Factors that affect your child's pre-adoption health. *Adoptive Families, 30,* 18–20.

16. Johnson, D. E. (2000). Medical and developmental sequelae of early childhood institutionalization in international adoptees from Romania and the Russian Federation. In C. A. Nelson (Ed.),

The effects of early adversity on neurobehavioral development (pp. 113–162). Mahwah, NJ: Erlbaum.

17. Johnson, D. E., Miller, L. C., Iverson, S., Thomas, W., Franchino, B., & Dole, K. (1992). The health of children adopted from Romania. *Journal of the American Medical Association, 268,* 3446–3451.

18. Maclean, K. (2003). The impact of institutionalization on child development. *Development and Psychopathology, 15,* 853–884.

19. Marshall, P. J., Fox, N. A., & The BEIP Core Group. (2004). A comparison of the electroencephalogram between institutionalized and community children in Romania. *Journal of Cognitive Neuroscience, 16,* 1327–1338.

20. Morison, S. J., Ames, E. W., & Chisholm, K. (1995). The development of children adopted from Romanian orphanages. *Merrill-Palmer Quarterly, 41,* 411–430.

21. Nelson, C. A., de Haan, M., & Thomas, K. M. (2006). *Neuroscience and cognitive development: The role of experience and the developing brain.* New York: Wiley.

22. Nelson, C. A., Zeanah, C., & Fox, N. A. (2007). The effects of early deprivation on brain-behavioral development: The Bucharest Early Intervention Project. In D. Romer & E. Walker (Eds.), *Adolescent psychopathology and the developing brain: Integrating brain and prevention science* (pp. 197–215). New York: Oxford University Press.

23. O'Connor, T. G., Bredenkamp, D., Rutter, M., & The English and Romanian Adoption Study Team. (1999). Attachment disturbances and disorders in children exposed to early severe deprivation. *Infant Mental Health Journal, 20,* 10–29.

24. O'Connor, T. G., & Rutter, M. (2000). Attachment disorder behavior following early severe deprivation: Extension and longitudinal follow-up. English and Romania Adopttes Study Team. *Journal of the American Academy of Child and Adolescent Psychiatry, 39,* 703–712.

25. Parker, S. W., Nelson, C. A., & The BEIP. Core Group. (2005a). An event-related potential study of the impact of institutional rearing on face recognition. *Development and Psychopathology, 17,* 621–639.

26. Parker, S. W., Nelson, C. A., & The BEIP. Core Group. (2005b). The impact of deprivation on the ability to discriminate facial expressions of emotion: An event-related potential study. *Child Development, 76,* 54–72.

27. Rutter, M. L. (1999). Psychosocial adversity and child psychopathology. *British Journal of Psychiatry, 174,* 480–493.

28. Rutter, M., Andersen-Wood, L., Beckett, C., Bredenkamp, D., Castle, J., Groothues, C., et al. (1999). Quasi-autistic patterns following severe early global privation. *Journal of Child Psychology, Psychiatry and Allied Disciplines, 40,* 537–549.

29. Rutter, M., & The English and Romanian Adoptees Study Team. (1998). Developmental catch-up, and delay, following adoption after severe global early privation. *Journal of Child Psychology and Psychiatry, 39,* 465–476.

30. Rutter, M., O'Connor, T., & The English and Romanian Adoptees Study Team. (2004). Are there biological programming effects for psychological Development? Findings from a study of Romanian adoptees. *Developmental Psychology, 40,* 81–94.

31. Suomi, S. J. (1997). Early determinants of behaviour: Evidence from primate studies. *British Medical Bulletin, 53,* 170–184.

32. Tizard, B. (1977). *Adoption: A second chance.* New York: Free Press.

33. Tizard, B., & Hodges, J. (1978). The effect of early institutional rearing on the development of eight-year-old children. *Journal of Child Psychology, Psychiatry, and Allied Disciplines, 19,* 99–118.

34. Tizard, B., & Rees, J. (1974). A comparison of the effects of adoption, restoration to the natural mother, and continued institutionalization on the cognitive development of four-year-old children. *Child Development, 45,* 92–99.

35. Tizard, B., & Rees, J. (1975). The effect of early institutional rearing on the behavior problems and affectional relationships of four-year-old children. *Journal of Child Psychology, Psychiatry, and Allied Disciplines, 16,* 61–73.

36. Wismer Fries, A. B., Ziegler, T. E., Kurian, J. R., Jacoris, S., & Pollak, S. D. (2005). Early experience in humans is associated with changes in neuropeptides critical for regulating social behavior. *Proceedings of the National Academy of Sciences, 102,* 17237–17240.

37. Zeanah, C. H., Nelson, C. A., Fox, N. A., Smyke, A. T., Marshall, P., Parker, S. W., et al. (2003). Designing research to study the effects of institutionalization on brain and behavioral development: The Bucharest Early Intervention Project. *Development and Psychopathology, 15,* 885–907.

CHARLES A. NELSON, Harvard Medical School, Development Medicine Center Laboratory of Cognitive Neuroscience, Children's Hospital Boston, Harvard Medical School, 1 Autumn Street, Mailbox #713, Office AU621, Boston, MA 02215-5365; e-mail: charles.nelson@childrens.harvard.edu.

Acknowledgments—This article was made possible in part by grants from the NIH (MH078829 to the author; MH068857 to Megan Gunnar).

Children's Capacity to Develop Resiliency
How to Nurture It

DEIRDRE BRESLIN

Today's world, full of change, uncertainty, and the unexpected challenges everyone's ability to cope. What coping skills must we nurture, enrich, and enhance to help children navigate successfully in a complex society? Resiliency must be primary. Not only is it essential for the children we teach, but it is a vital skill for ourselves as we strive to enable every child to become all that he or she is capable of.

By definition *resiliency* means the capability to rebound or recoil or to spring back, the power of recovery. How can a teacher help young children develop this capacity, the ability to bounce back from set-backs every child experiences in one form or another as a fact of everyday life?

Resiliency is a set of protective mechanisms that modify a person's response to risk situations.

Resiliency is not a fixed attribute. Rather it is a set of protective mechanisms that modify a person's response to risk situations. These mechanisms operate at turning points during the individual's life (Rutter 1984; Garmezy 1991). Resiliency is a valuable coping skill for all young children.

The Defeating Label "At Risk"

"Labeling matters, and the younger the person getting the label is, the more it matters" (Rosenthal & Jacobson 1968, 3). Some educators seek to help a child having difficulty by focusing on the child's inappropriate behavior patterns. The learning approaches and solutions emphasized perpetuate a problem perspective, and children are frequently labeled "at risk." In eradicating behaviors, massive doses of correction are administered to the child. As a result, we minimize or ignore strengths and competencies a child possesses that could promote adaptation and wellness.

Researcher Emmy Werner and her colleague Ruth Smith (1985) document that one in three children considered to be at risk develops into a competent, capable, caring young person by age 18. In their follow-up work (Werner & Smith 1992), they conclude that of the remaining two out of three high-risk adolescents, two-thirds are successful adults by age 32.

The growing body of research about resiliency provides concise information on the ways individuals develop successfully despite adversity and on the lack of predictive power in risk factors (Rutter 1979; Lanni 1989; McLaughlin, Irbey, & Langman 1994; Meier 1995). These facts have profound implications for deciding what approaches to emphasize when helping today's young children develop positive coping skills.

Children's Adaptive Approaches

For two years I systematically interviewed families and young children age five to eight who were identified by the school administration as functioning well in their urban school settings. Each interviewee had three and sometimes more major, ongoing life stressors in their lives: for example, homelessness, foster care, single parent family, alcohol and substance abuse, family problems, abandonment, and death in the family. Despite negative life events and stress, the children and their families seemed to be adapting and surviving. They displayed resilient behavior through their active participation in classroom activities, consistent high attendance, well-developed listening skills, and cooperative child-to-child and teacher-to-child interactions.

No group of families or individual children interviewed showed identical sets of coping behaviors. Although resiliency is an individualized skill, the resiliency of the individuals interviewed revealed some common factors that are important to examine. Four factors of resiliency that I identified are outlined here, with examples of classroom activities to help develop and enrich each aspect.

1. Heightened Sensory Awareness

The kindergarten boy who first alerted me to this quality of resiliency lived in a very poor area in which the streets contained a great deal of garbage and drug users' paraphernalia. As

Helping Children Realize Potential through Their Multiple Intelligences

Intelligences	Recognition and Reinforcement Suggestions
linguistic	Tell stories. Let children dictate their stories to the teacher or an adult volunteer. Transcribers read back each story and give the child his or her own print copy to illustrate.
	Create poetry orally and in writing. Imagine a character and play-act the role. Play word games and solve puzzles.
spatial	Ask children to describe the physical characteristics they see in a bird, squirrel, cat, dog. Draw visual likenesses of any objects.
logical-mathematical	Use numbers to create calendars. Make itemized, number listcounting anything and everything. Estimate how many of something (pennies, seeds, pebbles, acorns) are in a jar, box, bowl.
musical	Listen to various types of music. Sing songs and clap to the music. Hum, whistle, or use bodily response to the music. Write about whats fun in dancing or playing basketball and other sports. Make up skits or pantomimes in response to literature or music.
bodily-kinesthetic	Dance in all kinds of movement styles. Play pin-the-tail-on-the-donkey. Throw and catch a ball. Try all kinds of sports.
	Smell flowers and look closely to concentrate on their colors.
	Names flowers and notice the many differences (reds, pinks, etc.) Takes walks to focus on enhancing and heightening sensory awareness.
interpersonal	Act out situations that children encounter in classroom activities.
intrapersonal	Portray emotions such as sadness, regret, and so forth that everyone experiences.
naturalist	Make books identifying animals, birds, plants, and so on. Write stories and poetry about nature.

I walked to his school, I was startled by what I saw and could only focus on the unpleasantness of the journey. On meeting the child, I was so consumed with repugnance from the walk that my first question was, "What is it like coming to school each day?" He looked at me and smiled.

"It's wonderful," he said. "You know, the streets have been 'glassticized,' and all the little pieces of glass that are in the paving material shine and sparkle—it's like finely chopped diamonds. Every day my grandmother walks with me to school, and we look at the street and count the colors. On sunny days there is silver and gold, but on dark days there are purple and dark colors. We count the colors and name them."

With this boy's positive experience in mind, teachers can transform every trip home from school into an opportunity to heighten and enrich sensory awareness no matter where the child lives. The family member or other adult who accompanies the child to and from school can become an integral partner in the experience.

The walk provides a tool for observation as the teacher follows up on it the next day. How many squares did you see on the way home? How many circles? Where were they? Describe the circle. Which vocabulary words can you use in telling about your trip home? What new words can you teach us about your walk? What else do you do/see/feel on the way home from school?

The school setting provides many opportunities to encourage high, positive expectations.

2. High, Positive Expectations

One of the eight-year-old girls interviewed said that she was going to be a female basketball star. "I know I will be a star, because the gym teacher told me how good I am at basketball."

The importance of teacher expectations and feedback has been the focus of much research, starting with the classic study completed by Rosenthal and Jacobson (1968). This study showed that student performance was affected by teachers' expectations of the child. The effect on student performance was called the Pygmalion effect, referring to the growth in motivation that can occur when a teacher believes in and encourages a student. The name Pygmalion comes from the mythological story of a king who creates a female statue and then with the help of the gods brings it to life. The gym teacher's positive expectations and feedback heightened this girl's motivation and helped her to succeed.

Howard Gardner (1983) describes our multiple intelligences and outlines relevant behaviors that accompany each intelligence. Bodily kinesthetic intelligence is one of these, and the eight-year-old's performance at basketball indicates strength in that area. The gym teacher was reinforcing one of the intelligences this child displayed.

Children's self-concepts result partly from the expectations others have for them. Their self-concepts in turn affect the expectations they have for themselves. The school setting provides many opportunities to encourage high, positive expectations.

Gardner (1983) explores intelligence in terms of different "frames of mind." In the chart above, each of the eight intelligences (including Naturalist, which Gardner proposed later [1998]) is accompanied by suggestions that can be modified and enhanced to match the developmental and unique needs of young children.

3. A Clear and Developing Understanding of One's Strengths Relating to Accomplishment

The most powerful example of this concept came from an eight-year-old who said, "Well, you know I'm not so good at ball games, but I'm an awesome reader." This child understood the concept of knowing one's strengths and ably used his personal interactions with both adults and peers to cast success in the light of what he could accomplish. Developing such a clear understanding supports and reinforces children's high, positive expectations.

4. A Heightened, Developing Sense of Humor

All of the children I interviewed seemed to have a well-developed sense of the playful. Humor is not an innate gift, but it can and should be cultivated. It is a frame that can help keep things in perspective. The more children learn about humor, the more they become sensitized to it, and the more humor enters into everyday life (Kozol 2000). Philosopher Reinhold Neibuhr emphasized the importance of humor and the need for using it when trying to make sense out of some of the incongruities of life (Kleinman 2000). Children need this skill more than ever before.

In a second grade classroom I visited, each week the teacher featured an activity that highlighted humor. I joined the children on a humor walk. The teacher asked students to walk silently and listen for any sounds, notice sidewalk cracks, and watch for signs to present to the class in a humorous manner. After the walk the students shared what they saw and heard that was funny for them. One child imitated a bird in a marvelous way. In a few minutes, the entire class was trying to reproduce the sound, laughing and smiling happily.

The walk not only highlighted humor but also developed listening skills, interpersonal communication skills, and having the fun of a shared experience. The children told about another of their humor curriculum stories. For several weeks, children could act out something that happened to them or their family that they found funny. The class voted on the funniest story, and the humor prize of the week went to the winner. This activity enhanced coping skills, built vocabulary, honed presentation skills, and let the children act as critics and judges.

The more children learn about humor, the more they become sensitized to it, and the more humor enters into everyday life.

I believe that as part of a humor curriculum, each teacher and his students should develop together the group's criteria

Building Children's Resiliency

One effort that focuses on resiliency in children age two to six is an initiative of the Devereux Early Childhood Foundation in Villanova, Pennsylvania. The Devereux Early Childhood Initiative is a strength-based implemented in Head Start and other early childhood programs. The program consists of an integrated approach that not only provides a tool for assessing children's protective factors and screening challenging behaviors but also suggests strategies for fostering resiliency.

The Devereux Early Childhood Assessment (DECA), a nationally normed assessment of within-the-child protective factors in children age two to five, is the program's assessment tool. Supportive materials provide home and classroom approaches for supporting and enhancing resilient behaviors. An infant/toddler version of the DECA is under development.

More information is available online: www.devereuxearlychilhood.org.

for success. This is a meaningful way to introduce the importance of standards. In 2005, standards are critical in every facet of life.

Summary

This look at resiliency development through heightened sensory awareness; high, positive expectations; a clear understanding of one's strengths relating to accomplishment; and a developing sense of humor hopefully can encourage you to foster enriching coping behaviors in children. These four facets of resiliency seem critically important for young children.

But don't be trapped into thinking that there are precisely four resilience factors or seven or three. It is not possible to succinctly categorize human resiliency. Educators today need to help children search for the unique strengths that equip them, no matter the circumstances, to fulfill their individual potential.

However, we must avoid the urge to simplify as we strive to facilitate the resilience of children. Today's teacher must understand that development is part of a very complex unstable phenomenon. Garmezy and Rutter (1983), focusing on the study of competency, give insight into the fact that resiliency may not be fully attainable by all. However, Nobel laureate Albert Camus tells us the worth of trying: "In the midst of winter, I finally learned there was in me an invincible summer."

Educators today need to help children search for the unique strengths that equip them, no matter the circumstances, to fulfill their individual potential.

References

Gardner, H. 1983. *Frames of mind: The theory of multiple intelligences.* New York: Basic.

Gardner, H. 1998. Are there additional intelligences? *In Education, information, and transformation,* ed. J. Kane. Englewood, NJ: Prentice Hall.

Garmezy, N. 1991. Relevance and vulnerability to adverse developmental outcomes with poverty. *Behavioral Scientist* 34 (4): 416–30.

Garmezy, N., & M. Rutter. 1983. *Stress, coping and development in children.* New York: McGraw-Hill.

Kleinman, M.L. 2000. *A world of hope, a world of fear: Henry A. Wallace, Reinhold Neibuhr, and American liberalism.* Columbus: Ohio State University.

Kozol, J. 2000. *Ordinary resurrections.* New York: Crown.

Lanni, F. 1989. *The search for structure: A report on American youth today.* New York: Free Press.

McLaughlin, M., M. Irbey, & J. Langman. 1994. *Urban sanctuaries: Neighborhood organizations in the lives and futures of inner-city youth.* San Francisco: Jossey Bass.

Meier, D. 1995. *The power of their ideas: Lessons for America from a small school in Harlem.* Boston: Beacon.

Rosenthal, R., & L. Jacobson. 1968. *Pygmalion in the classroom.* New York: Rinehart & Winston.

Rutter, M. 1979. *Fifteen thousand hours.* Cambridge: Harvard University Press.

Rutter, M. 1984. Resilient children. *Psychology Today* (March): 57–65.

Werner, E.E., & R.S. Smith. 1985. *Vulnerable but invincible: A study of resilient children.* New York: McGraw-Hill.

Werner, E.E., & R.S. Smith. 1992. *Overcoming the odds.* New York: Cornell University Press.

DEIRDRE BRESLIN, PhD, is an urban educator and director of academic programs for Project ReConnect at St. John's University in New York City. Her primary area of research interest is resilient behavior, with a focus on inner-city children.

Emotions and the Development of Childhood Depression: Bridging the Gap

Pamela M. Cole, Joan Luby, and Margaret W. Sullivan

The mental health problems of young children are often unrecognized until they become severe and difficult to treat (e.g., Tolan & Dodge, 2005; U.S. Public Health Service, 2000a, 2000b). There is mounting evidence that early childhood behavioral and emotional difficulties are not always transient phases of normal development but can represent risk for or the presence of psychopathology (Briggs-Gowan, Carter, Bosson-Heenan, Guyer, & Horwitz, 2006; Egger & Angold, 2006; Keenan & Wakschlag, 2000). Yet, there is a significant gap in scientific knowledge that needs to be bridged to help us distinguish among these different developmental pathways. To bridge the gap, we need evidence that *integrates* knowledge of the wide range of individual differences in the functioning of typical children with clinical knowledge of the unique features of disordered functioning. Although this is a challenge during periods when children are going through rapid developmental changes, early identification is important for prevention because certain forms of behavioral and neural plasticity may permit intervention before symptoms crystallize into serious disorders (Cicchetti & Cohen, 2006).

We still have much to learn about when, why, and how early childhood problems constitute dysfunctional behavior that warrants formal diagnosis, signal risk for disorder, or reflect transient periods of difficulty that will resolve themselves without professional intervention. Recently, a published prevalence study indicated that approximately 6% to 7% of Danish toddlers qualified for a psychiatric diagnosis of emotional, behavioral, or attentional disorder on the basis of two recognized classification systems (Skovgaard, Houman, Christiansen, & Andreasen, 2007; see Egger & Angold, 2006, for discussion of the systems). Diagnosing such young children stimulates intense debate. What evidence demonstrates that we can distinguish disorder in processes such as executive attention and self-regulation when they are just emerging and rapidly developing (McClellan & Speltz, 2003)? In order to address this gap in knowledge, we need greater integration of developmental theory, knowledge, and methods with the study of individual differences that include significant risk or impairment. In this way, we avoid "pathologizing" individual differences among typically developing children and yet address the critical need for evidence-based early identification and intervention (Egger & Angold, 2006).

In this article, we illustrate an approach to the study of emotional development that can address the call for research that aids the accurate classification of problems and prediction of pathways to health, risk, and affective disorder (Costello et al., 2002). A comprehensive, comparative analysis of the emotional profiles of typically developing children and children with or at risk for clinical depression will help distinguish normal transitory problems (such as increased irritability as a developmental phase), indicators of risk or emerging psychopathology (such as predisposition to react negatively or difficulty regulating emotion), and symptom constellations that constitute clinical disorder (such as depression). We briefly summarize (a) what is known about early emotional development, (b) trends in research on childhood depression, and (c) new research directions that integrate the study of typical emotional development with clinical evidence of risk for and presence of affective disorders in young children.

Childhood Depression and Emotional Development

A leading developmental perspective views emotions as adaptive psychological processes that function to support goals for survival and well-being (Barrett & Campos, 1987), and yet, emotions are a salient feature of psychopathological functioning (Berenbaum, Raghavan, Le, Vernon, & Gomez, 2003; Cicchetti, Ganiban, & Barnett, 1991; Cole, Michel, & Teti, 1994; Gross & Muñoz, 1995; Keenan, 2000). Considerable evidence links heightened negative emotion, whether viewed as responses to challenging situations or as a stable temperamental characteristic, to the presence of or risk for psychological problems in children (Cole, Zahn-Waxler, Fox, Usher, & Welsh, 1996; Eisenberg et al., 1993; Luby et al., 2006; Zeman, Shipman, & Suveg, 2002). Yet, because heightened negative emotion is associated with several disorders, it does not identify specific pathways. We share the view that all emotions, including negative ones, are adaptive, and we advocate for research that identifies how normally functional processes become dysfunctional. Specifically, we believe that examining a full range of emotions, specific features of emotional processes (not just valence), and the nature and efficacy of strategies children use to regulate emotional reactions and moods will advance our knowledge of the development of psychopathology in early childhood (Cole & Hall, 2008; Luby & Belden, 2006).

Children who are diagnosed with depression exhibit prolonged sad or irritable mood or anhedonia (loss of pleasure and interest) along with concurrent symptoms involving four or more of the following: significant changes in eating and/or sleeping, changes in motor activity (restlessness or lethargy), difficulty concentrating, feelings of worthlessness or guilt, and recurrent thoughts of death. Although researchers once assumed that children under the age of 6 were too psychologically immature to experience clinical depression (Rie, 1966), evidence now indicates that depression often has a chronic and relapsing course of symptoms, underscoring the need to understand early precursors and first onset (Costello et al., 2002). Indeed, young children can suffer a constellation of symptoms that qualifies for a depressive disorder diagnosis (Luby et al., 2002); it is considerably similar to depression in older individuals and is relatively stable, specific, and distinguishable from disruptive disorders (Costello et al., 2002; Keenan & Wakschlag, 2004; Luby, Mrakotsky, Heffelfinger, Brown, & Spitznagel, 2004; Luby et al., 2003; Stalets & Luby, 2006). It is not clear how common depression is in early childhood, but one study estimated it at 2% (Egger & Angold, 2006).

Our view is that childhood depression results from dysfunctional patterns of normally adaptive emotional processes. Biological and environmental influences, and in most cases both, determine whether a pattern of emotional functioning deviates from the norm and further develops into symptoms that result in significant impairment in functioning. For instance, sadness, even intense or enduring, is not inherently maladaptive. Defined as (a) the appreciation that a goal for well-being is lost and (b) behavioral readiness to relinquish effort to attain it (e.g., Barrett & Campos, 1987), sadness supports realistic behavior in the face of unachievable goals. What distinguishes normal sadness from dysphoric mood is not the presence of sadness but such difficulty resolving it that it becomes pervasive and compromises other domains of functioning. It is therefore important to understand the regulation of emotion, or the ability to alter emotional responses (Cicchetti, Ackerman, & Izard, 1995; Cole, Martin, & Dennis, 2004; Thompson, 1994).

A Brief Synopsis of Early Emotional Development

Emotional development is rapid in the first 5 years of life. From the 1st weeks, nascent emotional capacities are evident (e.g., Gormally et al., 2001). A core set of emotions—anger, sadness, enjoyment, fear, interest, and surprise—and rudimentary strategies for regulating emotions, such as self-soothing, are discernible in infant behavior and expression before the end of the 1st year (Izard, 1991; Lewis & Michalson, 1983; Rothbart, Ziaie, & O'Boyle, 1992; Sroufe, 1996). In the 2nd year, the rudiments of guilt, shame, embarrassment, and pride emerge (Barrett, Zahn-Waxler, & Cole, 1993; Kochanska, 1997; Lewis & Sullivan, 2005; Lewis, Sullivan, Weiss, & Stanger, 1989). Around age 2, toddlers begin to understand prototypical expressions of happiness, sadness, and anger, and then other emotions; how they relate to situational contexts; and how they influence behavior (Lewis & Michalson, 1983). Between ages 2 and 5, children develop skill at regulating emotions (Kopp, 1989), such that by first grade, most children regulate emotion well enough to learn, form and maintain friendships, and obey classroom rules (Calkins & Hill, 2007; Denham, 1998; Shonkoff & Phillips, 2000).

This positive portrait is tempered by the fact that these same capacities contribute to the psychological vulnerability of young children. Emotional receptivity and responsiveness make young children vulnerable to environmental stress and conflict. Yet, young children lack the cognitive and social resources that help older persons cope with stress and conflict, including reflexive self-awareness, analytic reasoning, a social network, and personal autonomy. Thus, young children are emotionally sensitive but lack the skill, experience, and self-sufficiency to deal with strong emotions. Early exposure to adverse circumstances can have long-term deleterious effects on children's physiological and behavioral functioning, including debilitating effects on the neural, cardiovascular, and endocrine processes that support emotional functioning (Gunnar & Quevedo, 2007; Pollak, 2005; Porges, 2001), which is why it is critical for children to have external sources of emotion regulation, such as competent, sensitive caregivers.

During this period of rapid emotional development and vulnerability, it should be possible to specify qualities that distinguish the emotional functioning of typically developing children from those with disorder or risk for disorder. For example, typical children's tantrums appear to be composed of two related but distinct components—anger and distress—that are organized into initial quick peaks in anger intensity that decline as whining and comfort seeking appear (Potegal & Davidson, 2003; Potegal, Kosorok, & Davidson, 2003). The tantrums of depressed preschool-aged children, however, are more violent, self-injurious, destructive, and verbally aggressive, and they have a longer recovery time (Belden, Thompson, & Luby, 2008). Collectively, these findings suggest that the emotional dynamics of depressed and nondepressed children's tantrums differ, which may serve as one indicator of a need for early intervention.

Trends in Research on Emotional Functioning in Children with or at Risk for Depression

Research on emotional functioning in children with or at risk for depression has identified important emotional correlates of depressive symptoms but has not yet fully embraced a developmental perspective that would permit studying the thresholds that distinguish normal and atypical emotional functioning.

Approaches that examine a continuum of symptom profiles across ages, whether cross-sectional or longitudinal, are rare (but see Graber, Brooks-Gunn, & Warren, 2006).

Research on depressed children tends to draw from studies of adult depression rather than research on emotional development. Generally, it reveals that depressive symptoms in children and youth are associated with attending to and remembering both positive and negative emotional content differently (Bishop, Dalgleish, & Yule, 2004; Gotlib, Traill, Montoya, Joormann, & Chang, 2005; Joormann, Talbot, & Gotlib, 2007), reduced performance when other information is also presented that is emotional in nature (Jazbec, McClure, Hardin, Pine, & Ernst, 2005; LaDouceur et al., 2005), and less accurate, more inefficient processing of emotional information (LaDouceur et al., 2006; Pérez-Edgar, Fox, Cohn, & Kovacs, 2006; Pine et al., 2004; Reijntjes, Stegge, Terwogt, & Hurkens, 2007; but see Bishop et al., 2004, and Pine et al., 2004, for exceptions). However, much remains unknown about the consistency and specificity of such differences, as the same effects are often found for anxious children (Dalgleish et al., 2003; Hardin, Schroth, Pine, & Ernst, 2007).

Our view, that difficulty appropriately releasing from and resolving negative emotions is at the core of depression, has some empirical support (Forbes, Fox, Cohn, Galles, & Kovacs, 2006; Park, Goodyer, & Teasdale, 2004; Wilkinson & Goodyer, 2006). Childhood depressive symptoms are linked with less frequent use of and less confidence in effective strategies (such as problem solving and positive reappraisal; Garber, Braafladt, & Weiss, 1995; Garnefski, Rieffe, Jellesma, Terwogt, & Kraiij, 2007; Reijntjes et al., 2007). As with adults, neuroimaging evidence suggests that depression involves greater mental processing and/or less ability to draw on positive emotions or approach motivation when negative emotions are evoked (Forbes et al., 2006; Thibodeau, Jorgensen, & Kim, 2006).

Studies on infants or children who are offspring of depressed parents are particularly important as these groups have heightened risk for depression and, at young ages, it is possible to prospectively examine potential precursors because the children do not yet show symptoms (Goodman & Gotlib, 1999). Observational studies of young children at risk for depression indicate that they differ in emotional responsivity from healthy children, but the studies suggest nuances that are often not captured in neurophysiological and cognitive studies of responses to emotional information. For example, 4-months-olds of depressed mothers smile and vocalize less than infants of nondepressed women do during spontaneous interactions with their mothers (Field et al., 2007b; Moore, Cohn, & Campbell, 2001), a pattern that forecasts symptoms at 18 months (Moore et al., 2001). However, compared to infants who are not at risk, 5-month-old offspring of depressed mothers laugh *more* and fuss *less* when (a) maternal behavior is confined to imitating the infant (behavior that agitates infants of nondepressed mothers) or (b) the interaction is with an animated doll (Field et al., 2007a). Similarly, the emotional reactions of school-aged children with major depressive disorder differ in complex ways from those of children with other disorders. Casey (1996) reported that although depressed children expressed less emotion in peer interaction than children

with attenion deficit hyperactivity disorder (ADHD), they did not differ from children with oppositional defiant disorder (ODD). They were *slower* to express emotion than both ADHD and ODD children, although they eventually behaved similarly. Their emotion perception inaccuracies were not random (like those of ADHD children) but biased toward attributing negative emotions to other children.

In sum, evidence indicates unique emotional differences in children with or at risk for depression but does not fully distinguish childhood depression from other problems and does not address how emotional patterns uniquely associated with depression evolve from normal, adaptive emotional processes. An integration of developmental approaches with clinically pertinent aspects of emotional functioning may contribute to filling this gap. It may aid delineation of normal variations and normative boundaries, and the unique emotional characteristics that typify risk for and presence of childhood depression risk. To illustrate, we first take a brief look at the emotional problems of a troubled preschool-aged child.

The Emotional Profile of a Troubled Preschooler

Mr. and Mrs. B sought outpatient services for their 4-year-old son's impulsivity and excessive crying. They reported that A.B. was easily provoked, and that when provoked, he was impulsively aggressive. To illustrate the seriousness of the problem, they described an incident in which A.B. became very frustrated because his 2-year-old brother would not relinquish a toy immediately. In his frustration, A.B. poked his brother's eye with a stick.

In addition, A.B.'s parents stated that he was always unhappy, including frequent periods of excessive crying. They found him inconsolable, particularly during these periods, such that he required constant attention and support that disrupted family life. At these times, they tried unsuccessfully to soothe him or redirect his attention to pleasant activities. The excessive crying often followed his misbehavior, and their descriptions of his behavior suggested he felt intense guilt and shame. This pattern of unhappiness, frustration, misbehavior, and excessive crying was so well established and disruptive that his parents established a "cry room" in the home where A.B. often cried unabated for long periods.

A.B.'s emotional difficulties, which impair his interpersonal functioning, are atypical and, if left unchecked, will arguably compromise his ability to master later developmental tasks (Cicchetti et al., 1991; Cole & Hall, 2008). Typically developing 4-year-olds have their share of impulsive, angry, aggressive behavior with siblings (Dunn, 2002; Miller, Volling, & McElvain, 2000) and get angry when their goals are thwarted, but they modulate anger, frustration, and disappointment well enough that their behavior is easily redirected and not disruptive or destructive (Cole, 1986; Cole, Zahn-Waxler, & Smith, 1994; Skuban, Shaw, Gardner, Supplee, & Nichols, 2006). In fact, among typically developing 3- and 4-year-olds, low-intensity anger is followed by *appropriate* effort and problem solving (Dennis et al., 2008). A.B., in contrast, is not just angry; he is persistently, excessively sad and irritable, and his emotional difficulties may be compounded by anxiety, guilt, and/or shame, particularly in response to his own misbehavior. Furthermore, his capacity for interest and pleasure in typically enjoyable activities appears substantially diminished, including being unresponsive to parental soothing. The available data fail to address such atypical emotional functioning.

Future Directions

Our experience suggests research directions that we believe can shed more light on the clinically significant features of emotional dysfunction that is associated with early childhood depression and, in so doing, cast additional light on the nature of typical emotional development, including mechanisms underlying the development of trajectories toward and away from childhood depression.

Negative Emotions: Anger, Anxiety, Guilt, and Shame

A.B.'s aggression follows intense anger, a characteristic that may distinguish the aggression of young children with disruptive disorders from that of typically developing preschoolers (Wakschlag et al., 2007). What seems different for A.B. is his intense distress after acting angrily. We know little about individual differences in children's normal recovery from anger or the emotions that follow anger (Cole & Hall, 2008). A.B.'s intense and sustained postanger distress raises the question of whether he feels inordinate anxiety, shame, or guilt about his actions, reactions that are common in depressed adults (Gratz & Roemer, 2004). Typical youngsters become sad or clingy after intense anger (Potegal & Davidson, 2003), but A.B.'s responses are different. Emotions such as sadness and anxiety that follow anger are one area worthy of study for understanding clinical risk and dysfunction, as Izard (1972) and Tomkins (1963) first noted. For instance, infants who become sad when their goals are blocked have large cortisol responses, whereas those who express the most anger show little cortisol responses, a difference that suggests sadness in this context may reflect more stress (Lewis, Ramsay, & Sullivan, 2006; Lewis, Sullivan, Ramsay, & Alessandri, 1992). Relatively little is known about the experience and regulation of anger in children with major depression. Poorly regulated anger or persistent frustration can devolve into prolonged hopelessness and sadness or increased aggressiveness (Goodwin, 2006).

During the 2nd year, Children reveal sensitivity to standards, which supports the development of guilt, shame, and embarrassment (e.g., Barrett et al., 1993; Kagan, 1981; Lewis et al., 1989). Researchers have not explored the relation of these emotions to early presence of and risk for depression. Typically developing preschoolers show shame after they have been angry (Bennett, Sullivan, & Lewis, 2005); this may become dysfunctional, however, if it maintains a negative focus on the self and interferes with appropriate, instrumental problem-solving and

reparative behavior. Depressed preschoolers display high levels of guilt and shame and lower levels of reparative behavior than preschoolers with other clinical disorders and without disorder (Luby, Belden, Sullivan, Hayden, & McCadney, 2008). In A.B.'s case, his intense personal distress after being aggressive does not aid reparation or even appear to constitute empathic concern. Self-focused distress interferes with prosocial behavior, whereas empathic concern motivates it, probably alleviating shame or guilt (Eisenberg et al., 1988, 1990). Thus, a promising future direction for research is to understand individual differences in young children's emotions about their misbehavior, distinguishing among callousness, personal distress, and empathic concern, and how these relate to other emotions. For example, proneness to fear may inhibit empathic concern in early childhood (Young, Fox, & Zahn-Waxler, 1999).

Positive Emotions: Joy, Interest, and Pride

Another atypical feature of A.B.'s emotions is diminished positive emotion. Most upset 4-year-olds are responsive to efforts to redirect them toward pleasurable activities. A.B. does not enjoy, and is not readily diverted to, activities that most 4-year-olds greet with eagerness and delight. Young children who have or are at risk for depression may have difficulty generating positive emotions, such as enjoyment, enthusiasm, pride, and interest (Forbes & Dahl, 2005). Preschoolers who qualify for diagnosis of depression with anhedonia show the most severe depression (Luby et al., 2004), and the trait of low positive emotionality in 3-year-olds is associated with family history of depression (Durbin, Klein, Hayden, Buckley, & Moerk, 2005).

Temporal and Intensive Dynamics of Emotional Responding

Apart from studying the emotions involved, we also need to study atypical temporal and intensive features of emotional responses (Thompson, 1994). The speed, intensity, and duration of different emotions likely distinguish A.B.'s emotional responses from those of typically developing children. Yet, surprisingly few studies do service to Thompson's (1994) call for studying emotion dynamics (but see Luby & Belden, 2006). In part, this neglect may be due to the emphasis on aggregated negative emotions, such that threshold to a palpable emotional response, intensity (peak and average), and duration are highly correlated with total amount. A more detailed, time-sensitive study of *specific* emotions, and among children with risk or problems, will yield information on the clinical utility of studying temporal and intensive emotion dynamics.

Context Appropriateness

Negative emotions, even intense ones, are appropriate in certain circumstances (Saarni, 1999). A.B.'s lack of pleasure in contexts that please most children can be thought of as context-inappropriate emotion. Adults with major depressive disorder report higher levels of sadness than controls while watching films that generally evoke happy emotions (Rottenberg, Gross, & Gotlib, 2005). We know little about the context appropriateness of young children's emotional responses, although toddlers who react fearfully to situations that other children find enjoyable have more symptoms of anxiety (Buss, Kiel, Williams, & Leuty, 2005; Fox, Henderson, Marshall, Nichols, & Ghera, 2005). Diminished positive emotion in response to normally pleasant events then seems a particularly important aspect of context-inappropriate emotion in the study of depression (Forbes & Dahl, 2005).

Emotion Regulation Strategies

Finally, A.B. shows little effective, age-appropriate self-regulation of emotion, such as self-distraction or support seeking. It would be useful to know whether depressed children lack strategies or whether their strategic attempts are ineffective because of the intensity of emotional reactions. As we noted earlier, school-aged children with depression do not think of effective regulatory strategies and also report lacking confidence in those strategies. Multimethod, time-sensitive studies of strategies, their appropriateness, and their effectiveness are important for understanding typical and atypical emotional development.

In sum, A.B.'s emotional profile involves multiple emotions, with problematic temporal and intensive qualities, and clinically pertinent features such as resistance to change and few effective regulatory strategies (Cole & Hall, 2008; Luby & Belden, 2006). To fully develop a scientific basis for understanding emotional differences among typically developing children and those who are developing depression, research should (a) distinguish the emotional profiles of depressed and high-risk children; (b) specify the range of their emotional differences, including expressive and physiological qualities; (c) trace emotional profiles over time, from early risk to later outcomes; (d) examine the conditions that lead one child's symptoms to be transient and another's to develop into serious emotional dysfunction; and (e) integrate multiple levels of analysis, addressing the complex interplay among environmental, neurobehavioral, and cognitive factors. Integrating developmental and clinical science has enormous potential to address the complex and varied pathways to children's mental health and resilience, symptom development, and psychopathology. In doing so, the forward movement of our fields across the gap will be assured.

References

Barrett, K. C., & Campos, J. J. (1987). Perspectives on emotional development II: A functionalist perspective on emotions. In J. D. Osofsky (Ed.), *Handbook of infant development* (pp. 555–578). Oxford, England: Wiley.

Barrett, K. C., Zahn-Waxler, C., & Cole, P. M. (1993). Avoiders vs. amenders: Implications for the investigation of guilt and shame during toddlerhood? *Cognition and Emotion, 7*, 481–505.

Belden, A. C., Thompson, N. R., & Luby, J. L. (2008). Temper tantrums in healthy versus DSM-IV depressed and disruptive preschoolers: Defining tantrum behaviors associated with clinical problems. *Journal of Pediatrics, 152*, 117–122.

Bennett, D. B., Sullivan, M. W., & Lewis, M. (2005). Young children's emotional-behavioral adjustment as a function of maltreatment, shame, and anger. *Child Maltreatment, 10*, 311–324.

Berenbaum, H., Raghavan, C., Le, H., Vernon, L. L., & Gomez, J. J. (2003). A taxonomy of emotional disturbances. *Clinical Psychology: Science and Practice, 10*, 206–226.

Bishop, S. J., Dalgleish, T., & Yule, W. (2004). Memory for emotional stories in high and low depressed children. *Memory, 12*, 214–230.

Briggs-Gowan, M. J., Carter, A. S., Bosson-Heenan, J., Guyer, A. E., & Horwitz, S. M. (2006). Are infant-toddler socio-emotional and behavioral problems transient? *Journal of the American Academy of Child & Adolescent Psychiatry, 45*, 849–858.

Buss, K. A., Kiel, E. J., Williams, N. A., & Leuty, M. (2005, April). *Using context to identify toddlers with dysregulated fear responses.* Paper presented at the Society for Research in Child Development Conference, Atlanta, GA.

Calkins, S. D., & Hill, A. M. (2007). Caregiver influences on emerging emotion regulation: Biological and environmental transactions in early development. In J. J. Gross (Ed.), *Handbook of emotion regulation* (pp. 229–248). New York: Guilford.

Casey, R. J. (1996). Emotional competence in children with externalizing and internalizing disorders. In M. Lewis & M. W. Sullivan (Eds.), *Emotional development in atypical children* (pp. 161–183). Mahwah, NJ: Erlbaum.

Cicchetti, D., Ackerman, B., & Izard, C. E. (1995). Emotions and emotion regulation in developmental psychopathology. *Development and Psychopathology, 7*, 1–10.

Cicchetti, D., & Cohen, D. (2006). *Developmental psychopathology: Vol. 1. Theory and method.* New York: Wiley.

Cicchetti, D., Ganiban, J., & Barnett, D. (1991). Contributions from the study of high-risk populations to understanding the development of emotion regulation. In J. Garber & K. A. Dodge (Eds.), *The development of emotion regulation and dysregulation* (pp. 15–48). New York: Cambridge University Press.

Cole, P. M. (1986). Children's spontaneous control of facial expression. *Child Development, 57*, 1309–1321.

Cole, P. M., & Hall, S. E. (2008). Emotion dysregulation as a risk factor for psychopathology. In T. P. Beauchaine & S. P. Hinshaw (Eds.), *Child and adolescent psychopathology* (pp. 265–298). New York: Wiley.

Cole, P. M., Martin, S. E., & Dennis, T. D. (2004). Emotion regulation as a scientific construct: Methodological challenges and directions for child development research. *Child Development, 75*, 317–333.

Cole, P. M., Michel, M., & Teti, L. O. (1994). The development of emotion regulation and dysregulation: A clinical perspective. *Monographs of the Society for Research in Child Development, 59*(2–3, Serial No. 240).

Cole, P. M., Zahn-Waxler, C., Fox, N. A., Usher, B. A., & Welsh, J. D. (1996). Individual differences in emotion regulation and behavior problems in preschool children. *Journal of Abnormal Psychology, 105*, 518–529.

Cole, P. M., Zahn-Waxler, C., & Smith, K. D. (1994). Expressive control during a disappointment: Variations related to preschoolers' behavior problems. *Developmental Psychology, 30*, 835–846.

Costello, E. J., Pine, D. S., Hammen, C., March, J. S., Plotsky, P. M., Weissman, M. M., et al. (2002). Development and natural history of mood disorders. *Biological Psychiatry, 52*, 529–542.

Dalgleish, T., Taghavi, R., Neshat-Doost, H., Moradi, A., Canterbury, R., & Yule, W. (2003). Patterns of processing bias for emotional information across clinical disorders: A comparison of attention, memory, and prospective cognition in children and adolescents with depression, generalized anxiety, and posttraumatic stress disorder. *Journal of Clinical Child and Adolescent Psychology, 32,* 10–21.

Denham, S. E. (1998). *Emotional development in young children.* New York: Guilford.

Dennis, T. A., Wiggins, C. N., Cole, P. M., Myftaraj, L., Cushing, A., Cohen, L. C., et al. (2008). *Functional relations between preschool age children's emotions and actions in challenging situations.* Manuscript submitted for publication.

Dunn, J. (2002). Sibling relationships. In P. K. Smith & C. H. Hart (Eds.), *Blackwell handbook of childhood social development* (pp. 223–237). Malden, MA: Blackwell.

Durbin, C. E., Klein, D. N., Hayden, E. P., Buckley, M. E., & Moerk, K. C. (2005). Temperamental emotionality in preschoolers and parental mood disorders. *Journal of Abnormal Psychology, 114,* 28–37.

Egger, H. L., & Angold, A. (2006). Common emotional and behavioral disorders in preschool children: Presentation, nosology, and epidemiology. *Journal of the Child Psychology and Psychiatry, 47,* 313–337.

Eisenberg, N., Cumberland, A., Spinrad, T. L., Fabes, R. A., Shepard, S. A., Reiser, M., et al. (1993). The relations of regulation and emotionality to children's externalizing and internalizing problem behavior. *Child Development, 72,* 1112–1134.

Eisenberg, N., Fabes, R. A., Bustamante, D., Mathy, R., Miller, P. A., & Lindholm, E. (1988). Differentiation of vicariously induced emotional reactions in children. *Developmental Psychology, 24,* 237–246.

Eisenberg, N., Fabes, R. A., Miller, P. A., Shell, R., Shea R., May-Plumlee, T., et al. (1990). Preschoolers' vicarious responding and their situational and dispositional prosocial behavior. *Merrill-Palmer Quarterly, 36,* 507–529.

Field, T., Hernandez-Rief, M., Diego, M., Feijo, L., Vera, Y., Gil, K., et al. (2007a). Responses to animate and inanimate faces by infants of depressed mothers. *Early Childhood Development and Care, 177,* 533–539.

Field, T., Hernandez-Rief, M., Diego, M., Feijo, L., Vera, Y., Gil, K., et al. (2007b). Still-face and separation effects on depressed mother-infant interactions. *Infant Mental Health Journal, 28,* 314–323.

Forbes, E. E., & Dahl, R. E. (2005) Neural systems of positive affect: Relevance to understanding child and adolescent depression? *Development and Psychopathology, 17,* 827–850.

Forbes, E. E., Fox, N. A., Cohn, J. F., Galles, S. F., & Kovacs, M. (2006). Children's affect regulation during a disappointment: Psychophysiological responses and relation to parental history of depression. *Biological Psychiatry, 71,* 264–277.

Fox, N. A., Henderson, H. A., Marshall, P. J., Nichols, K. E., & Ghera, M. M. (2005). Behavioral inhibition: Linking biology and behavior within a developmental Framework. *Annual Review of Psychology, 56,* 235–262.

Garber, J., Braafladt, N., & Weiss, B. (1995). Affect regulation in depressed and nondepressed children and young adolescents. *Development and Psychopathology, 7,* 93–115.

Garnefski, N., Rieffe, C., Jellesma, F., Terwogt, M. M., & Kraiij, V. (2007). Cognitive emotion regulation strategies and emotional problems in 9-11-year-old children: The development of an instrument. *European Child and Adolescent Psychiatry, 16,* 1–9.

Goodman, S. H., & Gotlib, I. H. (1999). Risk for psychopathology in children of depressed mothers: A developmental model for understanding mechanisms of transmission. *Psychological Review, 106,* 458–490.

Goodwin, R. D. (2006). Association between coping with anger and feelings of depression among youth. *American Journal of Public Health, 96,* 664–669.

Gormally, S., Barr, R. G., Wertheim, L., Alkawaf, R., Calinoiu, N., & Young, S. N. (2001). Contact and nutrient caregiving effects on newborn pain responses. *Developmental Medicine and Child Neurology, 43,* 28–38.

Gotlib, I. H., Traill, S. K., Montoya, R. L., Joormann, J., & Chang, K. (2005). Attention and memory biases in offspring of parents with bipolar disorder: Implications from a pilot study. *Journal of Child Psychology and Psychiatry, 46,* 84–93.

Graber, J. A., Brooks-Gunn, J., & Warren, M. P. (2006). Pubertal effects on adjustment in girls: Moving from demonstrating effects to identifying pathways. *Journal of Youth and Adolescence, 35,* 413–423.

Gratz, K. L., & Roemer, L. (2004). Multidimensional assessment of emotion regulation and dysregulation: Development, factor structure, and initial validation of the difficulties in emotion regulation scale. *Journal of Psychopathology and Behavioral Assessment, 26,* 41–54.

Gross, J. J., & Muñoz, R. F. (1995). Emotion regulation and mental health. *Clinical Psychology: Science and Practice, 2,* 151–164.

Gunnar, M. R., & Quevedo, K. (2007). The neurobiology of stress and development. *Annual Review of Psychology, 58,* 145–173.

Hardin, M. G., Schroth, E., Pine, D. S., & Ernst, M. (2007). Incentive-related modulation of cognitive control in healthy, anxious, and depressed adolescents: Development and psychopathology related differences. *Journal of Child Psychology and Psychiatry, 48,* 446–454.

Izard, C. E. (1972). *Patterns of emotion in anxiety and depression.* New York: Academic Press.

Izard, C. E. (1991). *The psychology of emotions.* New York; Plenum.

Jazbec, S., McClure, E., Hardin, M., Pine, D. S., & Ernst, M. (2005). Cognitive control under contingencies in anxious and depressed adolescents: An antisaccade task. *Biological Psychiatry, 58,* 632–639.

Joormann, J., Talbot, L., & Gotlib, I. H. (2007). Mood regulation in depression: Differential effects of distraction and recall of happy and sad memories. *Journal of Abnormal Psychology, 116,* 484–490.

Kagan, J. (1981). *The second year: The emergence of self-awareness.* Cambridge, MA: Harvard University Press.

Keenan, K. (2000). Emotion dysregulation as a risk factor for child psychopathology. *Clinical Psychology: Science and Practice, 7,* 418–434.

Keenan, K., & Wakschlag, L. S. (2000). More than the terrible twos: The nature and severity of behavior problems in clinic-referred preschoolers. *Journal of Abnormal Child Psychology, 28,* 33–46.

Keenan, K., & Wakschlag, L. S. (2004). Are oppositional defiant and conduct disorder symptoms normative behaviors in preschoolers? A comparison of referred and non-referred children. *American Journal of Psychiatry, 161,* 356–358.

Kochanska, G. (1997). Multiple pathways to conscience for children with different temperaments: From toddlerhood to age 5. *Developmental Psychology, 33,* 228–240.

Kopp, C. B. (1989). The regulation of distress and negative emotions: A developmental view. *Developmental Psychology, 25,* 343–354.

LaDouceur, C. D., Dahl, R. E., Williamson, D. E., Birmaher, B., Axelson, D. A., Ryan, N. D., et al. (2006). Processing emotional facial expressions influences performance on a Go/No Go task in pediatric anxiety and depression. *Journal of Child Psychology and Psychiatry, 47,* 1107–1115.

LaDouceur, C. D., Dahl, R. E., Williamson, D. E., Birmaher, B., Ryan, N. D., & Casey, B. J. (2005). Altered emotional processing in pediatric anxiety, depression, and comorbid anxiety-depression. *Journal of Abnormal Child Psychology, 33,* 165–177.

Lewis, M., & Michalson, L. A. (1983). *Children's emotions and moods: Developmental theory and measurement.* New York: Plenum.

Lewis, M., Ramsay, D., & Sullivan, M. W. (2006). The relation of ANS and HPS activation to infant anger and sadness response to goal blockage. *Developmental Psychobiology, 48,* 397–405.

Lewis, M., & Sullivan, M. W. (2005). The development of self-conscious and evaluative emotions in early childhood. In A. Elliott and C. Dweck (Eds.), *Handbook of motivation* (pp. 185–201). New York: Guilford.

Lewis, M., Sullivan, M. W., Weiss, M., & Stanger, C. (1989). Self-cognition and the development of self-conscious emotions. *Child Development, 60,* 146–156.

Luby J. L., & Belden, A. (2006). Mood disorders: Phenomenology and a developmental emotion reactivity model. In J. L. Luby (Ed.), *Handbook of preschool mental health: Development, disorders and treatment* (pp. 200–230). New York: Guilford.

Luby, J. L., Belden, A., Sullivan, J., Hayden, R., & McCadney, A. (2008). *Guilt in preschool depression: Evidence for unique patterns in emotional development in early childhood psychopathology.* Manuscript submitted for publication.

Luby, J. L., Heffelfinger, A., Mrakotsky, C., Brown, K., Hessler, M., Wallis, J., et al. (2003). The clinical picture of depression in preschool children. *journal of the American Academy of Child and Adolescent Psychiatry, 42,* 340–348.

Luby, J. L., Heffelfinger, A., Mrakotsky, C., Hessler, M. J., Brown, K. M., & Hildebrand, T. (2002). Preschool major depressive disorder: Preliminary validation for developmentally modified DSM-IV criteria. *Journal of the American Academy of Child Adolescent Psychiatry, 41,* 928–937.

Luby J. L., Mrakotsky, C. M., Heffelfinger, A., Brown, K., & Spitznagel, E. (2004). Characteristics of depressed preschoolers with and without anhedonia: Evidence for a melancholic depressive sub-type in young children. *American Journal of Psychiatry, 161,* 1998–2004.

Luby, J. L., Sullivan, J., Belden, A., Stalets, M., Blankenship, S., & Spitznagel, E. (2006). An observational analysis of behavior in depressed preschoolers: Further validation of early-onset depression. *Journal of the American Academy of Child and Adolescent Psychiatry, 45,* 203–212.

McClellan, J., & Speltz, M. (2003). Psychiatric diagnosis in preschool children. *Journal of the American Academy of Child and Adolescent Psychiatry, 42,* 127–128.

Miller, A. L., Volling, B. L., & McElvain, N. L. (2000). Sibling jealousy in triadic context with mothers and fathers. *Social Development, 9,* 433–457.

Moore, G. A., Cohn, J. F., & Campbell, S. B. (2001). Infant affective responses to mother's still face at 6 months differentially predict externalizing and internalizing behaviors at 18 months. *Developmental Psychology, 37,* 706–714.

Park, R. J., Goodyer, I. M., & Teasdale, J. D. (2004). Effects of induced rumination and distraction on mood and overgeneral autobiographical memory in adolescent major depressive

disorder and controls. *Journal of Child Psychology and Psychiatry, 45,* 996–1006.

Pérez-Edgar, K., Fox, N. A., Cohn, J. F., & Kovacs, M. (2006). Behavioral and electrophysiological markers of selective attention in children of parents with a history of depression. *Biological Psychiatry, 60,* 1131–1138.

Pine, D. S., Lissek, S., Klein, R. G., Mannuzza, S., Mouton, J. L., III, Guardino, M., et al. (2004). Face-memory and emotion: Associations with major depression in children and adolescents. *Journal of Child Psychology and Psychiatry, 45,* 1199–1208.

Pollak, S. D. (2005). Early adversity and mechanisms of plasticity: Integrating affective neuroscience with developmental approaches to psychopathology. *Development and Psychopathology, 17,* 735–752.

Porges, S. W. (2001). The polyvagal theory: Phylogenetic substrates of a social nervous system. *International Journal of Psychophysiology, 42,* 123–126.

Potegal, M., & Davidson, R. J. (2003). Temper tantrums in young children: 2. Behavioral composition. *Journal of Developmental & Behavioral Pediatrics, 24,* 140–147.

Potegal, M., Kosorok, M., & Davidson, R. J. (2003). Tantrum duration and temporal organization. *Journal of Developmental & Behavioral Pediatrics, 24,* 148–154.

Reijntjes, A., Stegge, H. Terwogt, M. M., & Hurkens, E. (2007). Children's depressive symptoms and their regulation of negative affect in response to vignette depicted emotion-eliciting events. *International Journal of Behavioral Development, 31,* 49–58.

Rie, H. E. (1966). Depression in Childhood: A survey of some pertinent contributions. *Journal of the American Academy of Child and Adolescent Psychiatry, 5,* 653–685.

Rothbart, M. K., Ziaie, H., & O'Boyle, C. G. (1992). Self-regulation and emotion in infancy. In N. Eisenberg & R. A. Fabes (Eds.), *Emotion and its regulation in early development* (pp. 7–23). San Francisco: Jossey-Bass.

Rottenberg, J., Gross, J. J., & Gotlib, I. H. (2005). Emotion context insensitivity in major depressive disorder. *Journal of Abnormal Psychology, 114,* 627–639.

Saarni, C. (1999). *The development of emotional competence.* New York: Guilford.

Shonkoff, J. P., & Phillips, D. A. (2000). *From neurons to neighborhoods: The science of early child development.* Washington, DC: National Academy Press.

Skovgaard, A. M., Houman, T., Christiansen, E., & Andreasen, A. H. (2007). The reliability of the ICD-10 and the DC 0-3 in an epidemiological sample of children 1½ years of age. *Infant Mental Health Journal, 26,* 470–480.

Skuban, E. M., Shaw, D. S., Gardner, F., Supplee, L. H., & Nichols, S. R. (2006). The correlates of dyadic synchrony in high-risk, low-income toddler boys. *Infant Behavior & Development, 29,* 423–434.

Sroufe, L. A. (1996). *Emotional development: The organization of emotional life in the early years.* New York: Cambridge University Press.

Stalets, M. M., & Luby, J. L. (2006). Preschool depression. *Psychiatric Clinics of North America, 15,* 899–917.

Thibodeau, R., Jorgensen, R. S., & Kim, S. (2006). Depression, anxiety, and resting frontal EEG asymmetry: A meta-analytic review. *Journal of Abnormal Psychology, 115,* 715–729.

Thompson, R. A. (1994). Emotion regulation: In theme in search of definition. *Monographs of the Society for Research in Child Development, 59*(2–3, Serial No. 240).

Tolan, P. H., & Dodge, K. A. (2005). Children's mental health as a primary care and concern: A system for comprehensive support and services. *American Psychologist, 60,* 601–614.

Tomkins, S. S. (1963). *Affect, imager, and consciousness: Vol. 2. The negative affects.* New York: Springer.

U.S. Public Health Service. (2000a). *Infant mental health initiative agenda.* Washington, DC: Administration for Children, Youth, and Families. Retrieved November 15, 2007, from http://www.acf.hhs.gov/programs/opre/ehs/mental_health/mental_hth_overview.html

U.S. Public Health Service. (2000b). *Report of the Surgeon General's conference on children's mental health: A national agenda.* Washington, DC: Government Printing Office. Retrieved November 15, 2007, from http://www.surgeongeneral.gov/topics/cmh/childreport.htm

Wakschlag, L. S., Briggs-Gown, M. J., Carter, A. S., Hill, C., Danis, B., Keenan, K., et al. (2007). A developmental framework for distinguishing disruptive behavior from normative behavior in preschool children. *Journal of Child Psychology and Psychiatry, 48,* 976–987.

Wilkinson, P. O., & Goodyer, I. H. (2006). Attention difficulties and mood-related ruminative response style in adolescents with unipolar depression. *Journal of Child and Adolescent Psychiatry, 47,* 1284–1291.

Young, S. K, Fox, N. A., & Zahn-Waxler, C. (1999). The relations between temperament and empathy in 2-year-olds. *Developmental Psychology, 35,* 1189–1197.

Zeman, J., Shipman, K., & Suveg, C. (2002). Anger and sadness regulation: Predictions to internalizing and externalizing symptoms in children. *Journal of Clinical Child & Adolescent Psychology, 31,* 393–398.

This article began as a stimulating discussion among the authors at the National Institute of Mental Health Workshop, *Developmental and Translational Models of Emotion Regulation and Dysregulation: Links to Childhood Affective Disorders,* held April 3–4, 2006, in Bethesda, MD. The order of authorship is alphabetic. Support for this work includes National Institutes of Health awards to each of the authors: P. M.C. (MH61388), J.L. (MH64796), and M.W.S. (MH61778).

Correspondence concerning this article should be addressed to **Pamela M. Cole,** Department of Psychology, 309 Moore Building, The Pennsylvania State University, University Park, PA 16802; e-mail: pcole@la.psu.edu.

Children's Social and Moral Reasoning about Exclusion

Developmental research on social and moral reasoning about exclusion has utilized a social-domain theory, in contrast to a global stage theory, to investigate children's evaluations of gender- and race-based peer exclusion. The social-domain model postulates that moral, social-conventional, and personal reasoning coexist in children's evaluations of inclusion and exclusion, and that the priority given to these forms of judgments varies by the age of the child, the context, and the target of exclusion. Findings from developmental intergroup research studies disconfirm a general-stage-model approach to morality in the child, and provide empirical data on the developmental origins and emergence of intergroup attitudes regarding prejudice, bias, and exclusion.

MELANIE KILLEN

How early do individuals become capable of moral reasoning? What is the evidence for morality in the child? Over the past two decades, research on children's moral judgment has changed dramatically, providing new theories and methods for analysis. In brief, the change has been away from a global stage model toward domain-specific models of development. According to Kohlberg's foundational stage model of moral development (Kohlberg, 1984), which followed Piaget's research on moral judgment (Piaget, 1932), children justify acts as right or wrong first on the basis of consequences to the self (preconventional), then in terms of group norms (conventional), and finally in terms of a justice perspective in which individual principles of how to treat one another are understood (postconventional). This approach involved assessing an individual's general scheme (organizing principle) for evaluating social problems and dilemmas across a range of contexts.

By the mid-1980s, however, studies of contextual variation in judgments provided extensive evidence contesting broad stages (Smetana, 2006; Turiel, 1998). For example, young children's evaluations of transgressions and social events reflect considerations of the self, the group, and justice; these considerations do not emerge hierarchically (respectively) but simultaneously in development, each with its own separate developmental trajectory (e.g., self-knowledge, group knowledge, and moral knowledge). Thus, multiple forms of reasoning are applied to the evaluations of social dilemmas and interactions. Social judgments do not reflect one broad template or stage, such as Kohlberg's preconventional stage to characterize childhood morality. Instead, children use different forms of reasoning, moral, conventional, and psychological, simultaneously when evaluating transgressions and social events.

One area of recent empirical inquiry pertains to social and moral evaluations of decisions to exclude others, particularly on the basis of group membership (such as gender, race, or ethnicity), referred to as *intergroup exclusion*. What makes this form of exclusion a particularly compelling topic for investigation from a moral viewpoint is that it reflects, on the one hand, prejudice, discrimination, stereotyping, and bias about groups, and, on the other hand, judgments about fairness, equality, and rights (Killen, Lee-Kim, McGlothlin, & Stangor, 2002). Conceptually, these judgments are diametrically opposed; prejudice violates moral principles of fairness, discrimination violates equality, and stereotyping restricts individual rights. Do both forms of reasoning exist within the child? What do children do when confronted with an exclusion decision that involves moral considerations of fairness and equal treatment, on the one hand, and stereotypic and social-conventional expectations, on the other?

A social-domain model proposes that morality includes fairness, justice, rights, and others' welfare (e.g., when a victim is involved; "It wouldn't be fair to exclude him from the game"); social-conventional concerns involve conventions, etiquette, and customs that promote effective group functioning (e.g., when disorder in the group occurs; "If you let someone new in the group they won't know how it works or what it's about and it will be disruptive"); and psychological issues pertain to autonomy, individual prerogatives, and identity (e.g., acts that are not regulated but affect only the self; "It's her decision who she wants to be friends with"). Social-domain-theory approaches to moral reasoning, along with social-psychological theories about intergroup attitudes, provide a new approach to understanding social exclusion.

Social exclusion is a pervasive aspect of social life, ranging from everyday events (e.g., exclusion from birthday parties, sports teams, social organizations) to large-scale social tragedies (e.g., exclusion based on religion and ethnicity resulting in genocide). These forms of interindividual and intergroup exclusion create conflict, tension, and, in extreme cases, chronic suffering. In the child's world, exclusion has been studied most often in the context of interindividual, rather than intergroup, conflict. Research on peer rejection and victimization, for example, has focused on individual differences and the social deficits that contribute to being a bully (lack of social competence) or a victim (wariness, shyness, fearfulness; Rubin, Bukowski, & Parker, 1998). The findings indicate that the long-term consequences for children and adults who experience pervasive exclusion are negative, resulting in depression, anxiety, and loneliness.

Developmental Approaches

Recently, developmental researchers have investigated children's evaluations of intergroup exclusion (e.g., "You're an X and we don't want Xs in our group"). Decisions to exclude others involve a range of reasons, from group norms and stereotypic expectations to moral assessments about the fairness of exclusion. Much of what is known about group norms has been documented by social psychologists, who have conducted extensive studies on intergroup relationships. The findings indicate that social categorization frequently leads to intergroup bias and that explicit and implicit attitudes about others based on group membership contribute to prejudicial and discriminatory attitudes and behavior (Dovidio, Glick, & Rudman, 2005). Few researchers, however, have examined the developmental trajectory of exclusion from a moral-reasoning perspective.

Social-domain theory has provided a taxonomy for examining the forms of reasoning—moral, social-conventional, and psychological—that are brought to bear on intergroup exclusion decisions. One way that a social-domain model differs from the traditional stage model of moral reasoning, as formulated by Kohlberg in the late 1960s, is that the former provides a theory and a methodology for examining how individuals use different forms of reasons when evaluating everyday phenomena.

Social Reasoning about Exclusion

One of the goals of social-domain research is to identify the conditions under which children give priority to different forms of reasons when evaluating social decisions, events, and interactions. What are the major empirical findings on intergroup exclusion decisions by children? Most centrally, children do not use one scheme ("stage") to evaluate all morally relevant intergroup problems and scenarios; moreover, although some types of decisions are age related, others are not. In a study with children in the 1st, 4th, and 7th grades, the vast majority of students (95%) judged it wrong to exclude a peer from a group solely because of gender or race (e.g., a ballet club excludes a boy because he's a boy; a baseball club excludes a girl because she's a girl), and based their judgment on moral reasons, such as that such exclusion would be unfair and discriminatory (Killen & Stangor, 2001); there were no age-related differences, contrary to what a stage-model approach would predict.

Introducing complexity, however, revealed variation in judgments and justifications. As shown in Figure 1, in an equal-qualifications condition ("What if there was only room for one more to join the club, and a girl and a boy both were equally qualified, who should the group pick?"), most children used moral reasons ("You should pick the person who doesn't usually get a chance to be in the club because they're both equally good at it"); but in

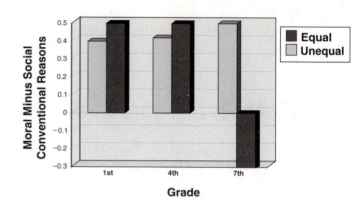

Figure 1 Proportion of moral minus social-conventional reasons given by 1st, 4th, and 7th graders for peer-exclusion judgments based on gender or race. In one condition (equal), participants stated which of two children should be excluded from an after-school club with only one available opening when a stereotypical and nonstereotypical applicant both were equally qualified. In the other (unequal) condition, participants stated which child should be excluded if the child who fit the stereotype for that activity was also more qualified. After-school clubs were baseball/ballet and basketball/math, reflecting gender- and race-associated stereotypes, respectively. Reprinted from Killen & Stangor (2001).

an unequal-qualification condition ("What if X was more qualified, who should the group pick?"), age-related increases in the use of social-conventional reasons ("The group won't work well if you pick the person who is not very good at it") were found. Young adolescents weighed individual merits and considered the functioning of the club or team. Qualifications (e.g., good at ballet or baseball) were considered to be more salient considerations than preserving the "equal opportunity" dimensions (e.g., picking a girl for baseball who has not had a chance to play).

In fact, how children interpret their group's ingroup and outgroup norms (conventions) appears to be related to prejudice and bias (moral transgressions; Abrams, Rutland, Cameron, & Ferrell, in press). Abrams et al. (in press) showed that children's view of whether exclusion is legitimate or wrong was contingent on whether they viewed an individual as supporting or rejecting an ingroup-identity norm. In other related developmental intergroup research, children's lay theories (conventional knowledge) about what it means to work in a group, and whether effort or intrinsic ability is what counts, have been shown to be significantly related to whether they view the denial of allocation of resources as fair or unfair (moral decision making); focusing on intrinsic ability in contrast to effort results in condoning prejudicial treatment (Levy, Chiu, & Hong, 2006). Moreover, adolescents' perceptions of the social status of membership in peer cliques (conventional knowledge) determine whether they view exclusion (e.g., excluding a "goth" from the cheerleading squad) as fair or legitimate (Horn, 2003). These findings demonstrate the nuanced ways in which children make judgments about groups and how group knowledge and group norms bear directly on moral judgments about exclusion and inclusion.

Research on intergroup contact in childhood provides information regarding how social experience influences the mani-

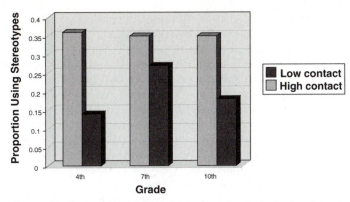

Figure 2 Proportion of European American students who explicitly used stereotypes to explain what it is about interracial interactions that makes their peers uncomfortable, as a function of positive intergroup contact. Positive intergroup contact included cross-race friendship in classrooms, schools, and neighborhoods (based on data reported in Killen et al., 2006).

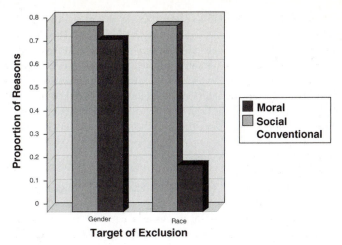

Figure 3 Proportion of moral and social-conventional reasons for gender and racial targets of exclusion in peer-group contexts. Peer-group contexts referred to after-school music clubs that excluded a target child from joining the club due to his or her gender or race. Reasons were moral (unfairness) or social-conventional (group functioning; based on data from Killen, Lee-Kim, McGlothlin, & Stangor, 2002).

festation of children's stereotypes and conventional reasoning to justify exclusion. Intergroup-contact theory states that under certain conditions, contact with members of outgroups decreases prejudice (Pettigrew & Tropp, 2005). In a developmental study with participants enrolled in 13 public schools ($N = 685$) of varying ethnic diversity (see Figure 2), European American students enrolled in heterogeneous schools were more likely to use explicit stereotypes to explain why interracial interactions make their peers uncomfortable, and were less likely to use moral reasons to evaluate peer exclusion, than were European Americans enrolled in homogeneous schools (Killen, Richardson, Kelly, Crystal, & Ruck, 2006). Children's positive experiences with students who are different from themselves, under certain conditions, facilitate moral reasoning about intergroup exclusion and suppress stereotypic expectations as a reason for an exclusion decision.

These findings support a domain-model view of social and moral judgment and challenge stage theory, which proposes that children are limited in their ability to make moral judgments by a general-processing scheme for assimilating information (their "stage"). From a stage view, one would expect children to use conventional or stereotypic (group-expectations) reasons, and expect older children to use moral reasons. Instead, researchers now find that children's reasoning varies by the context and a balance of priorities.

Context has many variables, and determining it involves investigating the role of the target of exclusion as well as participant variables (age, gender, race/ethnicity) on exclusion decisions. Regarding the target of exclusion, a series of findings reveals that gender exclusion is viewed as more legitimate than exclusion based on ethnicity, with more social-conventional reasons and stereotypic expectations used to support the former than the latter (Killen et al., 2002). As shown in Figure 3, children used fewer moral reasons to evaluate exclusion in a peer-group music context with a gender target ("What if the boys' music club will not let a girl join?") than with a race target ("What if the white students in a music club will not let a black student join?"). A significant proportion of students used social-conventional reasons, such as: "A girl/black student likes different music, so she/he won't fit in with the group." Not surprisingly, though, European American females, and minority participants (both males and females),

were more likely to reject these forms of exclusion and to use moral reasons than were European American males. This inclusive orientation may be due to the perspective, empathy, and reciprocity that result from experiencing prior exclusion. Thus, these findings support social-domain-theory propositions that the target of exclusion is influential on evaluations of exclusion, and that specific types of peer experiences may contribute to judgments that exclusion is wrong.

Children reject atypical peers based on stigmatized group identity (Nesdale & Brown, 2004). This finding further indicates that peer experience with exclusion is an important variable for investigation. Nesdale and Brown propose that children who experience extensive exclusion may be at risk for demonstrating prejudicial behavior toward others, and for perpetuating a cycle of negative intergroup attitudes. At the same time, however, adolescents are cognizant of the wrongfulness of discrimination regarding stigmatized peers (Verkuyten & Thijs, 2002).

Although stereotypes and conventions are powerful forces that legitimize exclusion, there is also extensive evidence of how adolescents explain the wrongfulness of discrimination in terms of social justice. Social-reasoning categories provide evidence for the types of norms that children use to justify or reject exclusion decisions and for the conditions that promote children's change from a priority on morality to group functioning, which may, at times, occur at the expense of fairness.

New Directions

Adults frequently use traditions and customs to justify exclusion. Tiger Woods' initial response to playing at the Augusta (Georgia) National Golf Club (host of the legendary Masters Tournament), which excludes women, was "That's just the way it is" (Brown, 2002)—categorized as social-conventional reasoning. More recently, Woods has stated, "Is it unfair? Yes. Do I want to see a female member? Yes" ("Woods Thinks Masters Debate Deserves a Private Meeting," 2005)—categorized as moral reasoning. Yet, he refuses to give up his participation in the event: "They're asking me to give up an opportunity to win the Masters three straight years" (Smith, 2003)—personal priority over the wrongfulness of exclusion. These quotes, which do not reflect coded responses from an in-depth systematic interview, nonetheless, reveal how an individual can give different priorities to exclusion decisions and how these priorities change depending on the context (Killen, Sinno, & Margie, in press). Social-conventional or personal reasons do not necessarily reflect a developmentally "primitive" response (as put forth by stage theory).

Are children moral? Yes, children demonstrate spontaneous and elaborated reasons for why it is wrong to exclude others based on group membership, referring to fairness, equality, and rights. Do children have stereotypes about others? Yes; how these stereotypes enter into moral decision making requires an in-depth analysis of how children weigh competing considerations, such as group functioning, traditions, customs, and cultural norms, when evaluating exclusion. What changes as children age is how these considerations are weighed, the contexts that become salient for children and adolescents, and the ability to determine when morality should take priority in a given situation.

What is not well known is how children's intergroup biases (those that are not explicit) influence their judgments about exclusion; what it is about intergroup contact that contributes to children's variation in reliance on stereotypes to evaluate exclusion; and how early intergroup attitudes influence children's awareness of justice, fairness, and equality. Given that stereotypes are very hard to change in adulthood, interventions need to be conducted in childhood. Understanding when children resort to stereotypic expectations is crucial information for creating effective interventions. Developmental findings on social reasoning about exclusion provide a new approach for addressing these complex issues in childhood and adulthood and for creating programs to reduce prejudice.

References

Abrams, D., Rutland, A., Cameron, L., & Ferrell, A. (in press). Older but wilier: Ingroup accountability and the development of subjective group dynamics. *Developmental Psychology.*

Brown, J. (2002, August 16). Should Woods carry the black man's burden? *The Christian Science Monitor* [electronic version]. Retrieved January 5, 2007, from http://www.csmonitor.com/2002/0816/p01s01-ussc.html

Dovidio, J.F., Glick, P., & Rudman, L. (Eds.). (2005). *Reflecting on the nature of prejudice: Fifty years after Allport.* Malden, MA: Blackwell.

Horn, S. (2003). Adolescents' reasoning about exclusion from social groups. *Developmental Psychology, 39,* 11–84.

Killen, M., Lee-Kim, J., McGlothlin, H., & Stangor, C. (2002). How children and adolescents evaluate gender and racial exclusion. *Monographs for the Society for Research in Child Development* (Serial No. 271, Vol. 67, No.4). Oxford, England: Blackwell.

Killen, M., Richardson, C., Kelly, M.C., Crystal, D., & Ruck, M. (2006, May). *European-American students' evaluations of interracial social exchanges in relation to the ethnic diversity of school environments.* Paper presented at the annual convention of the Association for Psychological Science, New York City.

Killen, M., Sinno, S., & Margie, N. (in press). Children's experiences and judgments about group exclusion and inclusion. In R. Kail (Ed.), *Advances in child psychology.* New York: Elsevier.

Killen, M., & Stangor, C. (2001). Children's social reasoning about inclusion and exclusion in gender and race peer group contexts. *Child Development, 72,* 174–186.

Kohlberg, L. (1984). *Essays on moral development: Vol. 2. The psychology of moral development—The nature and validity of moral stages.* San Francisco: Harper & Row.

Levy, S.R., Chiu, C.Y., & Hong, Y.Y. (2006). Lay theories and intergroup relations. *Group Processes and Intergroup Relations, 9,* 5–24.

Nesdale, D., & Brown, K. (2004). Children's attitudes towards an atypical member of an ethnic in-group. *International Journal of Behavioral Development, 28,* 328–335.

Pettigrew, T.F., & Tropp, L.R. (2005). Allport's intergroup contact hypothesis: Its history and influence. In J.F. Dovidio, P. Glick, & L. Rudman (Eds.), *Reflecting on the nature of prejudice: Fifty years after Allport* (pp. 262–277). Malden, MA: Blackwell.

Piaget, J. (1932). *The moral judgment of the child.* New York: Free Press.

Rubin, K.H., Bukowski, W., & Parker, J. (1998). Peer interactions, relationships and groups. In W. Damon (Ed.), *Handbook of child psychology: Vol. 3. Social, emotional, and personality development* (5th ed., pp. 619–700). New York: Wiley.

Smetana, J.G. (2006). Social domain theory: Consistencies and variations in children's moral and social judgments. In M. Killen & J.G. Smetana (Eds.), *Handbook of moral development* (pp. 119–154). Mahwah, NJ: Erlbaum.

Smith, T. (2003, February 20). A Master's challenge. *Online NewsHour.* Retrieved July 16, 2006, from http://www.pbs.org/newshour/bb/sports/jan-june03/golf_2-20.html

Turiel, E. (1998). The development of morality. In W. Damon (Ed.), *Handbook of child psychology: Vol. 3. Social, emotional, and personality development* (5th ed., pp. 863–932). New York: Wiley.

Verkuyten, M., & Thijs, J. (2002). Racist victimization among children in the Netherlands: The effect of ethnic group and school. *Ethnic and Racial Studies, 25,* 310–331.

Woods thinks Masters debate deserves a private meeting. (2005, February 14). *USA Today* [electronic version]. Retrieved January 10, 2007, from http://www.usatoday.com/sports/golf/2002-10-16-woods-masters_x.htm

Address correspondence to Melanie Killen, 3304 Benjamin Building, Department of Human Development, University of Maryland, College Park, MD 20742-1131; e-mail: mkillen@umd.edu.

Acknowledgments—The author would like to thank Judith G. Smetana, Stefanie Sinno, and Cameron Richardson, for helpful comments on earlier drafts of this manuscript, and the graduate students in the Social and Moral Development Laboratory for collaborative and insightful contributions to the research reported in this paper. The research described in this manuscript was supported, in part, by grants from the National Institute of Child Health and Human Development (IR01HD04121-01) and the National Science Foundation (#BCS0346717).

A Profile of Bullying at School

Bullying and victimization are on the increase, extensive research shows. The attitudes and routines of relevant adults can exacerbate or curb students' aggression toward classmates.

DAN OLWEUS

Bullying among schoolchildren is a very old and well-known phenomenon. Although many educators are acquainted with the problem, researchers only began to study bullying systematically in the 1970s (Olweus, 1973, 1978) and focused primarily on schools in Scandinavia. In the 1980s and early 1990s, however, studies of bullying among schoolchildren began to attract wider attention in a number of other countries, including the United States.

What Is Bullying?

Systematic research on bullying requires rigorous criteria for classifying students as bullies or as victims (Olweus, 1996; Solberg & Olweus, in press). How do we know when a student is being bullied? One definition is that

> a student is being bullied or victimized when he or she is exposed, repeatedly and over time, to negative actions on the part of one or more other students. (Olweus, 1993)

The person who intentionally inflicts, or attempts to inflict, injury or discomfort on someone else is engaging in *negative actions,* a term similar to the definition of *aggressive behavior* in the social sciences. People carry out negative actions through physical contact, with words, or in more indirect ways, such as making mean faces or gestures, spreading rumors, or intentionally excluding someone from a group.

Bullying also entails an *imbalance in strength* (or an *asymmetrical power relationship*), meaning that students exposed to negative actions have difficulty defending themselves. Much bullying is *proactive aggression,* that is, aggressive behavior that usually occurs without apparent provocation or threat on the part of the victim.

Some Basic Facts

In the 1980s, questionnaire surveys of more than 150,000 Scandinavian students found that approximately 15 percent of students ages 8–16 were involved in bully/victim problems with some regularity—either as bullies, victims, or both bully and victim (bully-victims) (Olweus, 1993). Approximately 9 percent of all students were victims, and 6–7 percent bullied other students regularly. In contrast to what is commonly believed, only a small proportion of the victims also engaged in bullying other students (17 percent of the victims or 1.6 percent of the total number of students).

In 2001, when my colleagues and I conducted a new large-scale survey of approximately 11,000 students from 54 elementary and junior high schools using the same questions that we used in 1983 (Olweus, 2002), we noted two disturbing trends. The percentage of victimized students had increased by approximately 50 percent from 1983, and the percentage of students who were involved (as bullies, victims, or bully-victims) in frequent and serious bullying problems—occurring at least once a week—had increased by approximately 65 percent. We saw these increases as an indication of negative societal developments (Solberg & Olweus, in press).

The surveys showed that bullying is a serious problem affecting many students in Scandinavian schools. Data from other countries, including the United States (Nansel et al., 2001; Olweus & Limber, 1999; Perry, Kusel, & Perry, 1988)—and in large measure collected with my Bully/Victim Questionnaire (1983, 1996)—indicate that bullying problems exist outside Scandinavia with similar, or even higher, prevalence (Olweus & Limber, 1999; Smith et al., 1999). The prevalence figures from different countries or cultures, however, may not be directly comparable. Even though the questionnaire gives a detailed definition of bullying, the prevalence rates obtained may be affected by language differences, the students' familiarity with the concept of bullying, and the degree of public attention paid to the phenomenon.

Boys bully other students more often than girls do, and a relatively large percentage of girls—about 50 percent—report that they are bullied mainly by boys. A somewhat higher percentage of boys are victims of bullying, especially in the junior high school grades. But bullying certainly occurs among girls as well. Physical bullying is less common among girls, who typically use more subtle and indirect means of harassment,

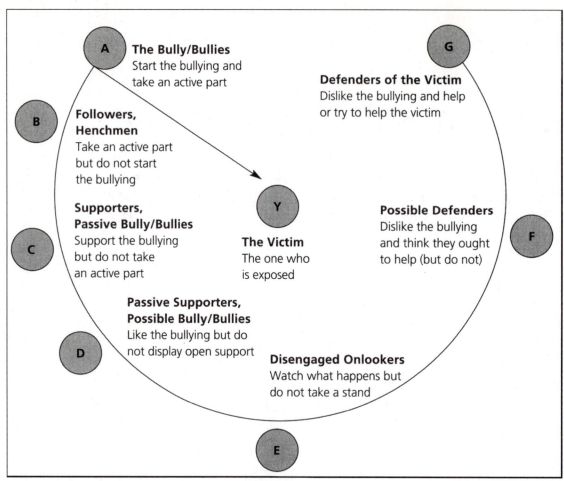

Figure 1 The Buylling Circle.   Students' Modes of Reaction/Roles in an Acute Buylling Situation

such as intentionally excluding someone from the group, spreading rumors, and manipulating friendship relations. Such forms of bullying can certainly be as harmful and distressing as more direct and open forms of harassment. Our research data (Olweus, 1993), however, clearly contradict the view that girls are the most frequent and worst bullies, a view suggested by such recent books as *Queen Bees and Wannabes* (Wiseman, 2002) and *Odd Girl Out* (Simmons, 2002).

Common Myths about Bullying

Several common assumptions about the causes of bullying receive little or no support when confronted with empirical data. These misconceptions include the hypotheses that bullying is a consequence of large class or school size, competition for grades and failure in school, or poor self-esteem and insecurity. Many also believe erroneously that students who are overweight, wear glasses, have a different ethnic origin, or speak with an unusual dialect are particularly likely to become victims of bullying.

All of these hypotheses have thus far failed to receive clear support from empirical data. Accordingly, we must look for other factors to find the key origins of bullying problems. The accumulated research evidence indicates that personality characteristics or typical reaction patterns, in combination with physical strength or weakness in the case of boys, are important in the development of bullying problems in individual students. At the same time, environmental factors, such as the attitudes, behavior, and routines of relevant adults—in particular, teachers and principals—play a crucial role in determining the extent to which bullying problems will manifest themselves in a larger unit, such as a classroom or school. Thus, we must pursue analyses of the main causes of bully/victim problems on at least two different levels: individual and environmental.

Victims and the Bullying Circle

Much research has focused on the characteristics and family backgrounds of victims and bullies. We have identified two kinds of victims, the more common being the *passive or submissive victim,* who represents some 80–85 percent of all victims. Less research information is available about *provocative victims,* also called *bully-victims* or *aggressive victims,* whose behavior may elicit negative reactions from a large part of the class. The dynamics of a classroom with a provocative victim are different from those of a classroom with a submissive victim (Olweus, 1978, 1993).

Bullies and victims naturally occupy key positions in the configuration of bully/victim problems in a classroom, but other students also play important roles and display different attitudes and reactions toward an acute bullying situation. Figure 1 outlines the "Bullying Circle" and represents the various ways in which most students in a classroom with bully/victim problems are involved in or affected by them (Olweus, 2001a, 2001b).

The Olweus Bullying Prevention Program

The Olweus Bullying Prevention Program,[1] developed and evaluated over a period of almost 20 years (Olweus, 1993, 1999), builds on four key principles derived chiefly from research on the development and identification of problem behaviors, especially aggressive behavior. These principles involve creating a school—and ideally, also a home—environment characterized by

- Warmth, positive interest, and involvement from adults;
- Firm limits on unacceptable behavior;
- Consistent application of nonpunitive, nonphysical sanctions for unacceptable behavior or violations of rules; and
- Adults who act as authorities and positive role models.

We have translated these principles into a number of specific measures to be used at the school, classroom, and individual levels (Olweus, 1993, 2001b). Figure 2 lists the set of core components that our statistical analyses and experience with the program have shown are particularly important in any implementation of the program.

Our research data clearly contradict the view that girls are the most frequent and worst bullies.

The program's implementation relies mainly on the existing social environment. Teachers, administrators, students, and parents all play major roles in carrying out the program and in restructuring the social environment. One possible reason for this intervention program's effectiveness is that it changes the opportunity and reward structures for bullying behavior, which results in fewer opportunities and rewards for bullying (Olweus, 1992).

Research-Based Evaluations

The first evaluation of the effects of the Olweus Bullying Prevention Program involved data from approximately 2,500 students in 42 elementary and junior high schools in Bergen, Norway, and followed students for two and one-half years, from 1983 to 1985 (Olweus, 1991, in press; Olweus & Alsaker, 1991). The findings were significant:

- Marked reductions—by 50 percent or more—in bully/victim problems for the period studied, measuring after 8 and 20 months of intervention.
- Clear reductions in general anti-social behavior, such as vandalism, fighting, pilfering, drunkenness, and truancy.
- Marked improvement in the social climate of the classes and an increase in student satisfaction with school life.

The differences between baseline and intervention groups were highly significant. The research concluded that the registered changes in bully/victim problems and related behavior patterns were likely to be a consequence of the intervention program and not of some other factor. Partial replications of the program in the United States, the United Kingdom, and Germany have resulted in similar, although somewhat weaker, results (Olweus & Limber, 1999; Smith & Sharp, 1994).

In 1997–1998, our study of 3,200 students from 30 Norwegian schools again registered clear improvements with regard to bully/victim problems in the schools with intervention programs. The effects were weaker than in the first project, with averages varying between 21 and 38 percent. Unlike the first study, however, the intervention program had been in place for only six months when we made the second measurement. In addition, we conducted the study during a particularly turbulent year in which Norway introduced a new national curriculum that made heavy demands of educators' time and resources.

Nonetheless, the intervention schools fared considerably better than the comparison schools. Surveys of the comparison schools, which had set up anti-bullying efforts according to their own plans, showed very small or no changes with regard to "being bullied" and a 35 percent increase for "bullying other students" (Olweus, in press). Because we have not yet analyzed the questionnaire information, we cannot fully explain this result, but it is consistent with findings from a number of studies showing that inexpert interventions intended to counteract delinquent and antisocial behavior often have unexpectedly negative effects (Dishion, McCord, & Poulin, 1999; Gottfredson, 1987; Lipsey, 1992).

Most students in a classroom with bully/victim problems are involved in or affected by the problems.

In the most recent (1999–2000) evaluation of the Olweus Bullying Prevention Program among approximately 2,300 students from 10 schools—some of which had large percentages of students with immigrant backgrounds—we found an average reduction by around 40 percent with regard to "being bullied" and by about 50 percent for "bullying other students" (Olweus, in press).

The Need for Evidence-Based Intervention Programs

Coping with bully/victim problems has become an official school priority in many countries, and many have suggested ways to handle and prevent such problems. But because most proposals have either failed to document positive results or have never been subjected to systematic research evaluation, it is difficult to know which programs or measures actually work and which do not. What counts is how well the program works for students, not how much the adults using the program like it.

Recently, when a U.S. committee of experts used three essential criteria (Elliott, 1999) to systematically evaluate more than 500 programs ostensibly designed to prevent violence or other problem behaviors, only 11 of the programs (four of which are school-based) satisfied the specified criteria.[2] The U.S. Department of Justice's Office of Juvenile Justice and Delinquency Prevention and other sources are now providing financial support for the implementation of these evidence-based "Blueprint" programs in a number of sites.

In Norway, an officially appointed committee recently conducted a similar evaluation of 56 programs being used in Norway's schools to counteract and prevent problem behavior (Norwegian Ministry of Education, Research, and Church Affairs, 2000) and recommended without reservation only one program for further use. The Olweus Bullying Prevention Program is one of the 11 Blueprint programs and the program selected by the Norwegian committee.

Norway's New National Initiative against Bullying

In late 2000, Norway's Department of Education and Research and Department of Children and Family Affairs decided to offer the Olweus Bullying Prevention Program on a large scale to Norwegian elementary and junior high schools over a period of several years. In building the organization for this national initiative, we have used a four-level train-the-trainer strategy of dissemination. At Norway's University of Bergen, the Olweus Group Against Bullying at the Research Center for Health Promotion trains and supervises specially selected *instructor candidates,* each of whom trains and supervises key persons from a number of schools. The key persons are then responsible for leading staff discussion groups at each participating school. These meetings typically focus on key components and themes of the program (Olweus, 1993, 2001b).

The training of the instructor candidates consists of 10–11 whole-day assemblies over 16 months. In between the whole-day meetings, the instructor candidates receive ongoing consultation from the Olweus Group by telephone or through e-mail.

In implementing this train-the-trainer model in the United States with financial support from the U.S. Department of

The Olweus Bullying Prevention Program

General Prerequisite

- Awareness and involvement of adults

Measures at the School Level

- Administration of the Olweus Bully/Victim Questionnaire (filled out anonymously by students)
- Formation of a Bullying Prevention Coordinating Committee
- Training of staff and time for discussion groups
- Effective supervision during recess and lunch periods

Measures at the Classroom Level

- Classroom and school rules about bullying
- Regular classroom meetings
- Meetings with students' parents

Measures at the Individual Level

- Individual meetings with students who bully
- Individual meetings with victims of bullying
- Meetings with parents of students involved
- Development of individual intervention plans

Figure 2

Justice and the U.S. Department of Health and Human Services, we have made some modifications to accommodate cultural differences and practical constraints. In particular, we have reduced the number of whole-day assemblies to four or five and have granted greater autonomy to individual schools' Bullying Prevention Coordinating Committees than is typical in Norway.

So far, 75 instructor candidates have participated in training, and more than 225 schools participate in the program. Recently, Norway's government substantially increased our funding to enable us to offer the program to more schools starting in 2003.

We see Norway's national initiative as a breakthrough for the systematic, long-term, and research-based work against bully/victim problems in schools. We hope to see similar developments in other countries.

Notes

1. More information about the Olweus Bullying Prevention Program is available at www.colorado.edu/cspv/blueprints/model/ BPPmaterials.html or by contacting nobully @clemson.edu or olweus@psych.uib.no.

2. The four school-based programs are Life Skills Training, Promoting Alternative Thinking Strategies (PATHS), the Incredible Years, and the Olweus Bullying Prevention Program. For more information about the Blueprints for Violence Prevention's model programs, visit www.colorado.edu/cspv/blueprints/model/overview.html.

References

Dishion, T. J., McCord, J., & Poulin, F. (1999). When interventions harm: Peer groups and problem behavior. *American Psychologist, 54,* 755–764.

Elliott, D. S. (1999). Editor's introduction. In D. Olweus & S. Limber, *Blueprints for violence prevention: Bullying Prevention Program.* Boulder, CO: Institute of Behavioral Science.

Gottfredson, G. D. (1987). Peer group interventions to reduce the risk of delinquent behavior: A selective review and a new evaluation. *Criminology, 25,* 671–714.

Lipsey, M. W. (1992). Juvenile delinquency treatment: A meta-analytic inquiry into the variability of effects. In T. D. Cook, H. Cooper, D. S. Corday, H. Hartman, L. V. Hedges, R. J. Light, T. A. Louis, & F. Mosteller (Eds.), *Meta-analysis for explanation: A casebook* (pp. 83–125). New York: Russell Sage.

Nansel, T. R., Overpeck, M., Pilla, R. S., Ruan, W. J., Simons-Morton, B., & Scheidt, P. (2001). Bullying behaviors among U.S. youth: Prevalence and association with psychosocial adjustment. *Journal of the American Medical Association, 285,* 2094–2100.

Norwegian Ministry of Education, Research, and Church Affairs. (2000). *Rapport 2000: Vurdering av program og tiltak for å redusere problematferd og utvikle sosial kompetanse.* (Report 2000: Evaluation of programs and measures to reduce problem behavior and develop social competence.) Oslo, Norway: Author.

Olweus, D. (1973). *Hackkycklingar och översittare. Forskning om skolmobbing.* (Victims and bullies: Research on school bullying.) Stockholm: Almqvist & Wicksell.

Olweus, D. (1978). *Aggression in the schools: Bullies and whipping boys.* Washington, DC: Hemisphere Press (Wiley).

Olweus, D. (1983). *The Olweus Bully/Victim Questionnaire.* Mimeo. Bergen, Norway: Research Center for Health Promotion, University of Bergen.

Olweus, D. (1991). Bully/victim problems among schoolchildren: Basic facts and effects of a school-based intervention program. In D. Pepler & K. Rubin (Eds.), *The development and treatment of childhood aggression* (pp. 411–448). Hillsdale, NJ: Erlbaum.

Olweus, D. (1992). Bullying among schoolchildren: Intervention and prevention. In R. D. Peters, R. J. McMahon, & V. L. Quincy (Eds.), *Aggression and violence throughout the life span.* Newbury Park, CA: Sage.

Olweus, D. (1993). *Bullying at school: What we know and what we can do.* Cambridge, MA: Blackwell. (Available from AIDC, P.O. Box 20, Williston, VT 05495; (800) 216-2522).

Olweus, D. (1996). *The Revised Olweus Bully/Victim Questionnaire.* Mimeo. Bergen, Norway: Research Center for Health Promotion, University of Bergen.

Olweus, D. (1999). Norway. In P. K. Smith, Y. Morita, J. Junger-Tas, D. Olweus, R. Catalano, & P. Slee (Eds.), *The nature of school bullying: A cross-national perspective* (pp. 28–48). London: Routledge.

Olweus, D. (2001a). Peer harassment: A critical analysis and some important issues. In J. Juvonen & S. Graham (Eds.), *Peer harassment in school* (pp. 3–20). New York: Guilford Publications.

Olweus, D. (2001b). *Olweus' core program against bullying and anti-social behavior: A teacher handbook.* Bergen, Norway: Research Center for Health Promotion, University of Bergen.

Olweus, D. (2002). *Mobbing i skolen: Nye data om omfang og forandring over tid.* (Bullying at school: New data on prevalence and change over time.) Manuscript. Research Center for Health Promotion, University of Bergen, Bergen, Norway.

Olweus, D. (in press). Bullying at school: Prevalence estimation, a useful evaluation design, and a new national initiative in Norway. *Association for Child Psychology and Psychiatry Occasional Papers.*

Olweus, D., & Alsaker, F. D. (1991). Assessing change in a cohort longitudinal study with hierarchical data. In D. Magnusson, L. R. Bergman, G. Rudinger, & B. Törestad (Eds.), *Problems and methods in longitudinal research* (pp. 107–132). New York: Cambridge University Press.

Olweus, D., & Limber, S. (1999). *Blueprints for violence prevention: Bullying Prevention Program.* Boulder, CO: Institute of Behavioral Science.

Perry, D. G., Kusel, S. J., & Perry, L. C. (1988). Victims of peer aggression. *Developmental Psychology, 24,* 807–814.

Simmons, R. (2002). *Odd girl out.* New York: Harcourt.

Smith, P. K., Morita, Y., Junger-Tas, J., Olweus, D., Catalano, R., & Slee, P. (Eds.). (1999). *The nature of school bullying: A cross-national perspective.* London: Routledge.

Smith, P. K., & Sharp, S. (Eds.). (1994). *School bullying: Insights and perspectives.* London: Routledge.

Solberg, M., & Olweus, D. (in press). Prevalence estimation of school bullying with the Olweus Bully/Victim Questionnaire. *Aggressive Behavior.*

Wiseman, R. (2002). *Queen bees and wannabes.* New York: Crown.

DAN OLWEUS is Research Professor of Psychology and Director of the Olweus Group Against Bullying at the Research Center for Health Promotion at the University of Bergen, Christies Gate 13, N-5015 Bergen, Norway; olweus@psych.uib.no.

When Girls and Boys Play: What Research Tells Us

Jeanetta G. Riley and Rose B. Jones

Research on play suggests that children of all ages benefit from engaging in play activities (Bergen, 2004). With the recent emphasis on standards and testing, however, many teachers have felt the increased pressure to spend time on structured learning events, leaving few moments of relaxation in a child's day (Chenfeld, 2006). Many elementary schools have even reduced or eliminated recess times in an effort to give children more time to work on academics (Clements, 2000). That is unfortunate, as findings from studies of play indicate that play helps children to develop social, language, and physical skills.

While beneficial for both, play often differs for girls and boys (see Gallas, 1998; Gurian & Stevens, 2005). This article reviews research related to the differences found between the genders as they play and the benefits that elementary children can gain from play. In addition, the authors include suggestions for educators regarding children's play at school.

Social Development
Girls and Boys Sharing Social Interactions during Play

Researchers have found differences in the way the genders socialize during play. In an early study examining gender and play, Lever (1978) found several differences in how 5th-grade girls and boys play. For example, boys played more competitive, rule-oriented, group games than did girls; girls interacted in smaller groups, had conversations, and walked and talked with friends more often than did boys. Lever concluded that the nature of boys' team games and their experiences with ruledictated play: 1) allowed for the development of cooperation skills between peers with differing ideas, 2) afforded them opportunities to work independently to accomplish a common task, and 3) provided motivation to abide by established rules.

Other recent studies have found results similar to those of Lever (1978). A study of elementary students at recess conducted by Butcher (1999) indicated that boys more often participated in competitive games, and girls chose activities that allowed them to have conversations. Likewise, Lewis and Phillipsen (1998) found that elementary-age boys at recess played physically active group games with rules more often than did girls.

However, in contrast to Lever's (1978) findings on groupings during recess, Lewis and Phillipsen (1998) noted that while girls tended to play in small groups, boys tended to play in groups of various sizes, from dyads to more than five children.

Also consistent with Lever's (1978) findings, a study of 4th-graders by Goodwin (2001) indicated that boys tended to form social structures, wherein the boys who were more skilled at the activity took the lead and directed the players. Boys with less skill were allowed to play but were not allowed a leadership role. In contrast, girls' leadership roles during games of jump rope did not depend on their ability to carry out the physical tasks of the game. Instead of one girl taking the lead, several girls directed the games; however, Goodwin (2001) found that the girls were more likely to exclude others from their play than were the boys.

Even very young children tend to be socially influenced by playing with same-sex peers. For example, Martin and Fabes' (2001) investigation of preschool and kindergarten children at play indicated that playing with same-gender peers affects play behaviors. Their research findings added to the evidence (e.g., Boyatzis, Mallis, & Leon, 1999; Thorne, 1993) that children often choose to play with same-sex peers. Additionally, Martin and Fabes found gender-typical behaviors for children who more often played with same-sex peers. For instance, the girls who most often played with other girls were generally less active during play and chose to play in areas close to adults. Boys who played with other boys more often engaged in play that was more aggressive and farther from adult supervision. This stereotypical play was found less often in children who tended to play with the opposite sex.

Not all students have positive social experiences during play activities. Some students may have difficulty developing the appropriate skills necessary for positive peer interactions. Children with inadequate social skills may tend to behave inappropriately during times of free play, such as recess (Blatchford, 1998). Rather than limit free play due to inappropriate behavior, however, these times can provide opportunities for conflict resolution interventions. In one study by Butcher (1999), the researchers trained college students to use conflict resolution strategies when interacting with 1st- through 6th-graders during recess times. The volunteers provided positive feedback, modeled appropriate social skills, and implemented strategies to increase cooperation among the children. As a result, when the numbers were analyzed, combining all grade levels, the means for the number of incidents of inappropriate targeted behaviors (i.e., violent behavior, verbal abuse, and inappropriate equipment use) declined during interventions. However, it is important to note that when the results were analyzed according to gender, significant differences were found in the reduction of targeted behaviors for boys only. No significant differences were found for girls' behavior. The researchers suggested that this lack of difference for the girls was due to the limited number of negative behaviors the girls initially exhibited (Butcher, 1999).

Overall Play and the Social Development of Children

By the time children reach school age, play typically becomes a social activity (Jarrett & Maxwell, 2000). As children play with others, they begin to learn what behaviors are expected and acceptable in their society. Playing with peers permits children to adjust to the expected norms (Fromberg, 1998).

Opportunities for free play with limited adult intervention provide time for children to explore which behaviors are accepted among their peers (Wortham, 2002). As younger children associate in play situations, they begin to realize that play ends if they do not negotiate behaviors and cooperate; therefore, play helps children learn to regulate their behaviors in order to continue playing together (Heidemann & Hewitt, 1992; Poole, Miller, & Church, 2004).

For older children, recess can be a time for learning about and adjusting to peer expectations. Pellegrini and Blatchford's (2002) findings suggest that recess play provides children with time to enter into social relationships early in the school year, which, in turn, helps them in social situations throughout the year. Pellegrini, Blatchford, Kato, and Baines (2004) also found that recess allowed opportunities for children to increase positive social experiences. For the 7- and 8-year-old participants in their study, basic games played at the beginning of the school year permitted the children time to get acquainted with peers, leading to more advanced play once the children became more familiar with each other. Additionally, Jarrett et al. (1998) speculated that children who move from one school to another find recess times helpful in adjusting and making new friends.

Language Development
Girls and Boys Expressing Language during Play

Research indicates that the types of games in which girls often engage may support language development differently than the types of games boys typically play. Blatchford, Baines, and Pellegrini (2003) studied playground activities of children in England during the year the children turned 8 years old. The researchers found that girls held significantly more conversations and played significantly more verbal games than did boys. Goodwin (2002) also found that 4th- through 6th-grade girls spent most of their playtime talking with one another. Their games tended to require close proximity to one another, thus allowing for extended conversations. Conversely, some studies found that the games boys tended to choose often involved language usage that was more instruction-oriented, with boys verbally directing the play actions of one another (Boyle, Marshall, & Robeson, 2003; Goodwin, 2001).

Overall Play and Language Skill Development of Children

Play is a natural environment for children's language development (Perlmutter & Burrell, 1995). Children use language during their solitary play as well as in social play encounters (Piaget, 1962). Both expressive and receptive language skills are needed to plan, explain, and execute play activities. Language skills give children the ability to cooperate in creating and prolonging their play episodes (Van Hoorn, Monighan-Nourot, Scales, & Alward, 2003).

Developing language skills facilitates peer relationships. Piaget (1962) theorized that the talk of preschool-age children is egocentric (i.e., talk that is not for the sake of communicating with others). Very young children verbalize without a need for others to enter into the conversation; however, as older children begin to interact more often with adults and peers, the need to communicate arises. Egocentric speech gradually subsides and social speech takes over as children practice using language (Ginsburg & Opper, 1979).

Language is a major factor in social play scenarios, such as sociodramatic play in which children create pretend play episodes and take on the roles of others. Language in the context of play provides children with the ability to develop strategies for cooperation, engage in varied and complex play themes, and share perspectives about their world (Van Hoorn et al., 2003). Children's language guides their play and provides the communication needed for the continuation of the play (Guddemi, 2000; Heidemann & Hewitt, 1992).

Language usage during play allows children to develop and test their verbal skills. Children experiment with language by telling jokes and riddles, reciting chants and poems, and making up words. As children use language during play, they create meaning for themselves concerning the nature of language and communication (Frost, 1992). Additionally, playing with language develops children's phonological awareness by allowing for experimentation with the sounds of words. Children learn that sounds can be manipulated as they rhyme words and create nonsense words (Johnson, Christie, & Wardle, 2005).

A more complicated form of play, games with rules, also requires children to expand their language skills. Once the egocentrism of earlier childhood diminishes, children can become more proficient at working together to negotiate the rules of games (Van Hoorn et al., 2003). Games with rules provide practice in cooperation, as well as opportunities to build language skills, as children create new games or discuss rules of known games.

Physical Development
Girls and Boys Engaging in Physical Activity during Play

Research indicates gender differences in physical activity during play. Studies have noted that boys, from infancy through adolescence, tend to participate in more physically active play than do girls (Campbell & Eaton, 1999; Frost, 1992; Lindsey & Colwell, 2003). For example, Lindsey and Colwell (2003) observed young children and found that boys playing with one other child engage in more physical play than girls playing with one other child. Additionally, a study by Sarkin, McKenzie, and Sallis (1997) compared gender differences in play levels of 5th-graders during physical education classes and recess. They found no significant differences between the boys' and the girls' activity levels during physical education classes. However, during recess times, boys more often played games requiring higher levels of physical activity than did girls. Girls played less strenuous games or held conversations as they walked around the playground. These results suggested that during times of unstructured activity, such as recess, boys tend to choose more active play than girls do.

Likewise, other researchers also concluded that the physical play of girls and boys often differs. Boys and girls tend to divide into gendered groups during outdoor play, and they often choose different types of activities (Thorne, 1993). Studies suggest that boys engage in play that involves more physical activity (Boyle, Marshall, & Robeson, 2003), more competition (Lever, 1978), and more space (Martin & Fabes, 2001) than do girls. Pellegrini and Smith (1993) suggested that boys tend to prefer playing outdoors, due to the need for open space to participate in their active games. One type of active play in which boys tend to engage in more frequently than girls is rough and tumble play (Martin & Fabes, 2001; Pellegrini, 1989; Thorne, 1993). Rough and tumble play involves such activities as grabbing and wrestling and may be a socially acceptable way for boys to physically demonstrate their feelings of friendship (Reed, 2000).

Overall Active Play and Physical Development in Children

The human body needs movement to stay healthy and well. Findings by the Centers for Disease Control and Prevention (2005) indicate that the incidence of childhood obesity is increasing. In today's world, many children spend most of their time in sedentary activities that do not enhance physical fitness. Active play encourages movement, thereby helping children's fitness. According to Huettig, Sanborn, DiMarco, Popejoy, and Rich (2004), young children need at least "thirty to sixty minutes of physical activity a day" (p. 54). Physical advantages that children gain from active play are increased motor control and flexibility (Brewer, 2001). Furthermore, with the added body control that develops as they play, children often become more competent in their skills and gain the self-confidence to play games with peers (Wortham, 2002).

Physical movement is necessary for the growth and development of the mind as well as the body. The brain needs movement in order to function properly (Gurian, 2001). Although indoor play encourages creativity and socialization, it provides only a limited amount of space for the type of physical movement children need each day. Time in outdoor play encourages physical activity, which, in turn, increases children's physical fitness. Consequently, outdoor recess periods provide the time and space for children to engage in the physically vigorous active play that is limited indoors (Sutterby & Frost, 2002).

Further Research Needs

Understanding more about how play benefits the social, language, and physical development of children can help teachers as they create learning environments; however, more research is needed to gain a clearer picture of how play enhances children's learning. For example, studies examining the influence of recess on classroom behaviors, such as concentration and amount of work produced, have yielded conflicting results (Jarrett et al., 1998; Pellegrini & Davis, 1993). Therefore, more work is necessary to determine how unstructured play correlates with behavior as well as academic achievement. Additionally, more research needs to be conducted about social interventions during play. Children who have been targeted as requiring assistance in developing positive social behaviors may have more difficulty during times of unstructured activity (Blatchford, 1998). Research to determine how to best assist these children, particularly during recess periods, is needed.

Finally, some researchers have included such variables as race and gender within the framework of their study of play; however, less often has the researcher's main purpose been to examine the educational implications based on the different ways girls and boys play. This aspect of play needs further examination if educators are to gain a better understanding of how to best structure learning environments for both genders.

Implications for Educators

Knowing the research about how children play and what they learn as they play can help educators and parents make sound decisions about how to provide appropriate play opportunities. To create learning environments in which children can thrive, adults must observe children's needs and try to accommodate those needs. The following are some suggestions for educators and parents.

- Importance of Observations of Play Experiences: Teachers can use playtimes to observe and assess children's social, emotional, physical, and cognitive development. Observing children's play can provide teachers with information about how to create appropriate learning environments. In some settings, recess may be a prime time to do this.
- Girls' Play: Girls have been found to engage in more sedentary, language-oriented activities during

recess play than boys. Although this type of activity is important, girls also need to be encouraged to be physically active. While many boys may participate in physical movement through rough and tumble play, educators may need to help girls create activities in which they become more active. Providing areas and equipment for active play is the first step; additionally, ensuring that girls have the opportunity to engage in this type of physical play is necessary.

- Boys' Play: Rough and tumble play may provide an outlet for boys' physical, social, emotional, and verbal expression. Schools where all physical contact during play has been banned may need to consider how to reduce aggressive behaviors while allowing for this type of physical contact between boys. Recess monitors may need to be trained to recognize differences between acts of aggression and rough and tumble play. Additionally, the exploration of language that girls enjoy during play may need to be encouraged for boys by creating play environments that support language development. For example, teachers can lead boys in discussing their play activities.

- Accommodations for Differences: Children have various interests and styles of play; therefore, schools can provide a variety of play materials and equipment to accommodate the differences. Additionally, an assortment of resources can encourage children to expand and extend their play. Children with special needs should be considered in this process.

- Parental Awareness: Parents may be concerned that their young children are "only playing" at school. During Open House, at PTA meetings, and through newsletters, educators can make parents aware of growth and development that takes place as children play, both in classrooms and at recess. It is necessary to make adults aware that natural outdoor play environments are important for girls and boys and that these areas do not always require equipment. Rustic, wooded settings can provide children with many opportunities for creative movement, imaginative growth, and cognitive learning as they participate in such activities as nature walks with adult supervision.

- Cooperative Activities: Although research indicates that girls tend to enjoy cooperative activities while boys pursue competitive games, children need to learn about both cooperation and competition. Teachers can incorporate each type of activity into classroom lessons.

Conclusion

While some adults dismiss play as mere fun, much growth and development occurs during playtimes. As children play, they gain knowledge of the world and an understanding of their place in it. Although play may differ generally for girls and boys, it offers both genders opportunities to test and refine their developing social, language, and physical skills, which leads not only to academic achievement but also to a lifetime of success. Thus, play does benefit children.

References

Bergen, D. (2004). *ACEI speaks: Play's role in brain development* [Brochure]. Olney, MD: Association for Childhood Education International.

Blatchford, P. (1998). The state of play in schools. *Child Psychology and Psychiatry Review, 3*(2), 58–67.

Blatchford, P., Baines, E., & Pellegrini, A. (2003). The social context of school playground games: Sex and ethnic differences, and changes over time after entry to junior school. *British Journal of Developmental Psychology, 21*(4), 481–505.

Boyatzis, C. J., Mallis, M., & Leon, I. (1999). Effects of game type on children's gender-based peer preferences: A naturalistic observational study. *Sex Roles: A Journal of Research, 40*(1–2), 93–105.

Boyle, D. E., Marshall, N. L., & Robeson, W. W. (2003). Gender at play: Fourth-grade girls and boys on the playground. *American Behavioral Scientist, 46*(10), 1326–1345.

Brewer, J. A. (2001). *Introduction to early childhood education: Preschool through primary grades* (4th ed.). Boston: Allyn and Bacon.

Butcher, D. A. (1999). Enhancing social skills through school social work interventions during recess: Gender differences. *Social Work in Education, 21*(4), 249–262.

Campbell, D. W., & Eaton, W. O. (1999). Sex differences in the activity level of infants. *Infant and Child Development, 8*(1), 1–17.

Centers for Disease Control and Prevention. (2005). Preventing chronic diseases through good nutrition and physical activity. Retrieved July 18, 2006, from www.cdc.gov/nccdphp/publications/factsheets/Prevention/obesity.htm

Chenfeld, M. B. (2006). Handcuff me, too! *Phi Delta Kappan, 87*(10), 745–747.

Clements, R. L. (Ed.). (2000). *Elementary school recess: Selected readings, games, and activities for teachers and parents.* Boston: American Press.

Fromberg, D. P. (1998). Play issues in early childhood education. In C. Seefeldt & A. Galper (Eds.), *Continuing issues in early childhood education* (2nd ed.)(pp. 190–212). Upper Saddle River, NJ: Merrill Prentice-Hall.

Frost, J. L. (1992). *Play and playscapes.* Albany, NY: Delmar.

Gallas, K. (1998). *Sometimes I can be anything: Power, gender, and identity in a primary classroom.* New York: Teachers College Press.

Ginsburg, H., & Opper, S. (1979). *Piaget's theory of intellectual development* (2nd ed.). Englewood Cliffs, NJ: Prentice-Hall.

Goodwin, M. H. (2001). Organizing participation in cross-sex jump rope: Situating gender differences within longitudinal studies of activities. *Research on Language & Social Interaction, 34*(1), 75–106.

Goodwin, M. H. (2002). Exclusion in girls' peer groups: Ethnographic analysis of language practices on the playground. *Human Development, 45*(6), 392–415.

Guddemi, M. P. (2000). Recess: A time to learn, a time to grow. In R. L. Clements (Ed.), *Elementary school recess: Selected readings, games, and activities for teachers and parents* (pp. 2–8). Boston: American Press.

Gurian, M. (2001). *Boys and girls learn differently! A guide for teachers and parents.* San Francisco: Jossey-Bass.

Gurian, M., & Stevens, K. (2005). *The minds of boys: Saving our sons from falling behind in school and life.* San Francisco: Jossey-Bass.

Heidemann, S., & Hewitt, D. (1992). *Pathways to play: Developing play skills in young children*. St. Paul, MN: Redleaf Press.

Huettig, C. I., Sanborn, C. R, DiMarco, N., Popejoy, A., & Rich, S. (2004). The O generation: Our youngest children are at risk for obesity. *Young Children, 59*(2), 50–55.

Jarrett, O. S., & Maxwell, D. M. (2000). What research says about the need for recess. In R. L. Clements (Ed.), *Elementary school recess: Selected readings, games, and activities for teachers and parents* (pp. 12–20). Boston: American Press.

Jarrett, O. S., Maxwell, D. M., Dickerson, C., Hoge, P., Davies, G., & Yetley, A. (1998). Impact of recess on classroom behavior: Group effects and individual differences. *The Journal of Educational Research, 92*(2), 121–126.

Johnson, J. E., Christie, J. R, & Wardle, F. (2005). *Play, development, and early education*. Boston: Pearson Education.

Lever, J. (1978). Sex differences in the complexity of children's play and games. *American Sociological Review, 43*(4), 471–483.

Lewis, T. E., & Phillipsen, L. C. (1998). Interactions on an elementary school playground: Variations by age, gender, race, group size, and playground area. *Child Study Journal, 2S*(4), 309–320.

Lindsey, E. W., & Colwell, M. J. (2003). Preschoolers' emotional competence links to pretend and physical play. *Child Study Journal, 33*(1), 39–52.

Martin, C. L., & Fabes, R. A. (2001). The stability and consequences of young children's same-sex peer interactions. *Developmental Psychology, 37*(3), 431–446.

Pellegrini, A. D. (1989). Elementary school children's rough-and-tumble play. *Early Childhood Research Quarterly, 4*(2), 245–260.

Pellegrini, A. D., & Blatchford, P. (2002). The developmental and educational significance of recess in schools. *Early Report, 29*(1). Retrieved March 16, 2004, from www.education.umn .edu/ceed/publications/earlyreport/spring02.htm

Pellegrini, A. D., Blatchford, P., Kato, K., & Baines, E. (2004). A short-term longitudinal study of children's playground games in primary school: Implications for adjustment to school and social adjustment in the USA and the UK. *Social/ Development, 13*(1), 107–123.

Pellegrini, A. D. & Davis, P. (1993). Relations between children's playground and classroom behaviour. *British Journal of Educational Psychology, 63*(1), 88–95.

Pellegrini, A. D., & Smith, P. K. (1993). School recess: Implications for education and development. *Review of Educational Research, 63*(1), 51–67.

Perlmutter, J. C., & Burrell, L. (1995). Learning through 'play' as well as 'work' in the primary grades. *Young Children, 50*(5), 14–21.

Piaget, J. (1962). *Play, dreams, and imitation in childhood* (G. Gattegno & F. M. Hodgson,Trans.). New York: W.W. Norton & Company.

Poole, C., Miller, S., & Church, E. B. (2004). Working through that "It's Mine" feeling. *Early Childhood Today, 18*(5), 28–32.

Reed, T. (2000). Rough and tumble play during recess: Pathways to successful social development. In R. L. Clements (Ed.), *Elementary school recess: Selected readings, games, and activities for teachers and parents* (pp. 45–48). Boston: American Press.

Sarkin, J. S., McKenzie, T. L., & Sallis, J. F. (1997). Gender differences in physical activity during fifth-grade physical education and recess periods. *Journal of Teaching in Physical Education, 17*(1), 99–106.

Sutterby, J. S., & Frost, J. L. (2002). Making playgrounds fit for children and children fit on playgrounds. *Young Children, 57*(3), 36–41.

Thorne, B. (1993). *Gender play: Girls and boys in school*. New Brunswick, NJ: Rutgers University Press.

Van Hoorn, J., Monighan-Nourot, P., Scales, B., & Alward, K. R. (2003). *Play at the center of the curriculum* (3rd ed.). Upper Saddle River, NJ: Merrill Prentice-Hall.

Wortham, S.C. (2002). *Early childhood curriculum: Developmental bases for learning and teaching* (3rd ed.). Upper Saddle River, NJ: Merrill PrenticeHall.

Jeanetta G. Riley is Assistant Professor, Department of Early Childhood and Elementary Education, Murray State University. **Rose B. Jones** is Assistant Professor of Early Childhood Education/Literacy, The University of Southern Mississippi.

Girls Just Want to Be Mean

MARGARET TALBOT

Today is Apologies Day in Rosalind Wiseman's class—so, naturally, when class lets out, the girls are crying. Not all 12 of them, but a good half. They stand around in the corridor, snuffling quietly but persistently, interrogating one another. "Why didn't you apologize to me?" one girl demands. "Are you stressed right now?" says another. "I am so stressed." Inside the classroom, which is at the National Cathedral School, a private girls' school in Washington, Wiseman is locked in conversation with one of the sixth graders who has stayed behind to discuss why her newly popular best friend is now scorning her.

"You've got to let her go through this," Wiseman instructs. "You can't make someone be your best friend. And it's gonna be hard for her too, because if she doesn't do what they want her to do, the popular girls are gonna chuck her out, and they're gonna spread rumors about her or tell people stuff she told them." The girl's ponytail bobs as she nods and thanks Wiseman, but her expression is baleful.

Wiseman's class is about gossip and cliques and ostracism and just plain meanness among girls. But perhaps the simplest way to describe its goals would be to say that it tries to make middle-school girls be nice to one another. This is a far trickier project than you might imagine, and Apologies Day is a case in point. The girls whom Wiseman variously calls the Alpha Girls, the R.M.G.'s (Really Mean Girls) or the Queen Bees are the ones who are supposed to own up to having back-stabbed or dumped a friend, but they are also the most resistant to the exercise and the most self-justifying. The girls who are their habitual victims or hangers-on—the Wannabes and Messengers in Wiseman's lingo—are always apologizing anyway.

But Wiseman, who runs a nonprofit organization called the Empower Program, is a cheerfully unyielding presence. And in the end, her students usually do what she wants: they take out their gel pens or their glittery feather-topped pens and write something, fold it over and over again into origami and then hide behind their hair when it's read aloud. Often as not, it contains a hidden or a not-so-hidden barb. To wit: "I used to be best friends with two girls. We weren't popular, we weren't that pretty, but we had fun together. When we came to this school, we were placed in different classes. I stopped being friends with them and left them to be popular. They despise me now, and I'm sorry for what I did. I haven't apologized because I don't really want to be friends any longer and am afraid if I apologize, then that's how it will result. We are now in completely different

leagues." Or: "Dear B. I'm sorry for excluding you and ignoring you. Also, I have said a bunch of bad things about you. I have also run away from you just because I didn't like you. A." Then there are the apologies that rehash the original offense in a way sure to embarrass the offended party all over again, as in: "I'm sorry I told everybody you had an American Girl doll. It really burned your reputation." Or: "Dear 'Friend,' I'm sorry that I talked about you behind your back. I once even compared your forehead/face to a minefield (only 2 1 person though.) I'm really sorry I said these things even though I might still believe them."

Wiseman, who is 32 and hip and girlish herself, has taught this class at many different schools, and it is fair to say that although she loves girls, she does not cling to sentimental notions about them. She is a feminist, but not the sort likely to ascribe greater inherent compassion to women or girls as a group than to men or boys. More her style is the analysis of the feminist historian Elizabeth Fox-Genovese, who has observed that "those who have experienced dismissal by the junior high school girls' clique could hardly, with a straight face, claim generosity and nurture as a natural attribute of women." Together, Wiseman and I once watched the movie "Heathers," the 1989 black comedy about a triad of vicious Queen Bees who get their comeuppance, and she found it "pretty true to life." The line uttered by Winona Ryder as Veronica, the disaffected non-Heather of the group, struck her as particularly apt: "I don't really like my friends. It's just like they're people I work with and our job is being popular."

Wiseman's reaction to the crying girls is accordingly complex. "I hate to make girls cry," she says. "I really do hate it when their faces get all splotchy, and everyone in gym class or whatever knows they've been crying." At the same time, she notes: "The tears are a funny thing. Because it's not usually the victims who cry; it's the aggressors, the girls who have something to apologize for. And sometimes, yes, it's relief on their part, but it's also somewhat manipulative, because if they've done something crappy, the person they've done it to can't get that mad at them if they're crying. Plus, a lot of the time they're using the apology to dump on somebody all over again."

Is dumping on a friend really such a serious problem? Do mean girls wield that much power? Wiseman thinks so. In May, Crown will publish her book-length analysis of girl-on-girl nastiness, "Queen Bees and Wannabes: Helping Your

Daughter Survive Cliques, Gossip, Boyfriends and other Realities of Adolescence." And her seminars, which she teaches in schools around the country, are ambitious attempts to tame what some psychologists are now calling "relational aggression"—by which they mean the constellation of "Heathers"-like manipulations and exclusions and gossip-mongering that most of us remember from middle school and through which girls, more often than boys, tend to channel their hostilities.

"My life is full of these ridiculous little slips of paper," says Wiseman, pointing to the basket of apologies and questions at her feet. "I have read thousands of these slips of paper. And 95 percent of them are the same. 'Why are these girls being mean to me?' 'Why am I being excluded?' 'I don't want to be part of this popular group anymore. I don't like what they're doing.' There are lots of girls out there who are getting this incredible lesson that they are not inherently worthy, and from someone—a friend, another girl—who was so intimately bonded with them. To a large extent, their definitions of intimacy are going to be based on the stuff they're going through in sixth and seventh grade. And that stuff isn't pretty."

> ## "Within the hidden culture of aggression, girls fight with body language and relationships instead of fists and knives."
>
> Rachel Simmons, from *Odd Girl Out: The Hidden Culture of Aggression in Girls*

This focus on the cruelty of girls is, of course, something new. For years, psychologists who studied aggression among schoolchildren looked only at its physical and overt manifestations and concluded that girls were less aggressive than boys. That consensus began to change in the early 90's, after a team of researchers led by a Finnish professor named Kaj Bjorkqvist started interviewing 11- and 12-year-old girls about their behavior toward one another. The team's conclusion was that girls were, in fact, just as aggressive as boys, though in a different way. They were not as likely to engage in physical fights, for example, but their superior social intelligence enabled them to wage complicated battles with other girls aimed at damaging relationships or reputations—leaving nasty messages by cellphone or spreading scurrilous rumors by e-mail, making friends with one girl as revenge against another, gossiping about someone just loudly enough to be overheard. Turning the notion of women's greater empathy on its head, Bjorkqvist focused on the destructive uses to which such emotional attunement could be put. "Girls can better understand how other girls feel," as he puts it, "so they know better how to harm them."

Researchers following in Bjorkqvist's footsteps noted that up to the age of 4 girls tend to be aggressive at the same rates and in the same ways as boys—grabbing toys, pushing, hitting. Later on, however, social expectations force their hostilities underground, where their assaults on one another are more indirect, less physical and less visible to adults. Secrets they share in one context, for example, can sometimes be used against them

in another. As Marion Underwood, a professor of psychology at the University of Texas at Dallas, puts it: "Girls very much value intimacy, which makes them excellent friends and terrible enemies. They share so much information when they are friends that they never run out of ammunition if they turn on one another."

In the last few years, a group of young psychologists, including Underwood and Nicki Crick at the University of Minnesota, has pushed this work much further, observing girls in "naturalistic" settings, exploring the psychological foundations for nastiness and asking adults to take relational aggression—especially in the sixth and seventh grades, when it tends to be worst—as seriously as they do more familiar forms of bullying. While some of these researchers have emphasized bonding as a motivation, others have seen something closer to a hunger for power, even a Darwinian drive. One Australian researcher, Laurence Owens, found that the 15-year-old girls he interviewed about their girl-pack predation were bestirred primarily by its entertainment value. The girls treated their own lives like the soaps, hoarding drama, constantly rehashing trivia. Owens's studies contain some of the more vivid anecdotes in the earnest academic literature on relational aggression. His subjects tell him about ingenious tactics like leaving the following message on a girl's answering machine—"Hello, it's me. Have you gotten your pregnancy test back yet?"—knowing that her parents will be the first to hear it. They talk about standing in "huddles" and giving other girls "deaths"—stares of withering condescension—and of calling one another "dyke," "slut" and "fat" and of enlisting boys to do their dirty work.

Relational aggression is finding its chroniclers among more popular writers, too. In addition to Wiseman's book, this spring will bring Rachel Simmons's "Odd Girl Out: The Hidden Culture of Aggression in Girls," Emily White's "Fast Girls: Teenage Tribes and the Myth of the Slut" and Phyllis Chesler's "Woman's Inhumanity to Woman."

In her book, the 27-year-old Simmons offers a plaintive definition of relational aggression: "Unlike boys, who tend to bully acquaintances or strangers, girls frequently attack within tightly knit friendship networks, making aggression harder to identify and intensifying the damage to the victims. Within the hidden culture of aggression, girls fight with body language and relationships instead of fists and knives. In this world, friendship is a weapon, and the sting of a shout pales in comparison to a day of someone's silence. There is no gesture more devastating than the back turning away." Now, Simmons insists, is the time to pull up the rock and really look at this seething underside of American girlhood. "Beneath a facade of female intimacy," she writes, "lies a terrain traveled in secret, marked with anguish and nourished by silence."

Not so much silence, anymore, actually. For many school principals and counselors across the country, relational aggression is becoming a certified social problem and the need to curb it an accepted mandate. A small industry of interveners has grown up to meet the demand. In Austin, Tex., an organization called GENaustin now sends counselors into schools to teach a course on relational aggression called Girls as Friends, Girls as Foes. In Erie, Pa., the Ophelia Project offers a similar curriculum, taught by high-school-aged mentors, that explores "how girls hurt each other" and how they can stop. A private Catholic school in Akron, Ohio, and a public-school district near Portland, Ore., have introduced programs aimed at rooting out girl meanness. And Wiseman and her Empower Program colleagues have taught their Owning Up class at 60 schools. "We are currently looking at relational aggression like domestic violence 20 years ago," says Holly Nishimura, the assistant director of the Ophelia Project. "Though it's not on the same scale, we believe that with relational aggression, the trajectory of awareness, knowledge and demand for change will follow the same track."

Whether this new hypervigilance about a phenomenon that has existed for as long as most of us can remember will actually do anything to squelch it is, of course, another question. Should adults be paying as much attention to this stuff as kids do or will we just get hopelessly tangled up in it ourselves? Are we approaching frothy adolescent bitchery with undue gravity or just giving it its due in girls' lives? On the one hand, it is kind of satisfying to think that girls might be, after their own fashion, as aggressive as boys. It's an idea that offers some relief from the specter of the meek and mopey, "silenced" and self-loathing girl the popular psychology of girlhood has given us in recent years. But it is also true that the new attention to girls as relational aggressors may well take us into a different intellectual cul-de-sac, where it becomes too easy to assume that girls do not use their fists (some do), that all girls are covert in their cruelties, that all girls care deeply about the ways of the clique—and that what they do in their "relational" lives takes precedence over all other aspects of their emerging selves.

After her class at the National Cathedral School, Wiseman and I chat for a while in her car. She has to turn down the India Arie CD that's blaring on her stereo so we can hear each other. The girl she had stayed to talk with after class is still on her mind, partly because she represents the social type for whom Wiseman seems to feel the profoundest sympathy: the girl left behind by a newly popular, newly dismissive friend. "See, at a certain point it becomes cool to be boy crazy," she explains. "That happens in sixth grade, and it gives you so much social status, particularly in an all-girls school, if you can go up and talk to boys."

"But often, an Alpha Girl has an old friend, the best friend forever elementary-school friend, who is left behind because she's not boy crazy yet," Wiseman goes on, pressing the accelerator with her red snakeskin boot. "And what she can't figure out is: why does my old friend want to be better friends with a girl who talks behind her back and is mean to her than with me, who is a good friend and who wouldn't do that?"

The subtlety of the maneuvers still amazes Wiseman, though she has seen them time and again. "What happens," she goes on, "is that the newly popular girl—let's call her Darcy—is hanging out with Molly and some other Alpha Girls in the back courtyard, and the old friend, let's call her Kristin, comes up to them. And what's going to happen is Molly's going to throw her arms around Darcy and talk about things that Kristin doesn't know anything about and be totally physically affectionate with Darcy so that she looks like the shining jewel. And Kristin is,

like, I don't exist. She doesn't want to be friends with the new version of Darcy—she wants the old one back, but it's too late for that."

So to whom, I ask Wiseman, does Kristin turn in her loneliness? Wiseman heaves a sigh as though she's sorry to be the one to tell me an obvious but unpleasant truth. "The other girls can be like sharks—it's like blood in the water, and they see it and they go, 'Now I can be closer to Kristin because she's being dumped by Darcy.' When I say stuff like this, I know I sound horrible, I know it. But it's what they do."

Hanging out with Wiseman, you get used to this kind of disquisition on the craftiness of middle-school girls, but I'll admit that when my mind balks at something she has told me, when I can't quite believe girls have thought up some scheme or another, I devise little tests for her—I ask her to pick out seventh-grade Queen Bees in a crowd outside a school or to predict what the girls in the class will say about someone who isn't there that day or to guess which boys a preening group of girls is preening for. I have yet to catch her out.

Once, Wiseman mentions a girl she knows whose clique of seven is governed by actual, enumerated rules and suggests I talk with this girl to get a sense of what reformers like her are up against. Jessica Travis, explains Wiseman, shaking her head in aggravated bemusement at the mere thought of her, is a junior at a suburban Maryland high school and a member of the Girls' Advisory Board that is part of Wiseman's organization. She is also, it occurs to me when I meet her, a curious but not atypical social type—an amalgam of old-style Queen Bee-ism and new-style girl's empowerment, brimming over with righteous self-esteem and cheerful cattiness. Tall and strapping, with long russet hair and blue eye shadow, she's like a Powerpuff Girl come to life.

When I ask Jessica to explain the rules her clique lives by, she doesn't hesitate. "O.K.," she says happily. "No 1: clothes. You cannot wear jeans any day but Friday, and you cannot wear a ponytail or sneakers more than once a week. Monday is fancy day—like black pants or maybe you bust out with a skirt. You want to remind people how cute you are in case they forgot over the weekend. O.K., 2: parties. Of course, we sit down together and discuss which ones we're going to go to, because there's no point in getting all dressed up for a party that's going to be lame. No getting smacked at a party, because how would it look for the rest of us if you're drunk and acting like a total fool? And if you do hook up with somebody at the party, please try to limit it to one. Otherwise you look like a slut and that reflects badly on all of us. Kids are not that smart; they're not going to make the distinctions between us. And the rules apply to all of us—you can't be like, 'Oh, I'm having my period; I'm wearing jeans all week.'"

She pauses for a millisecond. "Like, we had a lot of problems with this one girl. She came to school on a Monday in jeans. So I asked her, 'Why you wearing jeans today?' She said, 'Because I felt like it.' 'Because you felt like it? Did you forget it was a Monday?' 'No.' She says she just doesn't like the confinement. She doesn't want to do this anymore. She's the rebel of the group, and we had to suspend her a couple of times; she wasn't allowed to sit with us at lunch. On that first Monday, she didn't even try; she didn't even catch my eye—she knew better. But eventually she came back to us, and she was, like, 'I know, I deserved it.'"

Each member of Jessica's group is allowed to invite an outside person to sit at their table in the lunch room several times a month, but they have to meet at the lockers to O.K. it with the other members first, and they cannot exceed their limit. "We don't want other people at our table more than a couple of times a week because we want to bond, and the bonding is endless," Jessica says. "Besides, let's say you want to tell your girls about some total fool thing you did, like locking your hair in the car door. I mean, my God, you're not going to tell some stranger that."

For all their policing of their borders, they are fiercely loyal to those who stay within them. If a boy treats one of them badly, they all snub him. And Jessica offers another example: "One day, another friend came to school in this skirt from Express—ugliest skirt I've ever seen—red and brown plaid, O.K.? But she felt really fabulous. She was like, Isn't this skirt cute? And she's my friend, so of course I'm like, Damn straight, sister! Lookin' good! But then, this other girl who was in the group for a while comes up and she says to her: 'Oh, my God, you look so stupid! You look like a giant argyle sock!' I was like, 'What is wrong with you?'"

Jessica gets good grades, belongs to the B'nai B'rith Youth Organization and would like, for no particular reason, to go to Temple University. She plays polo and figure-skates, has a standing appointment for a once-a-month massage and "cried from the beginning of 'Pearl Harbor' till I got home that night." She lives alone with her 52-year-old mother, who was until January a consultant for Oracle. She is lively and loquacious and she has, as she puts it, "the highest self-esteem in the world." Maybe that's why she finds it so easy to issue dictums like: "You cannot go out with an underclassman. You just cannot—end of story." I keep thinking, when I listen to Jessica talk about her clique, that she must be doing some kind of self-conscious parody. But I'm fairly sure she's not.

On a bleary December afternoon, I attend one of Wiseman's after-school classes in the Maryland suburbs. A public middle school called William H. Farquhar has requested the services of the Empower Program. Soon after joining the class, I ask the students about a practice Wiseman has told me about that I find a little hard to fathom or even to believe. She had mentioned it in passing—"You know how the girls use three-way calling"—and when I professed puzzlement, explained: "O.K., so Alison and Kathy call up Mary, but only Kathy talks and Alison is just lurking there quietly so Mary doesn't know she's on the line. And Kathy says to Mary, 'So what do you think of Alison?' And of course there's some reason at the moment why Mary doesn't like Alison, and she says, Oh, my God, all these nasty things about Alison—you know, 'I can't believe how she throws herself at guys, she thinks she's all that, blah, blah, blah.' And Alison hears all this."

Not for the first time with Wiseman, I came up with one of my lame comparisons with adult life: "But under normal circumstances, repeating nasty gossip about one friend to another is not actually going to get you that far with your friends."

"Yeah, but in Girl World, that's currency," Wiseman responded. "It's like: Ooh, I have a dollar and now I'm more powerful and I can use this if I want to. I can further myself in the social hierarchy and bond with the girl being gossiped about by setting up the conference call so she can know about it, by telling her about the gossip and then delivering the proof."

In the classroom at Farquhar, eight girls are sitting in a circle, eating chips and drinking sodas. All of them have heard about the class and chosen to come. There's Jordi Kauffman, who is wearing glasses, a fleece vest and sneakers and who displays considerable scorn for socially ambitious girls acting "all slutty in tight clothes or all snotty." Jordi is an honor student whose mother is a teacher and whose father is the P.T.A. president. She's the only one in the class with a moderately sarcastic take on the culture of American girlhood. "You're in a bad mood one day, and you say you feel fat," she remarks, "and adults are like, 'Oh-oh, she's got poor self-esteem, she's depressed, get her help!'"

Next to Jordi is her friend Jackie, who is winsome and giggly and very pretty. Jackie seems more genuinely troubled by the loss of a onetime friend who has been twisting herself into an Alpha Girl. She will later tell us that when she wrote a heartfelt e-mail message to this former friend, asking her why she was "locking her out," the girl's response was to print it out and show it around at school.

On the other side of the room are Lauren and Daniela, who've got boys on the brain, big time. They happily identify with Wiseman's negative portrayal of "Fruit-Cup Girl," one who feigns helplessness—in Wiseman's example, by pretending to need a guy to open her pull-top can of fruit cocktail—to attract male attention. There's Courtney, who will later say, when asked to write a letter to herself about how she's doing socially, that she can't, because she "never says anything to myself about myself." And there's Kimberly, who will write such a letter professing admiration for her own "natural beauty."

They have all heard of the kind of three-way call Wiseman had told me about; all but two have done it or had it done to them. I ask if they found the experience useful. "Not always," Jordi says, "because sometimes there's something you want to hear but you don't hear. You want to hear, 'Oh, she's such a good person' or whatever, but instead you hear, 'Oh, my God, she's such a bitch."

I ask if boys ever put together three-way calls like that. "Nah," Jackie says. "I don't think they're smart enough."

Once the class gets going, the discussion turns, as it often does, to Jackie's former friend, the one who's been clawing her way into the Alpha Girl clique. In a strange twist, this girl has, as Daniela puts it, "given up her religion" and brought a witch's spell book to school.

"That's weird," Wiseman says, "because usually what happens is that the girls who are attracted to that are more outside-the-box types—you know, the depressed girls with the black fingernails who are always writing poetry—because it gives them some amount of power. The girl you're describing sounds unconfident; maybe she's looking for something that makes her seem mysterious and powerful. If you have enough social status, you can be a little bit different. And that's where she's trying to go with this—like, I am so in the box that I'm defining a new box."

Jackie interjects, blushing, with another memory of her lost friend. "I used to tell her everything," she laments, "and now she just blackmails me with my secrets."

"Sounds like she's a Banker," Wiseman says. "That means that she collects information and uses it later to her advantage."

"Nobody really likes her," chimes in Jordi. "She's like a shadow of her new best friend, a total Wannabe. Her new crowd's probably gonna be like, 'Take her back, pulleeze!'"

"What really hurts," Jackie persists, "is that it's like you can't just drop a friend. You have to dump on them, too."

"Yeah, it's true," Jordi agrees matter-of-factly. "You have to make them really miserable before you leave."

After class, when I concede that Wiseman was right about the three-way calling, she laughs. "Haven't I told you girls are crafty?" she asks. "Haven't I told you girls are evil?"

It may be that the people most likely to see such machinations clearly are the former masters of them. Wiseman's anthropological mapping of middle-school society—the way she notices and describes the intricate rituals of exclusion and humiliation as if they were a Balinese cockfight—seems to come naturally to her because she remembers more vividly than many people do what it was like to be an adolescent insider or, as she puts it, "a pearls-and-tennis-skirt-wearing awful little snotty girl."

It was different for me. When I was in junior high in the 70's—a girl who was neither a picked-on girl nor an Alpha Girl, just someone in the vast more-or-less dorky middle at my big California public school—the mean girls were like celebrities whose exploits my friends and I followed with interest but no savvy. I sort of figured that their caste was conferred at birth when they landed in Laurelwood—the local hillside housing development peopled by dentists and plastic surgeons—and were given names like Marcie and Tracie. I always noticed their pretty clothes and haircuts and the smell of their green-apple gum and cherry Lip Smackers and their absences from school for glamorous afflictions like tennis elbow or skiing-related sunburns. The real Queen Bees never spoke to you at all, but the Wannabes would sometimes insult you as a passport to popularity. There was a girl named Janine, for instance, who used to preface every offensive remark with the phrase "No offense," as in "No offense, but you look like a woofing dog." Sometimes it got her the nod from the Girl World authorities and sometimes it didn't, and I could never figure out why or why not.

Teachers would "guide students to the realization that most girls don't maliciously compete or exclude each other, but within their social context, girls perceive that they must compete with each other for status and power, thus maintaining the status system that binds them all."

Rosalind Wiseman,
Empower Program

Which is all to say that to an outsider, the Girl World's hard-core social wars are fairly distant and opaque, and to somebody like Wiseman, they are not. As a seventh grader at a private school in Washington, she hooked up with "a very powerful, very scary group of girls who were very fun to be with but who could turn on you like a dime." She became an Alpha Girl, but she soon found it alienating. "You know you have these moments where you're like, 'I hate this person I've become; I'm about to vomit on myself'? Because I was really a piece of work. I was really snotty."

When I ask Wiseman to give me an example of something wicked that she did, she says: "Whoa, I'm in such denial about this. But O.K., here's one. When I was in eighth grade, I spread around a lie about my best friend, Melissa. I told all the girls we knew that she had gotten together, made out or whatever, with this much older guy at a family party at our house. I must have been jealous—she was pretty and getting all this attention from guys. And so I made up something that made her sound slutty. She confronted me about it, and I totally denied it."

Wiseman escaped Girl World only when she headed off to California for college and made friends with "people who didn't care what neighborhood I came from or what my parents did for a living." After majoring in political science, she moved back to Washington, where she helped start an organization that taught self-defense to women and girls. "I was working with girls and listening to them, and again and again, before it was stories about boys, it was stories about girls and what they'd done to them. I'd say talk to me about how you're controlling each other, and I wrote this curriculum on cliques and popularity. That's how it all got started."

Wiseman's aim was to teach classes that would, by analyzing the social hierarchy of school, help liberate girls from it. Girls would learn to "take responsibility for how they treat each other," as Wiseman's handbook for the course puts it, "and to develop strategies to interrupt the cycle of gossip, exclusivity and reputations." Instructors would not let comments like "we have groups but we all get along" stand; they would deconstruct them, using analytic tools familiar from the sociology of privilege and from academic discourse on racism. "Most often, the 'popular' students make these comments while the students who are not as high in the social hierarchy disagree. The comments by the popular students reveal how those who have privilege are so accustomed to their power that they don't recognize when they are dominating and silencing others." Teachers would "guide students to the realization that most girls don't maliciously compete or exclude each other, but within their social context, girls perceive that they must compete with each other for status and power, thus maintaining the status system that binds them all."

The theory was sober and sociological, but in the hands of Wiseman, the classes were dishy and confessional, enlivened by role-playing that got the girls giggling and by Wiseman's knowing references to Bebe jackets, Boardwalk Fries and 'N Sync. It was a combination that soon put Wiseman's services in high demand, especially at some of the tonier private schools in the Washington area.

"I was just enthralled by her," says Camilla Vitullo, who as a headmistress at the National Cathedral School in 1994 was among the first to hire Wiseman. "And the girls gobbled up everything she had to say." (Vitullo, who is now at the Spence School in Manhattan, plans to bring Wiseman there.) Soon Wiseman's Empower Program, which also teaches courses on subjects like date rape, was getting big grants from the Liz Claiborne Foundation and attracting the attention of Oprah Winfrey, who had Wiseman on her show last spring.

Wiseman has been willing to immerse herself in Girl World, and it has paid off. (Out of professional necessity, she has watched "every movie with Kirsten Dunst or Freddie Prinze Jr." and innumerable shows on the WB network.) But even if it weren't her job, you get the feeling she would still know more about all that than most adults do. She senses immediately, for example, that when the girls in her Farquhar class give her a bottle of lotion as a thank-you present, she is supposed to open it on the spot and pass it around and let everybody slather some on. ("Ooh, is it smelly? Smelly in a good way?") When Wiseman catches sight of you approaching, she knows how to do a little side-to-side wave, with her elbow pressed to her hip, that is disarmingly girlish. She says "totally" and "omigod" and "don't stress" and "chill" a lot and refers to people who are "hotties" or "have it goin' on." And none of it sounds foolish on her yet, maybe because she still looks a little like a groovy high-schooler with her trim boyish build and her short, shiny black hair and her wardrobe—picked out by her 17-year-old sister, Zoe—with its preponderance of boots and turtlenecks and flared jeans.

Zoe. Ah, Zoe. Zoe is a bit of a problem for the whole Reform of Girl World project, a bit of a fly in the ointment. For years, Wiseman has been working on her, with scant results. Zoe, a beauty who is now a senior at Georgetown Day School, clearly adores her older sister but also remains skeptical of her enterprise. "She's always telling me to look inside myself and be true to myself—things I can't do right now because I'm too shallow and superficial" is how Zoe, in all her Zoe-ness, sums up their differences.

Once I witnessed the two sisters conversing about a party Zoe had given, at which she was outraged by the appearance of freshman girls—and not ugly, dorky ones, either! Pretty ones!

"And what exactly was the problem with that?" Wiseman asked.

"As long as education is mandatory, we have a huge obligation to make it socially safe."

Michael Thompson, author of
Best Friends, Worst Enemies

"If you're gonna be in high school," Zoe replied, with an attempt at patience, "you have to stay in your place. A freshman girl cannot show up at a junior party; disgusting 14-year-old girls with their boobs in the air cannot show up at your party going"—her voice turned breathy—"Uh, hi, where's the beer?"

Wiseman wanted to know why Zoe couldn't show a little empathy for the younger girls.

"No matter what you say in your talks and your little motivational speeches, Ros, you are not going to change how I feel when little girls show up in their little outfits at my party. I mean, I don't always get mad. Usually I don't care enough about freshmen to even know their names."

Wiseman rolled her eyes.

"Why would I know their names? Would I go out of my way to help freshmen? Should I be saying, 'Hey, I just want you to know that I'm there for you'? Would that make ya happy, Ros? Maybe in some perfect Montessori-esque, P.C. world, we'd all get along. But there are certain rules of the school system that have been set forth from time immemorial or whatever."

"This," said Wiseman, "is definitely a source of tension between us."

A little over a month after the last class at Farquhar, I go back to the school to have lunch with Jordi and Jackie. I want to know what they've remembered from the class, how it might have affected their lives. Wiseman has told me that she will sometimes get e-mail messages from girls at schools where she has taught complaining of recidivism: "Help, you have to come back! We're all being mean again"—that kind of thing.

The lunchroom at Farquhar is low-ceilinged, crowded and loud and smells like frying food and damp sweaters. The two teachers on duty are communicating through walkie-talkies. I join Jordi in line, where she selects for her lunch a small plate of fried potato discs and nothing to drink. Lunch lasts from 11:28 to 11:55, and Jordi always sits at the same table with Jackie (who bounds in late today, holding the little bag of popcorn that is her lunch) and several other girls.

I ask Jackie what she remembers best about Wiseman's class, and she smiles fondly and says it was the "in and out of the box thing—who's cool and who's not and why."

I ask Jordi if she thought she would use a technique Wiseman had recommended for confronting a friend who had weaseled out of plans with her in favor of a more popular girl's invitation. Wiseman had suggested sitting the old friend down alone at some later date, "affirming" the friendship and telling her clearly what she wanted from her. Jordi had loved it when the class acted out the scene, everybody hooting and booing at the behavior of the diva-girl as she dissed her social inferiors in a showdown at the food court. But now, she tells me that she found the exercise "kind of corny." She explains: "Not many people at my school would do it that way. We'd be more likely just to battle it out on the Internet when we got home." (Most of her friends feverishly instant-message after school each afternoon.) Both girls agree that the class was fun, though, and had taught them a lot about popularity.

Which, unfortunately, wasn't exactly the point. Wiseman told me once that one hazard of her trade is that girls will occasionally go home and tell their moms that they were in a class where they learned how to be popular. "I think they're smarter than that, and they must just be telling their moms that," she said. "But they're such concrete thinkers at this age that some could get confused."

I think Wiseman's right—most girls do understand what she's getting at. But it is also true that in paying such close attention to the cliques, in taking Queen Bees so very seriously, the relational-aggression movement seems to grant them a legitimacy and a stature they did not have when they ruled a world that was beneath adult radar.

Nowadays, adults, particularly in the upper middle classes, are less laissez-faire about children's social lives. They are more vigilant, more likely to have read books about surviving the popularity wars of middle school or dealing with cliques, more likely to have heard a talk or gone to a workshop on those topics. Not long ago, I found myself at a lecture by the best-selling author Michael Thompson on "Understanding the Social Lives of our Children." It was held inside the National Cathedral on a chilly Tuesday evening in January, and there were hundreds of people in attendance—attractive late-40's mothers in cashmere turtlenecks and interesting scarves and expensive haircuts, and graying but fit fathers—all taking notes and lining up to ask eager, anxious questions about how best to ensure their children's social happiness. "As long as education is mandatory," Thompson said from the pulpit, "we have a huge obligation to make it socially safe," and heads nodded all around me. He made a list of "the top three reasons for a fourth-grade girl to be popular," and parents in my pew wrote it down in handsome little leather notebooks or on the inside cover of Thompson's latest book, "Best Friends, Worst Enemies." A red-haired woman with a fervent, tremulous voice and an elegant navy blue suit said that she worried our children were socially handicapped by "a lack of opportunities for unstructured cooperative play" and mentioned that she had her 2-year-old in a science class. A serious-looking woman took the microphone to say that she was troubled by the fact that her daughter liked a girl "who is mean and controlling and once wrote the word murder on the bathroom mirror—and this is in a private school!"

I would never counsel blithe ignorance on such matters—some children are truly miserable at school for social reasons, truly persecuted and friendless and in need of adult help. But sometimes we do seem in danger of micromanaging children's social lives, peering a little too closely. Priding ourselves on honesty in our relationships, as baby-boomer parents often do, we expect to know everything about our children's friendships, to be hip to their social travails in a way our own parents, we thought, were not. But maybe this attention to the details can backfire, giving children the impression that the transient social anxieties and allegiances of middle school are weightier and more immutable than they really are. And if that is the result, it seems particularly unfortunate for girls, who are already more mired in the minutiae of relationships than boys are, who may already lack, as Christopher Lasch once put it, "any sense of an impersonal order that exists independently of their wishes and anxieties" and of the "vicissitudes of relationships."

I think I would have found it dismaying if my middle school had offered a class that taught us about the wiles of Marcie and Tracie: if adults studied their folkways, maybe they were

more important than I thought, or hoped. For me, the best antidote to the caste system of middle school was the premonition that adults did not usually play by the same rigid and peculiar rules—and that someday, somewhere, I would find a whole different mattering map, a whole crowd of people who read the same books I did and wouldn't shun me if I didn't have a particular brand of shoes. When I went to college, I found it, and I have never really looked back.

And the Queen Bees? Well, some grow out of their girly sense of entitlement on their own, surely; some channel it in more productive directions. Martha Stewart must have been a Q.B. Same with Madonna. At least one of the Q.B.'s from my youth—albeit the nicest and smartest one—has become a pediatrician on the faculty of a prominent medical school, I noticed when I looked her up the other day. And some Queen Bees have people who love them—dare I say it?—just as they are, a truth that would have astounded me in my own school days but that seems perfectly natural now.

On a Sunday afternoon, I have lunch with Jessica Travis and her mother, Robin, who turns out to be an outgoing, transplanted New Yorker—born in Brighton Beach, raised in Sheepshead Bay. Over white pizza, pasta, cannoli and Diet Cokes, I ask Robin what Jessica was like as a child.

"I was fabulous," Jessica says.

"She was," her mother agrees. "She was blond, extremely happy, endlessly curious and always the leader of the pack. She didn't sleep because she didn't want to miss anything. She was just a bright, shiny kid. She's still a bright, shiny kid."

After Jessica takes a call on her pumpkin-colored cellphone, we talk for a while about Jessica's room, which they both describe as magnificent. "I have lived in apartments smaller than her majesty's two-bedroom suite," Robin snorts. "Not many single parents can do for their children what I have done for this one. This is a child who asked for a pony and got two. I tell her this is the top of the food chain. The only place you can go from here is the royal family."

I ask if anything about Jessica's clique bothers her. She says no—because what she calls "Jess's band of merry men" doesn't "define itself by its opponents. They're not a threat to anyone. Besides, it's not like they're an A-list clique."

"Uh, Mom," Jessica corrects. "We are definitely an A-list clique. We are totally A-list. You are giving out incorrect information."

"Soooorry," Robin says. "I'd fire myself, but there's no one else lining up for the job of being your mom."

Jessica spends a little time bringing her mother and me up to date on the elaborate social structure at her high school. The cheerleaders' clique, it seems, is not the same as the pom-pom girls' clique, though both are A-list. All sports cliques are A-list, in fact, except—"of course"—the swimmers. There is a separate A-list clique for cute preppy girls who "could play sports but don't." There is "the white people who pretend to be black clique" and the drama clique, which would be "C list," except that, as Jessica puts it, "they're not even on the list."

"So what you are saying is that your high school is littered with all these groups that have their own separate physical and mental space?" Robin says, shaking her head in wonderment.

When they think about it, Jessica and her mom agree that the business with the rules—what you can wear on a given day of the week and all that—comes from Jessica's fondness for structure. As a child, her mom says she made up games with "such elaborate rules I'd be lost halfway through her explanation of them." Besides, there was a good deal of upheaval in her early life. Robin left her "goofy artist husband" when Jessica was 3, and after that they moved a lot. And when Robin went to work for Oracle, she "was traveling all the time, getting home late. When I was on the road, I'd call her every night at 8 and say: 'Sweet Dreams. I love you. Good Night.'"

"Always in that order," Jessica says. "Always at 8. I don't like a lot of change."

Toward the end of our lunch, Jessica's mother—who says she herself was more a nerd than a Queen Bee in school—returns to the subject of cliques. She wants, it seems, to put something to rest. "You know I realize there are people who stay with the same friends, the same kind of people, all their life, who never look beyond that," she says. "I wouldn't want that for my daughter. I want my daughter to be one of those people who lives in the world. I know she's got these kind of narrow rules in her personal life right now. But I still think, I really believe, that she will be a bigger person, a person who spends her life in the world." Jessica's mother smiles. Then she gives her daughter's hair an urgent little tug, as if it were the rip cord of a parachute and Jessica were about to float away from her.

MARGARET TALBOT, a contributing writer for the magazine, is a fellow at the New America Foundation.

The Role of Neurobiological Deficits in Childhood Antisocial Behavior

Stephanie H.M. van Goozen, Graeme Fairchild, and Gordon T. Harold

Antisocial behavior is a significant social and clinical concern. Every year, more than 1.6 million people are killed as a result of violence, and many more suffer from physical or mental health problems stemming from violence (World Health Organization, 2002). Antisocial behavior committed by youths is an issue of particular concern. A recent survey showed that citizens of European nations see themselves as having "significant" difficulties with antisocial behavior, and that the problem is above all associated with people under 25 years of age ("Bad behaviour," 2006).

The term *antisocial behavior* refers to the fact that people who are on the receiving end of the behavior are disadvantaged by it, and that social norms and values are violated. Not only aggression but also activities such as theft, vandalism, lying, truancy, running away from home, and oppositional behaviors are involved.

Most normally developing children will occasionally exhibit negative and disobedient behavior toward adults and engage in lying, fighting, and bullying other children. When antisocial behavior forms a pattern that goes beyond the "normal" realm and starts to have adverse effects on the child's functioning, psychiatrists tend to make a diagnosis of conduct disorder (CD) or oppositional defiant disorder (ODD; American Psychiatric Association, 1994). These disorders are relatively common in children, with estimated prevalences ranging from 5 to 10%. The extent to which these disorders can be treated via therapy is limited, and, as a result, these children are at risk for a host of negative outcomes in adolescence and adulthood, including dropping out of school, criminality unemployment, dependence on welfare, and substance abuse (Hill & Maughan, 2001).

There is a growing consensus that both child-specific (i.e., genetic, temperamental) and social (e.g., early adversity) factors contribute to the development and maintenance of antisocial behavior, although most research has focused on identifying specific contextual factors that impinge on the developing child. For example, negative life events, family stress, and parental relationship problems have been associated with antisocial-behavior problems in children. However, there is increasing evidence that factors organic to individual children exacerbate the risk of antisocial behavior to those who live with social adversity. Here, we review evidence relating to the role of neurobiological factors in accounting for the link between early adversity and childhood antisocial behavior and propose that consideration of biological factors underlying this stress-distress link significantly advances understanding of the mechanisms explaining individual differences in the etiology of antisocial behavior.

Research suggests that neurobiological deficits related to the functioning of the stress systems in children with CD are linked to antisocial behavior. We argue that familial factors (e.g., genetic influences, early adversity) are linked to negative outcomes through the mediating and transactional interplay with neurobiological deficits (see Figure 1) and propose that stress hyporeactivity is an index of persistent and serious antisocial behavior.

Stress-Response Systems

There are clear indications that stress plays an important role in explaining individual differences in antisocial behavior. The systems involved in the regulation of stress are the neuroendocrine hypothalamic-pituitary-adrenal (HPA) axis and the psychophysiological autonomic nervous system (ANS). Cortisol is studied in relation to HPA-axis activation, and heart rate (HR) and skin-conductance (SC) responses are used as markers of ANS (re)activity.

The starting point of our approach is that antisocial individuals are less sensitive to stress. This can be deduced from the fact that antisocial individuals engage in risky or dangerous behavior more often than other people do and seem less deterred by its possible negative consequences. There are two explanations for the proposed relationship between lower stress sensitivity and antisocial behavior. One theory claims that antisocial individuals are fearless (Raine, 1996). A lack of fear leads to antisocial behavior because individuals are less sensitive to the negative consequences of their own or other people's behavior in general and to the receipt of punishment in particular. The implications for treatment are clear: Antisocial individuals will have problems learning the association between behavior and punishment, such

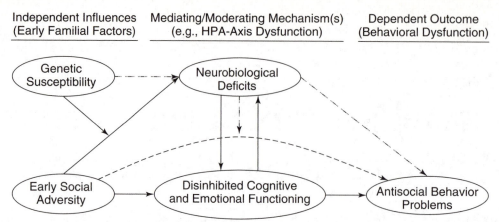

Independent Influences (Early Familial Factors) | Mediating/Moderating Mechanism(s) (e.g., HPA-Axis Dysfunction) | Dependent Outcome (Behavioral Dysfunction)

Figure 1 Theoretical model relating early social adversity to later antisocial behavior problems. It is hypothesized that this relationship is explained by the underlying mediating and moderating role of neurobiological factors. The dashed rolled lines emanating from genetic susceptibility to neurobiological deficits and from neurobiological deficits to antisocial behavior problems represent an indirect (or mediating) pathway between these factors. The bold line emanating from genetic susceptibility to the pathway linking early social adversity to neurobiological deficits, and the dashed-dotted line from neurobiological deficits to the pathway linking early social adversity to antisocial behavior problems, represent proposed moderating influences from each source variable (i.e., genetic susceptibility and neurobiological deficits). A moderating influence is the equivalent of statistical interaction between two theoretical constructs. Bold and dashed-dotted lines in all other instances represent direct and indirect pathways linking primary theoretical constructs. For a full exposition of this model, see van Goosen, Fairchild, Snoek, and Harold (2007).

that pointing out the negative consequences of behavior, or punishing unacceptable behavior, is likely to have little or no effect.

The second explanation focuses on stress thresholds and sensation-seeking behavior (Zuckerman, 1979), and argues that antisocial individuals have elevated thresholds for stress. They are more easily bored and less easily put off by situations that normal people find stressful or dangerous.

What evidence is there that dysfunctional stress systems play a role in antisocial behavior? Several studies (e.g., Virkkumen, 1985) have found that antisocial adults have low resting levels of cortisol, SC, and HR. There is also evidence of inverse relationships between these physiological variables and the severity of the behavioral problems shown. Studies investigating the relation between biological stress parameters and antisocial behavior have also been performed in children (e.g., van Goozen et al., 1998), and the predicted (inverse) relations have been found.

Stress variables can also predict antisocial behavior over time. Raine, Venables, and Mednick (1997) measured HR in more than 1,700 three-year-old children. Aggressive behavior was assessed at age 11. Raine et al. found that low resting HR at age 3 predicted aggressive behavior at age 11. In a study of criminals' sons (who are at risk of becoming delinquent), Brenman et al. (1997) found that boys who did not become delinquent had higher HR and SC than did boys who became delinquent. The authors concluded that the boys in the former group were biologically protected by their heightened autonomic responsivity.

Studies of youths who engage in antisocial behavior show that then like antisocial adults, have less reactive stress systems than do youths who do not engage in antisocial behavior. The question is whether the same applies to children with serious antisocial behavior who have been diagnosed with CD or ODD.

Stress Studies in CD Children

Most studies collect stress data under resting conditions rather than during stress exposure. Antisocial individuals might be different from normal individuals in two respects: A low resting stress level could result in failing to avoid, or even approaching, stressful situations; and low stress reactivity implies that one is more fearless and cares less about possible negative consequences.

Our studies use a paradigm in which psychosocial stress is evoked by exposing children to frustration, provocation, and competition (e.g., van Goozen et al., 1998). The participant competes against a fictitious videotaped "opponent" who behaves in an antagonistic manner. The participant and opponent perform computerized tasks on which they can earn points. The participant is told that the person who earns the most points will receive an attractive prize. Some tasks are impossible to complete, which induces frustration. HR and SC are measured continuously, and cortisol is collected repeatedly in saliva.

CD children show lower HR, SC, and cortisol reactivity to stress than do normal children. Although CD children appear to be less affected at a biological level, they react more angrily and aggressively to provocation than do non-CD children and report feeling quite upset. It is known that CD children are impulsive, have hostile appraisal patterns, and engage in conflictual situations. It is striking that this pattern of appraisal and behavior is not accompanied by contextually appropriate somatic changes.

Genetic factors likely play a role in the functioning of the HPA axis and ANS. There is also evidence that stressful event—by which we mean serious stressors like neglect and traumatization—play an important role in "programming" the stress systems, particularly the HPA axis. This evidence comes mainly from nonhuman animal studies, but the neurobiological consequences of the types of severe stress that can be manipulated in animal studies also occur in humans.

Early Experience and Family Adversity

Physical and biological problems during important phases in development (e.g., birth complications, stress or illness during pregnancy), together with early adversity (e.g., malnutrition, neglect, abuse), contribute importantly to the development of personality and psychopathology. There is increasing evidence that interactions between biological and environmental factors affect the developing brain (Huizink, Mulder, & Buitelaar, 2004).

Nonhuman animal studies show that stressors in early life can have permanent effects on the functioning of the HPA axis, resulting in altered basal and stress-reactivity levels. For example, Liu et al. (1997) varied the amount of licking and grooming behavior in mothers of newborn rats. In adulthood, offspring who had been exposed to normal maternal care were more capable of handling stress than were rats that had received less care. The former also expressed more stress-hormone receptors in the hippocampus, an area important for stress regulation, than did rats that had received less care. Thus, maternal behavior had a direct and lasting effect on the development of the stress systems of the offspring.

Such conclusions are based on data from nonhuman animals, and for obvious reasons it is difficult to conduct similar studies on humans. However, evidence from a handful of studies involving institutionalized children suggests that the processes at work are similar (Carlson & Earls, 1997; Gunnar, Morison, Chisolm, & Schuder, 2001).

Antisocial children are more likely to come from adverse rearing environments involving atypical caregiver–child interactions (Rutter & Silberg, 2002). It is known that CD children are more likely to experience compromised pre- or perinatal development due to maternal smoking, poor nutrition, or exposure to alcohol and/or drugs. It is possible that these factors have affected such children's stress-response systems and resulted in children with a difficult temperament.

Stress Hyporeactivity as a Mediating Factor

We have suggested that physiological hyporeactivity may reflect an inability to generate visceral signals to guide behavior and, in particular, to regulate anger and reactive aggression (van Goozen), Fairchild, Snoek, & Harold, 2007). Evidence from nonhuman animals indicates that abolishing the hormonal response to stress may impair processing of social signals and lead to abnormal patterns of aggression (Haller, Halász, Mikics, & Kruk, 2004). These studies also showed that abnormal aggressive behavior can be prevented by mimicking the hormonal response normally seen during aggressive encounters. These findings have clear parallels with abnormal aggression in humans, in the sense that the behavior is not only excessive but also often risky, badly judged, and callous.

We have proposed an integrative theoretical model linking genetic factors, early adversity, cognitive and neurobiological regulatory mechanisms, and childhood antisocial behavior (van Goozen et al., 2007; see Figure 1). Interactions between genetic predispositions and the environment in which they are expressed appear to be crucial in the etiology of antisocial-behavior problems. A genetic predisposition toward antisocial behavior may be expressed in adverse rearing environments in which the child receives harsh or inconsistent discipline or is exposed to high levels of interparental conflict or marital breakdown (Moffitt, 2005). It is likely that the origin of antisocial behavior in young children lies in this combination of a difficult temperament and a harsh environment in which there is ineffective socialization: A difficult child elicits harsh, inconsistent, and negative socialization behaviors, as a result of which a difficult temperament develops into antisocial behavior (Lykken, 1995). Conversely, the effects of a genetic predisposition may be minimized if the child is raised in an environment in which the parents express warmth or adopt a consistent, authoritative parenting style.

Some children are born with a more easygoing temperament than others. In cases of "hard-to-manage" children, a child's genotype can evoke negative behavior from the environment because genetic influences lead the individual to create, seek out, or otherwise end up in environments that match the genotype (Rutter & Silberg, 2002). These active, evocative gene–environment processes are extremely important in understanding the development and continuity of antisocial behavior (Moffitt, 2005). Social factors occurring independently of the child's genetic makeup or temperament can serve as contributory factors (Harold, Aitken, & Shelton, 2008).

We noted above that early brain development is vulnerable to the effects of environmental stress (Huizink et al., 2004), and that CD children are likely to have been exposed to early stress. A down-regulation of the stress-response system in the face of chronic stress in early life would be an adaptive mechanism, avoiding chronic arousal and excessive energy expenditure that could ultimately result in serious pathophysiological consequences. Given what we know about the background of CD children, it is plausible that these processes have occurred.

We propose that physiological hyporeactivity is a mediating and/or moderating factor for persistent and severe antisocial behavior and that the effects of variations in genetic makeup and early adversity on childhood antisocial behavior occur via this deficit. The primary pathway by which familial factors are linked to antisocial outcome is the reciprocal interplay with neurobiological deficits and resulting disinhibited cognitive (e.g., impulsivity, hostile bias) and emotional (e.g., increased anger) processing, with the latter serving as the psychological gateway through which neurobiological deficits find their expression in antisocial behavior.

Conclusion

Antisocial behavior in children can be persistent and difficult to treat. Although behavioral interventions have been shown to be effective in milder forms of problem behavior, they have limited effectiveness in more seriously disturbed children (Hill & Maughan, 2001).

At present, we do not know what causes the pattern of neuro-biological impairments observed in antisocial children, although it is clear that genetic factors are involved (Caspi et al., 2002). An important line of research suggests that psychosocial adversity affects brain development. Knowing that many CD children have problematic backgrounds, it seems possible that exposure to severe stress has had an effect on the development of their stress systems. Longitudinal research in high-risk children is needed to shed more light on this issue.

Future interventions and treatments should benefit from a neurobiological approach: Neurobiological assessment of high-risk children could indicate whether their deficits are such that interventions involving "empathy induction" or "learning from punishment," for example, are unlikely to work. In such cases, pharmacological interventions could be considered as a treatment option. An important line of future research is to establish whether CD children with attenuated stress (re)activity would be more effectively treated by using pharmacological therapies that reinstate normal HPA-axis functioning.

Current interventions for childhood antisocial behavior have limited success because we lack knowledge of the cognitive–emotional problems of these children and their neurobiological bases. We also fail to assess the environmental risk factors that affect individual neurodevelopment. Furthermore, available treatment options do not target the individual's specific neurobiological vulnerabilities. It seems prudent to identify subgroups of children in whom different causal processes initiate and maintain behavioral problems. This should result in a better match between patient and treatment.

A final point is that the understandable tendency to focus on persistence of antisocial behavior runs the risk of overlooking the fact that a substantial proportion of antisocial children do not grow up to be antisocial adults (with prevalence rates for antisocial children who persist into adulthood ranging from 35 to 75%). Neurobiological factors could also account for this: Promising data from a handful of studies show that neurobiological factors differ between children who persist in and desist from antisocial behavior (Brennan et al., 1997; van de Wiel, van Goozen, Matthys, Snoek, & van Engeland, 2004). Expanding on this research base is essential if we are to reach a more adequate understanding of the causes, course, and consequences of childhood antisocial behavior and, most importantly, devise effective ways of reducing the negative consequences for society.

Recommended Reading

Hill, J., & Maughan, B. (2001). *Conduct disorders in childhood and adolescence.* Cambridge, UK: Cambridge University Press. A clearly written and comprehensive review for readers who wish to expand their knowledge on conduct disorders in youngsters.

Moffitt, T.E. (2005). The new look of behavioral genetics in developmental psychopathology: Gene–environment interplay in antisocial behaviors. *Psychological Bulletin, 131, 533–554.* Explains and discusses the gene–environment interplay in antisocial behavior in more detail.

van Goozen, S.H.M., Fairchild, G., Snoek, H., & Harold, G.T. (2007). The evidence for a neurobiological model of childhood antisocial behavior. *Psychological Bulletin, 133,* 149–182. Discusses the neurobiological basis of antisocial behavior in greater detail than the current paper.

References

American Psychiatric Association. (1994). *Diagnostic and statistical manual of mental disorders* (4th ed.). Washington, DC: Author.

Bad behaviour 'worst in Europe'. (2006). BBC News. Downloaded April 30, 2008, from http://news.bbc.co.uk/l/hi/uk/4751315.stm

Brennan, P.A., Raine, A., Schulsinger, F., Kirkegaard-Sorensen, L., Knop, J., Hutchings, B., et al. (1997). Psychophysiological protective factors for male subjects at high risk for criminal behavior. *American Journal of Psychiatry, 154,* 853–855.

Carlson, M., & Earls, F. (1997). Psychological and neuroendocrinological sequelae of early social deprivation in institutionalized children in Romania. *Annals of the New York Academy of Sciences, 807,* 419–428.

Caspi, A., McClay J., Moffitt, T.E., Mill, J., Martin, J., Craig, I.W., et al. (2002). Role of the genotype in the cycle of violence in maltreated children. *Science, 297,* 851–854.

Gunnar, M.R., Morison, S.J., Chisholm, K., & Schuder, M. (2001). Salivary cortisol levels in children adopted from Romanian orphanages. *Development and Psychopathology, 13,* 611–628.

Harold, G.T, Aitken, J.J., & Shelton, K.H. (2008). Inter-parental conflict and children's academic attainment: A longitudinal analysis. *Journal of Child Psychology and Psychiatry, 48,* 1223–1232.

Haller, J., Halász, J., Mikics, E., & Kruk, M.R. (2004). Chronic glucocorticoid deficiency-induced abnormal aggression, autonomic hypoarousal, and social deficit in rats. *Journal of Neuroendocrinology, 16,* 550–557.

Hill, J., & Maughan, B. (2001). *Conduct disorders in childhood and adolescence.* Cambridge, UK: Cambridge University Press.

Huizink, A.C., Mulder, E.J.H., & Buitelaar, J.K. (2004). Prenatal stress and risk for psychopathology: Specific effects or induction of general susceptibility. *Psychological Bulletin, 130,* 115–142.

Liu, D., Diorio, J., Tannenbaum, B., Caldji, C., Francis, D., Freedman, A., et al. (1997). Maternal care, hippocampal glucocorticoid receptors, and hypothalamic-pituitary-adrenal responses to stress. *Science, 277,* 1659–1662.

Lykken, D.T (1995). *The antisocial personalities.* Hillsdale, NJ: Erlbaum.

Moffitt, T.E. (2005). The new look of behavioral genetics in developmental psychopathology: Gene–environment interplay in antisocial behaviors. *Psychological Bulletin, 131,* 533–554.

Raine, A. (1996). Autonomic nervous system activity and violence. In D.M. Stoff & R.B. Cairns (Eds.), *Aggression and violence: Genetic, neurobiological and biological perspectives* (pp. 145–168). Mahwah, NJ: Erlbaum.

Raine, A., Venables, P.H., & Mednick, S.A. (1997). Low resting heart rate at age 3 years predisposes to aggression at age 11 years: Evidence from the Mauritius Child Health Project. *Journal of the American Academy of Child and Adolescent Psychiatry, 36,* 1457–1464.

Rutter, M., & Silberg, J. (2002). Gene–environment interplay in relation to emotional and behavioral disturbance. *Annual Review of Psychology, 53,* 463–490.

van de Wiel, N.M.H., van Goozen, S.H.M., Matthys, W., Snoek, H., & van Engeland, H. (2004). Cortisol and treatment effect in children with disruptive behavior disorders: A preliminary study. *Journal of the American Academy of Child and Adolescent Psychiatry, 43,* 1011–1018.

van Goozen, S.H.M., Fairchild, G., Snoek, H., & Harold, G.T (2007). The evidence for a neurobiological model of childhood antisocial behaviour. *Psychological Bulletin, 133,* 149–182.

van Goozen, S.H.M., Matthys, W., Cohen-Kettenis P.T, Gispen-de Wied, C., Wiegant, V.M., & van Engeland, H. (1998). Salivary cortisol and cardiovascular activity during stress in oppositional-defiant disorder boys and normal controls. *Biological Psychiatry, 43,* 531–539.

Virkkunen, M. (1985). Urinary free cortisol secretion in habitually violent offenders. *Acta Psychiatrica Scandinavica, 72,* 40–44.

World Health Organization (2002). *World report on violence and health.* E.G. Krug, L.L. Dahlman, J.A. Mercy, A.B. Zwi, & R. Lozano (Eds.). Geneva, Switzerland: Author.

Zuckerman, M. (1979). *Sensation seeking: Beyond the optimum level of arousal.* Hillsdale, NJ: Erlbaum.

Address correspondence to STEPHANIE H.M. VAN GOOZEN, School of Psychology Cardiff University, Tower Building, Park Place, Cardiff CF1O 3AT, United Kingdom; e-mail: vangoozens@cardiff.ac.uk.

UNIT 4

Parenting and Family Issues

Unit Selections

Key Points to Consider

• If you have brothers or sisters, have you ever felt your parents favor your siblings or yourself? Does this favoritism continue today as an adult? How does this favoritism affect your feelings and relationships with your parents or your siblings?

• A significant number of children in the United States will experience the divorce of their parents. Have you or do you know of children who have experienced their parents' divorce? How does divorce impact children? Describe factors that can ameliorate the negative effects of divorce.

• Given that effective parenting is not a function of one's sexual orientation, how might you help children raised by gay parents cope with this kind of discrimination? What steps could you take to help educate others of these results?

• IQ, intelligence, and school performance have been shown to increase for children adopted into families with higher education and socioeconomic status. Why do you think this is the case? Given this research, do you think that families who do not possess high socioeconomic status should be permitted to adopt?

Student Website
www.mhcls.com

Internet References

The National Association for Child Development (NACD)
http://www.nacd.org

National Council on Family Relations
http://www.ncfr.com

Parenting and Families
http://www.cyfc.umn.edu

Parentsplace.com: Single Parenting
http://www.parentsplace.com/family/archive/0,10693,239458,00.html

National Stepfamily Resource Center
http://www.stepfam.org

ew people today realize that the potential freedom to choose parenthood—deciding whether to become a parent, deciding when to have children, or deciding how many children to have—is a development due to the advent of reliable methods of contraception and other recent sociocultural changes. Moreover, unlike any other significant job to which we may aspire, few, if any, of us will receive any formal training or information about the lifelong responsibility of parenting. For most of us, our behavior is generally based on our own conscious and subconscious recollections of how we were parented as well as on our observations of the parenting practices of others around us. In fact, our society often behaves as if the mere act of producing a baby automatically confers upon the parents an innate parenting ability, furthermore, that a family's parenting practices should remain private and not be subjected to scrutiny or criticism by outsiders.

Given this climate, it is not surprising that misconceptions about many parenting practices persist. Only within the last 40 years or so have researchers turned their lenses on the scientific study of the family. Social, historical, cultural, and economic forces also have dramatically changed the face of the American family today. In fact, the vast majority of parents never take courses or learn of the research on parenting. This unit helps present some of the research on the many complex factors related to successful parenting.

A majority of parents in the United States today admit to relying on spanking as a form of discipline for their children and do not view spanking as inappropriate. Researchers are beginning to amass evidence on the consequences for children. The authors of "Physical Discipline and Children's Adjustment" present evidence that mothers' use of physical discipline has differential consequences on children depending on larger cultural factors.

Between 43% and 50% of first marriages will end in divorce in the United States. Researcher Jennifer Lansford summarizes the wealth of data on the effects of divorce on children's development in "Parental Divorce and Children's Adjustment" and makes recommendations that might improve children's adjustment to divorce in the areas of child custody and child support policies and enforcement.

Parental favoritism for some of their children over others is discussed by researchers in "Within-Family Differences in Parent-Child Relations across the Life Course." They review research studies showing that parental favoritism can begin very early in children's development and often continues and grows stronger when children become adults. The authors discuss factors that influence favoritism including gender, birth order, temperament, and health status as well as the positive and negative effects of parental favoritism.

Research on lesbian and gay parents demonstrates that children's adjustment and development are not negatively affected by having same-sex parents. In fact, the studies show that children from same-sex parents are equally likely to thrive as children from heterosexual parents. What matters more is the

© image 100/PunchStock

quality of the parenting relationships as described in Patterson's article, "Children of Lesbian and Gay Parents." This important data is being used to assist judges when awarding custody and helping to develop sound family policies.

Sadly, an estimated quarter of all children in the United States have suffered from parental alcohol abuse or dependency. The authors of "Children of Alcoholics" examine the risk factors, child outcomes, and ameliorating factors and preventive intervention possibilities.

IQ and intelligence appear to have strong genetic determinants. However, as the authors of "Adoption Is a Successful Natural Intervention Enhancing Adopted Children's IQ and School Performance" attest, the environment can exert an extremely powerful influence. Even children coming from at-risk situations will show significant improvement in their intelligence and school performance if they are able to move to a high-functioning, nurturing, and supportive environment in infancy or early childhood.

Children of Lesbian and Gay Parents

Does parental sexual orientation affect child development, and if so, how? Studies using convenience samples, studies using samples drawn from known populations, and studies based on samples that are representative of larger populations all converge on similar conclusions. More than two decades of research has failed to reveal important differences in the adjustment or development of children or adolescents reared by same-sex couples compared to those reared by other-sex couples. Results of the research suggest that qualities of family relationships are more tightly linked with child outcomes than is parental sexual orientation.

CHARLOTTE J. PATTERSON

Does parental sexual orientation affect child development, and if so, how? This question has often been raised in the context of legal and policy proceedings relevant to children, such as those involving adoption, child custody, or visitation. Divergent views have been offered by professionals from the fields of psychology, sociology, medicine, and law (Patterson, Fulcher, & Wainright, 2002). While this question has most often been raised in legal and policy contexts, it is also relevant to theoretical issues. For example, does healthy human development require that a child grow up with parents of each gender? And if not, what would that mean for our theoretical understanding of parent–child relations? (Patterson & Hastings, in press) In this article, I describe some research designed to address these questions.

Early Research

Research on children with lesbian and gay parents began with studies focused on cases in which children had been born in the context of a heterosexual marriage. After parental separation and divorce, many children in these families lived with divorced lesbian mothers. A number of researchers compared development among children of divorced lesbian mothers with that among children of divorced heterosexual mothers and found few significant differences (Patterson, 1997; Stacey & Biblarz, 2001).

These studies were valuable in addressing concerns of judges who were required to decide divorce and child custody cases, but they left many questions unanswered. In particular, because the children who participated in this research had been born into homes with married mothers and fathers, it was not obvious how to understand the reasons for their healthy development. The possibility that children's early exposure to apparently heterosexual male and female role models had contributed to healthy development could not be ruled out.

When lesbian or gay parents rear infants and children from birth, do their offspring grow up in typical ways and show healthy development? To address this question, it was important to study children who had never lived with heterosexual parents. In the 1990s, a number of investigators began research of this kind.

An early example was the Bay Area Families Study, in which I studied a group of 4- to 9-year-old children who had been born to or adopted early in life by lesbian mothers (Patterson, 1996, 1997). Data were collected during home visits. Results from in-home interviews and also from questionnaires showed that children had regular contact with a wide range of adults of both genders, both within and outside of their families. The children's self-concepts and preferences for same-gender playmates and activities were much like those of other children their ages. Moreover, standardized measures of social competence and of behavior problems, such as those from the Child Behavior Checklist (CBCL), showed that they scored within the range of normal variation for a representative sample of same-aged American children. It was clear from this study and others like it that it was quite possible for lesbian mothers to rear healthy children.

Studies Based on Samples Drawn from Known Populations

Interpretation of the results from the Bay Area Families Study was, however, affected by its sampling procedures. The study had been based on a convenience sample that had been assembled by word of mouth. It was therefore impossible to rule out the possibility that families who participated in the research were especially well adjusted. Would a more representative sample yield different results?

To find out, Ray Chan, Barbara Raboy, and I conducted research in collaboration with the Sperm Bank of California

(Chan, Raboy, & Patterson, 1998; Fulcher, Sutfin, Chan, Scheib, & Patterson, 2005). Over the more than 15 years of its existence, the Sperm Bank of California's clientele had included many lesbian as well as heterosexual women. For research purposes, this clientele was a finite population from which our sample could be drawn. The Sperm Bank of California also allowed a sample in which, both for lesbian and for heterosexual groups, one parent was biologically related to the child and one was not.

We invited all clients who had conceived children using the resources of the Sperm Bank of California and who had children 5 years old or older to participate in our research. The resulting sample was composed of 80 families, 55 headed by lesbian and 25 headed by heterosexual parents. Materials were mailed to participating families, with instructions to complete them privately and return them in self-addressed stamped envelopes we provided.

Results replicated and expanded upon those from earlier research. Children of lesbian and heterosexual parents showed similar, relatively high levels of social competence, as well as similar, relatively low levels of behavior problems on the parent form of the CBCL. We also asked the children's teachers to provide evaluations of children's adjustment on the Teacher Report Form of the CBCL, and their reports agreed with those of parents. Parental sexual orientation was not related to children's adaptation. Quite apart from parental sexual orientation, however, and consistent with findings from years of research on children of heterosexual parents, when parent–child relationships were marked by warmth and affection, children were more likely to be developing well. Thus, in this sample drawn from a known population, measures of children's adjustment were unrelated to parental sexual orientation (Chan et al., 1998; Fulcher et al., 2005).

Even as they provided information about children born to lesbian mothers, however, these new results also raised additional questions. Women who conceive children at sperm banks are generally both well educated and financially comfortable. It was possible that these relatively privileged women were able to protect children from many forms of discrimination. What if a more diverse group of families were to be studied? In addition, the children in this sample averaged 7 years of age, and some concerns focus on older children and adolescents. What if an older group of youngsters were to be studied? Would problems masked by youth and privilege in earlier studies emerge in an older, more diverse sample?

Studies Based on Representative Samples

An opportunity to address these questions was presented by the availability of data from the National Longitudinal Study of Adolescent Health (Add Health). The Add Health study involved a large, ethnically diverse, and essentially representative sample of American adolescents and their parents. Data for our research were drawn from surveys and interviews completed by more than 12,000 adolescents and their parents at home and from surveys completed by adolescents at school.

Parents were not queried directly about their sexual orientation but were asked if they were involved in a "marriage, or marriage-like relationship." If parents acknowledged such a relationship, they were also asked the gender of their partner. Thus, we identified a group of 44 12- to 18-year-olds who lived with parents involved in marriage or marriage-like relationships with same-sex partners. We compared them with a matched group of adolescents living with other-sex couples. Data from the archives of the Add Health study allowed us to address many questions about adolescent development.

Consistent with earlier findings, results of this work revealed few differences in adjustment between adolescents living with same-sex parents and those living with opposite-sex parents (Wainright, Russell, & Patterson, 2004; Wainright & Patterson, 2006). There were no significant differences between teenagers living with same-sex parents and those living with other-sex parents on self-reported assessments of psychological well-being, such as self-esteem and anxiety; measures of school outcomes, such as grade point averages and trouble in school; or measures of family relationships, such as parental warmth and care from adults and peers. Adolescents in the two groups were equally likely to say that they had been involved in a romantic relationship in the last 18 months, and they were equally likely to report having engaged in sexual intercourse. The only statistically reliable difference between the two groups—that those with same-sex parents felt a greater sense of connection to people at school—favored the youngsters living with same-sex couples. There were no significant differences in self-reported substance use, delinquency, or peer victimization between those reared by same- or other-sex couples (Wainright & Patterson, 2006).

Although the gender of parents' partners was not an important predictor of adolescent well-being, other aspects of family relationships were significantly associated with teenagers' adjustment. Consistent with other findings about adolescent development, the qualities of family relationships rather than the gender of parents' partners were consistently related to adolescent outcomes. Parents who reported having close relationships with their offspring had adolescents who reported more favorable adjustment. Not only is it possible for children and adolescents who are parented by same-sex couples to develop in healthy directions, but—even when studied in an extremely diverse, representative sample of American adolescents—they generally do.

These findings have been supported by results from many other studies, both in the United States and abroad. Susan Golombok and her colleagues have reported similar results with a near-representative sample of children in the United Kingdom (Golombok et al., 2003). Others, both in Europe and in the United States, have described similar findings (e.g., Brewaeys, Ponjaert, Van Hall, & Golombok, 1997).

The fact that children of lesbian mothers generally develop in healthy ways should not be taken to suggest that they encounter no challenges. Many investigators have remarked upon the fact that children of lesbian and gay parents may encounter anti-gay sentiments in their daily lives. For example, in a study of 10-year-old children born to lesbian mothers, Gartrell, Deck, Rodas, Peyser, and Banks (2005) reported that a substantial minority had encountered anti-gay sentiments among their peers. Those who had had such encounters were likely to report having felt angry, upset, or sad about these experiences. Children of lesbian and gay parents may be exposed to prejudice against their parents in some settings, and this may be painful for them, but evidence for the idea that such encounters affect children's overall adjustment is lacking.

Conclusions

Does parental sexual orientation have an important impact on child or adolescent development? Results of recent research provide no evidence that it does. In fact, the findings suggest that parental sexual orientation is less important than the qualities of family relationships. More important to youth than the gender of their parent's partner is the quality of daily interaction and the strength of relationships with the parents they have.

One possible approach to findings like the ones described above might be to shrug them off by reiterating the familiar adage that "one cannot prove the null hypothesis." To respond in this way, however, is to miss the central point of these studies. Whether or not any measurable impact of parental sexual orientation on children's development is ever demonstrated, the main conclusions from research to date remain clear: Whatever correlations between child outcomes and parental sexual orientation may exist, they are less important than those between child outcomes and the qualities of family relationships.

Although research to date has made important contributions, many issues relevant to children of lesbian and gay parents remain in need of study. Relatively few studies have examined the development of children adopted by lesbian or gay parents or of children born to gay fathers; further research in both areas would be welcome (Patterson, 2004). Some notable longitudinal studies have been reported, and they have found children of same-sex couples to be in good mental health. Greater understanding of family relationships and transitions over time would, however, be helpful, and longitudinal studies would be valuable. Future research could also benefit from the use of a variety of methodologies.

Meanwhile, the clarity of findings in this area has been acknowledged by a number of major professional organizations. For instance, the governing body of the American Psychological Association (APA) voted unanimously in favor of a statement that said, "Research has shown that the adjustment, development, and psychological well-being of children is unrelated to parental sexual orientation and that children of lesbian and gay parents are as likely as those of heterosexual parents to flourish" (APA, 2004). The American Bar Association, the American Medical Association, the American Academy of Pediatrics, the American Psychiatric Association, and other mainstream professional groups have issued similar statements.

The findings from research on children of lesbian and gay parents have been used to inform legal and public policy debates across the country (Patterson et al., 2002). The research literature on this subject has been cited in amicus briefs filed by the APA in cases dealing with adoption, child custody, and also in cases related to the legality of marriages between same-sex partners. Psychologists serving as expert witnesses have presented findings on these issues in many different courts (Patterson et al., 2002). Through these and other avenues, results of research on lesbian and gay parents and their children are finding their way into public discourse.

The findings are also beginning to address theoretical questions about critical issues in parenting. The importance of gender in parenting is one such issue. When children fare well in two-parent lesbian-mother or gay-father families, this suggests that the gender of one's parents cannot be a critical factor in child development. Results of research on children of lesbian and gay parents cast doubt upon the traditional assumption that gender is important in parenting. Our data suggest that it is the quality of parenting rather than the gender of parents that is significant for youngsters' development.

Research on children of lesbian and gay parents is thus located at the intersection of a number of classic and contemporary concerns. Studies of lesbian- and gay-parented families allow researchers to address theoretical questions that had previously remained difficult or impossible to answer. They also address oft-debated legal questions of fact about development of children with lesbian and gay parents. Thus, research on children of lesbian and gay parents contributes to public debate and legal decision making, as well as to theoretical understanding of human development.

References

American Psychological Association (2004). Resolution on sexual orientation, parents, and children. Retrieved September 25, 2006, from http://www.apa.org/pi/lgbc/policy/parentschildren.pdf

Brewaeys, A., Ponjaert, I., Van Hall, E.V., & Golombok, S. (1997). Donor insemination: Child development and family functioning in lesbian mother families. *Human Reproduction, 12,* 1349–1359.

Chan, R.W., Raboy, B., & Patterson, C.J. (1998). Psychosocial adjustment among children conceived via donor insemination by lesbian and heterosexual mothers. *Child Development, 69,* 443–457.

Fulcher, M., Sutfin, E.L., Chan, R.W., Scheib, J.E., & Patterson, C.J. (2005). Lesbian mothers and their children: Findings from the Contemporary Families Study. In A. Omoto & H. Kurtzman (Eds.), *Recent research on sexual orientation, mental health, and substance abuse* (pp. 281–299). Washington, DC: American Psychological Association.

Gartrell, N., Deck., A., Rodas, C., Peyser, H., & Banks, A. (2005). The National Lesbian Family Study: 4. Interviews with the 10-year-old children. *American Journal of Orthopsychiatry, 75,* 518–524.

Golombok, S., Perry, B., Burston, A., Murray, C., Mooney-Somers, J., Stevens, M., & Golding, J. (2003). Children with lesbian parents: A community study. *Developmental Psychology, 39,* 20–33.

Patterson, C.J. (1996). Lesbian mothers and their children: Findings from the Bay Area Families Study. In J. Laird & R.J. Green (Eds.), *Lesbians and gays in couples and families: A handbook for therapists* (pp. 420–437). San Francisco: Jossey-Bass.

Patterson, C.J. (1997). Children of lesbian and gay parents. In T. Ollendick & R. Prinz (Eds.), *Advances in clinical child psychology* (Vol. 19, pp. 235–282). New York: Plenum Press.

Patterson, C.J. (2004). Gay fathers. In M.E. Lamb (Ed.), *The role of the father in child development* (4th ed., pp. 397–416). New York: Wiley.

Patterson, C.J., Fulcher, M., & Wainright, J. (2002). Children of lesbian and gay parents: Research, law, and policy. In B.L. Bottoms, M.B. Kovera, & B.D. McAuliff (Eds.), *Children, social science and the law* (pp. 176–199). New York: Cambridge University Press.

Patterson, C.J., & Hastings, P. (in press). Socialization in context of family diversity. In J. Grusec & P. Hastings (Eds.), *Handbook of socialization*. New York: Guilford Press.

Stacey, J., & Biblarz, T.J. (2001). (How) Does sexual orientation of parents matter? *American Sociological Review, 65,* 159–183.

Wainright, J.L., & Patterson, C.J. (2006). Delinquency, victimization, and substance use among adolescents with female same-sex parents. *Journal of Family Psychology, 20,* 526–530.

Wainright, J.L., Russell, S.T., & Patterson, C.J. (2004). Psychosocial adjustment and school outcomes of adolescents with same-sex parents. *Child Development, 75,* 1886–1898.

Address correspondence to Charlotte J. Patterson, Department of Psychology, P.O. Box 400400, University of Virginia, Charlottesville, VA 22904; e-mail: cjp@virginia.edu.

From *Current Directions in Psychological Science*, October 2006, pp. 241–244. Copyright © 2006 by the Association for Psychological Science. Reprinted by permission of Wiley-Blackwell.

Evidence of Infants' Internal Working Models of Attachment

Susan C. Johnson, Carol S. Dweck, and Frances S. Chen

Nearly half a century ago, psychiatrist John Bowlby proposed that the instinctual behavioral system that underpins an infant's attachment to his or her mother is accompanied by "internal working models" of the social world—models based on the infant's own experience with his or her caregiver (Bowlby, 1958, 1969/1982). These mental models were thought to mediate, in part, the ability of an infant to use the caregiver as a buffer against the stresses of life, as well as the later development of important self-regulatory and social skills.

Hundreds of studies now testify to the impact of caregivers' behavior on infants' behavior and development: Infants who most easily seek and accept support from their parents are considered secure in their attachments and are more likely to have received sensitive and responsive caregiving than insecure infants; over time, they display a variety of socioemotional advantages over insecure infants (Cassidy & Shaver, 1999). Research has also shown that, at least in older children and adults, individual differences in the security of attachment are indeed related to the individual's representations of social relations (Bretherton & Munholland, 1999). Yet no study has ever directly assessed internal working models of attachment in infancy. In the present study, we sought to do so.

Method

Using a visual habituation technique, we tested expectations of caregivers' responsiveness in 10 securely and 11 insecurely attached 12- to 16-month-old infants (mean age = 403 days; 13 females). Attachment security was measured in the lab using the Strange Situation (Ainsworth, Blehar, Waters, & Wall, 1978).

Following Bowlby (1958, 1969/1982) and Ainsworth (Ainsworth et al., 1978), we predicted that different experiences with their own primary caregivers would lead infants to construct different internal working models, including different expectations of caregivers' responsiveness. Thus, we expected that secure infants, compared with insecure infants, would look longer at a display of an unresponsive caregiver (relatively unexpected) relative to a display of a responsive caregiver (relatively expected).

Given recent demonstrations of the abstractness and generality of infants' reasoning about agents (Gergely, Nádasdy, Csibra, & Bíró, 1995; Johnson, 2003; Kuhlmeier, Wynn, & Bloom, 2003), we chose to test infants' expectations with displays of animated geometric characters, rather than actual people. Infants were habituated to a video of two animated ellipses enacting a separation event. The large "mother" and small "child" appeared together at the bottom of a steep incline, and then the mother traveled halfway up the incline to a small plateau. As the mother came to rest there, the child below began to cry, an event depicted by a slight pulsation and bouncing and an actual human infant cry. The animation then paused, allowing the participant to look at the scene as long as he or she desired. Once the participant looked away, the sequence was repeated until his or her visual attention to the event declined to half of its initial amount, as measured by the duration of the participant's looks. When an infant reached this criterion of habituation, each of two test outcomes was shown twice. Each test outcome opened with the mother still positioned halfway up the incline, as the child continued to cry. In the *responsive* outcome, the mother returned to the child. In the *unresponsive* outcome, the mother continued up the slope, away from the child. The order in which the outcomes were presented was counterbalanced. Interest in each outcome was measured by looking time.

The Strange Situation sessions of all 21 infants were blind-coded by the third author after training at the Institute of Child Development's Attachment Workshop. A second blind coder, the first author, scored 10 randomly selected sessions. The coders' agreement was 90%, and kappa was .83.

The visual looking times of all infants were coded on-line by an observer blind to attachment status and test event. A second blind observer, also on-line, coded the looking times of 13 of the infants, achieving 93% agreement and a kappa of .82.

Results

Mean looking times for the last three trials of habituation and each outcome were calculated for each infant (see Figure 1). Securely attached infants looked for 5.9 s ($SD = 4.1$) at the last three habituation events, 10.2 s ($SD = 8.9$) at the unresponsive-caregiver outcome, and 7.3 s ($SD = 7.0$) at the responsive-caregiver outcome. The comparable times in insecurely attached infants were 5.4 s ($SD = 2.9$), 6.6 s ($SD = 3.5$), and 8.0 s

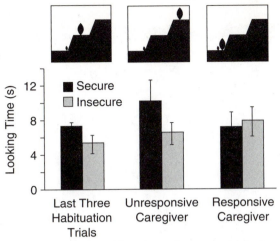

Figure 1 Mean looking times (in seconds) to habituation and test events among secure and insecure infants. Standard error bars are shown. Each illustration depicts the final scene in the video corresponding to the graph below. The large oval represents the "mother," and the small oval represents the "child."

($SD = 5.4$). Preliminary analyses showed no effect of gender or order of presentation on looking times in the outcome trials.

A mixed analysis of variance with attachment status (secure, insecure) and outcome (responsive, unresponsive) as variables revealed no differences between secure and insecure infants in the overall amount of time that they looked at the test displays, $F(1, 19) = 0.31$, n.s., and no differences between the overall looking times (secure and insecure infants combined) to responsive versus unresponsive outcomes, $F(1, 19) = 0.48$, n.s. However, as predicted, infants' relative interest in the two outcomes did vary by group. Secure infants looked relatively longer at the unresponsive outcome than the responsive outcome compared with the insecure infants, $F(1, 19) = 4.76$, $p = .042$.[1] These results constitute direct positive evidence that infants' own personal attachment experiences are reflected in abstract mental representations of social interactions.

The current method opens a new window onto the nature of internal working models of attachment. In addition, these representations can now be traced as they emerge, well before existing behavioral measures of attachment can be employed. The literature on attachment has shown the profound impact of early experience. The method used in the present study provides a means of looking into the mind upon which that experience has left its imprint.

Note

1. Results of additional analyses converged. One-tailed, pair-wise comparisons revealed a significant effect of outcome within the secure group, $t(9) = 1.99$, $p < .04$, but not the insecure group. Also, 7 of the 10 secure infants looked longer at the unresponsive than at the responsive outcome, whereas 7 of the 11 insecure infants showed the opposite result, $p < .07$, Mann-Whitney test. The looking behaviors of the two subtypes of insecure infants (6 avoidant, 5 resistant) did not differ.

References

Ainsworth, M.D.S., Blehar, M.C., Waters, E., & Wall, S. (1978). *Patterns of attachment: A psychological study of the strange situation.* Hillsdale, NJ: Erlbaum.

Bowlby, J. (1958). The nature of the child's ties to his mother. *International Journal of Psychoanalysis, 39,* 350.

Bowlby, J. (1982). *Attachment and loss: Vol. 1. Attachment.* New York: Basic Books. (Original work published 1969)

Bretherton, I., & Munholland, K.A. (1999). Internal working models revisited. In J. Cassidy & P.R. Shaver (Eds.), *Handbook of attachment: Theory, research, and clinical applications* (pp. 89–111). New York: Guilford Press.

Cassidy, J., & Shaver, P.R. (Eds.). (1999). *Handbook of attachment: Theory, research, and clinical applications.* New York: Guilford Press.

Gergely, G., Nádasdy, Z., Csibra, G., & Bíró, S. (1995). Taking the intentional stance at 12 months of age. *Cognition, 56,* 165–193.

Johnson, S.C. (2003). Detecting agents. *Philosophical Transactions of the Royal Society B, 358,* 549–559.

Kuhlmeier, V.A., Wynn, K., & Bloom, P. (2003). Attribution of dispositional states by 12-month-olds. *Psychological Science, 14,* 402–408.

SUSAN C. JOHNSON, CAROL S. DWECK, and FRANCES S. CHEN
Stanford University.

Address correspondence to Susan C. Johnson, Department of Psychology, Jordan Hall, Bldg. 420, Stanford University, Stanford, CA 94305; e-mail: scj@psych.stanford.edu.

Acknowledgments—We thank C. Lai, P. Romera, C. Titchenal, and L. Weitzel for assistance.

Children of Alcoholics
Risk and Resilience

CARA E. RICE, MPH, ET AL.

In 2002, over 17 million people in the United States were estimated to suffer from alcohol abuse or alcohol dependence (NIAAA, 2006). These alcohol disorders have devastating effects on the individuals, their families, and society. It has been reported that one in four children in the United States has been exposed to alcohol abuse or dependence in the family (Grant, 2000). A 1992 survey revealed that over 28 million children in the United States lived in households with one or more adults who had an alcohol disorder at some time in their lives, while nearly 10 million children lived with adults who reported alcohol disorders in the past year (Grant, 2000). Children of alcoholics (COAs) are at increased risk for a variety of negative outcomes, including fetal alcohol syndrome, substance use disorders, conduct problems, restlessness and inattention, poor academic performance, anxiety, and depression (West & Prinz, 1987). Furthermore, children of alcoholics are more likely to be exposed to family stressors such as divorce, family conflict, parental psychopathology, and poverty, which, in turn, may contribute to their negative outcomes.

In particular, COAs show increased risk of alcoholism and other substance use disorders. Genetic factors have been identified as increasing the risk of developing substance use problems among COAs (Schuckit, 2000). However, the risk faced by COAs is best understood as resulting from the interplay of both genetic and environmental factors (McGue, Elkins, & Iacano, 2000). We will discuss the factors that influence the development of substance abuse and other negative outcomes in COAs. We will also review three models in the development of substance disorders for COAs. These models are not mutually exclusive, and all three may influence a child. We will also discuss protective factors that may decrease COAs' risk for the development of future negative outcomes.

Prenatal Risk

One pathway for increased risk among COAs is through prenatal exposure to alcohol. Fetal alcohol syndrome (FAS), which can occur if a woman drinks alcohol during pregnancy, is a condition characterized by abnormal facial features, growth retardation, and central nervous system problems. Children with FAS may have physical disabilities and problems with learning, memory, attention, problem solving, and social/behavioral problems (Bertrand et al., 2004).

Pathways of Risk for the Development of Substance Disorders

Multiple pathways have been studied in the development of substance use disorders. Three important ones are the deviance proneness model, the stress/negative affect model, and the substance use effects model (Sher, 1991). Although these models were originally proposed to explain the development of alcohol disorders among COAs, they can also be extended to a consideration of other negative outcomes.

Deviance Proneness Pathway

The deviance proneness pathway theorizes that parental substance abuse produces poor parenting, family conflict, difficult child temperament and cognitive dysfunction. Poor parenting along with conflicted family environment are thought to interact with a child's difficult temperament and cognitive dysfunctions, which raises the child's risk for school failure and for associating with peers who themselves have high levels of conduct problems. Affiliation with these antisocial peers then increases the likelihood of antisocial behavior by COAs, including substance use (Dishion, Capaldi, Spracklen, & Li, 1995). Conduct problems in childhood and later adolescence predict the development of substance use disorders in young adulthood (Chassin et al., 1999; Molina, Bukstein, & Lynch, 2002).

One component of the deviance proneness model is difficult temperament or personality. The temperament and personality traits that are associated with adolescent substance use include sensation seeking, aggression, impulsivity, and an inability to delay gratification (Gerra et al., 2004; Wills,

Windle, & Cleary, 1998). For example, 3-year-old boys observed to be distractible, restless, and impulsive were more likely to be diagnosed with alcohol dependence at the age of 21 (Caspi, Moffitt, Newman, & Silva, 1996). Importantly, these characteristics, which are associated with adolescent substance use, have also been shown to be more common among COAs and children of drug users. (e.g., Carbonneau et al., 1998). This suggests that COAs may be at risk for substance use, in part, because of their personality traits.

One in four children in the United States has been exposed to alcohol abuse or dependence in the family.

Another component of the deviance proneness model is a deficit in cognitive function. Children of alcoholics may also be at risk for substance abuse because of deficits in cognitive functioning that have been called "executive" functions. Executive functioning refers to the ability to adjust behavior to fit the demands of individual situations and executive functioning includes planning, working memory and the ability to inhibit responses (Nigg et al., 2004). COAs have demonstrated poor response inhibition (Nigg et al., 2004), and impairments in executive functioning have found to predict drinking among young adult COAs (Atyaclar, Tarter, Kirisci, & Lu, 1999).

The deviance proneness pathway also suggests that COAs may be at risk because of the poor parenting that they receive. Decreased parental monitoring of the child's behavior, inconsistent discipline, and low levels of social support from parents are associated with increased levels of adolescent substance use and conduct problems (Brody, Ge, Conger, Gibbons, Murry, Gerrard, & Simons, 2001; Wills, McNamara, Vaccaro, & Hirky, 1996). These negative parenting behaviors have been found in substance-abusing families (Chassin, Curran, Hussong, & Colder, 1996; Curran & Chassin, 1996), suggesting that alcoholic parents may engage in poor parenting practices, which may in turn place their children at risk for substance use and/or conduct problems.

Most researchers have assumed that poor parenting leads to behavior problems in children, making it the basis for many prevention and intervention programs. However, developmental researchers have suggested that child behavior also affects parenting (Bell & Chapman, 1986). For example, Stice and Barrera (1995) found that low levels of parental control and support predicted adolescent substance use. However, adolescent substance use, in turn, predicted decreases in parental control and support. Therefore, the link between parenting and adolescent conduct problems and substance use may best be thought of as a system in which parents affect children, and children affect parents.

Stress and Negative Affect Pathway

The stress and negative affect pathway suggests that parental substance abuse increases children's exposure to stressful life events such as parental job instability, familial financial difficulty, parental legal problems, etc. (Chassin et al., 1993; Sher, 1991). These potentially chronic stressors may lead to emotional distress in COAs such as depression and/or anxiety. Substance use may then be used to control this distress.

Research has shown a link between negative affect and substance use in adolescence (see Zucker, 2006, for a review). For example, depression has been found to co-occur with adolescent substance abuse (Deykin, Buka, & Zeena, 1992) and heavy alcohol use (Rohde, Lewinson, & Seely, 1996). Moreover, negative life events have been associated with adolescent substance use (Wills, Vaccaro, & McNamara, 1992). However, not all findings support a negative affect pathway to adolescent substance use problems.

One explanation for the conflicting findings is that not all adolescents with negative affect will be at risk for substance use. Rather, adolescents who suffer from negative affect may only use alcohol and drugs if they also lack good strategies to cope with their negative moods and/or if they believe that alcohol or drugs will help them cope. Therefore, helping COAs to develop coping strategies can potentially serve as an intervention. There may also be gender differences in the extent to which COAs use substance use to cope with stress and negative mood (Chassin et al., 1999).

Substance Use Effects Model

The substance use effects model focuses on individual differences in the pharmacological effects of substances. It is hypothesized that some individuals are more sensitive to the pleasurable effects of alcohol and substance use and/or less sensitive to the adverse effects. For example, Schuckit and Smith (1996) found that male COAs with extremely low levels of negative responses to alcohol were more likely be to diagnosed with alcohol abuse/dependence almost a decade later. It is possible that individuals who do not experience negative effects from drinking may lack the "natural brakes" that limit drinking behavior. Some researchers have also suggested that COAs receive greater stress reduction effects from drinking alcohol (Finn, Zeitouni, & Pihl, 1990). Thus, COAs would be expected to engage in more stress-induced drinking than non-COAs because they derive greater physiological benefit from it. It is important to note, however, that not all studies have supported this finding and more research is needed to draw concrete conclusions concerning COAs' physiological response to alcohol (see Sher, 1991, for a review).

Resilience/Protective Factors

Despite the risks presented by genetic, social, and psychological variables, not all COAs experience negative outcomes. These individuals who, despite high-risk status, manage to defeat the odds, are labeled resilient (Garmezy & Neuchterlein, 1972). Resilience has been extensively studied in a variety of populations, but resilience among COAs remains an area that needs further research (Carle & Chassin, 2004). Sher (1991) hypothesized that factors that can help protect COAs from developing alcoholism include social class, preservation of family rituals, amount of attention received from primary caregivers, family harmony during infancy, parental support, personality, self-awareness, cognitive-intellectual functioning, and coping skills.

COAs show increased risk of alcoholism and other substance use disorders.

Carle and Chassin (2004) examined competence and resilience of COAs and found a significant difference between COAs and non-COAs in competence with regards to rule-abiding and academic behaviors, but no differences in social competence. A small subset of resilient COAs demonstrated at or above average levels of academic and rule-abiding competence. These resilient COAs also had fewer internalizing symptoms and reported increased levels of positive affect than did the general COA population (Carle & Chassin, 2004). This suggests that COAs with average or above average academic and rule-abiding competence as well as low levels of internalizing symptoms and high positive affect may be resilient to the risk associated with having an alcoholic parent.

Another potential source of resilience for COAs may be the recovery of the alcoholic parent. Hussong and colleagues (2005) found support for this idea in a study of social competence in COAs. Results from this study indicated that children of recovered alcoholics demonstrated comparable levels of social competence when compared to children of nonalcoholic parents, suggesting again that not all COAs are at equivalent levels of risk.

Along with recovery of parental alcohol symptoms, previous research has also demonstrated the importance of a number of familial factors in buffering the risk associated with parental alcoholism. For example, parental social support, consistency of parental discipline, family harmony, and stability of family rituals have all been shown to protect COAs from the development of alcohol and drug use and abuse (King & Chassin, 2004; Marshal & Chassin, 2000; Stice, Barrera, & Chassin, 1993).

Although there is evidence to suggest that family factors play a protective role in children's risk for substance use and substance use disorders, there is evidence to suggest that this protection may not be equal for all children (Luthar, Cicchetti, & Becker, 2000). In other words, the protective family factor may reduce the negative effect of parental alcoholism for some children, but may lose its effectiveness at the highest levels of risk. For example, King and Chassin (2004) found that parental support reduced the negative effect of family alcoholism for children with low and average levels of impulsivity and sensation seeking, but not for children with high levels of impulsivity and sensation seeking. In other words, parental support was protective for most children, but not for those with the highest levels of risk. Similarly, Zhou, King, and Chassin (2006) found that the protective effect of family harmony was lost for those children with high levels of family alcoholism. Together these studies provide evidence that consistent and supportive parenting and family harmony are protective for many children of alcoholics, but those children at especially high risk may not benefit from these familial protective factors.

Family relationships, though clearly an important aspect of resilience in COAs, are not the only relationships that appear to contribute to positive outcomes in children of alcoholics. There is also evidence to suggest that, for older children, peer relationships may be as influential as family relationships on adolescents' decision to use substances (Mayes & Suchman, 2006). Therefore, peer relationships may also provide protection against the risk associated with having an alcoholic parent. For example, Ohannessian and Hesselbrock (1993) found that COAs with high levels of social support from friends drank at levels similar to non-COAs, indicating that friendships may also work to reduce the negative effects of parent alcoholism.

Conclusion

Although much work remains to be done in understanding both risk and resilience among COAs, the work that has been done provides important implications for preventive interventions. For example, family factors appear to protect many COAs from negative outcomes. This knowledge supports the need for family-based preventive interventions, which seek to improve both parenting practices and family relationships among families of alcoholics. As research in this area continues to uncover the complex interplay of both the genetic and environmental factors that contribute to COA risk and resilience, prevention researchers will be afforded the opportunity to design and implement interventions to assist this prevalent and heterogeneous population of children.

References

Atyaclar, S., Tarter, R.E., Kirisci, L., & Lu, S. (1999). Association between hyperactivity and executive cognitive functioning in childhood and substance use in childhood and substance use in early adolescence. *Journal of the American Academy of Child and Adolescent Psychiatry, 38,* 172–178.

Bell, R.Q., & Chapman, M. (1986). Child effects in studies using experimental or brief longitudinal approaches to socialization. *Developmental Psychology, 22,* 595–603.

Bertrand, J., Floyd, R.L., Weber, M.K., O'Connor, M., Riley, E.P., Johnson, K.A., Cohen, D.E., National Task Force on FAS/FAE.

(2004). *Fetal Alcohol Syndrome: Guidelines for Referral and Diagnosis.* Atlanta, GA: Centers for Disease Control and Prevention. Available online at http://www.cdc.gov/ncbddd/fas/documents/FAS_guidelines_accessible.pdf

Brody, G.H., Ge, X., Conger, R., Gibbons, F.X., Murry, V.M., Gerrard, M., & Simons, R.L. (2001). The influence of neighborhood disadvantage, collective socialization, and parenting on African American children's affiliation with deviant peers. *Child Development, 72*(4), 1,231–1,246.

Carbonneau, R., Tremblay, R.E., Vitaro, F., Dobkin, P.L., Saucier, J.F., & Pihl, R.O. (1998). Paternal alcoholism, paternal absence, and the development of problem behaviors in boys from age 6 to 12 years. *Journal of Studies on Alcohol, 59,* 387–398.

Carle, A.C., & Chassin, L. (2004) Resilience in a community sample of children of alcoholics: Its prevalence and relation to internalizing symptomatology and positive affect. *Applied Developmental Psychology, 25,* 577–595.

Caspi, A., Moffitt, T., Newman, D., & Silva, P. (1996). Behavioral observations at age 3 years predict adult psychiatric disorders. *Archives of General Psychiatry, 53,* 1,033–1,039.

Chassin, L., Curran, P., Hussong, A., & Colder, C. (1996). The relation of parent alcoholism to adolescent substance use: A longitudinal follow-up study. *Journal of Abnormal Psychology, 105,* 70–80.

Chassin, L., Pillow, D., Curran, P., Molina, B., & Barrera, M. (1993). The relation between parent alcoholism and adolescent substance use: A test of three mediating mechanisms. *Journal of Abnormal Psychology, 102,* 1–17.

Chassin, L., Pitts, S.C., DeLucia, C., & Todd, M. (1999). A longitudinal study of children of alcoholics: Predicting young adult substance use disorders, anxiety, and depression. *Journal of Abnormal Psychology, 108,* 106–118.

Curran, P.J., & Chassin, L. (1996). Longitudinal study of parenting as a protective factor for children of alcoholics. *Journal of Studies on Alcohol, 57,* 305–313.

Deykin, E.Y., Buka, S.L., & Zeena, T.H. (1992). Depressive illness among chemically dependent adolescents. *American Journal of Psychiatry, 149,* 1,341–1,347.

Dishion, T.J., Capaldi, D., Spracklen, K.M., & Li, F. (1995). Peer ecology of male adolescent drug use. *Development and Psychopathology. Special Issue: Developmental Processes in Peer Relations and Psychopathology, 7*(4), 803–824.

Finn, P., Zeitouni, N., & Pihl, R.O. (1990). Effects of alcohol on psychophysiological hyperreactivity to nonaversive and aversive stimuli in men at high risk for alcoholism. *Journal of Abnormal Psychology, 99,* 79–85.

Garmezy, N., & Neuchterlein, K. (1972). Invulnerable children: The fact and fiction of competence and disadvantage. *American Journal of Orthopsychiatry, 42,* 328–329.

Gerra, G., Angioni, L., Zaimovic, A., Moi, G., Bussandri, M., Bertacca, S., Santoro, G., Gardini, S., Caccavari, R., & Nicoli, M.A. (2004). Substance use among high-school students: Relationships with temperament, personality traits, and personal care perception. *Substance Use & Misuse, 39,* 345–367.

Grant, B.F. (2000). Estimates of U.S. children exposed to alcohol use and dependence in the family. *American Journal of Public Health, 90,* 112–115.

Hussong, A.M., Zucker, R.A., Wong, M.M., Fitzgerald, H.E., & Puttler, L.I. (2005). Social competence in children on alcoholic parents over time. *Developmental Psychology, 41,* 747–759.

King, K.M., & Chassin, L. (2004). Mediating and moderated effects of adolescent behavioral under control and parenting in the prediction of drug use disorders in emerging adulthood. *Psychology of Addictive Behaviors, 18,* 239–249.

Luthar, S.S., Cicchetti D., & Becker, B. (2000). The construct of resilience: A critical evaluation and guidelines for future work. *Child Development, 71*(3), 543–562.

Marshal, M.P., & Chassin, L. (2000). Peer influence on adolescent alcohol use: The moderating role of parental support and discipline. *Applied Developmental Science, 4,* 80–88.

Mayes, L.C., & Suchman, N.E. (2006). Developmental pathways to substance use. In D. Cicchetti & D.J. Cohen (Eds.), *Developmental Psychopathology: Vol. 3. Risk, Disorder, and Adaptation* (2nd ed., pp. 599–619). New Jersey: John Wiley & Sons.

McGue, M., Elkins, I., Iacono, W.G. (2000). Genetic and environmental influences on adolescent substance use and abuse. *American Journal of Medical Genetics, 96,* 671–677.

Molina, B.S.G., Bukstein, O.G., & Lynch, K.G. (2002). Attention-deficit/hyperactivity disorder and conduct disorder symptomatology in adolescents with alcohol use disorder. *Psychology of Addictive Behaviors, 16,* 161–164.

National Institute on Alcohol Abuse and Alcoholism. (2006). NIAAA 2001–2002 NESARC [Data File]. Accessed August 1, 2006. from http://niaaa.census.gov/index.html.

Nigg, J.T., Glass, J.M., Wong, M.M., Poon, E., Jester, J.M., Fitzgerald, H.E., Puttler, L.I., Adams, K.A., & Zucker, R.A., (2004). Neuropsychological executive functioning in children at elevated risk for alcoholism: Findings in early adolescence. *Journal of Abnormal Psychology, 113,* 302–314.

Ohannessian, C.M., & Hesselbrock, V.M. (1993). The influence of perceived social support on the relationship between family history of alcoholism and drinking behaviors. *Addiction, 88,* 1,651–1,658.

Rohde, P., Lewinson, P.M., & Seeley, J.R. (1996). Psychiatric comorbidity with problematic alcohol use in high school students. *Journal of the American Academy of Child and Adolescent Psychiatry, 35,* 101–109.

Schuckit, M.A. (2000). Genetics of the risk for alcoholism. *The American Journal on Addictions 9,* 103–112.

Schuckit, M.A., & Smith, T.L. (1996). An 8-year follow-up of 450 sons of alcoholic and control subjects. *Archives of General Psychiatry, 53*(3), 202–210.

Sher, K.J. (1991). *Children of Alcoholics: A Critical Appraisal of Theory and Research.* Chicago: University of Chicago Press.

Stice, E., & Barrera, M. (1995). A longitudinal examination of the reciprocal relations between perceived parenting and adolescents' substance use and externalizing behaviors. *Developmental Psychology, 31*(2), 322–334.

Stice, E., Barrera, M., & Chassin, L. (1993). Relation of parental support and control to adolescents' externalizing symptomatology and substance use: A longitudinal examination of curvilinear effects. *Journal of Abnormal Child Psychology, 21,* 609–629.

West, M.O., & Prinz, R.J. (1987). Parental alcoholism and childhood psychopathology. *Psychological Bulletin, 102*(2), 204–218.

Wills, T.A., McNamara, G., Vaccaro, D., & Hirky, A.E. (1996). Escalated substance use: A longitudinal grouping analysis from early to middle adolescence. *Journal of Abnormal Psychology, 105,* 166–180.

Wills, T.A., Vaccaro, D., & McNamara, G. (1992). The role of life events, family support, and competence in adolescent substance use: A test of vulnerability and protective factors. *American Journal of Community Psychology, 20,* 349–374.

Wills, T.A., Windle, M., & Cleary, S.D. (1998). Temperament and novelty seeking in adolescent substance use: Convergence of dimensions of temperament with constructs from Cloninger's theory. *Journal of Personality and Social Psychology, 74*(2), 387–406.

Zhou, Q., King, K.M., & Chassin, L. (2006). The roles of familial alcoholism and adolescent family harmony in young adults' substance dependence disorders: mediated and moderated relations. *Journal of Abnormal Psychology, 115,* 320–331.

Zucker, R.A. (2006). Alcohol use and the alcohol use disorders: A developmental-biopsychosocial systems formulation covering the life course. In D. Cicchetti & D.J. Cohen (Eds.), *Developmental Psychopathology: Vol 3. Risk, Disorder, and Adaptation* (2nd ed., pp. 620–656). New Jersey: John Wiley & Sons.

CARA E. RICE, MPH, is Project Director of the Adult and Family Development Project at Arizona State University. **DANIELLE DANDREAUX,** MS, is a doctoral student in applied developmental psychology at the University of New Orleans and is currently employed by the Department of Psychology at Arizona State University. **ELIZABETH D. HANDLEY,** MA, is a doctoral student in clinical psychology at Arizona State University. Her research and clinical training are focused on at-risk children and families. **LAURIE CHASSIN,** PhD, is Professor of Psychology at Arizona State University. Her research focuses on longitudinal, multigenerational studies of risk for substance use disorders and intergenerational transmission of that risk.

Preparation of this article was supported by grant AA16213 from the National Institute of Alcohol Abuse and Alcoholism to Laurie Chassin.

Within-Family Differences in Parent–Child Relations across the Life Course

J. JILL SUITOR ET AL.

D espite a powerful social norm that parents should treat offspring equally, beginning in early childhood and continuing through adulthood, parents often differentiate among their children in such domains as closeness, support, and control. We review research on how parent–child relationships differ within families, focusing on issues of parental favoritism and differential treatment of children. We begin by examining within-family differences in childhood and adolescence and then explore differentiation by older parents among adult children. Overall, we find considerable similarities across the life course in the prevalence, predictors, and consequences of parents' differentiation among their offspring.

Literature and history abound with stories of parental favoritism, beginning with the Biblical story of Israel favoring his lastborn son Joseph and continuing to Pat Conroy's novel *Beach Music*. In the early 20th century, both Sigmund Freud, who was his mother's favorite, and Alfred Adler, who was not, noted the potential consequences of such favoritism for children's development. Despite the attention that these two eminent psychoanalysts gave to this issue, scholars showed little interest in the topic until the early 1980s. In fact, according to Harris and Howard (1983), who published one of the earliest pieces on differential treatment, neither *Psychological Abstracts* nor the *Psychoanalytic Study of the Child* contained any references to parental favoritism in the preceding 20 years.

Since that time, within-family differentiation among offspring has gained widespread attention across a range of disciplines including evolutionary biology, psychology, sociology, and economics. Although much of this work has emphasized the ways in which birth order affects characteristics such as intelligence, personality, and social attitudes, an increasing focus has been on within-family differences in parent–child relationships. In this article, we explore the patterns and consequences of such differentiation in parents' relationships with their offspring across the life course, drawing upon a review of more than 120 articles and books.

We examined literature on both "parental favoritism" and "parental differential treatment" (PDT), given that the study of within-family differences encompasses these closely related areas of research. The primary distinction between these two phenomena is that favoritism generally refers to parents' differential affect and preferences among their children, whereas PDT typically describes ways in which parents differentiate among their children behaviorally, such as displays of affection, discipline, and the distribution of other interpersonal and instrumental resources. The literature on the early stages of the life course has included studies of both favoritism and PDT, whereas scholarship on within-family differences after children have entered adulthood has focused primarily on favoritism.

Within-Family Differences in Childhood and Adolescence

Parents are commonly exhorted not to favor some of their children over others, yet beginning in early childhood they often differentiate in terms of closeness, support, and control. Although the exact figures vary widely across studies, reports suggest that, in one third to two thirds of families, parents favor one or more of their children in at least one domain (Shebloski, Conger, & Widaman, 2005; Volling & Elins, 1998).

There is obviously considerable variation in reporting of PDT. One of the most important sources of this variation can be attributed to the diversity of methodologies. For example, studies of families with preschoolers often include some combination of in-person interviews with the parents, videotaping of interactions between family members, and parents' completion of written questionnaires. In studies in which offspring are of school age or older, interviews are frequently conducted with the children.

Researchers have also examined whether reports of parental differentiation vary by the structural position of the family member responding. For instance, children tend to report favoritism more frequently than do their parents (Feinberg, Neiderhiser, Howe, & Hetherington, 2000), consistent with Bengtson's (Bengtson & Kuypers, 1971) argument that parents have a greater stake than children in portraying their intergenerational relations as harmonious. Although there is often overlap between parents' and children's perceptions, there is also substantial incongruence, highlighting the importance of collecting data from multiple family members. For example, in one recent investigation (Kowal, Krull, & Kramer, 2006), only about 60% of parents' and children's reports agreed about whether parents differentiated regarding affection.

Even across studies using subjects in the same structural position in the family and the same mode of data collection (e.g., interview), the measurement of PDT varies considerably. Few studies ask parents directly to differentiate among their children, instead typically asking the same questions about each child and using those data to create difference scores. No single measure of parents' reports of PDT has become standard, although a large number of investigations have used the Parent–Child Relationship Survey (Hetherington & Clingempeel, 1992). When studying children's perceptions of PDT, scholars have increasingly used the Sibling Inventory of Differential Experience (Daniels & Plomin, 1985), which asks subjects to compare their experiences directly to those of one of their siblings.

Explaining Differentiation: The Role of Family and Individual Characteristics

The literature provides a rich body of findings regarding which children are most often favored, the forms that favoritism takes, and the conditions under which particular patterns occur. We provide an overview of those findings that are the most uniform across studies.

One factor that predicts families in which parents differentiate is high levels of stress, particularly in the lives of parents. For example, favoritism is more common when parents experience marital problems and when children have serious health problems (Singer & Weinstein, 2000).

A second set of factors associated with PDT involves family structure and composition. Birth order is one of the structural factors that has received substantial attention in the study of PDT. The preponderance of evidence regarding comparisons of first- and last-borns suggests that youngest children are advantaged in terms of parental affection (Tucker, McHale, & Crouter, 2003), supporting theories that last-borns develop more sensitive social skills in an attempt to create a special position in families (Sulloway, 1996). However, the findings of other first-versus last-born comparisons are less consistent. In contrast, the literature is quite uniform regarding middle children, who are much less likely to be favored than are their eldest and youngest siblings across multiple domains (Hertwig, Davis, & Sulloway, 2002). Another important family-composition factor is the presence of both biological and nonbiological children, particularly in blended families (O'Conner, Dunn, Jenkins, & Rasbash, 2006). Parents in such families, especially mothers, tend to favor their biological children.

Finally, studies show that parents' differential responses reflect variations in the children's behaviors and personalities. In particular, mothers and fathers have been found to direct more control and discipline toward children whose behaviors are disruptive or aggressive, and express more warmth toward children who show greater positive affect toward their parents (Tucker et al., 2003). Perhaps because of the tendency for boys to display more aggression and for girls to show more warmth, studies have often found greater differential treatment in families with mixed offspring than in families with single-gender offspring (O'Conner et al., 2006; McHale, Updegraff, Tucker, & Crouter, 2000), particularly regarding affection and time spent with children. In some studies, this gender difference has been reduced by controlling for children's aggression and affection (Tucker et al., 2003).

Consequences of Within-Family Differentiation in Childhood and Adolescence

From the review we have presented, it is clear that parents often favor one or more of their children in childhood and adolescence—but does such differentiation have any consequences? Research has shown that least-favored children experience lower levels of self-esteem, self-worth, and sense of social responsibility, and higher levels of aggression, depression, and externalizing behaviors (Feinberg et al., 2000; Singer & Weinstein, 2000).

The evidence for effects of being most favored is less clear than for the effects of being unfavored. Although being favored has been shown to produce positive outcomes under particular sets of circumstances (McHale, Crouter, McGuire, & Updegraff, 1995; McHale et al., 2000), in most cases, it appears that regardless of which child is favored, PDT is problematic for the well-being of all offspring in the family (Singer & Weinstein, 2000). Findings regarding the effects of PDT on the quality of siblings' relationships are among the most consistent in this body of research. With few exceptions, the literature indicates that siblings express less warmth and greater hostility toward one another when parents show favoritism (McHale et al., 1995).

One important line of inquiry involves the role of children's perceptions of fairness. The evidence suggests that perceptions of fairness moderate the relationship between PDT and both well-being and sibling relations. In some cases, perceptions of fairness have positive consequences. For example, children express less hostility toward siblings who receive more attention if they believe the other children are needier. However, perceptions of fairness can have detrimental consequences as well, such as when these perceptions lead unfavored children to feel that they deserve less affection from their parents than do their siblings (McHale et al., 2000).

It might be tempting to interpret these findings as evidence that difficult children increase parents' differentiation and sibling tensions, rather than differentiation affecting children's outcomes. Although it is clear that children's behaviors and temperaments affect these patterns (Tucker et al., 2003), our review leads us to believe that offspring characteristics alone cannot adequately account for the association between PDT and children's outcomes. First, as noted above, the literature demonstrates that PDT, regardless of the form it takes, typically increases hostility among siblings (McHale et al., 1995). Second, the findings of longitudinal investigations suggest that, over time, being unfavored by parents produces behavior problems in children (Richmond, Stocker, & Rienks, 2005).

Within-Family Differences in Adulthood

There is a vast literature on the quality of relationships between parents and their adult children; however, with few exceptions, this work is based on studies using between-family designs. In this review, we restrict our discussion to findings from studies that have used within-family designs and are therefore comparable to investigations of PDT in earlier life-course stages. Unlike research on children and adolescents, there are fewer than 20 articles on within-family differences in adult child–parent relations, about half of which are based upon only one study; thus, it is impossible to answer questions about PDT in adulthood as fully as those about earlier stages of the life course.

Do Parents Continue to Differentiate among Adult Children?

Studies of the middle and later stages of the life course have shown that parents are more likely to differentiate among their offspring in adulthood than in childhood. For example, in a recent study of 556 families, more than three quarters of mothers named a particular child whom they would choose as a confidant, nearly three quarters named a child whom they would prefer provide them assistance when ill or disabled, and nearly two thirds named a child to whom they were most emotionally close (Suitor & Pillemer, 2007). Fathers' reports closely mirrored those of the mothers. The majority of mothers also differentiated among their adult children regarding providing emotional and instrumental support (Suitor, Pillemer, & Sechrist, 2006). Studies using smaller and less representative samples (Aldous, Klaus, & Klein, 1985) have shown similar patterns. Such high levels of favoritism are particularly striking given that, in these studies, parents were asked directly to differentiate among their children.

Reports from offspring reveal that adult children often believe that their parents favor some children (Bedford, 1992; Suitor, Sechrist, Steinhour, & Pillemer, 2006). Suitor and colleagues found that 66% of children accurately reported that their mothers differentiated regarding closeness, but only 44% were correct about *which* offspring were favored (Suitor et al., 2006); most children reported themselves as the favorite.

Explaining Differentiation in Adulthood

Intergenerational relationships change as children move into adulthood, bringing with them the history from childhood onto which is superimposed a new set of expectations. Despite this different context, the factors that best explain within-family differences in parent–adult-child relations are related, conceptually, to those from earlier stages of the life course. These are (a) similarity between parents and children, (b) developmental histories, (c) equity and exchange, and (d) family structure and composition. Specifically, parents are more likely to favor daughters, children who share their values, children who have achieved

normative adult statuses and avoided deviant behaviors, children who have provided parents with support, and children who are more geographically proximate (Aldous et al., 1985; Suitor et al., 2006). Mothers are also closest to last-borns and least close to middle-borns (Suitor & Pillemer, 2007). Further, these patterns are similar for Blacks and Whites. Thus, these patterns mirror those in childhood in terms of normative societal and parental expectations, positive affect, gender, and birth order.

Consequences of Within-Family Differentiation in Adulthood

There has been less attention to the effects of PDT in adulthood than to its effects in childhood. However, the few studies that have examined this issue reveal patterns similar to those of earlier stages of the life course. For example, adults who perceive that they have been unfavored in childhood or adulthood have less close relations with their parents (Bedford, 1992; Boll, Ferring, & Filipp, 2003). Being slightly favored improves adult children's relations with their parents; however, being highly favored also reduces relationship quality.

Consistent with earlier stages, sibling relations are most positive when adult children are treated equally (Boll et al., 2003). Also similar to studies in childhood, perceptions of fairness moderate the relationship between PDT and relations with parents and siblings (Boll et al., 2003). Whether PDT in adulthood has consequences for well-being remains to be investigated.

Future Directions

There is clear evidence that many parents differentiate among their offspring from the earliest stages of childhood through adulthood. Further, several factors explain PDT across the life course, such as children's behaviors, birth order, and gender. Because data do not yet exist to examine whether consistency in differentiation occurs within the same families across several decades, we can only speculate about this possibility. Some patterns we might expect would change over time; for example, comparisons across studies of families with preschoolers, adolescents, and adult children suggest that parents may differentiate more as their children mature. However, several of the factors that play important roles in PDT remain stable within families throughout the life course, perhaps leading some families to be more prone to continued favoritism. Thus, we would expect continued favoritism in families with more than two children, with children of both genders, and with children who engage in deviant behaviors in both adolescence and adulthood.

Another important research question that has yet to be answered is how PDT is moderated by socioeconomic status and race. Only a handful of investigations at any point in the life course have included minorities, and studies of the early life course have relied almost exclusively on middle-class families.

Finally, future research may show that PDT and parental favoritism have long-term effects on outcomes affecting both parents and adult children. An important dynamic in parent–child relations in later life revolves around both the anticipation of and actual provision of care for older parents. Further, most parents have strong preferences regarding which children will provide care to them in the later years (Suitor & Pillemer, 2007). It is possible that such expectations will affect both parents' and children's well being. For example, it is possible that greater caregiver stress and burden may result if circumstances require a nonpreferred child to become the primary caregiver. Thus the match between parental preference for caregiving and actual outcomes for both parties is likely to be a fruitful topic for research.

In sum, we know a great deal about the existence and predictors of parental favoritism across the life course and about the consequences of these patterns in childhood. We hope that future research will help us to better understand the ways in which these patterns change across time, are moderated by social factors, and have effects on children's and parents' well-being across the life course.

Recommended Reading

Downey, D.B. (1995). When bigger is not better: Family size, parental resources, and children's educational performance. *American Sociological Review, 60,* 746–761. A theoretically driven study demonstrating the role of family composition on children's outcomes.

Shanahan, L., McHale, S.M., Crouter, A.C., & Osgood, D.W. (2007). Warmth with mothers and fathers from middle childhood to late adolescence: Within- and between-families comparisons. *Developmental Psychology, 43,* 551–563. A representative study that provides further detail regarding changes in parental differential treatment from childhood through adolescence.

Steelman, L.C., Powell, B., Werum, R. & Carter, S. (2002). Reconsidering the effect of sibling configuration: Recent advances and challenges. *Annual Review of Sociology, 28,* 243–269. A clearly-written comprehensive review of the consequences of sibling composition.

Sulloway, F.J. (1996). (See References). A highly accessible overview of history, theory, and research on birth order.

References

Aldous, J., Klaus, E., & Klein, D.M. (1985). The understanding heart: Aging parents and their favorite children. *Child Development, 56,* 303–316.

Bedford, V.H. (1992). Memories of parental favoritism and the quality of parent–child ties in adulthood. *Journal of Gerontology: Social Sciences, 47,* S149–S155.

Bengtson, V.L., & Kuypers, J.A. (1971). Generational differences and the developmental stake. *Aging and Human Development, 2,* 249–260.

Boll, T., Ferring, D., & Filipp, S.H. (2003). Perceived parental differential treatment in middle adulthood: Curvilinear relations with individuals' experienced relationship quality to sibling and parents. *Journal of Family Psychology, 17,* 472–487.

Daniels, D., & Plomin, R. (1985). Differential experience of siblings in the same family. *Developmental Psychology, 21,* 747–760.

Feinberg, M.E., Neiderhiser, J.M., Howe, G., & Hetherington, E.M. (2000). Adolescent, parent, and observer perceptions of parenting: Genetic and environmental influences on shared and distinct perceptions. *Child Development, 72,* 1266–1284.

Harris, I.D., & Howard, K.I. (1983). Correlates of perceived parental favoritism. *Journal of Genetic Psychology, 1461,* 45–56.

Hertwig, R., Davis, J.N., & Sulloway, F.J. (2002). Parental investment: How an equity motive can produce inequality. *Psychological Bulletin, 128,* 728–745.

Hetherington, E.M., & Clingempeel, W.G. (1992). Coping with marital transitions: A family systems perspective. *Monographs of the Society for Research in Child Development, 57*(2–3, Serial No. 227).

Kowal, A.K., Krull, J.L., & Kramer, L. (2006). Shared understanding of parental differential treatment in families. *Social Development, 15,* 277–295.

McHale, S.M., Crouter, A.C., McGuire, S.A., & Updegraff, K.A. (1995). Congruence between mothers' and fathers' differential treatment of siblings: Links with family relations and children's well-being. *Child Development, 66,* 116–128.

McHale, S.M., Updegraff, K.A., Tucker, C.J., & Crouter, A.C. (2000). When does parents' differential treatment have negative implications for siblings? *Social Development, 9,* 149–172.

O'Conner, T.G., Dunn, J., Jenkins, J.M., & Rasbash, J. (2006). Predictors of between-family and within-family variation in parent-child relationships. *Journal of Child Psychology and Psychiatry, 47,* 498–510.

Richmond, M.K., Stocker, C.M., & Rienks, S.L. (2005). Longitudinal associations between sibling relationship quality, parental differential treatment, and children's adjustment. *Journal of Family Psychology, 19,* 550–559.

Shebloski, B., Conger, K.J., & Widaman, K.F. (2005). Reciprocal links among differential parenting, perceived partiality, and self-worth: A three-wave longitudinal study. *Journal of Family Psychology, 19,* 633–642.

Singer, A.T., & Weinstein, R. (2000). Differential parental treatment predicts achievements and self-perceptions in two cultural contexts. *Journal of Family Psychology, 14,* 491–509.

Suitor, J.J., & Pillemer, K. (2007). Mothers' favoritism in later life: The role of children's birth order. *Research on Aging, 29,* 32–55.

Suitor, J.J., Pillemer, K., & Sechrist, J. (2006). Within-family differences in mothers' support to adult children. *Journal of Gerontology: Social Science, 61,* S10–S17.

Suitor, J.J., Sechrist, J., Steinhour, M., & Pillemer, K. (2006). 'I'm sure she chose me!' Consistency in intergenerational reports of mothers' favoritism in later-life families. *Family Relations, 55,* 526–538.

Sulloway, F.J. 1996. *Born To Rebel.* New York: Pantheon Books.

Tucker, C.J., McHale, S.M., & Crouter, A.C. (2003). Dimensions of mothers' and fathers' differential treatment of siblings: Links with adolescents' sex-typed personal qualities. *Family Relations, 52,* 82–89.

Volling, B.L., & Elins, J.L. (1998). Family relationships and children's emotional adjustment as correlates of maternal and paternal differential treatment: A replication with toddler and preschool siblings. *Child Development, 69,* 1640–1656.

Address correspondence to **J. JILL SUITOR,** Department of Sociology and Anthropology, Purdue University, 700 Stone Hall, Purdue University, West Lafayette, IN 47907; e-mail: jsuitor@purdue.edu.

Adoption Is a Successful Natural Intervention Enhancing Adopted Children's IQ and School Performance

Is the cognitive development of adopted children different from that of (a) children who have remained in institutional care or in their birth families or (b) their current (environmental) nonadopted siblings or peers? We attempt to answer these questions on the basis of a meta-analysis of 62 studies including 17,767 adopted children. Compared to their nonadopted siblings or peers who stayed behind, adopted children scored substantially higher on IQ tests and they performed much better at school. Compared to their current nonadopted environmental peers or siblings, adopted children showed similar IQ scores but their school performance and language abilities lagged somewhat behind. Most importantly, we found a twofold increase in special-education referrals in adopted children compared to their nonadopted peers. Taken together, the findings document the positive impact of adoption on children's cognitive development and adopted children's remarkably normal cognitive competence but somewhat delayed school performance.

MARINUS H. VAN IJZENDOORN AND FEMMIE JUFFER

More than 30 years ago, Dennis (1973) conducted a pioneering study to answer the question: Does the cognitive development of adopted children lag behind that of their nonadopted peers? He studied children who were abandoned immediately after birth and who were raised in the Creche, an orphanage in Lebanon founded by French nuns. The Creche was a traditional institutional setting with minimal individual care and interaction. The babies were put on a potty in long rows to empty their bowels, and they slept in cribs in long rows in a large room. Child care in the Creche satisfied hygienic requirements but it was impersonal. Dennis found 136 former children of the Creche, a large number of whom (85) were adopted by families around their third birthday.

Around their 11th birthday, all 136 former Creche children completed an IQ test. The results were remarkable. The 85 adopted children scored on average much higher than the orphans who stayed behind. The average IQ of adopted children was just within the range of normally developing children, with an average IQ of about 85. The IQ of the nonadopted orphans was about 65, well within the range of mentally retarded children. Large-scale and intensive enrichment programs such as Head Start have shown considerably smaller effects on children's cognitive development than this "natural intervention experiment."

Protection by Adoption

Only a few studies such as Dennis's (1973) pioneering Creche investigation compared adoptees' IQ with the IQ of their non-adopted birth siblings or nonadopted peers from the same institution, but the outcomes were similar (Schiff et al., 1978; Colombo, de la Parra, & Lopez, 1992). Colombo et al. (1992) studied 35 school-aged children (5–21 years) with a history of early malnutrition. Three groups were compared: The first group consisted of children who were raised after recovery by adoptive families, the second group of children remained in institutional care, and the third group were children restored to their birth families. Adopted children had IQs in the normal range, and they outperformed the other groups. The authors concluded that early malnutrition may not cause irreversible damage for children but instead can be compensated for by environmental improvement (i.e., adoption into a stable and enriched environment).

The influence of the adoption experience may become larger when the change of environment becomes more drastic. Scarr and Weinberg (1976) studied IQ and school achievement of 130 black children adopted before the age of 12 months by advantaged white families. The adoptees from educationally average birth families scored above the average level of IQ and school achievement of the white population. The high IQ scores of the black adoptees suggested that IQ is malleable under rearing conditions that prepare children for high performance on achievement tests and in school and that deviate drastically from the preadoption social backgrounds.

However, age at adoption and previous adverse experiences or deprivation may make a substantial difference for the influence of the adoption experience. O'Connor et al. (2000) studied Romanian adopted children in the United Kingdom who had experienced early malnutrition and circumstances of severe deprivation, particularly in institutional care. They found that children adopted at older ages and institutionalized children had lower IQ scores than younger and noninstitutionalized adopted children (see also Rutter et al., 1998). This may indicate that the positive outcomes of adoption may be reduced by severe negative experiences before adoptive placement.

Meta-Analytic Findings

Is the cognitive development of adopted children more advanced compared to that of children who remained in institutional care or in the birth family? Do adopted children show less advanced cognitive development compared with their current environmental nonadopted siblings or peers (Van IJzendoorn, Juffer, & Klein Poelhuis, 2005)?

Our first hypothesis concerned the potential cognitive advantages of adoption over staying behind. With regard to IQ scores, the adopted children outperformed their siblings or peers left behind (a large effect size, $d = -1.17$, in 6 studies including 253 participants).[1] In terms of school achievement, the adopted children also outperformed their left-behind siblings and peers (a substantial effect size, $d = -0.55$, in 3 studies including 523 participants). Although the number of pertinent studies is small, they nevertheless suggest that adopted children are able to profit substantially from the positive change of environment offered by adoption and subsequent upbringing in educationally more stimulating adoptive families (see Figure 1).

Our second hypothesis concerned the potential cognitive delays of adopted children compared with their current, environmental siblings or peers. Overall, we found that studies reported a negligible difference in the IQ of adopted children and their nonadopted environmental siblings or peers (a nonsignificant $d = 0.13$, in 42 studies with 6,411 participants). Comparing their school achievement, we documented that the adopted children did somewhat less well in school, but the effect size was rather small ($d = 0.19$, in 52 studies, with 78,662 participants). Their language abilities also showed a significant delay compared with their environmental siblings or peers, but again the effect size was small ($d = 0.09$, significant across 14 studies due to the large number of participants: 15,418).

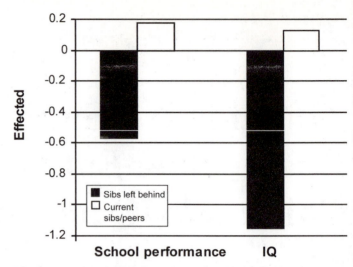

Figure 1 School performance and IQ of adopted children compared with siblings and peers left behind and with current peers and siblings. Larger *ds* mean larger differences between adopted and nonadopted children ($d = 0.20$ points to small differences; $d = 0.50$, to medium sized differences; and $d = 0.80$, to large differences). The negative *ds* mean that the adopted-away children showed better school performance and higher IQ scores than did their nonadopted siblings who stayed behind. The positive *ds* mean that the adopted children scored lower than their current siblings and peers.

The largest delay was found in a set of eight studies comparing the learning problems of adopted children with their environmental peers ($d = 0.55$, in 8 studies with 13,291 participants; see Figure 2). The percentage of adopted children struggling with learning problems is significantly larger than that of nonadopted children. We found that, in each country studied, adopted children were referred to special education twice as often as nonadopted children were. However, it should be noted that the percentage of children with learning problems that need treatment or referral to special education is generally rather small—both in the adopted group (12.8%) and in the general population (5.5%)—and that this finding is based on a small number of studies. Moreover, adoptive parents may be more readily inclined to perceive learning problems, as they are often more aware of available services and more alert to potential problems than nonadoptive parents are (Warren, 1992). Adoptive parents may be more likely to seek treatment or special education for their child.

Taken together, this series of meta-analyses document the potential positive impact of the adoption experience on the adopted children's cognitive development compared to that of the children left behind. The studies also show the nearly normal cognitive competence and only somewhat delayed school performance of adopted children. Because the number of pertinent studies addressing these issues is large, only through meta-analyses are we able to find commonalities (Van

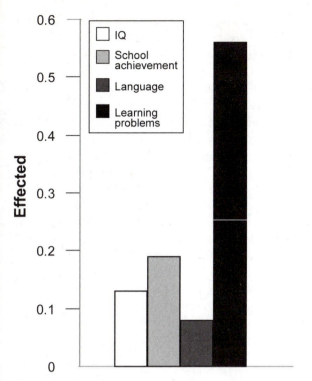

Figure 2 Adopted children compared with nonadopted siblings and peers on IQ, school achievement, language, and learning problems. Larger *ds* mean larger differences between adopted and nonadopted children.

IJzendoorn et al., 2005). It should be noted, however, that the studies included in the meta-analyses were not always of high quality, and that most studies did not present sufficiently detailed data on preadoption status of their participants, thus making a balanced comparison difficult. Although meta-analyses frequently are conducted on correlational data, their use on randomized experiments may allow for somewhat firmer conclusions about causal effects. Meta-analyses remain powerful in finding explanations for discrepancies between study outcomes, in particular by partitioning the set of studies into smaller subsets on the basis of some core study characteristics such as age at adoption or preadoption background.

Important factors that indeed influence children's cognitive development are the age at which they are adopted and whether or not the adoptees came from abusive and/or neglecting backgrounds. Age at adoption does not seem to matter for adopted children's IQ, but it does matter for their school performance. Children adopted in their first year of life do not show any delays in school performance, whereas children adopted after their first birthday lag behind. Thus, early adoption may be a protective factor, not so much for cognitive competence (IQ) as for cognitive performance. This may occur because the positive effects of the adoptive environment have greater impact during an important period in the children's lives. It may also indicate the importance of

the first attachment relationships (with the adoptive parents) developing around 10 to 14 months after birth. These early attachment relationships may function as protective factors, buffering against the stress of "adoption losses."

Another interpretation is that briefer preadoption time may imply shorter exposure to risk factors such as abuse or neglect. This interpretation converges with the significant effect we found for the impact of preadoption malnutrition, abuse, or neglect on school performance. Adopted children who were exposed to these adversities lagged farther behind in school achievement than did adopted children without such backgrounds, although their IQ scores did not show a corresponding difference. Of course, preadoption abuse or neglect is a major risk factor that appears to leave its marks on children's school performance even after adoption into less deprived social contexts. In fact, it is surprising that we did not find a similar negative effect on IQ, considering the negative effects of these early circumstances on brain growth and development (Chugani et al., 2001). Our findings may be taken as evidence for the impressive plasticity of the human brain after drastic improvement of the child-rearing environment (Miller, 2005).

Cognitive Decalage

The discrepancy between adopted children's positive attainment in terms of IQ and their somewhat delayed school achievement (in children adopted after their first birthday) may indicate an *adoption decalage*—that is, a gap between adopted children's competence and their actual school performance. We found that the adoption decalage was largest for those children who came from extremely deprived backgrounds, because their school achievements lagged farther behind than those of adopted children from less deprived backgrounds, but their IQ was higher than that of their nonadopted comparisons. Adopted children appear to show the same cognitive potentials as their environmental comparisons, as these two groups do not differ in IQ. However, they are not able to catch up completely in school performance. Also, a larger number of adopted children develop learning problems causing them to require referrals to special educational or therapeutic services.

We speculate that the adoption decalage is intensified by the socioemotional demands required by the achievement orientation in a group setting at school. In middle childhood, some adopted children may begin to struggle with the loss of their birth parents (Brodzinsky, Schechter, & Henig, 1992) and the burden of grief may hamper or slow down their progress through school. Unresolved loss is associated with intrusive thoughts and ruminations that limit the ability to focus on the tasks at hand (Main, 1999). An alternative explanation is that, in general, adopted children are able to profit from the favorable circumstances offered by the adoptive family, but that for some children, in particular those who experienced more extreme deprivation or later adoption, catch-up is incomplete. Socioemotional problems may affect school performance in a direct way, for example because behavior problems interfere with school attendance. Genetically determined problems and enduring effects of deprivation may result in concentration problems and cognitive delays, hampering successful progress at school.

Future Directions

In sum, our meta-analyses lead to three theoretically and practically important findings. First, for many adopted children adoption involves a drastic change of environment and this change is an effective intervention that improves their cognitive development. In a cognitively richer and emotionally safer environment, on average adopted children may recover and nearly get back on a normal track. While it is possible that children with higher cognitive skills are more likely to be adopted, it is more plausible that adoption is associated with a remarkable recovery from often extremely adverse preadoption circumstances, which could be considered as evidence for children's resilience. It should be noted, however, that the number of studies comparing adopted children with their siblings or peers who stayed behind is small, and more research is needed to confirm the recovery hypothesis.

Second, adopted children do not completely catch up in school performance with their nonadopted environmental peers. The discrepancy between the adopted children's development in terms of IQ and their school achievement indicates an adoption decalage similar to the socioemotional problems presented by a minority of adopted children (e.g., Bimmel, Juffer, Van IJzendoorn, & Bakermans-Kranenburg, 2003). Although the decalage is generally small, it is a robust finding. The mechanisms behind this remarkable decalage should be investigated, and the specific socioemotional problems affecting adoptees' cognitive performance require careful study (Juffer & Van IJzendoorn, 2005).

Third, in a small set of studies we found that the percentage of adopted children who need special education for their learning problems is about twice as large as the percentage in nonadopted children. This minority of adopted children with learning problems is clinically important because they suffer from these problems and need special treatment. Future studies should examine the reasons for this overrepresentation: Are the learning problems of adoptees really larger, or are parents and teachers more sensitive to the potential problems of adopted children?

Clinical and Practical Implications

The large majority of adopted children, either internationally adopted or placed within the country, are expected to show similar levels of cognitive development as nonadopted children. In contrast to popular beliefs, most adopted children overcome their developmental delays and are able to profit from the educational opportunities offered by their adoptive families and by the schools.

However, a small minority of adopted children, in particular children adopted after their first birthday and children who experienced severe malnutrition or neglect before adoptive placement, are expected to show lower levels of school performance or to struggle with learning problems, resulting in higher rates of referrals to special education or educational services. Adoptive parents may have lower thresholds to seek help for their adopted children, but these referrals may also prevent the emergence of even more serious problems. Teachers, educationalists, mental health practitioners, and parents should acknowledge the special needs of late-adopted children from deprived backgrounds and offer them sufficient remedial support.

We conclude that, in terms of their cognitive development, most adopted children do remarkably well—certainly much better than their siblings or peers who had to stay behind in poor institutions or deprived families. Adoption is a natural intervention with great success.

Note

1. It should be noted that d is the standardized difference between the means of the adopted group versus that of the nonadopted group. An effect size of $d = .50$ means that the groups differ half a standard deviation, according to conventional criteria a substantial effect size; $d = .20$ is considered to be only a weak effect size; $d = .80$ is considered to be large.

References

Bimmel, N., Juffer, F., Van IJzendoorn, M.H., & Bakermans-Kranenburg, M.J. (2003). Problem behavior of internationally adopted adolescents: A review and meta-analysis. *Harvard Review of Psychiatry, 11,* 64–77.

Brodzinsky, D.M., Schechter, M.D., & Henig, R.M. (1992). *Being adopted: The lifelong search for self.* New York: Anchor Books.

Chugani, H.T., Behen, M.E., Muzik, O., Juhász, C., Nagy, F., & Chugani, D.C. (2001). Local brain functional activity following early deprivation: A study of postinstitutionalized Romanian orphans. *NeuroImage, 14,* 1290–1301.

Colombo, M., de la Parra, A., & Lopez, I. (1992). Intellectual and physical outcome of children undernourished in early life is influenced by later environmental conditions. *Developmental Medicine and Child Neurology, 34,* 611–622.

Dennis, W. (1973). *Children of the Creche.* New York: Appleton-Century-Crofts.

Juffer, F., & Van IJzendoorn, M.H. (2005). Behavior problems and mental health referrals of international adoptees: A meta-analytic approach. *JAMA, the Journal of the American Medical Association, 293,* 2501–2515.

Main, M. (1999). Epilogue. Attachment theory: Eighteen points with suggestions for future studies. In J. Cassidy & P.R. Shaver (Eds.), *Handbook of attachment: Theory, research, and clinical applications* (pp. 845–887). New York: Guilford.

Miller, L.C. (2005). *The handbook of international adoption medicine.* Oxford: Oxford University Press.

O'Connor, T.G., Rutter, M., Beckett, C., Keaveney, L., & Kreppner, J.M. & the English and Romanian Adoptees Study Team (2000). The effects of global severe privation on cognitive competence: Extension and longitudinal follow-up. *Child Development, 71,* 376–390.

Rutter, M., Andersen-Wood, L., Beckett, C., Bredenkamp, D., Castle, J., Dunn, J., & the English and Romanian Adoptees Study Team (1998). Developmental catch-up, and deficit, following adoption after severe global early privation. *Journal of Child Psychology and Psychiatry, 39,* 465–476.

Scarr, S., & Weinberg, R.A. (1976). IQ test performance of Black children adopted by White families. *American Psychologist, 31,* 726–739.

Schiff, M., Duyme, M., Dumaret, A., Stewart, J., Tomkiewicz, S., & Feingold, J. (1978). Intellectual status of working-class children adopted early into upper-middle-class families. *Science, 200,* 1503–1504.

Van IJzendoorn, M.H., Juffer, F., & Klein Poelhuis, C.W. (2005). Adoption and cognitive development: A meta-analytic comparison of adopted and non-adopted children's IQ and school performance. *Psychological Bulletin, 131,* 301–316.

Warren, S.B. (1992). Lower threshold for referral for psychiatric treatment for adopted adolescents. *Journal of the American Academy for Child and Adolescent Psychiatry, 31,* 512–527.

Address correspondence to Marinus H. van IJzendoorn, PO Box 9555, NL-2300RB Leiden, The Netherlands, e-mail: vanijzen@fsw.leidenuniv.nl; or to Femmie Juffer, e-mail: juffer@fsw.leidenuniv.nl.

Acknowledgments—We gratefully acknowledge the assistance of Caroline W. Klein Poelhuis. The Adoption Meta-Analysis Project (ADOPTION MAP) is supported by grants from Stichting VSBfonds, Stichting Fonds 1818, Nationaal Fonds Geestelijke Volksgezondheid, and Stichting Kinderpostzegels to F.J. and M.H.vIJ in cooperation with the Adoptie Driehoek Onderzoeks Centrum (ADOC; www.adoptionresearch.nl). Marinus van IJzendoorn is supported by the NWO/SPINOZA Prize of the Netherlands Organization for Scientific Research. Femmie Juffer is supported by Wereldkinderen.

The Case against Breast-Feeding

In certain overachieving circles, breast-feeding is no longer a choice— it's a no-exceptions requirement, the ultimate badge of responsible parenting. Yet the actual health benefits of breast-feeding are surprisingly thin, far thinner than most popular literature indicates. Is breast-feeding right for every family? Or is it this generation's vacuum cleaner— an instrument of misery that mostly just keeps women down?

HANNA ROSIN

One afternoon at the playground last summer, shortly after the birth of my third child, I made the mistake of idly musing about breast-feeding to a group of new mothers I'd just met. This time around, I said, I was considering cutting it off after a month or so. At this remark, the air of insta-friendship we had established cooled into an icy politeness, and the mothers shortly wandered away to chase little Emma or Liam onto the slide. Just to be perverse, over the next few weeks I tried this experiment again several more times. The reaction was always the same: circles were redrawn such that I ended up in the class of mom who, in a pinch, might feed her baby mashed-up Chicken McNuggets.

In my playground set, the urban moms in their tight jeans and oversize sunglasses size each other up using a whole range of signifiers: organic content of snacks, sleekness of stroller, ratio of tasteful wooden toys to plastic. But breast-feeding is the real ticket into the club. My mother friends love to exchange stories about subversive ways they used to sneak frozen breast milk through airline security (it's now legal), or about the random brutes on the street who don't approve of breast-feeding in public. When Angelina Jolie wanted to secure her status as America's ur-mother, she posed on the cover of *W* magazine nursing one of her twins. Alt-rocker Pete Wentz recently admitted that he tasted his wife, Ashlee Simpson's, breast milk ("soury" and "weird"), after bragging that they have a lot of sex—both of which must have seemed to him markers of a cool domestic existence.

From the moment a new mother enters the obstetrician's waiting room, she is subjected to the upper-class parents' jingle: "Breast Is Best." Parenting magazines offer "23 Great Nursing Tips," warnings on "Nursing Roadblocks," and advice on how to find your local lactation consultant (note to the childless: yes, this is an actual profession, and it's thriving). Many of the stories are accompanied by suggestions from the ubiquitous parenting

guru Dr. William Sears, whose Web site hosts a comprehensive list of the benefits of mother's milk. "Brighter Brains" sits at the top: "I.Q. scores averaging seven to ten points higher!" (Sears knows his audience well.) The list then moves on to the dangers averted, from infancy on up: fewer ear infections, allergies, stomach illnesses; lower rates of obesity, diabetes, heart disease. Then it adds, for good measure, stool with a "buttermilk-like odor" and "nicer skin"—benefits, in short, "more far-reaching than researchers have even dared to imagine."

In 2005, *Babytalk* magazine won a National Magazine Award for an article called "You *Can* Breastfeed." Given the prestige of the award, I had hoped the article might provide some respite from the relentlessly cheerful tip culture of the parenting magazines, and fill mothers in on the real problems with nursing. Indeed, the article opens with a promisingly realistic vignette, featuring a theoretical "You" cracking under the strain of having to breast-feed around the clock, suffering "crying jags" and cursing at your husband. But fear not, You. The root of the problem is not the sudden realization that your ideal of an equal marriage, with two parents happily taking turns working and raising children, now seems like a farce. It turns out to be quite simple: You just haven't quite figured out how to fit "Part A into Part B." Try the "C-hold" with your baby and some "rapid arm movement," the story suggests. Even Dr. Sears pitches in: "Think 'fish lips,'" he offers.

In the days after my first child was born, I welcomed such practical advice. I remember the midwife coming to my hospital bed and shifting my arm here, and the baby's head there, and then everything falling into place. But after three children and 28 months of breast-feeding (and counting), the insistent cheerleading has begun to grate. Buttermilk-like odor? Now Dr. Sears is selling me too hard. I may have put in fewer parenting years than he has, but I do have *some* perspective. And when I look around my daughter's second-grade class, I can't seem to pick out the unfortunate ones: "Oh, poor little Sophie, whose mother couldn't breast-feed. What dim eyes she has. What a sickly pallor. And already sprouting acne!"

I dutifully breast-fed each of my first two children for the full year that the American Academy of Pediatrics recommends. I have experienced what the *Babytalk* story calls breast-feeding-induced "maternal nirvana." This time around, *nirvana* did not describe my state of mind; I was launching a new Web site and I had two other children to care for, and a husband I would occasionally like to talk to. Being stuck at home breast-feeding as he walked out the door for work just made me unreasonably furious, at him and everyone else.

In Betty Friedan's day, feminists felt shackled to domesticity by the unreasonably high bar for housework, the endless dusting and shopping and pushing the Hoover around—a vacuum cleaner being the obligatory prop for the "happy housewife heroine," as Friedan sardonically called her. When I looked at the picture on the cover of Sears's *Breastfeeding Book*—a lady lying down, gently smiling at her baby and *still in her robe,* although the sun is well up—the scales fell from my eyes: it was not the vacuum that was keeping me and my 21st-century sisters down, but another sucking sound.

Still, despite my stint as the postpartum playground crank, I could not bring myself to stop breast-feeding—too many years of Sears's conditioning, too many playground spies. So I was left feeling trapped, like many women before me, in the middle-class mother's prison of vague discontent: surly but too privileged for pity, breast-feeding with one hand while answering the cell phone with the other, and barking at my older kids to get their own organic, 100 percent juice—the modern, multitasking mother's version of Friedan's "problem that has no name."

And in this prison I would have stayed, if not for a chance sighting. One day, while nursing my baby in my pediatrician's office, I noticed a 2001 issue of the *Journal of the American Medical Association* open to an article about breast-feeding: "Conclusions: There are inconsistent associations among breast-feeding, its duration, and the risk of being overweight in young children." Inconsistent? There I was, sitting half-naked in public for the tenth time that day, the hundredth time that month, the millionth time in my life—and the associations were *inconsistent?* The seed was planted. That night, I did what any sleep-deprived, slightly paranoid mother of a newborn would do. I called my doctor friend for her password to an online medical library, and then sat up and read dozens of studies examining breast-feeding's association with allergies, obesity, leukemia, mother-infant bonding, intelligence, and all the Dr. Sears highlights.

After a couple of hours, the basic pattern became obvious: the medical literature looks nothing like the popular literature. It shows that breast-feeding is probably, maybe, a *little* better; but it is far from the stampede of evidence that Sears describes. More like tiny, unsure baby steps: two forward, two back, with much meandering and bumping into walls. A couple of studies will show fewer allergies, and then the next one will turn up no difference. Same with mother-infant bonding, IQ, leukemia, cholesterol, diabetes. Even where consensus is mounting, the meta studies—reviews of existing studies—consistently complain about biases, missing evidence, and other major flaws in study design. "The studies do not demonstrate a universal phenomenon, in which one method is superior to another in all instances," concluded one of the first, and still one of the broadest, meta studies, in a 1984 issue of *Pediatrics,* "and they do not support making a mother feel that she is doing psychological harm to her child if she is unable or unwilling to breast-feed." Twenty-five years later, the picture hasn't changed all that much. So how is it that every mother I know has become a breast-feeding fascist?

Like many babies of my generation, I was never breast-fed. My parents were working-class Israelis, living in Tel Aviv in the '70s and aspiring to be modern. In the U.S., people were already souring on formula and passing out NO NESTLÉ buttons, but in Israel, Nestlé formula was the latest thing. My mother had already ditched her fussy Turkish coffee for Nescafé (just mix with water), and her younger sister would soon be addicted to NesQuik. Transforming soft, sandy grains from solid to magic liquid must have seemed like the forward thing to do. Plus, my mom believed her pediatrician when he said that it was important to precisely measure a baby's food intake and stick to a schedule. (To this day she pesters me about whether I'm *sure* my breast-fed babies are getting enough to eat; the parenting magazines would classify her as "unsupportive" and warn me to stay away.) Formula grew out of a late-19th-century effort to combat atrocious rates of infant mortality by turning infant feeding into a controlled science. Pediatrics was then a newly minted profession, and for the next century, the men who dominated it would constantly try to get mothers to welcome "enlightenment from the laboratory," writes Ann Hulbert in *Raising America.* But now and again, mothers would fight back. In the U.S., the rebellion against formula began in the late '50s, when a group of moms from the Chicago suburbs got together to form a breast-feeding support group they called La Leche League. They were Catholic mothers, influenced by the Christian Family Movement, who spoke of breast-feeding as "God's plan for mothers and babies." Their role model was the biblical Eve ("Her baby came. The milk came. She nursed her baby," they wrote in their first, pamphlet edition of *The Womanly Art of Breastfeeding,* published in 1958).

They took their league's name, La Leche, from a shrine to the Madonna near Jacksonville, Florida, called Nuestra Señora de La Leche y Buen Parto, which loosely translates into "Our Lady of Happy Delivery and Plentiful Milk." A more forthright name was deemed inappropriate: "You didn't mention *breast* in print unless you were talking about Jean Harlow," said co-founder Edwina Froehlich. In their photos, the women of La Leche wear practical pumps and high-neck housewife dresses, buttoned to the top. They saw themselves as a group of women who were "kind of thinking crazy," said co-founder Mary Ann Cahill. "Everything we did was radical."

La Leche League mothers rebelled against the notion of mother as lab assistant, mixing formula for the specimen under her care. Instead, they aimed to "bring mother and baby together again." An illustration in the second edition shows a woman named Eve—looking not unlike Jean Harlow—exposed to the waist and caressing her baby, with no doctor hovering nearby. Over time the group adopted a feminist edge. A 1972 publication rallies mothers to have "confidence in themselves and their sisters rather than passively following the advice of licensed professionals." As one woman wrote in another league publication, "Yes, I want to be liberated! I want to be free! I want to be free to be a woman!"

In 1971, the Boston Women's Health Book Collective published *Our Bodies, Ourselves,* launching a branch of feminism known as the women's-health movement. The authors were more groovy types than the La Leche League moms; they wore slouchy jeans, clogs, and bandanas holding back waist-length hair. But the two movements had something in common; *Our Bodies* also grew out of "frustration and anger" with a medical establishment that was "condescending, paternalistic, judgmental and non-informative." Teaching women about their own bodies would make them "more self-confident, more autonomous, stronger," the authors wrote. Breasts were not things for men to whistle and wink at; they were made for women to feed their babies in a way that was "sensual and fulfilling." The book also noted, in passing, that breast-feeding could "strengthen the infant's resistance to infection and disease"—an early hint of what would soon become the national obsession with breast milk as liquid vaccine.

Pediatricians have been scrutinizing breast milk since the late 1800s. But the public didn't pay much attention until an international scandal in the '70s over "killer baby bottles." Studies in South America and Africa showed that babies who were fed formula instead of breast milk were more likely to die. The mothers, it turned out, were using contaminated water or rationing formula because it was so expensive. Still, in the U.S., the whole episode turned breast-feeding advocates and formula makers into Crips and Bloods, and introduced the take-no-prisoners turf war between them that continues to this day. Some of the magical thinking about breast-feeding stems from a common misconception. Even many doctors believe that breast milk is full of maternal antibodies that get absorbed into the baby's bloodstream, says Sydney Spiesel, a clinical professor of pediatrics at Yale University's School of Medicine. That is how it works for most mammals. But in humans, the process is more pedestrian, and less powerful. A human baby is born with antibodies already in place, having absorbed them from the placenta. Breast milk dumps another layer of antibodies, primarily secretory IgA, directly into the baby's gastrointestinal tract. As the baby is nursing, these extra antibodies provide some added protection against infection, but they never get into the blood.

Since the identification of sIgA, in 1961, labs have hunted for other marvels. Could the oligosaccharides in milk prevent diarrhea? Do the fatty acids boost brain development? The past few decades have turned up many promising leads, hypotheses, and theories, all suggestive and nifty but never confirmed in the lab. Instead, most of the claims about breast-feeding's benefits lean on research conducted outside the lab: comparing one group of infants being breast-fed against another being breast-fed less,

or not at all. Thousands of such studies have been published, linking breast-feeding with healthier, happier, smarter children. But they all share one glaring flaw.

An ideal study would randomly divide a group of mothers, tell one half to breast-feed and the other not to, and then measure the outcomes. But researchers cannot ethically tell mothers what to feed their babies. Instead they have to settle for "observational" studies. These simply look for differences in two populations, one breast-fed and one not. The problem is, breast-fed infants are typically brought up in very different families from those raised on the bottle. In the U.S., breast-feeding is on the rise—69 percent of mothers initiate the practice at the hospital, and 17 percent nurse exclusively for at least six months. But the numbers are much higher among women who are white, older, and educated; a woman who attended college, for instance, is roughly twice as likely to nurse for six months. Researchers try to factor out all these "confounding variables" that might affect the babies' health and development. But they still can't know if they've missed some critical factor. "Studies about the benefits of breast-feeding are extremely difficult and complex because of who breast-feeds and who doesn't," says Michael Kramer, a highly respected researcher at McGill University. "There have been claims that it prevents everything—cancer, diabetes. A reasonable person would be cautious about every new amazing discovery."

The study about obesity I saw in my pediatrician's office that morning is a good example of the complexity of breast-feeding research—and of the pitfalls it contains. Some studies have found a link between nursing and slimmer kids, but they haven't proved that one causes the other. This study surveyed 2,685 children between the ages of 3 and 5. After adjusting for race, parental education, maternal smoking, and other factors—all of which are thought to affect a child's risk of obesity—the study found little correlation between breast-feeding and weight. Instead, the strongest predictor of the child's weight was the mother's. Whether obese mothers nursed or used formula, their children were more likely to be heavy. The breast-feeding advocates' dream—that something in the milk somehow reprograms appetite—is still a long shot.

In the past decade, researchers have come up with ever more elaborate ways to tease out the truth. One 2005 paper focused on 523 sibling pairs who were fed differently, and its results put a big question mark over all the previous research. The economists Eirik Evenhouse and Siobhan Reilly compared rates of diabetes, asthma, and allergies; childhood weight; various measures of mother-child bonding; and levels of intelligence. Almost all the differences turned out to be statistically insignificant. For the most part, the "long-term effects of breast feeding have been overstated," they wrote.

Nearly all the researchers I talked to pointed me to a series of studies designed by Kramer, published starting in 2001. Kramer followed 17,000 infants born in Belarus throughout their childhoods. He came up with a clever way to randomize his study, at least somewhat, without doing anything unethical. He took mothers who had already started nursing, and then subjected half of them to an intervention strongly encouraging them to nurse exclusively for several months. The intervention worked:

many women nursed longer as a result. And extended breast-feeding did reduce the risk of a gastrointestinal infection by 40 percent. This result seems to be consistent with the protection that sIgA provides; in real life, it adds up to about four out of 100 babies having one less incident of diarrhea or vomiting. Kramer also noted some reduction in infant rashes. Otherwise, his studies found very few significant differences: none, for instance, in weight, blood pressure, ear infections, or allergies—some of the most commonly cited benefits in the breast-feeding literature.

Both the Kramer study and the sibling study did turn up one interesting finding: a bump in "cognitive ability" among breast-fed children. But intelligence is tricky to measure, because it's subjective and affected by so many factors. Other recent studies, particularly those that have factored out the mother's IQ, have found no difference at all between breast-fed and formula-fed babies. In Kramer's study, the mean scores varied widely and mysteriously from clinic to clinic. What's more, the connection he found "could be banal," he told me—simply the result of "breast-feeding mothers' interacting more with their babies, rather than of anything in the milk."

The IQ studies run into the central problem of breast-feeding research: it is impossible to separate a mother's decision to breast-feed—and everything that goes along with it—from the breast-feeding itself. Even sibling studies can't get around this problem. With her first child, for instance, a mother may be extra cautious, keeping the neighbor's germy brats away and slapping the nurse who gives out the free formula sample. By her third child, she may no longer breast-feed—giving researchers the sibling comparison that they crave—but many other things may have changed as well. Maybe she is now using day care, exposing the baby to more illnesses. Surely she is not noticing that kid No.2 has the baby's pacifier in his mouth, or that the cat is sleeping in the crib (trust me on this one). She is also not staring lovingly into the baby's eyes all day, singing songs, reading book after infant book, because she has to make sure that the other two kids are not drowning each other in the tub. On paper, the three siblings are equivalent, but their experiences are not.

What does all the evidence add up to? We have clear indications that breast-feeding helps prevent an extra incident of gastrointestinal illness in some kids—an unpleasant few days of diarrhea or vomiting, but rarely life-threatening in developed countries. We have murky correlations with a whole bunch of long-term conditions. The evidence on IQs is intriguing but not all that compelling, and at best suggests a small advantage, perhaps five points; an individual kid's IQ score can vary that much from test to test or day to day. If a child is disadvantaged in other ways, this bump might make a difference. But for the kids in my playground set, the ones whose mothers obsess about breast-feeding, it gets lost in a wash of Baby Einstein videos, piano lessons, and the rest. And in any case, if a breast-feeding mother is miserable, or stressed out, or alienated by nursing, as many women are, if her marriage is under stress and breast-feeding is making things worse, surely that can have a greater effect on a kid's future success than a few IQ points.

So overall, yes, breast is probably best. But not so much better that formula deserves the label of "public health menace,"

alongside smoking. Given what we know so far, it seems reasonable to put breast-feeding's health benefits on the plus side of the ledger and other things—modesty, independence, career, sanity—on the minus side, and then tally them up and make a decision. But in this risk-averse age of parenting, that's not how it's done.

In the early '90s, a group of researchers got together to revise the American Academy of Pediatrics' policy statement on breast-feeding. They were of the generation that had fought the formula wars, and had lived through the days when maternity wards automatically gave women hormone shots to stop the flow of breast milk. The academy had long encouraged mothers to make "every effort" to nurse their newborns, but the researchers felt the medical evidence justified a stronger statement. Released in 1997, the new policy recommended exclusive breast-feeding for six months, followed by six more months of partial breast-feeding, supplemented with other foods. The National Organization for Women complained that this would tax working mothers, but to no avail. "The fact that the major pediatric group in the country was taking a definitive stance made all the difference," recalls Lawrence Gartner, a pediatrician and neonatologist at the University of Chicago, and the head of the committee that made the change. "After that, every major organization turned the corner, and the popular media changed radically."

In 2004, the Department of Health and Human Services launched the National Breastfeeding Awareness Campaign. The ads came out just after my second child was born, and were so odious that they nearly caused me to wean him on the spot. One television ad shows two hugely pregnant women in a logrolling contest, with an audience egging them on. "You wouldn't take risks before your baby is born," reads the caption. "Why start after?" The screen then flashes: "Breastfeed exclusively for 6 months." A second spot shows a pregnant woman—this time African American—riding a mechanical bull in a bar while trying to hold on to her huge belly. She falls off the bull and the crowd moans.

To convey the idea that failing to breast-feed is harmful to a baby's health, the print ads show ordinary objects arranged to look like breasts: two dandelions (respiratory illness), two scoops of ice cream with cherries on top (obesity), two otoscopes (ear infections). Plans were made to do another ad showing rubber nipples on top of insulin syringes (suggesting that bottle-feeding causes diabetes), but then someone thought better of it. The whole campaign is so knowing, so dripping with sexual innuendo and condescension, that it brings to mind nothing so much as an episode of *Mad Men,* where Don Draper and the boys break out the whiskey at day's end to toast another victory over the enemy sex.

What's most amazing is how, 50 years after La Leche League's founding, "enlightenment from the laboratory"—judgmental and absolutist—has triumphed again. The seventh edition of *The Womanly Art,* published in 2004, has ballooned to more than 400 pages, and is filled with photographs in place of the original hand drawings. But what's most noticeable is the shift in attitude. Each edition of the book contains new expert testimony about breast milk as an "arsenal against illness." "The resistance to disease that human milk affords a baby cannot be duplicated in any other way," the authors scold. The experience of reading the 1958 edition is like talking with your bossy but charming neighbor, who has some motherly advice to share. Reading the latest edition is like being trapped in the office of a doctor who's haranguing you about the choices you make.

In her critique of the awareness campaign, Joan Wolf, a women's-studies professor at Texas A&M University, chalks up the overzealous ads to a new ethic of "total motherhood." Mothers these days are expected to "optimize every dimension of children's lives," she writes. Choices are often presented as the mother's selfish desires versus the baby's needs. As an example, Wolf quotes *What to Expect When You're Expecting,* from a section called the "Best-Odds Diet," which I remember quite well: "Every bite counts. You've got only nine months of meals and snacks with which to give your baby the best possible start in life . . . Before you close your mouth on a forkful of food, consider, 'Is this the best bite I can give my baby?' If it will benefit your baby, chew away. If it'll only benefit your sweet tooth or appease your appetite put your fork down." To which any self-respecting pregnant woman should respond: "I am carrying 35 extra pounds and my ankles have swelled to the size of a life raft, and now I would like to eat some coconut-cream pie. So you know what you can do with this damned fork."

About seven years ago, I met a woman from Montreal, the sister-in-law of a friend, who was young and healthy and normal in every way, except that she refused to breast-feed her children. She wasn't working at the time. She just felt that breast-feeding would set up an unequal dynamic in her marriage—one in which the mother, who was responsible for the very sustenance of the infant, would naturally become responsible for everything else as well. At the time, I had only one young child, so I thought she was a kooky Canadian—and selfish and irresponsible. But of course now I know she was right. I recalled her with sisterly love a few months ago, at three in the morning, when I was propped up in bed for the second time that night with my new baby (note the *my*). My husband acknowledged the ripple in the nighttime peace with a grunt, and that's about it. And why should he do more? There's no use in both of us being a wreck in the morning. Nonetheless, it's hard not to seethe.

The Bitch in the House, published in 2002, reframed *The Feminine Mystique* for my generation of mothers. We were raised to expect that co-parenting was an attainable goal. But who were we kidding? Even in the best of marriages, the domestic burden shifts, in incremental, mostly unacknowledged ways, onto the woman. Breast-feeding plays a central role in the shift. In my set, no husband tells his wife that it is her womanly duty to stay home and nurse the child. Instead, both parents together weigh the evidence and then make a rational, informed decision that she should do so. Then other, logical decisions follow: she alone fed the child, so she naturally knows better how to comfort the child, so she is the better judge to pick a school for the child

and the better nurse when the child is sick, and so on. Recently, my husband and I noticed that we had reached the age at which friends from high school and college now hold positions of serious power. When we went down the list, we had to work hard to find any women. Where had all our female friends strayed? Why had they disappeared during the years they'd had small children?

The debate about breast-feeding takes place without any reference to its actual context in women's lives. Breast-feeding exclusively is not like taking a prenatal vitamin. It is a serious time commitment that pretty much guarantees that you will not work in any meaningful way. Let's say a baby feeds seven times a day and then a couple more times at night. That's nine times for about a half hour each, which adds up to more than half of a working day, every day, for at least six months. This is why, when people say that breast-feeding is "free," I want to hit them with a two-by-four. It's only free if a woman's time is worth nothing.

That brings us to the subject of pumping. Explain to your employer that while you're away from your baby, "you will need to take breaks throughout the day to pump your milk," suggest the materials from the awareness campaign. Demand a "clean, quiet place" to pump, and a place to store the milk. A clean, quiet place. So peaceful, so spa-like. Leave aside the preposterousness of this advice if you are, say, a waitress or a bus driver. Say you are a newspaper reporter, like I used to be, and deadline is approaching. Your choices are (a) leave your story to go down to the dingy nurse's office and relieve yourself; or (b) grow increasingly panicked and sweaty as your body continues on its merry, milk-factory way, even though the plant shouldn't be operating today and the pump is about to explode. And then one day, the inevitable will happen. You will be talking to a male colleague and saying to yourself, "Don't think of the baby. Please don't think of the baby." And then the pump *will* explode, and the stigmata will spread down your shirt as you rush into the ladies' room.

This year alone I had two friends whose babies could not breast-feed for one reason or another, so they mostly had to pump. They were both first-time mothers who had written themselves dreamy birth plans involving hot baths followed by hours of intimate nursing. When that didn't work out, they panicked about their babies' missing out on the milky elixir. One of them sat on my couch the other day hooked up to tubes and suctions and a giant deconstructed bra, looking like some fetish ad, or a footnote from the Josef Mengele years. Looking as far as humanly possible from Eve in her natural, feminine state.

In his study on breast-feeding and cognitive development, Michael Kramer mentions research on the long-term effects of mother rats' licking and grooming their pups. Maybe, he writes, it's "the physical and/or emotional act of breastfeeding" that might lead to benefits. This is the theory he prefers, he told me, because "it would suggest something the formula companies can't reproduce." No offense to Kramer, who seems like a great guy, but this gets under my skin. If the researchers just want us to lick and groom our pups, why don't they say so? We can find our own way to do that. In fact, by insisting that milk is some kind of vaccine, they make it less likely that we'll experience nursing primarily as a loving maternal act—"pleasant and relaxing," in the words of *Our Bodies, Ourselves* and more likely that we'll view it as, well, dispensing medicine.

I continue to breast-feed my new son some of the time—but I don't do it slavishly. When I am out for the day working, or out with friends at night, he can have all the formula he wants, and I won't give it a second thought. I'm not really sure why I don't stop entirely. I know it has nothing to do with the science; I have no grandiose illusions that I'm making him lean and healthy and smart with my milk. Nursing is certainly not pure pleasure, either; often I'm tapping my foot impatiently, waiting for him to finish. I do it partly because I can get away with breast-feeding part-time. I work at home and don't punch a clock, which is not the situation of most women. Had I been more closely tied to a workplace, I would have breast-fed during my maternity leave and then given him formula exclusively, with no guilt.

My best guess is something I can't quite articulate. Breast-feeding does not belong in the realm of facts and hard numbers; it is much too intimate and elemental. It contains all of my awe about motherhood, and also my ambivalence. Right now, even part-time, it's a strain. But I also know that this is probably my last chance to feel warm baby skin up against mine, and one day I will miss it.

From *The Atlantic,* April, 2009, pp. 64–70. Copyright © 2009 by Atlantic Monthly Group. Reprinted by permission.

UNIT 5

Cultural and Societal Influences

Unit Selections

Key Points to Consider

- Have you noticed the trend of product marketing, the media, and the music and entertainment industries in sexualizing younger and younger girls? How do you feel about this increasing trend? What is the fallout for this pop culture depiction on the development of young girls and how can we more effectively counter these negative effects? Similarly, how do you feel about aggressive marketing and consumerism targeting young children?

- When you were growing up, do you think you had high self-esteem? Why or why not? The general wisdom is that children with high self-esteem enjoy many other positive outcomes. However, can you think back to your childhood and remember any other children who were aggressive bullies and who had high self-esteem? Explain how this might be.

- Do you know anyone with autism? Describe their patterns of behavior. How did the parents and family cope with this child? What treatments did this child get and did they help? What would you do if you had a child with autism?

- What can be done to help safeguard children both in our country and on other shores from the ravages of hunger, malnutrition, disease, poor medical care, violence, and child sexual trafficking for children?

- At no other time in human history have we seen such an explosion and epidemic of child obesity, and it appears we are losing the battle. What can schools and parents to do help children adopt healthier lifestyles and connect with nature?

Student Website
www.mhcls.com

Internet References

Association to Benefit Children (ABC)
   http://www.a-b-c.org
Children's Defense Fund
   http://www.childrensdefense.org/
Children Now
   http://www.childrennow.org
Council for Exceptional Children
   http://www.cec.sped.org
Prevent Child Abuse America
   http://www.preventchildabuse.org

Social scientists and developmental psychologists have come to realize that children are influenced by a multitude of social forces. In this unit we present articles to illuminate how children and adolescents are influenced by broad factors such as economics, culture, politics, and the media. These influences also affect the family, which is a major context of child development, and many children are now faced with more family challenges than ever. In addition, analysis of exceptional or atypical children gives the reader a more comprehensive account of child development. Thus, articles are presented on special challenges of development, such as the effects of sexual trafficking, autism, wartime violence, and other circumstances.

Other external societal factors that influence children's development include the powerful influence of the media and advertising shaping children's young minds. The authors of "Goodbye to Girlhood" decry merchandisers who are encouraging younger and younger girls, to see themselves in sexualized terms. This aggressive, targeted marketing fills our stores with inappropriately sexualized clothing for younger and younger girls, putting an unhealthy emphasis on appearance and beauty.

Our fast-paced, convenience-fueled lifestyles have forever changed America's palate and eating habits and in many ways have contributed to an epidemic of child obesity. In the past, experts have advocated for parents to help restrict their obese children's diets in order to see a drop in weight. Unfortunately, these efforts generally do not produce enduring and sustained weight loss in children. Instead, today experts are calling for parents, families, schools, and society to reshift the focus from weight loss to making lifestyle changes for children that include integrating exercise into a daily routine and reconnecting children with nature and outdoor activity. The authors of two articles describe some of these efforts in "How to Win the Weight Battle" and "Getting Back to the Great Outdoors."

Some children must cope with special psychological, emotional, and cognitive challenges such as ADHD, autism, emotional, psychological, or linguistic disorders. Such children are often misunderstood and mistreated and pose special challenges. The authors of the articles "What Autistic Girls Are Made Of," "Three Reasons Not to Believe in an Autism Epidemic," "Trials for Parents Who Choose Faith Over Medicine," and "What Causes Specific Language Impairment in Children?" describe the research and evidence to better inform us of some of the myths and truths about the incidence, potential causes, and interventions for various disorders.

Still other children both here and abroad face terrible conditions related to international poverty, malnutrition, and coping with situations such as the horrors of child sexual trafficking,

© Brand X Pictures/Alamy

wartime violence, and fetal drug exposure. "The Impact of Trafficking on Children: Psychological and Social Policy Perspectives", "The Epidemic That Wasn't," and "Treatment and Prevention of Posttraumatic Stress Reactions in Children and Adolescents Exposed to Disasters and Terrorism: What Is the Evidence?" address these challenges. Although these articles are sometimes unpleasant to read, as future parents, teachers, and professionals it is important for us to learn more about these difficult and challenging situations in order to find ways to improve and solve future problems.

Goodbye to Girlhood

As pop culture targets ever younger girls, psychologists worry about a premature focus on sex and appearance.

STACY WEINER

Ten-year-old girls can slide their low-cut jeans over "eye-candy" panties. French maid costumes, garter belt included, are available in preteen sizes. Barbie now comes in a "bling-bling" style, replete with halter top and go-go boots. And it's not unusual for girls under 12 to sing, "Don't cha wish your girlfriend was hot like me?"

American girls, say experts, are increasingly being fed a cultural catnip of products and images that promote looking and acting sexy.

"Throughout U.S. culture, and particularly in mainstream media, women and girls are depicted in a sexualizing manner," declares the American Psychological Association's Task Force on the Sexualization of Girls, in a report issued Monday. The report authors, who reviewed dozens of studies, say such images are found in virtually every medium, from TV shows to magazines and from music videos to the Internet.

While little research to date has documented the effect of sexualized images specifically on *young* girls, the APA authors argue it is reasonable to infer harm similar to that shown for those 18 and older; for them, sexualization has been linked to "three of the most common mental health problems of girls and women: eating disorders, low self-esteem and depression."

Said report contributor and psychologist Sharon Lamb: "I don't think because we don't have the research yet on the younger girls that we can ignore that [sexualization is] of harm to them. Common sense would say that, and part of the reason we wrote the report is so we can get funding to prove that."

Boys, too, face sexualization, the authors acknowledge. Pubescent-looking males have posed provocatively in Calvin Klein ads, for example, and boys with impossibly sculpted abs hawk teen fashion lines. But the authors say they focused on girls because females are objectified more often. According to a 1997 study in the journal Sexual Abuse, 85 percent of ads that sexualized children depicted girls.

Even influences that are less explicitly erotic often tell girls who they are equals how they look and that beauty commands power and attention, contends Lamb, co-author of "Packaging Girlhood: Rescuing Our Daughters from Marketers' Schemes" (St. Martin's, 2006). One indicator that these influences are reaching girls earlier, she and others say: The average age for adoring the impossibly proportioned Barbie has slid from preteen to preschool.

When do little girls start wanting to look good for others? "A few years ago, it was 6 or 7," says Deborah Roffman, a Baltimore-based sex educator. "I think it begins by 4 now."

While some might argue that today's belly-baring tops are no more risque than hip huggers were in the '70s, Roffman disagrees. "Kids have always emulated adult things," she says. "But [years ago] it was, 'That's who I'm supposed to be as an adult.' It's very different today. The message to children is, 'You're already like an adult. It's okay for you to be interested in sex. It's okay for you to dress and act sexy, right now.' That's an entirely different frame of reference."

It's not just kids' exposure to sexuality that worries some experts; it's the kind of sexuality they're seeing. "The issue is that the way marketers and media present sexuality is in a very narrow way," says Lamb. "Being a sexual person isn't about being a pole dancer," she chides. "This is a sort of sex education girls are getting, and it's a misleading one."

Clothes Encounters

Liz Guay says she has trouble finding clothes she considers appropriate for her daughter Tanya, age 8. Often, they're too body-hugging. Or too low-cut. Or too short. Or too spangly.

Then there are the shoes: Guay says last time she visited six stores before finding a practical, basic flat. And don't get her started on earrings.

"Tanya would love to wear dangly earrings. She sees them on TV, she sees other girls at school wearing them, she sees them in the stores all the time. . . . I just say, 'You're too young.'"

"It's not so much a feminist thing," explains Guay, a Gaithersburg medical transcriptionist. "It's more that I want her to be comfortable with who she is and to make decisions based on what's right for her, not what everybody else is doing. I want her to develop the strength that when she gets to a point where kids are offering her alcohol or drugs, that she's got enough self-esteem to say, 'I don't want that.'"

Some stats back up Guay's sense of fashion's shrinking modesty. For example, in 2003, tweens—that highly coveted marketing segment ranging from 7 to 12—spent $1.6 million on thong underwear, *Time* magazine reported. But even more-innocent-seeming togs, toys and activities—like tiny "Beauty Queen" T-shirts, Hello Kitty press-on nails or preteen make-overs at Club Libby Lu—can be problematic, claim psychologists. The reason: They may lure young girls into an unhealthy focus on appearance.

Studies suggest that female college students distracted by concerns about their appearance score less well on tests than do others. Plus, some experts say, "looking good" is almost culturally inseparable for girls from looking sexy: Once a girl's bought in, she's hopped onto a consumer conveyor belt in which marketers move females from pastel tiaras to hot-pink push-up bras.

Where did this girly-girl consumerism start? Diane Levin, an education professor at Wheelock College in Boston who is writing an upcoming book, "So Sexy So Soon," traces much of it to the deregulation of children's television in the mid-1980s. With the rules loosened, kids' shows suddenly could feature characters who moonlighted as products (think Power Rangers, Care Bears, My Little Pony). "There became a real awareness," says Levin, "of how to use gender and appearance and, increasingly, sex to market to children."

Kids are more vulnerable than adults to such messages, she argues.

The APA report echoes Levin's concern. It points to a 2004 study of adolescent girls in rural Fiji, linking their budding concerns about body image and weight control to the introduction of television there.

In the United States, TV's influence is incontestable. According to the Kaiser Family Foundation, for example, nearly half of American kids age 4 to 6 have a TV in their bedroom. Nearly a quarter of teens say televised sexual content affects their own behavior.

And that content is growing: In 2005, 77 percent of prime-time shows on the major broadcast networks included sexual material, according to Kaiser, up from 67 percent in 1998. In a separate Kaiser study of shows popular with teenage girls, women and girls were twice as likely as men and boys to have their appearance discussed. They also were three times more likely to appear in sleepwear or underwear than their male counterparts.

Preteen Preening

It can be tough for a parent to stanch the flood of media influences.

Ellen Goldstein calls her daughter Maya, a Rockville fifth-grader, a teen-mag maniac. "She has a year's worth" of *Girls' Life* magazine, says Goldstein. "When her friends come over, they pore over this magazine." What's Maya reading? There's "Get Gorgeous Skin by Tonight," "Crush Confidential: Seal the Deal with the Guy You Dig," and one of her mom's least faves: "Get a Fierce Body Fast."

"Why do you want to tell a kid to get a fierce body fast when they're 10? They're just developing," complains Goldstein. She also bemoans the magazines' photos, which Maya has plastered on her ceiling.

"These are very glamorous-looking teenagers. They're wearing lots of makeup. They all have very glossy lips," she says. "They're generally wearing very slinky outfits. . . . I don't think those are the best role models," Goldstein says. "When so much emphasis is placed on the outside, it minimizes the importance of the person inside."

So why not just say no?

"She loves fashion," explains Goldstein. "I don't want to take away her joy from these magazines. It enhances her creative spirit. [Fashion] comes naturally to her. I want her to feel good about that. We just have to find a balance."

Experts say her concern is warranted. Pre-adolescents' propensity to try on different identities can make them particularly susceptible to media messages, notes the APA report. And for some girls, thinking about how one's body stacks up can be a real downer.

In a 2002 study, for example, seventh-grade girls who viewed idealized magazine images of women reported a drop in body satisfaction and a rise in depression.

Such results are disturbing, say observers, since eating disorders seem to strike younger today. A decade ago, new eating disorder patients at Children's National Medical Center tended to be around age 15, says Adelaide Robb, director of inpatient psychiatry. Today kids come in as young as 5 or 6.

Mirror Images

Not everyone is convinced of the uglier side of beauty messages.

Eight-year-old Maya Williams owns four bracelets, eight necklaces, about 20 pairs of earrings and six rings, an assortment of which she sprinkles on every day. "Sometimes, she'll stand in front of the mirror and ask, "Are these pretty, Mommy?""

Her mom, Gaithersburg tutor Leah Haworth, is fine with Maya's budding interest in beauty. In fact, when Maya "wasn't sure" about getting her ears pierced, says Haworth, "I talked her into it by showing her all the pretty earrings she could wear."

What about all these sexualization allegations? "I don't equate looking good with attracting the opposite sex," Haworth says. Besides, "Maya knows her worth is based on her personality. She knows we love her for who she is."

"Looking good just shows that you care about yourself, care about how you present yourself to the world. People are judged by their appearance. People get better service and are treated better when they look better. That's just the way it is," she says. "I think discouraging children from paying attention to their appearance does them a disservice."

Magazine editor Karen Bokram also adheres to the beauty school of thought. "Research has shown that having skin issues at [her readers'] age is traumatic for girls' self-esteem," says Bokram, founder of *Girls' Life*. "Do we think girls need to be gorgeous in order to be worthy? No. Do we think girls' feeling good about how they look has positive effects in other areas of their lives, meaning that they make positive choices academically, socially and in romantic relationships? Absolutely."

Some skeptics of the sexualization notion also argue that kids today are hardier and savvier than critics think. Isaac Larian, whose company makes the large-eyed, pouty-lipped Bratz dolls, says, "Kids are very smart and know right from wrong." What's more, his testing indicates that girls want Bratz "because they are fun, beautiful and inspirational," he wrote in an e-mail. "Not once have we ever heard one of our consumers call Bratz 'sexy.'" Some adults "have a twisted sense of what they see in the product," Larian says.

"It is the parents' responsibility to educate their children," he adds. "If you don't like something, don't buy it."

But Genevieve McGahey, 16, isn't buying marketers' messages. The National Cathedral School junior recalls that her first real focus on appearance began in fourth grade. That's when classmates taught her: To be cool, you needed ribbons. To be cool, you needed lip gloss.

Starting around sixth grade, though, "it took on a more sinister character," she says. "People would start wearing really short skirts and lower tops and putting on more makeup. There's a strong pressure to grow up at this point."

"It's a little scary being a young girl," McGahey says. "The image of sexuality has been a lot more trumpeted in this era. . . . If you're not interested in [sexuality] in middle school, it seems a little intimidating." And unrealistic body ideals pile on extra pressure, McGahey says. At a time when their bodies and their body images are still developing, "girls are not really seeing people [in the media] who are beautiful but aren't stick-thin," she notes. "That really has an effect."

Today, though, McGahey feels good about her body and her style.

For this, she credits her mom, who is "very secure with herself and with being smart and being a woman." She also points to a wellness course at school that made her conscious of how women were depicted. "Seeing a culture of degrading women really influenced me to look at things in a new way and to think how we as high school girls react to that," she says.

"A lot of girls still hold onto that media ideal. I think I've gotten past it. As I've gotten more comfortable with myself and my body, I'm happy not to be trashy," McGahey says. "But most girls are still not completely or even semi-comfortable with themselves physically. You definitely still feel the pressure of those images."

STACY WEINER writes frequently for *Health* about families and relationships. Comments: health@washpost.com.

Trials for Parents Who Chose Faith over Medicine

DIRK JOHNSON

Weston, Wis.—Kara Neumann, 11, had grown so weak that she could not walk or speak. Her parents, who believe that God alone has the ability to heal the sick, prayed for her recovery but did not take her to a doctor.

After an aunt from California called the sheriff's department here, frantically pleading that the sick child be rescued, an ambulance arrived at the Neumann's rural home on the outskirts of Wausau and rushed Kara to the hospital. She was pronounced dead on arrival.

The county coroner ruled that she had died from diabetic ketoacidosis resulting from undiagnosed and untreated juvenile diabetes. The condition occurs when the body fails to produce insulin, which leads to severe dehydration and impairment of muscle, lung and heart function.

"Basically everything stops," said Dr. Louis Philipson, who directs the diabetes center at the University of Chicago Medical Center, explaining what occurs in patients who do not know or "are in denial that they have diabetes."

About a month after Kara's death last March, the Marathon County state attorney, Jill Falstad, brought charges of reckless endangerment against her parents, Dale and Leilani Neumann. Despite the Neumanns' claim that the charges violated their constitutional right to religious freedom, Judge Vincent Howard of Marathon County Circuit Court ordered Ms. Neumann to stand trial on May 14, and Mr. Neumann on June 23. If convicted, each faces up to 25 years in prison.

"The free exercise clause of the First Amendment protects religious belief," the judge wrote in his ruling, "but not necessarily conduct."

Wisconsin law, he noted, exempts a parent or guardian who treats a child with only prayer from being criminally charged with neglecting child welfare laws, but only "as long as a condition is not life threatening." Kara's parents, Judge Howard wrote, "were very well aware of her deteriorating medical condition."

About 300 children have died in the United States in the last 25 years after medical care was withheld on religious grounds, said Rita Swan, executive director of Children's Health Care Is a Legal Duty, a group based in Iowa that advocates punishment for parents who do not seek medical help when their children need it. Criminal codes in 30 states, including Wisconsin, provide some form of protection for practitioners of faith healing in cases of child neglect and other matters, protection that Ms. Swan's group opposes.

Shawn Peters, the author of three books on religion and the law, including *When Prayer Fails: Faith Healing, Children and the Law* (Oxford, 2007), said the outcome of the Neumann case was likely to set an important precedent.

"The laws around the country are pretty unsettled," said Mr. Peters, who teaches religion at the University of Wisconsin Oshkosh and has been consulted by prosecutors and defense lawyers in the case.

In the last year, two other sets of parents, both in Oregon, were criminally charged because they had not sought medical care for their children on the ground that to do so would have violated their belief in faith healing. One couple were charged with manslaughter in the death of their 15-month-old daughter, who died of pneumonia last March. The other couple were charged with criminally negligent homicide in the death of their 16-year-old son, who died from complications of a urinary tract infection that was severely painful and easily treatable.

"Many types of abuses of children are motivated by rigid belief systems," including severe corporal punishment, said Ms. Swan, a former Christian Scientist whose 16-month-old son, Matthew, died after she postponed taking him to a hospital for treatment of what proved to be meningitis. "We learned the hard way."

All states give social service authorities the right to go into homes and petition for the removal of children, Ms. Swan said, but cases involving medical care often go unnoticed until too late. Parents who believe in faith healing, she said, may feel threatened by religious authorities who oppose medical treatment. Recalling her own experience, she said, "we knew that once we went to the doctor, we'd be cut off from God."

The crux of the Neumanns' case, Mr. Peters said, will be whether the parents could have known the seriousness of their daughter's condition.

Investigators said the Neumanns last took Kara to a doctor when she was 3. According to a police report, the girl had lost the strength to speak the day before she died. "Kara laid down and was unable to move her mouth," the report said, "and merely made moaning noises and moved her eyes back and forth."

The courts have ordered regular medical checks for the couple's other three children, ages 13 to 16, and Judge Howard ordered all the parties in the case not to speak to members of the news media. Neither Ms. Falstad nor the defense lawyers, Gene Linehan and Jay Kronenwetter, would agree to be interviewed.

The Neumanns, who had operated a coffee shop, Monkey Mo's, in this middle-class suburb in the North Woods, are known locally as followers of an online faith outreach group called Unleavened Bread Ministries, run by a preacher, David Eells. The site shares stories of faith healing and talks about the end of the world.

An essay on the site signed Pastor Bob states that the Bible calls for healing by faith alone. "Jesus never sent anyone to a doctor or a hospital," the essay says. "Jesus offered healing by one means only! Healing was by faith."

A link from the site, helptheneumanns.com, asserts that the couple is being persecuted and "charged with the crime of praying." The site also allows people to contribute to a legal fund for the Neumanns.

In the small town of Weston, many people shake their heads with dismay when Kara Neumann is mentioned. Tammy Klemp, 41, who works behind the counter at a convenience store here, said she disagreed with the Neumanns' passive response to their daughter's illness but said she was not sure they should go to prison.

"I've got mixed feelings," Ms. Klemp said. "It's just such a terribly sad case."

Chris Goebel, 30, a shipping department worker for a window maker, said many people in the area felt strongly that the parents should be punished.

"That little girl wasn't old enough to make the decision about going to a doctor," Mr. Goebel said. "And now, because some religious extremists went too far, she's gone."

How Many Fathers Are Best for a Child?

After 40 years of visiting the Barí Indians in Venezuela, anthropologists have discovered a new twist on family values.

Meredith F. Small

Anthropologist Stephen Beckerman was well into his forties before he finally understood how babies are made. He had thought, as most people do, that a sperm from one man and an egg from one woman joined to make a child. But one summer day, as he and his colleague Roberto Lizarralde lounged around in hammocks, chatting with Rachel, an elderly woman of the Barí tribe of Venezuela, she pointed out his error. Babies, she explained, can easily have more than one biological father. "My first husband was the father of my first child, my second child, and my third child," Rachel said, recalling her life. "But the fourth child, actually, he has two fathers." It was clear that Rachel didn't mean there was a stepfather hanging around or a friendly uncle who took the kid fishing every weekend. She was simply explaining the Barí version of conception to these ignorant anthropologists: A fetus is built up over time with repeated washes of sperm—which means, of course, that more than one man can contribute to the endeavor. This interview changed not only the way Beckerman and Lizarralde viewed Barí families but also brought into question the very way that anthropologists portray human coupling. If biological fatherhood can be shared—an idea accepted by many indigenous groups across South America and in many other cultures across the globe—then the nuclear family with one mom and one dad might not be the established blueprint for a family that we have been led to expect. If so, the familiar story of traditional human mating behavior, in which man the hunter brings home the bacon to his faithful wife, loses credibility. And if the Barí and other groups work perfectly well with more flexible family styles, the variety of family structures that are increasingly common in Western culture these days—everything from single-parent households to blended families—may not be as dangerous to the social fabric as we are led to believe. People in this culture may simply be exercising the same family options that humans have had for millions of years, options that have been operating in other cultures while the West took a stricter view of what constitutes a family.

Stephen Beckerman folds his 6-foot-4-inch frame into a chair and turns to the mountainous topography of papers on his desk at Pennsylvania State University. Once he manages to locate a map under all the piles, he points to a spot on the border between Venezuela and Colombia where he spent 20 years, off and on, with the indigenous Barí Indians. The traditional Barí culture, Beckerman explains, has come under attack by outside forces, starting with the conquistadors who arrived in the early 16th century. Today Catholic missionaries interact with the Barí, coal and oil companies are trying to seize their land, and drug traffickers and guerrillas are threats. Western influences are apparent: Most families have moved from traditional long-houses to single-family dwellings, and everyone wears modern Western clothes and uses Western goods. However, the Barí continue to practice their traditions of manioc farming, fishing, and hunting, according to Roberto Lizarralde, an anthropologist at the Central University of Venezuela who has been visiting the Barí regularly since 1960. Lizarralde also says that the Barí still have great faith in traditional spirits and ancestral wisdom, including their notion that a child can have multiple biological fathers. The Barí believe that the first act of sex, which should always be between a husband and wife, plants the seed. Then the fledgling fetus must be nourished by repeated anointings of semen; the woman's body is viewed as a vessel where men do all the work. "One of the reasons women give you for taking lovers is that they don't want to wear out their husbands," Beckerman says. "They claim it's hard work for men to support a pregnancy by having enough sex, and so lovers can help." Just look, the Barí say. Women grow fat during a pregnancy, while men grow thin from all their work.

Women grow fat during a pregnancy, while men grow thin from all their work.

125

Anthropologists study a culture's ideas about conception because those ideas have a profound impact on the way people run their lives. In our culture, for example, conceiving children incurs long-term economic responsibility for both the mother and father. We take this obligation so seriously that when a parent fails to provide for a child, it is usually a violation of law. In the Barí system, when a man is named as a secondary biological father he is also placed under an obligation to the mother and the child. In addition, he is expected to give gifts of fish and game. These gifts are a significant burden because the man must also provide for his own wife and primary children. Beckerman and his colleagues have discovered that naming secondary fathers has evolutionary consequences. A team of ethnographers led by Beckerman, Roberto Lizarralde, and his son Manuel, an anthropologist at Connecticut College who has been visiting the Barí since he was 5 years old, interviewed 114 Barí women past childbearing years and asked them about their full reproductive histories. "These interviews were a lot of fun," Beckerman says, laughing. "Randy old ladies talking about their lovers." In total, the researchers recorded claims of 916 pregnancies, an average of eight pregnancies for each woman. But child mortality was high—about one-third of the children did not survive to age 15. Naming secondary fathers was a critical factor in predicting which babies made it to adulthood. Secondary fathers were involved in 25 percent of pregnancies, and the team determined that two fathers were the ideal number. Children with one father and one secondary father made it to their teens most often; kids with only one father or those with more than two fathers didn't fare as well. The researchers also found that this decrease in mortality occurred not during the child's life but during fetal development: Women were less likely to have a miscarriage or stillbirth if they had a husband and an additional male contributing food. This result was a surprise because researchers had expected that help during childhood would be more important. "The Barí are not hungry; they are not close to the bone. But it must be the extra fat and protein that they get from secondary fathers during gestation that makes the difference," Beckerman explains as he points to photographs of Barí women who look well nourished, even downright plump. Barí women seem to use this more flexible system of paternity when they need it. Within families, some children have secondary fathers, while their siblings belong to the husband alone. The team discovered that mothers are more likely to take on a secondary father when a previous child has died in infancy. Manuel Lizarralde claims the strategy makes perfect sense, given the Barí belief that the best way to cure a sick child is for the father to blow tobacco smoke over the child's body. "It is easy to imagine a bereaved mother thinking to herself that if she had only provided a secondary father and so more smoke for her dead child, she might have saved him—and vowing to provide that benefit for her next child." Beckerman says extra fathers may have always been insurance for uncertain times: "Because the Barí were once hunted as if they were game animals—by other Indians, conquistadors, oilmen, farmers, and ranchers—the odds of a woman being widowed when she still had young children were one in three, according to data we gathered about the years 1930 to 1960. The men as well as the women knew this. None of these

guys can go down the street to Mutual of Omaha and buy a life insurance policy. By allowing his wife to take a lover, the husband is doing all he can to ensure the survival of his children." Barí women are also freer to do as they wish because men need their labor—having a wife is an economic necessity because women do the manioc farming, harvesting, and cooking, while men hunt and fish. "The sexual division of labor is such that you can't make it without a member of the opposite sex," says Beckerman. Initially, the researchers worried that jealousy on the part of husbands would make Barí women reticent about discussing multiple sexual partners. "In our first interviews, we would wait until the husband was out of the house," says Beckerman. "But one day we interviewed an old couple who were enjoying thinking about their lives; they were lying in their hammocks, side by side, and it was obvious he wasn't going anywhere. So we went down the list of her children and asked about other fathers. She said no, no, no for each child, and then the husband interrupted when we got to one and said, 'That's not true, don't you remember, there was that guy. . .' And the husband was grinning." Not all women take lovers. Manuel Lizarralde has discovered through interviews that one-third of 122 women were faithful to their husbands during their pregnancies. "These women say they don't need it, or no one asked, or they have enough support from family and don't require another father for their child," Lizarralde says. "Some even admit that their husbands were not that happy about the idea." Or it may be a sign of changing times. Based on his most recent visits to the Barí, Lizarralde thinks that under the influence of Western values, the number of people who engage in multiple fatherhood may be decreasing. But his father, who has worked with the Barí for more than 40 years, disagrees. He says the practice is as frequent but that the Barí discuss it less openly than before, knowing that Westerners object to their views. After all, it took the anthropologists 20 years to hear about other fathers, and today the Barí are probably being even more discreet because they know Westerners disapprove of their beliefs. "What this information adds up to," Beckerman says, "is that the Barí may be doing somewhat less fooling around within marriage these days but that most of them still believe that a child can have multiple fathers." More important, the Barí idea that biological paternity can be shared is not just the quirky custom of one tribe; anthropologists have found that this idea is common across South America. The same belief is shared by indigenous groups in New Guinea and India, suggesting that multiple paternity has been part of human behavior for a long time, undermining all previous descriptions of how human mating behavior evolved.

Since the 1960s, when anthropologists began to construct scenarios of early human mating, they had always assumed that the model family started with a mom and dad bonded for life to raise the kids, a model that fit well with acceptable Western behavior. In 1981 in an article titled "The Origin of Man," C. Owen Lovejoy, an anthropologist at Kent State University, outlined the standard story of human evolution as it was used in the field—and is still presented in textbooks today: Human infants with their big brains and long periods of growth and learning have always been dependent on adults, a dependence that separates the humans from the apes. Mothers alone couldn't possibly find enough food for these dependent young, so women have always needed to find a mate who would stick close to home and bring in supplies for the family. Unfortunately for women, as evolutionary psychologists suggest, men are compelled by their biology to mate with as many partners as possible to pass along their genes. However, each of these men might be manipulated into staying with one woman who offered him sex and a promise of fidelity. The man, under those conditions, would be assured of paternity, and he might just stay around and make sure his kids survived. This scenario presents humans as naturally monogamous, forming nuclear families as an evolutionary necessity. The only problem is that around the world families don't always operate this way. In fact, as the Barí and other cultures show, there are all sorts of ways to run a successful household. The Na of Yunnan Province in China, for example, have a female-centric society in which husbands are not part of the picture. Women grow up and continue to live with their mothers, sisters, and brothers; they never marry or move away from the family compound. As a result, sisters and brothers rather than married pairs are the economic unit that farms and fishes together. Male lovers in this system are simply visitors. They have no place or power in the household, and children are brought up by their mothers and by the mothers' brothers. A father is identified only if there is a resemblance between him and the child, and even so, the father has no responsibilities toward the child. Often women have sex with so many partners that the biological father is unknown. "I have not found any term that would cover the notion of father in the Na language," writes Chinese anthropologist Cai Hua in his book *A Society Without Fathers or Husbands: The Na of China.* In this case, women have complete control over their children, property, and sexuality. Across lowland South America, family systems vary because cultures put their beliefs into practice in different ways. Among some native people, such as the Canela, Mehinaku, and Araweté, women control their sex lives and their fertility, and most children have several fathers. Barí women are also sexually liberated from an early age. "Once she has completed her puberty ritual, a Barí girl can have sex with anyone she wants as long as she doesn't violate the incest taboo," Beckerman explains. "It's nobody's business, not even Mom's and Dad's business." Women can also turn down prospective husbands. In other cultures in South America, life is not so free for females, although members of these cultures also believe that babies

As the Barí and other cultures show, there are all sorts of ways to run a successful household.

can have more than one father. The Curripaco of Amazonia, for instance, acknowledge multiple fatherhood as a biological possibility and yet frown on women having affairs. Paul Valentine, a senior lecturer in anthropology at the University of East London who has studied the Curripaco for more than 20 years, says, "Curripaco women are in a difficult situation. The wives come into the village from different areas, and it's a very patrilineal system." If her husband dies, a widow is allowed to turn only to his brothers or to clan members on his side of the family for a new husband. The relative power of women and men over their sex lives has important consequences. "In certain social and economic systems, women are free to make mate choices," says Valentine. In these cultures women are often the foundation of society, while men have less power in the community. Sisters tend to stay in the same household as their mothers. The women, in other words, have power to make choices. "At the other extreme, somehow, it's the men who try to maximize their evolutionary success at the expense of the women," says Valentine. Men and women often have a conflict of interest when it comes to mating, marriage, and who should invest most in children, and the winners have sometimes been the men, sometimes the women. As Beckerman wryly puts it, "Anyone who believes that in a human mating relationship the man's reproductive interests always carry the day has obviously never been married." The Barí and others show that human systems are, in fact, very flexible, ready to accommodate any sort of mating system or type of family. "I think that human beings are capable of making life extremely complicated. That's our way of doing business," says Ian Tattersall, a paleoanthropologist and curator in the division of anthropology at the American Museum of Natural History in New York City. Indeed, such flexibility suggests there's no reason to assume that the nuclear family is the natural, ideal, or even most evolutionarily successful system of human grouping. As Beckerman says, "One of the things this research shows is that human beings are just as clever and creative in assembling their kin relations as they are putting together space shuttles or symphonies."

Childhood for Sale

Consumer culture is pervasive and invasive. It is targeting kids in surprising and troubling ways—with harmful consequences. Here's what to do about it.

MICHELE STOCKWELL

For today's children, the world is a parade of brand names. They wake up in the morning to breakfasts of Kellogg's *Star Wars* cereal, and go to sleep at night in Hello Kitty or *Spiderman* pajamas. In between, snack-food companies vie for vending positions in the hallways of their schools; pop stars and celebrities beckon them in designer-label clothes; and popular TV shows, movies, books, and music pelt them with subliminal product placements—from soft drinks to computers. McDonald's has even hired an entertainment marketing firm to help it buy mentions of Big Mac sandwiches in hip-hop songs.

Advertising and marketing campaigns aimed at children are nothing new, of course. Baseball cards go back more than a century, and TV ads during Saturday morning cartoons have been a staple for decades. America is, after all, a capitalist society; marketing is a central part of our economic system. But the scale and sophistication of today's campaigns far exceeds anything that has come before. The consumer culture has turned pervasive and invasive, and it is targeting kids in increasingly surprising and troubling ways to entice them to spend their pocket money—more than $200 billion per year—and then become lifelong customers.

Indeed, analysts say children are the new darlings of Madison Avenue. Marketers hire psychologists and child development experts to help them devise strategies that take advantage of children's deeply impressionable nature. The modern marketing repertoire now includes word-of-mouth campaigns in which companies identify the "alpha kids" on playgrounds and in malls and hire them to generate enthusiasm about new products among their friends—without ever telling those friends they've been recruited to do so.

Another technique takes advantage of young people's enthusiasm for video and computer games: Marketers develop hybrid "advergames" that are specifically designed CO promote certain products and brands. While children play these games, brand logos and product images flash at them repeatedly. After a few rounds of an online advergame associated with candy or junk food, for example, a child is likely to remember a brand well enough to ask for it at the grocery store.

At the same time, marketers survey kids' interests by prompting them to participate in online contests, chat rooms, and the like, culling their personal information and preferences in order to design more tailored, personalized marketing strategies.

And then there is the next frontier: cell phones. Nearly one-half of all 10- to 18-year-olds have them, and they are evolving into mini-personal entertainment centers for playing games, listening to music, and watching videos. Cell phones have the dual virtue for marketers of offering (a) direct communication with children, either by voice or touch-key interactive programs, and (b) a clear path around the protective eyes of gatekeeper parents. Maybelline and Timex have both announced plans for cell phone-based marketing campaigns aimed at teenagers.

Some of the techniques for marketing to children may not seem particularly odious. But the cumulative effect is to commercialize childhood to an unprecedented degree—with unhealthy consequences.

In fact, a growing body of research indicates that the consumer culture's harmful effects on children can run the gamut from physical and emotional problems to increased parent-child conflicts over spending decisions, distorted value systems, and strained family budgets. One study found a strong correlation between children's immersion in the consumer culture their feelings of depression, anxiety, and low self-esteem. Meanwhile ads for alcohol and tobacco have, not surprisingly, been linked to underage alcohol and tobacco use. Studies have also found correlations between child obesity rates and the prevalence of TV ads for junk food; research has specifically shown that children's exposure to food advertising and marketing may be influencing their food choices.

Equally troubling is children's frequent exposure to ads for violent entertainment—adult-rated movies, TV shows, video games, and music—because watching violent media has been linked to childhood displays of violent and aggressive behavior. Sexual imagery in marketing campaigns and consumer products geared for kids (like padded push-up bras and high-heeled shoes for young girls) is also hyper-charging children's sexuality before they may be cognitively or emotionally ready.

Parents may not be aware of every last marketing practice, but they see enough to know basically what is happening, and they don't like it. As Sen. Hillary Clinton (D-N.Y.) said in a speech last March, "Parents worry that their children will not grow up with the same values that they did or that they believe in because of the overwhelming presence of the media telling them to buy this and that, or conveying negative messages filled with explicit sex content and violence."

There is no doubt that the primary responsibility for shielding America's children from the damaging effects of a rampant commercial culture lies with parents. But they can't—and shouldn't—do it alone. Helping parents do their job better represents both a policy challenge and a political opportunity. Democrats, in particular, would do well to become champions for children's and parents' interests, because, as Progressive Policy Institute senior fellow Barbara Dafoe Whitehead explained in the April 2005 issue of *Blueprint,* parents doubt Democrats' commitment on these cultural issues. That's one big reason they have been voting Republican in recent presidential elections. (*See a longer report, "Closing the Parent Gap," at* ppionline.org.)

For more on these policy proposals, look for the forthcoming report "Childhood for Sale: Consumer Culture's Bid for Our Kids" at *ppionline.org.*

So what is there to do? Here are some ideas:

Ensure that marketing practices aimed at children are fair. Experts argue that a well-established principle in communications law holds that for an ad to be considered fair, an audience must be able to recognize that it is an ad and must be able to identify the seller. But psychological research concludes that children—particularly children younger than 8—may be able to associate Ronald McDonald with McDonald's restaurants, but they lack the cognitive maturity to understand the persuasive intent of marketing, or to view ads with skepticism. They are likely to see advertising as truthful and entertaining, not as a come-on. Because children are developmentally vulnerable to advertising, child health experts, including the American Academy of Pediatrics, argue that ads aimed at them are inherently unfair, particularly for children under 8.

The Federal Trade Commission (FTC) has traditionally had the regulatory authority to uphold U.S. laws that prohibit "unfair or deceptive" commercial practices. But Congress In 1980 explicitly stripped the commission of the power to regulate unfair advertising to children. That was after it proposed banning TV ads for children on the grounds that children were not discerning enough to keep the ads in perspective. The commission was particularly concerned that most ads aimed at children were for sugary foods, and children did not understand the health risks of excessive sugar consumption. Congress balked after industry and marketers reacted strongly. It passed a blanket restriction, prohibiting the FTC from issuing any sort of rule in the area of children's advertising on the grounds of unfairness.

But since then, a growing body of scientific evidence has more conclusively shown how children in certain stages of cognitive development react to advertising, and what its harmful effects may be. Equally important, marketers have found more surreptitious means than traditional print ads for reaching children. They are capitalizing in particular on children's comfort with technology and their immersion in the new interactive environment of the web. More research is needed on the effects of all this marketing and consumerism, but enough is known to conclude that Congress should lift its restriction on the FTC's authority, and direct it to investigate all forms of marketing aimed at children. Once started, the FTC should issue a report on its findings within a year, and then issue rules to guide marketing practices directed at children.

Ensure that advertising is appropriate for the media in which it appears. General-audience entertainment should include only general-audience advertising. Ads for beer and R-rated movies, for example, shouldn't be aired during prime-time sitcoms, when children are watching. To stop that practice, Congress should direct the Department of Health and Human Services (HHS) to monitor the advertising that appears in media that are popular among young people. The HHS should then begin systematically naming and shaming companies that advertise adult-rated entertainment or adult products like alcohol or tobacco on TV shows, in magazines, and in other popular media that have large youth audiences. And if a pattern emerges in which some companies continue to advertise adult-restricted products to large youth audiences, Congress should give the FTC the authority to impose fines on repeat offenders.

Require toys and other products based on movies and TV shows to carry consistent age ratings. Consider the slew of *Star Wars: Episode III* toys now being marketed to children ages 4 and up, despite the fact that the movie is rated PG-13, and its director has discouraged parents from taking young children to see it because of its violent content. Or, consider the line of toys based the on R-rated Arnold Schwarzenegger movie *Terminator 3—Rise of the Machines.* One toy, recommended for kids 12 and up, is an action figure that depicts Schwarzenegger's character with a bloody face. Other toys based on the movie are designed for children as young as 5. Why not ensure that the age recommendations displayed on packaging match the age ratings of the original movies, and let parents decide if the toys are appropriate for their children?

Protect children's privacy. Providing consumers information to help them make purchasing decisions is always a sound policy principle. But when information flows in the other direction—from consumers to marketers—there should be appropriate safeguards to ensure the consumers' privacy. That is particularly true when the information in question is about children: their names and addresses, personal preferences, and more. In the burgeoning interactive marketplace of websites, cell phones, digital TV, and other communication devices, marketers have many opportunities to collect personal data from children. Congress established protections for children under 13 in the Children's Online Privacy Protection Act of 1998. That law dictates the circumstances under which companies may collect information from children. Congress should now extend the same protections to everyone under 16. It should also ban corporations from selling or purchasing the personal information of children under 16 for commercial marketing purposes, unless parents give express consent.

Curtail marketing activities inside public schools. The consumerism that children encounter daily is by no means confined to TV, the Internet, and pocket-sized gadgetry. The parade also marches straight through schools. Cash-strapped school districts open their doors to marketers to generate much-needed revenues—sometimes millions of dollars. Beverage contracts alone may generate up to $1.5 million per year for a large school district. The National Soft Drink Association estimates that 62 percent of U.S. principals have signed "pouring rights" contracts, giving soda companies exclusive access to their schools. Advertising also shows up on billboards, yearbooks, newsletters, textbook covers, screen savers, team uniforms, vending machines, and school buses. (San Francisco students have in past years ridden to and from school in buses sponsored by Old Navy, for example.)

Companies even create educational materials. Oil companies, for example, sponsor lessons about energy. Consumer products companies donate packets of deodorant sticks and feminine hygiene products to kids in 5th grade sex education classes, a time when many are struggling with adolescent insecurities. Some packets include testimonials like this one from an adolescent boy: "I used to be really worried about sweating a lot, but since I started using an antiperspirant every morning, I'm dry all day."

A Government Accountability Office report found that few states have laws or comprehensive regulations governing in-school marketing. Schools and school districts have widely varying policies. So Congress should direct the secretary of education to investigate all forms of marketing in schools and then develop a set of voluntary recommendations for states to use in establishing comprehensive policies on marketing. Why not set a goal of completely eliminating marketing in elementary schools, where many children don't yet understand what advertising is?

End the practice of using children's friendships for marketing purposes. Of course, it is doubly hard for children to understand that they are being marketed to when the pitch is coming from their peers who have been recruited to spread enthusiasm for products by word-of-mouth on playgrounds and in malls, either for pay or for freebies. That technique is a new variation on the concept that experts call "viral" marketing, which spreads information from person to person, like a virus. (A more innocuous type of viral marketing is common on websites: links that say, "email this article to a friend.") But taking commercial advantage of children's friendships crosses a line into ethically murky territory.

Congress should require companies to disclose what they are doing when they use adolescents in these viral marketing campaigns. And the FTC should require marketers to ensure that the "alpha kids" they enlist to promote products tell their peers up front that they are working for a sponsor.

Protect children involved in product research. Many of the products marketed to children today are based on focus groups, demonstrations, and other trials with children. We should demand that the marketing industry protect children by following the same standards that federally funded researchers must follow. Those standards include oversight by diverse and credible professional review boards, which approve and monitor research projects, and protect the rights and welfare of child participants.

Ask more from broadcasters. We are way beyond old-fashioned TV ads now. But TV is still a very important conduit for the consumer culture. Congress should strike a new bargain with broadcasters: In exchange for free use of the public spectrum, they should provide more—and better—children's programming. Broadcasters are now required to air three hours of children's programming per week. That should double to six hours. Broadcasters should also make it commercial-free programming, target it to 6 to 12 year olds, and schedule it to air after school, when children are most likely to be watching.

Ask more from cable and satellite TV providers, too. Striking a new bargain with broadcasters is a good start, but 85 percent of American households subscribe to cable or satellite TV. Regardless of how they get it, polls show that parents are deeply concerned about sex and violence on TV. Furthermore, most are unaware of, or confused by, parental control technologies like the V-chip. Therefore, Congress should give cable and satellite TV companies a choice: Start offering parents the option of subscribing to family-friendly channel packages, or face the same indecency regulations that apply to over-the-air broadcasters, as some powerful lawmakers are proposing. Family-friendly channel packages could include channels like Nickelodeon, The Learning Channel, Animal Planet, and news channels, but not MTV and other channels that tend to be inappropriate for younger children.

There is no way to totally eliminate marketing from the culture—nor should that be the goal. A highly developed market economy needs advertising. But policymakers can help parents shield their children from some of the culture's corrosive influences by demanding more responsible and age-appropriate marketing that does not exploit children's psychological and cognitive weak spots or push them too quickly into adulthood.

MICHELE STOCKWELL is director of social and family policy at the Progressive Policy Institute.

Childhood's End

For 19 years, Joseph Kony has been enslaving, torturing, raping, and murdering Ugandan children, many of whom have become soldiers for his "Lord's Resistance Army," going on to torture, rape, and kill other children. The author exposes the vicious insanity—and cynical politics—behind one of Africa's greatest nightmares.

CHRISTOPHER HITCHENS

In William Faulkner's story "Raid," set in Alabama and Mississippi in the closing years of the Civil War, a white family becomes aware of a sudden, vast, nighttime migration through the scorched countryside. They can hear it and even smell it before they can see it; it's the black population voting with its feet and heading, so it fervently believes, for the river Jordan: "We couldn't see them and they did not see us; maybe they didn't even look, just walking fast in the dark with that panting, hurrying murmuring, going on . . ."

Northern Uganda is centered on the headstreams of the Nile rather than the Jordan, and is a strange place for me to find myself put in mind of Faulkner, but every evening at dusk the main town of Gulu starts to be inundated by a mass of frightened humanity, panting, hurrying, and murmuring as it moves urgently through the crepuscular hours. Most of the "night commuters," as they are known locally, are children. They leave their outlying villages and walk as many as eight kilometers to huddle for safety in the towns. And then, in the morning, often without breakfast and often without shoes, they walk all the way back again to get to their schools and their families. That's if the former have not been burned and the latter have not been butchered. These children are not running toward Jordan and the Lord; they are running for their lives from the "Lord's Resistance Army" (L.R.A.). This grotesque, zombie-like militia, which has abducted, enslaved, and brainwashed more than 20,000 children, is a kind of Christian Khmer Rouge and has for the past 19 years set a standard of cruelty and ruthlessness that—even in a region with a living memory of Idi Amin—has the power to strike the most vivid terror right into the heart and the other viscera.

Here's what happens to the children who can't run fast enough, or who take the risk of sleeping in their huts in the bush. I am sitting in a rehab center, talking to young James, who is 11 and looks about 9. When he actually was nine and

sleeping at home with his four brothers, the L.R.A. stormed his village and took the boys away. They were roped at the waist and menaced with bayonets to persuade them to confess what they could not know—the whereabouts of the Ugandan Army's soldiers. On the subsequent forced march, James underwent the twin forms of initiation practiced by the L.R.A. He was first savagely flogged with a wire lash and then made to take part in the murder of those children who had become too exhausted to walk any farther. "First we had to watch," he says. "Then we had to join in the beatings until they died." He was spared from having to do this to a member of his family, which is the L.R.A.'s preferred method of what it calls "registration." And he was spared from being made into a concubine or a sex slave, because the L.R.A. doesn't tolerate that kind of thing for boys. It is, after all, "faith-based." Excuse me, but it does have its standards.

Talking to James about the unimaginable ruin of his childhood, I notice that when I am speaking he stays stock-still, with something a bit dead behind his eyes. But when it comes his turn to tell his story, he immediately starts twisting about in his chair, rubbing his eyes and making waving gestures with his arms. The leader of the L.R.A., a former Catholic acolyte in his 40s named Joseph Kony, who now claims to be a spirit medium with a special mission to impose the Ten Commandments, knows what old Fagin knew: that little boys are nimble and malleable if you catch them young enough, and that they make good thieves and runners. Little James was marched all the way to Sudan, whose Muslim-extremist government offers shelter and aid—such an ecumenical spirit!—to the Christian fanatics. There he was put to work stealing food from neighboring villages, and digging and grinding cassava roots. Soon enough, he was given a submachine gun almost as big as himself. Had he not escaped during an ambush, he would have gotten big enough to be given a girl as well, to do with what he liked.

I drove out of Gulu—whose approach roads can be used only in the daytime—to a refugee camp nearer the Sudanese border. A few Ugandan shillings and a few packets of cigarettes procured me a Ugandan Army escort, who sat heavily armed in the back of the pickup truck. As I buckled my seat belt, the driver told me to unbuckle it in spite of the parlous condition of the road. "If you have to jump out," he said, "you will have to jump out very fast." That didn't make me feel much safer, but only days after I left, two Ugandan aid workers were murdered in daylight on these pitted, dusty highways. We bounced along until we hit Pabbo, where a collection of huts and shanties huddle together as if for protection. In this place are packed about 59,000 of the estimated 1.5 million "internally displaced persons" (I.D.P.'s) who have sought protection from the savagery of the L.R.A. Here, I had the slightly more awkward task of interviewing the female survivors of Joseph Kony's rolling Jonestown: a campaign of horror and superstition and indoctrination.

The women of Uganda are naturally modest and reserved, and it obviously involved an effort for them to tell their stories to a male European stranger. But they stood up as straight as spears and looked me right in the eye. Forced to carry heavy loads through the bush and viciously caned—up to 250 strokes—if they dropped anything. Given as gifts or prizes to men two or three times their age and compelled to bear children. Made to watch, and to join in, sessions of hideous punishment for those who tried to escape. Rose Atim, a young woman of bronze Nubian Nefertiti beauty, politely started her story by specifying her primary-school grade (grade five) at the time of her abduction. Her nostrils still flared with indignation when she spoke, whereas one of her fellow refugees, Jane Akello, a young lady with almost anthracite skin, was dull and dead-eyed and monotonous in her delivery. I was beginning to be able to distinguish symptoms. I felt a strong sense of indecency during these interviews, but this was mere squeamish self-indulgence on my part, since the women were anxious to relate the stories of their stolen and maimed childhoods. It was as if they had emerged from some harrowing voyage on the Underground Railroad.

Kony appointed himself the Lord's anointed prophet in 1987.

Very few people, apart from his victims, have ever met or even seen the enslaving and child-stealing Joseph Kony, and the few pictures and films of him are amateur and indistinct. This very imprecision probably helps him to maintain his version of charisma. Here is what we know and (with the help of former captives and a Scotland Yard criminal profiler) what we speculate. Kony grew up in a Gulu Province village called Odek. He appointed himself the Lord's anointed prophet for the Acholi people of northern Uganda in 1987, and by the mid-90s was receiving arms and cash from Sudan. He probably suffers from multiple-personality disorder, and he takes his dreams for prophecies. He goes into trances in which he speaks into a tape recorder and plays back the resulting

words as commands. He has helped himself to about 50 captives as "wives," claiming Old Testament authority for this (King Solomon had 700 spouses), often insisting—partly for biblical reasons and partly for the more banal reason of AIDS dread—that they be virgins. He used to anoint his followers with a holy oil mashed from indigenous shea-butter nuts, and now uses "holy water," which he tells his little disciples will make them invulnerable to bullets. He has claimed to be able to turn stones into hand grenades, and many of his devotees say that they have seen him do it. He warns any child tempted to run away that the baptismal fluids are visible to him forever and thus they can always be found again. (He can also identify many of his "children" by the pattern of lashes that they earned while under his tender care.) Signs of his disapproval include the cutting off of lips, noses, and breasts in the villages he raids and, to deter informers, a padlock driven through the upper and lower lips. This is the sort of deranged gang—flagellant, hysterical, fanatical, lethal, underage—that an unfortunate traveler might have encountered on the roads of Europe during the Thirty Years' War or the last Crusade. "Yes," says Michael Oruni, director of the Gulu Children of War Rehabilitation Center, who works on deprogramming these feral kids, "children who have known pain know how to inflict it." We were sitting in a yard that contained, as well as some unreformed youngsters, four random babies crawling about in the dust. These had been found lying next to their panga-slashed mothers or else left behind when their mothers were marched away.

Children who have known pain know how to inflict it.

In October, the Lord of the Flies was hit, in his medieval redoubt, by a message from the 21st century. Joseph Kony and four other leaders of the L.R.A. were named in the first arrest warrants ever issued by the new International Criminal Court (I.C.C.). If that sounds like progress to you, then consider this. The whereabouts of Kony are already known: he openly uses a satellite phone from a base across the Ugandan border in southern Sudan. Like the United States, Sudan is not a signatory to the treaty that set up the I.C.C. And it has sponsored the L.R.A. because the Ugandan government—which *is* an I.C.C. signatory—has helped the people of southern Sudan fight against the theocracy in Khartoum, the same theocracy that has been sponsoring the genocide against Muslim black Africans in Darfur. Arrest warrants look pretty flimsy when set against ruthless cynicism of this depth and intensity. Kony has evidently made some kind of peace with his Sudanese Islamist patrons: in addition to his proclamation of the Ten Commandments, he once banned alcohol and announced that all pigs were unclean and that those who farm them, let alone eat them, were subject to death. So, unless he has undergone a conversion to Judaism in the wilderness, we can probably assume that he is repaying his murderous armorers and protectors.

I had a faintly nerve-racking drink with Francis Ongom, one of Kony's ex-officers, who defected only recently and who would not agree to be questioned about his own past crimes. "Kony has refused Sudan's request that he allow his soldiers to convert to Islam," said this hardened-looking man as he imbibed a Red Bull through a straw, "but he has found Bible justifications for killing witches, for killing pigs because of the story of the Gadarene swine, and for killing people because god did the same with Noah's flood and Sodom and Gomorrah." Nice to know that he is immersed in the Good Book.

The terrifying thing about such violence and cruelty is that only a few dedicated practitioners are required in order to paralyze everyone else with fear. I had a long meeting with Betty Bigombe, one of those staunch and beautiful women—it is so often the women—who have helped restore Uganda's pulse after decades of war and famine and tyranny and Ebola and West Nile fever and AIDS. She has been yelled at by Joseph Kony, humiliated by corrupt and hypocritical Sudanese "intermediaries," dissed by the Ugandan political elite, and shamefully ignored by the international "human rights" community. She still believes that an amnesty for Kony's unindicted commanders is possible, which will bring the L.R.A. children back from the bush, but she and thousands like her can always be outvoted by one brutalized schoolboy with a machete. We are being forced to watch yet another Darfur, in which the time supposedly set aside for negotiations is used by the killers and cleansers to complete their work.

The Acholi people are the chief sufferers in all this.

The Acholi people of northern Uganda, who are the chief sufferers in all this, have to suffer everything twice. Their children are murdered or abducted and enslaved and then come back to murder and abduct and enslave even more children. Yet if the Ugandan Army were allowed to use extreme measures to destroy the L.R.A., the victims would be . . . Acholi children again. It must be nightmarish to know that any feral-child terrorist who is shot could be one of your own. "I and the public know," wrote W. H. Auden in perhaps his greatest poem, "September 1, 1939":

> *What all schoolchildren learn,*
> *Those to whom evil is done*
> *Do evil in return.*

And that's what makes it so affecting and so upsetting to watch the "night commuter" children when they come scuttling and scampering into town as the sun departs from the sky. These schoolchildren have not yet had evil done to them, nor are they ready to inflict any evil. It's not too late for them, in other words.

I sat in the deepening gloom for a while with one small boy, Jimmy Opioh, whose age was 14. He spoke with an appalling gravity and realism about his mother's inability to pay school fees for himself and his brother both, about the fatigue and time-wasting of being constantly afraid and famished and continually on the run. In that absurd way that one does, I asked him what he wanted to be when he grew up. His unhesitating answer was that he wanted to be a politician—he had his party, the Forum for Democratic Change, all picked out as well. I shamefacedly arranged, along with the admirable John Prendergast of the International Crisis Group, to get him the meager sum that would pay for his schooling, tried not to notice the hundreds of other eyes that were hungrily turned toward me in the darkness, wondered what the hell the actual politicians, here or there, were doing about his plight, and managed to get out of the night encampment just before the equatorial rains hit and washed most of the tents and groundsheets away.

How to Win the Weight Battle

DEBORAH KOTZ

Families now stuffing backpacks and greeting the children's new teachers face a crisis that makes falling test scores and rising college costs dull by comparison. Ten years and billions of dollars into the fight against childhood fat, it's clear that the campaign has been a losing battle. According to a report released last week by the research group Trust for America's Health, one third of kids nationwide are overweight now; other stats show that the percentage of children who are obese has more than tripled since the 1970s. Now, experts are worrying about the collateral damage, too: A 2006 University of Minnesota study found that 57 percent of girls and 33 percent of boys used cigarettes, fasting, or skipping meals to control their weight and that diet-pill intake by teenage girls had nearly doubled in five years. Last year, nearly 5,000 teens opted for liposuction, according to the American Society of Plastic Surgeons—more than three times the number in 1998, when experts first warned of a "childhood obesity epidemic."

"We've taken the approach that if we make children feel bad about being fat or scare them half to death, they'll be motivated to lose excess weight," says Joanne Ikeda, nutritionist emeritus at the University of California-Berkeley, who studies pediatric obesity prevention. "It hasn't worked in adults, so what makes us think it will work in kids?" Many experts now believe that an emphasis on dropping weight rather than adding healthful nutrients and exercise is doing more harm than good.

Failure to end—or even slow—the epidemic has public-health experts, educators, and politicians in a near panic. All told, some 17 percent of kids are now obese, which means they're at or above the 95th percentile for weight in relation to height for their age; an additional 17 percent are overweight, or at or over the 85th percentile. This is despite massive government-funded education campaigns in schools, in libraries, and on TV to alert parents and kids to the dangers. "In the early 1980s, I used to see one or two kids a year with type 2 diabetes, and now I see one or two a month," says Alan Lake, an associate professor of pediatrics at the Johns Hopkins University School of Medicine. "Evidence now suggests that this type 2 diabetes progresses more rapidly in kids, which means we could be soon seeing 20-year-olds developing severe heart disease." Already, high blood pressure affects more than 2 million youngsters.

Long haul. Obesity is hard to outgrow, so about 50 percent of elementary-school kids and 80 percent of teens who are obese will battle the scales—and the greatly increased risk of disease—for the rest of their lives. A number of authorities have warned that today's youth could be the first ever to have a shorter life span than their parents.

What explains both the problem and the elusiveness of a solution? Blame the American "toxic environment." Cinnamon buns and candy are far cheaper and easier to sell at the local mall than, say, a fresh fruit cup or a packet of sliced almonds. Half of kids walked or biked to school a generation ago; today, only about 10 percent do—then they come home and plop down in front of their various screens. As if the inactivity weren't bad enough, preteens absorb more than 7,600 commercials a year for candy, sugary cereal, and fast food, according to the Kaiser Family Foundation. "They're surrounded by circumstances where the default behavior is one that encourages obesity," says Marlene Schwartz, deputy director of the Rudd Center for Food Policy and Obesity at Yale University. Busy parents contribute by stocking pantries with quick energy—sugary cereal, Fruit Roll-Ups, and Oreos—while bringing home Kentucky Fried Chicken for dinner.

Schools have taken a stab at introducing the basics of good nutrition and the four food groups. But such efforts pale beside a cutback of gym time in favor of academics and vending machines stocked with high-calorie (and high-profit-margin) snack foods. More than 90 percent of elementary schools don't provide daily physical education, according to the Robert Wood Johnson Foundation, and the share of high school students participating in daily gym has dropped from 42 percent in 1991 to 33 percent in 2005. Some states have reconsidered and passed laws to increase phys ed, but plenty of schools have yet to figure out how to comply; in California, more than half the school districts have failed to implement the 20 minutes a day of physical activity that the state law now requires, according to the California Center for Public Health Advocacy.

While eating too much and exercising too little clearly put children's health in jeopardy, so might the methods used to change their behavior. As with any losing war, this one lacks a battle plan that everyone agrees upon. Robert Jeffery, director of the Obesity Prevention Center at the University of Minnesota School of Public Health, is one of many who believe that the solution lies in focusing more attention on body weight by screening kids at school and educating them about the dangers of obesity. One Minnesota high school last year showed the documentary *Super Size Me,* for example, to illustrate the ill effects that greasy burgers and fries have on the body. And proactive states like Florida and Pennsylvania mandate that schools weigh students yearly and send letters home warning parents if their child's body mass index, a number that relates weight to height, is too high. Down the hall and around the corner from Jeffery, meanwhile, Minnesota's Dianne Neumark-Sztainer, who studies adolescent eating behaviors, argues that such "overzealous efforts" may push teens to seek a quick and unhealthful weight-loss remedy. "Overweight teens are far more likely to turn to these risky behaviors instead of incorporating exercise or a more nutritious diet," she says.

Jillian Croll, a nutritionist who treats eating disorders at the Anna Westin House, a private facility in Chaska, Minn., has seen the evidence. "We find ourselves unteaching" girls raised to believe that their self-worth is measured by how much they weigh, she says. On a June afternoon tour of the suburban house filled with handmade quilts and stuffed teddy bears, the mood is tense as the eight residents sit down to sloppy Joes and buttered broccoli.

50% of obese elementary-school kids and 80% of obese teens are apt to battle the scales for the rest of their lives.

No joke. The path to an eating disorder is often paved with the good intentions of parents and educators who presume that warning and cajoling or joking will motivate children to lose weight. Neumark-Sztainer's findings suggest just the opposite in a study of 130 previously overweight teens. About 65 percent of the teens reported being teased about their body weight, and they were more likely to engage in binge eating, which leads to weight gain over time. And when parents harp on children's body weight, kids are also likely to become preoccupied with achieving thinness, says Neumark-Sztainer. Her research found that approaches that may be effective weight-loss strategies in adults, like daily weigh-ins and attempting a restricted diet, may trigger diet-pill use and purging in teens.

Shaming kids is prevalent in schools as well, and it's just as counterproductive there. A review paper published in the July issue of the journal *Psychological Bulletin* found that teachers perceive obese people to be sloppy and less likely to succeed than thinner people. Gym teachers usually have higher expectations for normal-weight kids, which means they might let heavier kids languish on the sidelines. "When kids are made to feel ashamed of themselves for being fat, they will cope by finding ways to make themselves feel better, often turning to food," says Schwartz. Studies have shown they're more likely to be depressed and dissatisfied with their bodies and develop other health problems like high blood pressure and eating disorders. "Yet I still hear educators and health professionals at conferences saying that weight bias serves a purpose."

School weight screenings, now performed in 16 states, have yielded mixed reviews. Though the report cards sent home with kids who have high body mass indexes work to inform parents about the problem, they don't provide effective solutions. "Many parents assume they should put their child on a diet," says Berkeley's Ikeda.

Preteens absorb over 7,600 commercials a year for candy, and fast food.

What's worse, the reports may be inaccurate. A government analysis found that 17 percent of kids who have a BMI that nudges them into the overweight category actually have a normal percentage of body fat but are large boned or have a greater

muscle mass. Nine-year-old Ben Baturka, an avid swimmer who does up to 2 miles of laps while training for his swim meets, was put in the BMI "at risk" zone last year by Hillcrest Elementary School in Drexel Hill, Pa. "He's always been a big boy, but he's a healthy eater and as fit as he can be, so I'm going to ignore the school letter," says Ben's mother, Angie. The American Medical Association recently recommended that doctors perform BMI screenings during annual physicals, looking for weight-related health risks like hypertension or high cholesterol, too.

Some families go too far by turning healthful eating into a new religion. "Anorexia often starts with healthy eating behaviors, like cutting down on bread and other starches, that evolve to become too restrictive," says pediatrician Tania Heller, director of the Washington Center for Eating Disorders and Adolescent Obesity in Bethesda, Md. "My mom was always into organic food, so she didn't notice when I got on a health kick, running more miles and avoiding all fat in my diet," says Marina Leith, 17, who was treated by Heller for anorexia after dropping 30 pounds in less than two months four years ago. She's now a high school senior, back to a normal weight.

Think positive. How to get a child to a healthy weight in the healthiest possible way? Most experts now favor a positive approach—showing, for example, ways that exercise strengthens the body and refreshes the mind and how certain nutrients in foods help cells, organs, and bones grow properly. Hundreds of schools are now trying out Planet Health, a curriculum developed by Harvard University researchers that disguises obesity prevention by integrating healthful messages about the power of food and exercise into various subjects. Students in math class, for example, come to appreciate the importance of reducing TV viewing by calculating the hours they've spent over their lifetime in front of the set. A 2005 study published in the *Archives of Pediatrics & Adolescent Medicine* found that middle school girls who had Planet Health in their schools were half as likely to purge or use diet pills as those in schools without it.

Half of kids walked or biked to school a generation ago; today, some 10% do.

A second program adopted by 7,000 elementary schools nationwide, the Coordinated Approach to Child Health, similarly puts the focus on good health habits instead of weight. In class, students use a traffic-light system to identify "go," "slow," and "whoa" foods and take breaks to do jumping jacks. In the cafeteria, fruits, vegetables, low-fat milk, and whole-grain starches are labeled with green-light tags, and pizza gets a yellow light. Gym activities are designed to keep students constantly moving. "Every kid gets a ball to dribble or a hula hoop; there's no lining up and waiting to take a turn," says Philip Nader, professor of pediatrics emeritus at the University of California-San Diego, who helped develop CATCH. One study found that the program succeeded at preventing the growth in number of overweight students that normally occurs from grade 3 to grade 5. CATCH schools in El Paso, Texas (with one of the highest obesity rates in the nation), held the line between those grades; elsewhere in the city, the share of overweight girls increased from 26 percent to 40 percent and of overweight boys from 39 percent to 49 percent.

Five Comments Parents Should Never Make

Teens Who Overcame Anorexia Consider How They Might Have Avoided It

Even gentle and well-meant comments about your kids' weight can have an unintended downside: an increased likelihood that they'll turn to dangerous dieting behaviors. U.S. *News* recently sat down with five teens who were treated for anorexia at the Emily Program, a private eating disorders facility in Minneapolis-St. Paul, to find out what sent their weight plunging. Their moms sat in, too. Here are some of the comments the girls wish they'd never heard.

1. You're Big Boned Compared to Your Sister

Even offhand comparisons can cause a harmful overreaction. "I'd overhear my mom saying to her friends, 'Katie's the bigger one,'" recalls Katie Million, a 19-year-old from Lino Lakes, Minn., whose shame contributed to her weight falling below 95 pounds during her sophomore year of high school. Although there's no way to protect children from every hurtful comment, parents can certainly avoid remarking on a child's weight—and insist that siblings do, too. Research has shown that kids who are teased are more prone to binge eating and other eating disorders.

2. Maybe This New Diet Will Help

"I'm always hearing about how bad food is," says Leah Schumacher, 18, of St. Paul. "I would have liked to have learned about the positives of food, like why I need some fat to build cells and what fruits and vegetables do for my body." Million recently had a roommate whose mother sent her diet products and then complained on visits that her daughter hadn't lost enough weight. "I couldn't stick around for those conversations," she says.

3. I Hated My Body, Too, When I Was Your Age

With the best of intentions, Natalie Durbin shared the insecurities she'd had as a teen with her daughter Hannah, now 16, when Hannah was going through puberty. "I told her that I'd always been really thin but then started hating my body when I developed curves. I wanted to be really open about it in case she was feeling the same way," Durbin explains. Hannah, though, took it as a cue for how she should feel about her own developing body—especially since her mother was still uncomfortable with her weight. "She would tell me not to focus on my body image, but then she'd talk about how she hated her body all the time," says Hannah. "Now I think it's best if my mom never talks about these things with me."

4. You're Such a Talented Athlete; Let's Crank It up a Notch

One Emily mom who recognized running talent in her daughter encouraged her to join the track team and began to run with her to help her train. "I praised her, thinking I was building up her self-esteem, but never realized she hated [running] and was only doing it for me," says the mother, who prefers not to be identified. When the girl began adding extra miles and rapidly shedding weight, her mother was shocked to discover the response was a statement of how much her daughter hated the pressure of the track meets. Some kids have a natural drive to excel in sports, but if parents are doing the pushing, they may need to stop and reassess.

5. You Look Great! Have You Lost Weight?

Nearly all the teens said they got praise from family and friends when they began restricting their food intake and dropping pounds. "You can put up with how painfully cold you are all the time," says 18-year-old Edie Kuss from Minneapolis, "and that you're so weak you can't stand up. What you crave is the praise—and that's what you remember even when it stops because you've gotten too thin."

—D.K.

Grass-roots efforts can make a difference, too. Hillcrest Elementary School nurse Kim Glielmi implemented a voluntary walking program last year in which 200 students, parents, and teachers put in 1 mile a day around the neighborhood to reach a grand total for the group. "Our goal had been to walk enough miles to get to California by the end of the year," she says, "but we actually got as far as Hawaii." A community garden project in New York City's Harlem section has increased inner-city kids' appreciation of fresh fruits and vegetables. A program to build bike paths and sidewalks in Marin County, Calif., is prompting more kids to transport themselves to school.

At home. Parents, of course, will have the biggest impact. In her book *"I'm, Like, So Fat!"* Neumark-Sztainer says the most important thing parents can do is to model healthful behaviors—not preach them—by avoiding fad diets, skipped meals, and too much junk food and by hitting the gym and planning active family outings on a regular basis. A slew of studies have shown that teens who regularly eat home-cooked family dinners enjoy healthier weights, higher grades, lower rates of smoking, less depression, and a lower risk of developing an eating disorder.

The home environment should be conducive to good habits: a fruit bowl on the kitchen counter, cut-up vegetables in the fridge, jump-ropes in the garage, a basketball hoop in the driveway. Lake advises introducing healthful foods again and again even if a child refuses to eat them, since research shows it may take 10 to 12 sightings before a picky eater lifts fork to mouth. And he recommends against enforcing a clean-plate rule, pointing out that toddlers up to age 4 naturally and wisely regulate their own intake and that older kids eat out of habit, even if they're feeling full. "Parents should choose when to eat and what to eat, while a child should choose when to stop," says Lake.

How to Succeed at Losing

It's Tough, but Kids Can Get to—and Stay at—a Healthy Weight

A focus on body weight may be necessary when a seriously overweight child's well-being is at stake. But parents need to be respectful and supportive, since pressuring kids—especially teens—to lose weight could cause them to overeat more or develop an eating disorder. After seeing her 18-year-old son, Wes, shave 65 pounds off his 270-pound frame, registered dietitian Anne Fletcher set out to discover the secret of other teens' success. In her recent book *Weight Loss Confidential,* she studies how 104 seriously overweight preteens and teens, 41 boys and 63 girls, got to a healthier weight and stayed there for two years or longer. The kids on average lost 58 pounds each, and one quarter lost 75 pounds or more. Here's how they did it:

They Took the Initiative

Readiness is everything, says Fletcher, and the teens she studied decided on their own when and how they were going to lose the weight. They were motivated by wanting to improve their health, look better, feel better about themselves, and improve their performance at sports and other activities.

They Got Active

Exercise was by far the most popular slimming strategy, with 83 percent of the teens reporting that they upped their calorie-burning efforts to lose and then to maintain. Running, walking, and lifting weights were the most common choices. Nearly two thirds of the kids continued to exercise three to five times a week.

They Got Real about Portions

These teens know that a proper portion of meat is the size of a deck of cards and that a cup of pasta is the size of their fist. Using smaller plates and cups helped them impose limits, as did avoiding eating directly out of a bag.

They Drew on Support from Their Parents

Never underestimate the power of a cheering section. Encouraging parents who stocked the kitchen with nutritious low-calorie fare and exercised with their kids were a key to these teens' success.

They Discovered What Worked Best for Them

Some of the teens went to nutritionists for one-on-one counseling or attended summer weight camps that emphasized the importance of a healthful lifestyle. Others created their own structure, by cutting portions or giving up certain foods like french fries or soda. Fletcher's son counted calories. "Wes had always been able to eat a huge amount of food without feeling full, so this really made him start paying attention to portion sizes," she says.

They Connected

Some teens discovered the power of bonding with peers in support groups like Take Off Pounds Sensibly. One girl went to meetings with her mother, and they both lost weight together.

They Gave Themselves Time

Some of the teens lost the weight over many months or, in some cases, years. Gradual weight loss, explains Fletcher, doesn't demand the kind of deprivation required for quick results.

They Didn't Use the Scale as Their Only Measure of Success

Although they were certainly motivated by drops in clothing sizes, the successful losers were also encouraged by feeling less winded when they climbed a flight of stairs, by improvements in their blood pressure, and by closer relationships with friends and relatives and greater self-confidence. Most realized that they were never going to reach society's thin ideal. So they chose to appreciate their assets and aimed for good health instead.

—D.K

Experts also emphasize the importance of fostering a positive body image since, according to the Minnesota data, 46 percent of teenage girls and 26 percent of boys are dissatisfied with the way they look. Parents should both avoid making negative comments about their own bodies and put a stop to any teasing (box, Page 136). They should also discuss healthful behaviors without focusing too much on size or body fat. Liza Miller, a lean and sprightly 10-year-old, shows the level of understanding that parents might wish to achieve. (Her father, Dirk Miller, heads the Emily Program, a private eating disorders organization that runs the Anna Westin House.) She has trained herself to say no at slumber parties to bowls of potato chips and ice cream. And she has made a firm decision not to use celebrities as role models. Witness the sign posted on her bedroom door: "I won't allow people like Nicole Richie to make me feel fat."

Note

"How to Win the Weight Battle" [September 10] stated that 17 percent of kids are now obese, which means they're at or above the 95th percentile for weight in relation to height. The reason that a greater percentage of kids now fall into the "top 5 percent" category is that the standard measurement charts that define obesity were created using data from the 1960s and '70s, when kids weighed less than they do now.

The Epidemic That Wasn't

Susan Okie

Baltimore—One sister is 14; the other is 9. They are a vibrant pair: the older girl is high-spirited but responsible, a solid student and a devoted helper at home; her sister loves to read and watch cooking shows, and she recently scored well above average on citywide standardized tests.

There would be nothing remarkable about these two happy, normal girls if it were not for their mother's history. Yvette H., now 38, admits that she used cocaine (along with heroin and alcohol) while she was pregnant with each girl. "A drug addict," she now says ruefully, "isn't really concerned about the baby she's carrying."

When the use of crack cocaine became a nationwide epidemic in the 1980s and '90s, there were widespread fears that prenatal exposure to the drug would produce a generation of severely damaged children. Newspapers carried headlines like "Cocaine: A Vicious Assault on a Child," "Crack's Toll Among Babies: A Joyless View" and "Studies: Future Bleak for Crack Babies."

But now researchers are systematically following children who were exposed to cocaine before birth, and their findings suggest that the encouraging stories of Ms. H.'s daughters are anything but unusual. So far, these scientists say, the long-term effects of such exposure on children's brain development and behavior appear relatively small.

"Are there differences? Yes," said Barry M. Lester, a professor of psychiatry at Brown University who directs the Maternal Lifestyle Study, a large federally financed study of children exposed to cocaine in the womb. "Are they reliable and persistent? Yes. Are they big? No."

Cocaine is undoubtedly bad for the fetus. But experts say its effects are less severe than those of alcohol and are comparable to those of tobacco—two legal substances that are used much more often by pregnant women, despite health warnings.

Surveys by the Department of Health and Human Services in 2006 and 2007 found that 5.2 percent of pregnant women reported using any illicit drug, compared with 11.6 percent for alcohol and 16.4 percent for tobacco.

"The argument is not that it's O.K. to use cocaine in pregnancy, any more than it's O.K. to smoke cigarettes in pregnancy," said Dr. Deborah A. Frank, a pediatrician at Boston University. "Neither drug is good for anybody."

But cocaine use in pregnancy has been treated as a moral issue rather than a health problem, Dr. Frank said. Pregnant women who use illegal drugs commonly lose custody of their children, and during the 1990s many were prosecuted and jailed.

Cocaine slows fetal growth, and exposed infants tend to be born smaller than unexposed ones, with smaller heads. But as these children grow, brain and body size catch up.

At a scientific conference in November, Dr. Lester presented an analysis of a pool of studies of 14 groups of cocaine-exposed children—4,419 in all, ranging in age from 4 to 13. The analysis failed to show a statistically significant effect on I.Q. or language development. In the largest of the studies, I.Q. scores of exposed children averaged about 4 points lower at age 7 than those of unexposed children.

In tests that measure specific brain functions, there is evidence that cocaine-exposed children are more likely than others to have difficulty with tasks that require visual attention and "executive function"—the brain's ability to set priorities and pay selective attention, enabling the child to focus on the task at hand.

Cocaine exposure may also increase the frequency of defiant behavior and poor conduct, according to Dr. Lester's analysis. There is also some evidence that boys may be more vulnerable than girls to behavior problems.

But experts say these findings are quite subtle and hard to generalize. "Just because it is statistically significant doesn't mean that it is a huge public health impact," said Dr. Harolyn M. Belcher, a neurodevelopmental pediatrician who is director of research at the Kennedy Krieger Institute's Family Center in Baltimore.

And Michael Lewis, a professor of pediatrics and psychiatry at the Robert Wood Johnson Medical School in New Brunswick, N.J., said that in a doctor's office or a classroom, "you cannot tell" which children were exposed to cocaine before birth.

He added that factors like poor parenting, poverty and stresses like exposure to violence were far more likely to damage a child's intellectual and emotional development—and by the same token, growing up in a stable household, with parents who do not abuse alcohol or drugs, can do much to ease any harmful effects of prenatal drug exposure.

Possession of crack cocaine, the form of the drug that was widely sold in inner-city, predominantly black neighborhoods, has long been punished with tougher sentences than possession of powdered cocaine, although both forms are identically metabolized by the body and have the same pharmacological effects.

Dr. Frank, the pediatrician in Boston, says cocaine-exposed children are often teased or stigmatized if others are aware of their exposure. If they develop physical symptoms or behavioral problems, doctors or teachers are sometimes too quick to blame the drug exposure and miss the real cause, like illness or abuse.

"Society's expectations of the children," she said, "and reaction to the mothers are completely guided not by the toxicity, but by the social meaning" of the drug.

Research on the health effects of illegal drugs, especially on unborn children, is politically loaded. Researchers studying children exposed to cocaine say they struggle to interpret their findings for the public without exaggerating their significance—or minimizing it, either.

Dr. Lester, the leader of the Maternal Lifestyle Study, noted that the evidence for behavioral problems strengthened as the children in his study and others approached adolescence. Researchers in the study are collecting data on 14-year-olds, he said, adding: "Absolutely, we need to continue to follow these kids. For the M.L.S., the main thing we're interested in is whether or not prenatal cocaine exposure predisposes you to early-onset drug use in adolescence" or other mental health problems.

Researchers have long theorized that prenatal exposure to a drug may make it more likely that the child will go on to use it. But so far, such a link has been scientifically reported only in the case of tobacco exposure.

Teasing out the effects of cocaine exposure is complicated by the fact that like Yvette H., almost all of the women in the studies who used cocaine while pregnant were also using other substances.

Moreover, most of the children in the studies are poor, and many have other risk factors known to affect cognitive development and behavior—inadequate health care, substandard schools, unstable family situations and exposure to high levels of lead. Dr. Lester said his group's study was large enough to take such factors into account.

Ms. H., who agreed to be interviewed only on the condition that her last name and her children's first names not be used, said she entered a drug and alcohol treatment program about six years ago, after losing custody of her children.

Another daughter, born after Ms. H. recovered from drug and alcohol abuse, is thriving now at 3. Her oldest, a 17-year-old boy, is the only one with developmental problems: he is autistic. But Ms. H. said she did not use cocaine, alcohol or other substances while pregnant with him.

After 15 months without using drugs or alcohol, Ms. H. regained custody and moved into Dayspring House, a residential program in Baltimore for women recovering from drug abuse, and their children.

There she received psychological counseling, parenting classes, job training and coaching on how to manage her finances. Her youngest attended Head Start, the older children went to local schools and were assigned household chores, and the family learned how to talk about their problems.

Now Ms. H. works at a local grocery, has paid off her debts, has her own house and is actively involved in her children's schooling and health care. She said regaining her children's trust took a long time. "It's something you have to constantly keep working on," she said.

Dr. Belcher, who is president of Dayspring's board of directors, said such programs offered evidence-based interventions for the children of drug abusers that can help minimize the chances of harm from past exposure to cocaine or other drugs.

"I think we can say this is an at-risk group," Dr. Belcher said. "But they have great potential to do well if we can mobilize resources around the family."

Three Reasons Not to Believe in an Autism Epidemic

According to some lay groups, the nation is experiencing an autism epidemic—a rapid escalation in the prevalence of autism for unknown reasons. However, no sound scientific evidence indicates that the increasing number of diagnosed cases of autism arises from anything other than purposely broadened diagnostic criteria, coupled with deliberately greater public awareness and intentionally improved case finding. Why is the public perception so disconnected from the scientific evidence? In this article we review three primary sources of misunderstanding: lack of awareness about the changing diagnostic criteria, uncritical acceptance of a conclusion illogically drawn in a California-based study, and inattention to a crucial feature of the "child count" data reported annually by the U.S. Department of Education.

MORTON ANN GERNSBACHER, MICHELLE DAWSON, AND H. HILL GOLDSMITH

I f you have learned anything about autism lately from the popular media, you most likely have learned—erroneously—that there is "a mysterious upsurge" in the prevalence of autism (*New York Times,* October 20, 2002, Section 4, p. 10), creating a "baffling . . . outbreak" (CBSnews.com, October 18, 2002), in which new cases are "exploding in number" (*Time,* May 6, 2002, p. 48), and "no one knows why" (*USA Today,* May 17, 2004, p. 8D). At least a handful of U.S. Congress members decree on their .gov Web sites that the nation is facing an autism epidemic. Several national media have erroneously concluded that a set of data from California "confirms the autism epidemic," and the largest autism-advocacy organization in the world has expressed alarm over astronomical percentage increases in the number of autistic children served in the public schools since 1992. However, no sound scientific evidence indicates that the increase in the number of diagnosed cases of autism arises from anything other than intentionally broadened diagnostic criteria, coupled with deliberately greater public awareness and conscientiously improved case finding. How did public perception become so misaligned from scientific evidence? In this article, we review three major sources of misunderstanding.

The Changing Diagnosis of Autism

The phenomenon of autism has existed most likely since the origins of human society. In retrospect, numerous historical figures—for instance, the 18th-century "wild boy of Aveyron"—fit autism diagnostic criteria but were not so diagnosed in their

day (Frith, 1989). Only in the 1940s did a constellation of differences in social interaction, communication, and focused interests come to be categorized by Leo Kanner as "autism." However, another 40 years would elapse before American psychiatric practice incorporated criteria for autism into what was by then the third edition of its *Diagnostic and Statistical Manual of Mental Disorders* (*DSM-III;* American Psychiatric Association, APA, 1980). Thus, estimates of the prevalence of autism prior to 1980 were based on individual clinicians' (e.g., Kanner & Eisenberg, 1956) or specific researchers' (e.g., Rutter, 1978) conceptions—and fluctuated because of factors that continue to introduce variation into current-day estimates (e.g., variation in the size of the population sampled and the manner of identification).

Autism has remained in the *DSM* (under the title, Pervasive Developmental Disorders), but not without modification through subsequent editions. Whereas the 1980 *DSM-III* entry required satisfying six mandatory criteria, the more recent 1994 *DSM-IV* (APA, 1994) offers 16 optional criteria—only half of which need to be met. Moreover, the severe phrasing of the 1980 mandatory criteria contrasts with the more inclusive phrasing of the 1994 optional criteria. For instance, to qualify for a diagnosis according to the 1980 criteria an individual needed to exhibit "*a pervasive lack of responsiveness* to other people" (emphasis added; APA, 1980, p. 89); in contrast, according to 1994 criteria an individual must demonstrate only "a lack of spontaneous seeking to share . . . achievements with other people" (APA, 1994, p. 70) and peer relationships less sophisticated than would be predicted by the individual's developmental level. The 1980

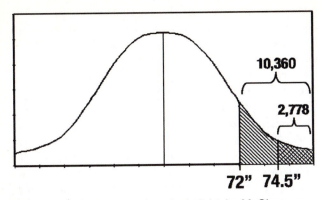

Figure 1 Distribution of male height in McClennan county, Texas. Shaded areas represent segments of the population defined as "tall" according to two standards: men over 74.5 in. (2,778) versus men over 72 in. (10,360).

mandatory criteria of "*gross deficits* in language development" (emphasis added; APA, 1980, p. 89) and "if speech is present, peculiar speech patterns such as immediate and delayed echolalia, metaphorical language, pronominal reversal" (APA, 1980, p. 89) were replaced by the 1994 options of difficulty "sustain[ing] a conversation" (APA, 1994, p. 70) or "lack of varied . . . social imitative play" (p. 70). "*Bizarre responses* to various aspects of the environment" (emphasis added; APA, 1980, p. 90) became "persistent preoccupation with parts of objects" (APA, 1994, p. 71).

Furthermore, whereas the earlier 1980 (*DSM-III*) entry comprised only two diagnostic categories (infantile autism and childhood onset pervasive developmental disorder), the more recent 1994 (*DSM-IV*) entry comprises five. Three of those five categories connote what is commonly called autism: Autistic Disorder, Pervasive Developmental Disorder Not Otherwise Specified (PDDNOS), and Asperger's Disorder. Autistic Disorder requires meeting half of the 16 criteria, but Asperger's Disorder, which did not enter the *DSM* until 1994, involves only two thirds of that half, and PDDNOS, which entered the *DSM* in 1987, is defined by subthreshold symptoms. Therefore, Asperger's Disorder and PDDNOS are often considered "milder variants." These milder variants can account for nearly three fourths of current autism diagnoses (Chakrabarti & Fombonne, 2001). Consider also the recent practice of codiagnosing autism alongside known medical and genetic conditions (e.g., Down syndrome, Tourette's syndrome, and cerebral palsy; Gillberg & Coleman, 2000); the contemporary recognition that autism can exist among people at every level of measured intelligence (Baird et al., 2000), the deliberate efforts to identify autism in younger and younger children (Filipek et al., 2000), and the speculation that many individuals who would meet present-day criteria were previously mis- or undiagnosed (Wing & Potter, 2002), including some of the most accomplished, albeit idiosyncratic, historical figures such as Isaac Newton, Lewis Carroll, W.B. Yeats, Thomas Jefferson, and Bill Gates (Fitzgerald, 2004).

The California Data

In California, persons diagnosed with autism (and other developmental disabilities) qualify for services administered by the statewide Department of Developmental Services (DDS). In 1999, the California DDS reported that from 1987 to 1998 the number of individuals served under the category of "autism" had increased by 273% (California DDS, 1999). Alarmed by this 273% increase, the California legislature commissioned the University of California Medical Investigation of Neurodevelopmental Disorders (M.I.N.D.) Institute to determine whether the increase could be explained by changes in diagnostic criteria. The M.I.N.D. Institute (2002) concluded, on the basis of data we describe next, that there was "no evidence that a loosening in the diagnostic criteria has contributed to the increased number of autism clients served by the [California DDS] Regional Centers" (p. 5). Although this unrefereed conclusion made national headlines and continues to be articulated on innumerable Web sites, it is unwarranted.

The study involved two samples of children who had been served under the California DDS category of "autism": One sample was born between 1983 and 1985 (the earlier cohort); the other sample was born between 1993 and 1995 (the more recent cohort). Both cohorts were assessed with the same autism diagnostic instrument (an interview conducted with care providers). However, the autism diagnostic instrument was based on *DSM-IV* criteria—criteria that were not even published until 1994. When the same percentage of children in the earlier and the more recent cohort met the more recent *DSM-IV* criteria, the researchers imprudently concluded that the "observed increase in autism cases cannot be explained by a loosening in the criteria used to make the diagnosis" (M.I.N.D. Institute, 2002, p. 7).

To understand the fallacy of the conclusion, consider the following analogy, based on male height and graphically illustrated in Figure 1. Suppose the criterion for "tall" was 74.5 in. and taller in the mid-1980s, but the criterion was loosened to 72 in. and taller in the mid-1990s. A diagnostic instrument based on the looser, more recent criterion of 72 in. would identify males who met the 74.5-in. criterion as well as those who met the 72-in. criterion.[1] Although a perfectly reliable diagnostic instrument based on a looser criterion would identify 100% of the individuals who meet the looser criterion along with 100% of the individuals who meet the more restricted criterion, a highly reliable instrument might identify about 90% of each group; this is the percentage of each cohort in the California study who met the more recent autism criteria.

Most crucially, broadening the criterion will result in a dramatic increase in diagnosed cases. For instance, census data allow us to estimate that 2,778 males in McClennan County, Texas would be called tall by the more restricted 74.5-in. criterion, and 10,360 males would be called tall by the broader 72-in. criterion; if those two criteria had been applied a decade apart, a 273% increase in the number of males called tall would have emerged—without any real increase in Texans' height. In the same way, the 273% increase from 2,778 versus 10,360

California children who received services for "autism" in 1987 versus 1998 could well be a function of broadened criteria.

As we have already detailed, the commonly applied diagnostic criteria for autism broadened nationally from the 1980s to the 1990s; thus, it would be unusual if the criteria used for eligibility in California had not also broadened during this time. Two further aspects of the California data suggest that the criteria must have broadened. First, children in the more recent cohort were dramatically less likely to have intellectual impairment: Whereas 61% of the children in the earlier cohort were identified as having intellectual impairments, only 27% of the children in the more recent cohort were so identified. The lower rate of intellectual impairment in the more recent cohort matches recent epidemiological data, and the difference between the two rates suggests a major difference between the two cohorts (e.g., that the more recent cohort was drawn from a less cognitively impaired population).

Second, on two of the three dimensions measured by the autism diagnostic instrument, the children in the more recent cohort were, on average, less symptomatic than the children from the earlier cohort. The researchers stated that although these differences were statistically significant (i.e., they exceeded the criterion of a statistical test), they were likely not clinically significant (i.e., they were likely not of significance to the clinical presentation); therefore, the researchers suggested that these differences should not be taken as evidence that the diagnostic criteria had broadened. However, refer again to the tallness analogy: Comparing two cohorts of males in McClennan County diagnosed according to our more restricted (74.5-in.) versus our broader (72-in.) criterion would probably result in a statistically significant difference between the two cohorts' average height—but the difference would be just about an inch (i.e., most likely not a clinically significant difference).

The "Child Count" Data

The purpose of the federal Individuals With Disabilities Education Act (IDEA), passed in 1991, is to ensure that all children with disabilities are provided a free, appropriate, public education including an individually designed program. Schools comply with the IDEA by reporting to the federal Department of Education an annual "child count" of the number of children with disabilities served. It is the data from these annual child counts that have been the most egregiously misused in arguments for an autism epidemic.

For example, in October 2003, the Autism Society of America sent its 20,000 members the following electronic message: "Figures from the most recent U. S. Department of Education's 2002 Report to Congress on IDEA reveal that the number of students with autism [ages 6 to 21] in America's schools *jumped an alarming 1,354% in the eight-year period from the school year 1991–92 to 2000–01*" (emphasis added). What the Autism Society failed to note is the following fact (available in the *Report to Congress,* immediately under the autism data entries): Prior to the 1991–1992 school year, there was no child count of students with autism; autism did not even exist as an IDEA reporting category. Moreover, in 1991–1992, use of the autism reporting category was optional (it was required only in subsequent years).

Whenever a new category is introduced, if it is viable, increases in its usage will ensue. Consider another IDEA reporting category introduced along with autism in 1991–1992: "traumatic brain injury." From 1991–1992 to 2000–2001, this category soared an astronomical 5,059%. Likewise, the reporting category "developmental delay," which was introduced only in 1997–1998, grew 663% in only 3 years.

After the initial year, the number of children reported under the IDEA category of autism has increased by approximately 23% annually. Why the continuing annual increase? As is the case with new options in the marketplace, like cellular phones and high-speed Internet, new reporting categories in the annual child count are not capitalized upon instantaneously; they require incrementally magnified awareness and augmentation or reallocation of resources. Currently no state reports the number of children with autism that would be expected based on the results of three recent, large-scale epidemiological studies, which identified 5.8 to 6.7 children per 1,000 for the broader autism spectrum (Baird et al., 2000; Bertrand et al., 2001; Chakrabarti & Fombonne, 2001). In 2002–2003, front-runners Oregon and Minnesota reported 4.3 and 3.5 children with autism per 1,000, respectively, while Colorado, Mississippi, and New Mexico reported only 0.8, 0.7, and 0.7 children with autism per 1,000. Thus, most likely IDEA child counts will continue to increase until the number reported by each state approaches the number of children identified in the epidemiological studies.

Why do states vary so widely in the number of children reported (or served)? Each state's department of education specifies its own diagnostic criteria, and states differ (as do school districts within states, and individual schools within school districts) in the value given to a diagnosis in terms of services received. States also vary from year to year in the number of children served and reported. For instance, Massachusetts historically reported the lowest percentage of children with autism: only 0.4 or 0.5 per 1,000 from 1992 through 2001. Then, in 2002, Massachusetts reported a 400% increase in one year, when it began using student-level data (i.e., actually counting the students) rather than applying a ratio, which was calculated in 1992, based on the proportion of students in each disability classification as reported in 1992. In their 2002 IDEA report to Congress, Massachusetts state officials warned that the increase will continue for several years as "districts better understand how to submit their data at the student level" (IDEA, 2002, p. 4) and "all districts comply completely with the new reporting methods" (IDEA, 2002, p. 4).

Other Reasons Not to Believe in an Autism Epidemic

In this article we have detailed three reasons why some laypersons mistakenly believe that there is an autism epidemic. They are unaware of the purposeful broadening of diagnostic criteria, coupled with deliberately greater public awareness; they accept the unwarranted conclusions of the M.I.N.D. Institute study; and they fail to realize that autism was not even an IDEA reporting category until the early 1990s and incremental increases will most likely continue until the schools are identifying and serving the number of children identified in epidemiological studies. Apart from a desire to be aligned with scientific reasoning, there are other reasons not to believe in an autism epidemic.

Epidemics solicit causes; false epidemics solicit false causes. Google *autism* and *epidemic* to witness the range of suspected causes of the mythical autism epidemic. Epidemics also connote danger. What message do we send autistic children and adults when we call their increasing number an epidemic? A pandemic? A scourge? Realizing that the increasing prevalence rates are most likely due to noncatastrophic mechanisms, such as purposely broader diagnostic criteria and greater public awareness, should not, however, diminish societal responsibility to support the increasing numbers of individuals being diagnosed with autism. Neither should enthusiasm for scientific inquiry into the variety and extent of human behavioral, neuroanatomical, and genotypic diversity in our population be dampened.

Note

1. Wing and Potter (2002) provide a similar illustration. The same percentage of children who met Kanner's earlier, more restricted criteria met *DSM-IV*'s more recent, broadened criteria; if the child was autistic according to Kanner's restricted criteria, the child was autistic according to *DSM-IV*'s broadened criteria. Of course, the reverse was not true. Only 33 to 45% of the children who met more recent *DSM-IV* criteria met earlier Kanner criteria.

References

American Psychiatric Association. (1980). *Diagnostic and statistical manual of mental disorders* (3rd ed.). Washington, DC: Author.

American Psychiatric Association. (1994). *Diagnostic and statistical manual of mental disorders* (4th ed.). Washington, DC: Author.

Baird, G., Charman, T., Baron-Cohen, S., Cox, A., Swettenham, J., Wheelwright, S., & Drew, A. (2000). A screening instrument for autism at 18 months of age: A 6 year follow-up study. *Journal of the American Academy of Child and Adolescent Psychiatry, 39,* 694–702.

Bertrand, J., Mars, A., Boyle, C., Bove, F., Yeargin-Allsopp, M., & Decoufle, P. (2001). Prevalence of autism in a United States population: The Brick Township, New Jersey, investigation. *Pediatrics, 108,* 1155–1161.

California Department of Developmental Services. (1999). *Changes in the population with autism and pervasive developmental disorders in California's developmental services system: 1987–1998.* A report to the legislature. Sacramento, CA: California Health and Human Services Agency.

Chakrabarti, S., & Fombonne, E. (2001). Pervasive developmental disorders in preschool children. *Journal of the American Medical Association, 285,* 3093–3099.

Filipek, P.A., Accardo, P.J., Ashwal, S., Baranek, G.T., Cook, E.H. Jr., Dawson, G., Gordon, B., Gravel, J.S., Johnson, C.P., Kallen, R.J., Levy, S.E., Minshew, N.J., Ozonoff, S., Prizant, B.M., Rapin, I., Rogers, S.J., Stone, W.L., Teplin, S.W., Tuchman, R.F., & Volkmar, F.R. (2000). Practice parameter: Screening and diagnosis of autism: Report of the Quality Standards Subcommittee of the American Academy of Neurology and the Child Neurology Society. *Neurology, 55,* 468–479.

Fitzgerald, M. (2004). *Autism and creativity: Is there a link between autism in men and exceptional ability?* London: Brunner-Routledge.

Frith, U. (1989). *Autism: Explaining the enigma.* Oxford, England: Blackwell.

Gillberg, C., & Coleman, M. (2000). *The biology of the autistic syndromes* (3rd ed.). London: MacKeith Press.

IDEA. (2002). *Data Notes for IDEA, Part B.* Retrieved April 22, 2005, from IDEAdata Web side: http://www.ideadata.org/docs/bdatanotes2002.doc

Kanner, L., & Eisenberg, J. (1956). Early infantile autism 1943–1955. *American Journal of Orthopsychiatry, 26,* 55–65.

M.I.N.D. Institute. (2002). *Report to the Legislature on the principal findings from The Epidemiology of Autism in California: A Comprehensive Pilot Study.* Davis: University of California-Davis.

Rutter, M. (1978). Diagnosis and definition. In M. Rutter & E. Schopler (Eds.), *Autism: A reappraisal of concepts and treatments* (pp. 1–25). New York: Plenum Press.

U.S. Department of Education. (2002). *Twenty-fourth annual report to Congress on the implementation of the Individuals With Disabilities Education Act.* Washington, DC: Author.

Wing, L., & Potter, D. (2002). The epidemiology of autistic spectrum disorders: Is the prevalence rising? *Mental Retardation and Developmental Disabilities Research Reviews, 8,* 151–162.

MORTON ANN GERNSBACHER: University of Wisconsin-Madison; **MICHELLE DAWSON:** University of Montreal, Montreal, Quebec, Canada; **H. HILL GOLDSMITH:** University of Wisconsin-Madison

Address correspondence to Morton Ann Gernsbacher, Department of Psychology, University of Wisconsin-Madison, 1202 W. Johnson St., Madison, WI 53706; e-mail: MAGernsb@wisc.edu

Getting Back to the Great Outdoors

With children spending less time in nature than ever before, the biggest victim may be Mother Earth. Psychologists are helping kids connect.

AMY NOVOTNEY

Martha Erickson, PhD, always believed that her frequent nature outings with her children, and her encouragement of their independent play and exploration outdoors, helped them mature into well-rounded adults. These days, she's getting confirmation of that fact.

"As many young people were spending increasing amounts of time watching television or playing video games, my kids were much more likely to head off on their bikes, canoe down the creek that flows through our city or rally some friends to create an outdoor adventure," she says. "Now, as young adults, they are fit, creative, adventurous and striving to protect the environment."

Increasing evidence demonstrates the many benefits of nature on children's psychological and physical well-being, including reduced stress, greater physical health, more creativity and improved concentration.

"The basic finding seems to be yes, nature does seem to be really good for kids," says Frances Kuo, PhD, founder of the Landscape and Human Health Laboratory at the University of Illinois at Urbana-Champaign.

Beyond the health and cognitive benefits children may gain from free and unstructured play outdoors, nature also provides them with a sense of wonder and a deeper understanding of our responsibility to take care of the Earth, says Richard Louv, author of "Last Child in the Woods: Saving Our Children from Nature Deficit-Disorder" (Algonquin Books, 2005). Yet increasingly, nature is the last place you'll find children, research shows.

Many factors have come together to push children indoors, he says, including land development and more people living in cities, additional demands on children's time—such as more homework and structured activities—video games and the Internet, and parental fear, particularly of strangers. In today's society of indoor children, personal connections with nature seem hard to come by, which threatens to lessen future generations' concerns about the environment, Louv says.

"Last time I checked, it was pretty tough to have a sense of wonder when you're playing 'Grand Theft Auto,'" Louv says.

"If we're raising a generation of children under protective house arrest, where does that lead us in terms of our connection to the natural world?"

As experts in child development and learning, psychologists are helping children reconnect with nature by conducting research, incorporating the outdoors into clinical interventions and educating parents, says Erickson, a director of early childhood mental health training programs at the University of Minnesota in Minneapolis.

"People often listen to what psychologists have to say when it comes to kids' learning and development," she says. "We really need to work as advocates and in our practices to think about the potential of nature to improve the health and well-being of children."

Green Is Good

Psychologists have actively studied the role nature plays in children's mental health since the early 1980s, when Harvard University biologist Edward O. Wilson, PhD, introduced his theory of "biophilia," which argues that humans have an innate affinity for the natural world. Now, a host of studies are showing just how essential outdoor activities are for the developing mind.

One of the most influential longitudinal studies, led by Cornell University environmental psychologist Nancy M. Wells, PhD, found that children who experienced the biggest increase in green space near their home after moving improved their cognitive functioning more than those who moved to areas with fewer natural resources nearby (*Environment and Behavior* (Vol. 32, No. 6). Similarly, in a study of 337 school-age children in rural upstate New York, Wells found that the presence of nearby nature bolsters a child's resilience against stress and adversity, particularly among those children who experience a high level of stress (*Environment and Behavior*, Vol. 35, No. 3).

But while such studies support the notion that nature is good for children, psychologists may need to act fast to get children back outside. A study by University of Maryland sociologist

Sandra Hofferth, PhD, shows that between 1997 and 2003, the amount of time children ages 9 to 12 spent participating in outdoor activities such as hiking, horseback riding, fishing, camping and gardening declined by 50 percent.

What are children doing instead? Playing video games, watching TV and spending time on the computer, Hofferth found.

Such activities are, of course, linked with the rise in childhood obesity. A 2004 National Health and Nutrition Examination Survey found that one-third of children and teens, ages 2 to 19, were overweight or at risk of becoming overweight. By 2010, about half of school-age children in North and South America will be overweight or obese, predicts an article in the *International Journal of Pediatric Obesity* (Vol. 1, No. 1).

Without building a connection to the natural world when they're young, it seems unlikely that children will possess much of an affiliation with Mother Earth as adults, says Wells. In fact, a 2006 study—led by Wells and published in *Children, Youth and Environments* (Vol. 16, No. 1)—suggests that childhood participation with nature may set individuals on a trajectory toward adult environmentalism.

"Kids are already hearing that polar bears don't have anywhere to rest. If we don't have them outside thinking that squirrels are fascinating, they may get overwhelmed and close down completely."

Meg Houlihan
Charlotte, N.C.

"This study shows that there really may be a connection between kids' experiences in nature and their later life attitudes and behaviors," Wells says.

Erickson agrees. "It's a principle of human nature that you care for what you know and what you love," says Erickson. "Learning about climate change just by studying it on the Internet or reading about it in books is one thing, but to come to know and love the natural world firsthand from an early age just gives you a different kind of motive [for preserving it]."

Reinventing Children of Nature

Practitioners can use this research as strong evidence for incorporating nature into their client interventions, says Erickson.

"Making time to get outside to play, run and explore could be a really important part of a treatment plan," she says.

Psychologists can also encourage school administrators to get children outside during the school day, by working with their state psychological associations to develop briefing papers for local school boards, contacting local news media to encourage coverage of the benefits of nature to children or leading volunteer efforts to plant gardens at a local schools, Erickson

recommends. Creative exploration and firsthand experience discovering nature appear to be the best ways for children to learn about a host of subjects—particularly, Erickson says. More recess time and greener playgrounds might also enable children to learn more effectively and improve a child's ability to concentrate in the classroom, says Kuo. In a study published in the September 2004 issue of the *American Journal of Public Health* (Vol. 94, No. 9), Kuo and her colleague, Andrea Faber Taylor, PhD, found that green outdoor activities reduced attention-deficit hyperactivity disorder symptoms significantly more than activities in built outdoor and indoor settings.

"If we had kids moving around and burning off energy, I think we would have much less difficulty with kids having trouble paying attention in the classroom," Erickson says.

Wells says research by psychologists and others may help determine whether there may be a "critical period" for children's exposure to the natural environment, and if so, when that might be.

Perhaps most importantly, psychologists are among those helping to educate the public—particularly parents—on the importance of getting children outside. In April, Erickson will help kick off a statewide children and nature awareness campaign in Minnesota, which will include television and radio coverage and public events—such as moonlight walks at a Minneapolis-area nature center—focused on specific steps parents and other caregivers can take to help renew children's interest in the natural world. Similar public outreach initiatives are also under way in New Hampshire, Massachusetts and California, among other states, according to the Children and Nature Network (www.cnaturenet.org), a national organization that Louv and Erickson help lead, dedicated to reconnecting children with nature.

Often, parents aren't aware of nature's benefits to their children, or they aren't sure how to tear their children away from the computer or television screen, says Meg Houlihan, PhD, a private practitioner in Charlotte, N.C., who speaks locally to parents and teachers about overcoming barriers to getting kids outside. She emphasizes gradual change: taking children out on the front lawn for an hour, for example.

"It's important to give the message to parents that it doesn't have to be a huge trip to Yellowstone to be nature," says Houlihan.

She tells parents to pick up a handful of paint chips from the hardware store and have their children find things in the backyard that match those colors, or to host a neighborhood scavenger hunt in the park. These types of activities help children build a love for nature through everyday interactions—with birds, trees and community gardens, for example. Only then will they be able to fully appreciate—and hopefully take action against—issues such as climate change, Houlihan says.

"Kids are already hearing that polar bears don't have anywhere to rest," she says. "If we don't have them outside thinking that squirrels are fascinating, they may get overwhelmed and close down completely."

What Causes Specific Language Impairment in Children?

Specific language impairment (SLI) is diagnosed when a child's language development is deficient for no obvious reason. For many years, there was a tendency to assume that SLI was caused by factors such as poor parenting, subtle brain damage around the time of birth, or transient hearing loss. Subsequently it became clear that these factors were far less important than genes in determining risk for SLI. A quest to find "the gene for SLI" was undertaken, but it soon became apparent that no single cause could account for all cases. Furthermore, although fascinating cases of SLI caused by a single mutation have been discovered, in most children the disorder has a more complex basis, with several genetic and environmental risk factors interacting. The clearest evidence for genetic effects has come from studies that diagnosed SLI using theoretically motivated measures of underlying cognitive deficits rather than conventional clinical criteria.

DOROTHY V. M. BISHOP

Talking comes so naturally to most children that one seldom pauses to consider the enormous complexity of the achievement. Understanding just how the human brain manages to learn language—typically in the space of around 4 short years—is still a long way off. Perhaps as remarkable as the speed with which young humans learn language is the robustness of this process in the face of adverse conditions (Bishop & Mogford, 1993). Most children will learn to talk adequately even if they are exposed to impoverished language input from adults or are visually impaired and thus unable to see what is being talked about. Children who are unable to speak because of physical disability, and those who cannot hear what others say to them, will nevertheless learn to communicate by other means, provided they are exposed to alternative systems of communication such as sign language.

There are, however, exceptions to this general rule of speedy and robust language acquisition: Children with specific language impairment (SLI) have major problems in learning to talk, despite showing normal development in all other areas (see Table 1). Thus, a typical 7- or 8-year-old child with SLI may talk like a 3-year-old, using simplified speech sounds, with words strung together in short, ungrammatical strings—e.g., "me go there," rather than "I went there." SLI is a heterogeneous category, varying in both severity and profile of disorder, but in most cases it is possible to demonstrate problems with both understanding and producing spoken language; for example, the child may have difficulty using toys to act out a sentence such as "the boy is chased by the dog," showing confusion as to who is doing what to whom. Language impairment in SLI is puzzling precisely because it occurs in children who are otherwise normally developing, with no hearing problems or physical handicaps that could explain the difficulties.

The prevalence of SLI has been estimated at around 7% (Tomblin et al., 1997), although this will vary with both the diagnostic criteria and children's age: Long-term language impairments that persist into adulthood are less common than milder delays in preschoolers, which may resolve with time (Bishop & Adams, 1990).

SLI as a Strongly Genetic Disorder

When I started out studying SLI in the mid-1970s, very little was known about its causes. Possibilities that had been suggested included inadequate parenting, subtle brain damage acquired around the time of birth, or recurrent ear disease in early childhood. However, none of these theories has had much support. Instead, it has become increasingly clear that genetic makeup exerts a strong influence in determining which children will develop SLI. Studies showing that SLI tends to run in families are suggestive of genetic influence, but they are not watertight, because family members share environments as well as genes. More compelling evidence comes from twin studies showing that monozygotic (MZ) twins, who are genetically identical, resemble each other in terms of SLI diagnosis more closely than do dizygotic (DZ) twins, who have 50% of their segregating genes (genes that can take different forms, or alleles, in different people) in common. Statistical analysis of twin data shows that the environment shared by the twins is

Table 1 Characteristics of Specific Language Impairment (SLI)

Diagnostic criteria

- Language is significantly below level expected from age and IQ, usually interpreted as scoring in the lowest 10% on a standardized test of expressive and/or receptive language
- Nonverbal IQ and nonlinguistic aspects of development (self-help skills, social skills) fall within broadly normal limits
- Language difficulties cannot be accounted for by hearing loss, physical abnormality of the speech apparatus, or environmental deprivation
- Language difficulties are not caused by brain damage

Common presenting features*

- Delay in starting to talk; first words may not appear until 2 years of age or later
- Immature or deviant production of speech sounds, especially in preschool children
- Use of simplified grammatical structures, such as omission of past tense endings or the auxiliary "is," well beyond the age when this is usually mastered
- Restricted vocabulary, in both production and comprehension
- Weak verbal short-term memory, as evidenced in tasks requiring repetition of words or sentences
- Difficulties in understanding complex language, especially when the speaker talks rapidly

*SLI shows substantial heterogeneity, as well as age-related change, and diagnosis does not depend on presence or absence of specific language characteristics.

relatively unimportant in causing SLI, whereas genes exert a significant effect, with heritability estimates (i.e., the proportion of variance in a trait that is attributable to genetic factors) typically ranging from around .5 to .75 for school-aged children (see Bishop, 2002, for review).

Is There a "Gene for Language"?

When it first became apparent that genes are implicated in SLI, there was a lot of popular interest in the idea that researchers might discover a "gene for language" that had evolved in humans and that distinguished humans from other primates. The idea would be that this gene was defective in some children, who consequently lacked a natural capacity for language learning. However, subsequent research on SLI has not supported this interpretation. For one thing, it is unusual to find families in which SLI is inherited in a simple fashion. In this regard, SLI resembles *complex genetic disorders,* such as asthma and diabetes, which run in families but for which patterns of inheritance do not correspond to any known dominant or recessive pattern.

There is, however, one remarkable family that is an exception: the three-generational KE family from London, England, that has been extensively studied by geneticists. SLI affects 50% of the children of an affected parent, and it is caused by a mutation affecting a tiny piece of DNA on a gene on chromosome 7. The KE family excited a great deal of interest from researchers, because, once the defective gene was identified, it was possible to study its effect on the developing brain. However, research on this gene, known as *FOXP2,* makes it clear that it is not a gene for language—rather, it is a gene that regulates the activity of other genes, having an effect on the development of many organs, including brain systems important for speech and language (Fisher, 2005). Structural and functional brain-imaging studies have shown that affected family members have abnormalities in the caudate nuclei and cerebellum as well as in

Broca's area, a classic language center (Vargha-Khadem, Gadian, Copp, & Mishkin, 2005). Studies of the KE family have helped to identify one route by which genetic variation affects brain development and subsequent language capability, but it is clear that this is only part of the picture. Most people with SLI do not have any abnormality of the *FOXP2* gene, and it seems likely that in the majority of cases the disorder is caused by the interaction of several genes together with environmental risk factors.

Genetic Influences on Different Aspects of Language Impairment

The first step in unravelling the causes of a condition such as SLI does not involve any direct DNA analysis, but rather uses methods such as twin studies, which allow the comparison of phenotypes (observed characteristics) in people who differ in their degree of genetic similarity. One issue is how to define the SLI phenotype. In one of the first twin studies that I did on this topic, I found that it was very common to find MZ twin pairs in which one twin met clinical criteria for SLI and the other did not. However, the non-SLI twin typically had evidence of language difficulties: These simply were not selective enough or persistent enough to meet conventional diagnostic criteria for the disorder. This suggested that simply categorising children as affected or unaffected on the basis of conventional language tests was not an effective approach to phenotype definition. An alternative approach is to look for *endophenotypes,* measures of underlying factors thought to play a causal role in the disorder (Gottesman & Gould, 2003). I adopted such an approach by doing genetic analysis using experimental measures that were derived from particular theoretical accounts of SLI.

One such measure, nonword repetition, was derived from a theory that attributes SLI to impairment in a system that is specialised for holding verbal material in memory for short periods of time—phonological short-term memory (STM). An

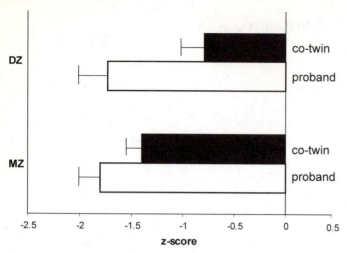

Figure 1 Mean z-scores on nonword repetition for individuals with specific language impairment (probands, defined as those with z-score less than 1.0) and their co-twins, in relation to whether they are monozygotic (MZ) or dizygotic (DZ) twins. The population mean score is zero. Insofar as similar environmental influences affect both twins, two members of a twin pair would be expected to resemble one another. However, if, as shown here, the similarity between MZ probands and their co-twins is greater than that between DZ probands and their co-twins, this points to a genetic influence on low scores. Data from Bishop, North, & Donlan (1996).

estimate of phonological STM capacity can be obtained by asking children to repeat meaningless sequences of syllables, such as "perplisteronk" or "blonterstaping." Children with SLI are usually extremely poor at this task, even if they can produce the individual speech sounds accurately. The longer the nonsense word, the worse they do. The task also reveals deficits in people who appear to have overcome early developmental language difficulties, and so it acts as a good marker of resolved language difficulties. When we used this task in a twin study (Bishop, North, & Donlan, 1996), we found evidence of strong genetic influence on impaired nonword repetition (see Figure 1). Subsequently, molecular geneticists have homed in on an area of chromosome 16 that appears to harbor a gene associated with poor phonological STM (Newbury, Bishop, & Monaco, 2005).

We know that phonological STM is poor in SLI, but there has been debate as to whether this can be traced to a more general deficit affecting perception of auditory input. One account proposes that the fundamental problem in SLI is a difficulty in distinguishing or identifying sounds that are brief or that occur in rapid succession, be they nonverbal or verbal. Accordingly, in one twin study we included a measure of nonverbal auditory perception (identification of tone sequences), as well as a test of nonword repetition. Although we found evidence for poor performance in SLI on both tasks, the twin analysis suggested they were not different manifestations of the same problem. Deficient nonword repetition again showed strong genetic influence, but poor ability to identify tone sequences was not significantly heritable. Twins tended to resemble one another on

the non-verbal auditory task, but this was equally true for DZ as for MZ twins, suggesting the twin similarity was the result of environmental influences that they shared. One possibility is that this task is affected by the child's musical experiences: I showed that the effect of shared environment on the tone-sequence task accounted for about 60% of the variance, but almost half of this effect could be accounted for by a measure of the amount of live music experienced at home (as assessed by a parental questionnaire asking whether family members played a musical instrument; Bishop, 2001).

In a recent study with a sample of 6-year-old twins, we again measured phonological STM, but this time we also took a measure of children's ability to add appropriate inflectional endings to verbs (Bishop, Adams, & Norbury, 2006). Many English-speaking children with SLI have unusual difficulty with some aspects of grammar, and will tend to omit the appropriate verb inflection in sentences such as "Yesterday my brother walk(ed) to school," or "Every day John ride(s) his bike." There has been debate in the field as to whether this grammatical difficulty is a consequence of weak phonological STM or has separate origins. We found evidence for strong genetic influence on poor performance on the verb-inflection task: If a MZ twin had a low score, his or her co-twin also tended to do poorly, whereas if a DZ twin did poorly, the result for the co-twin was much more variable. However, there was no association between this effect and that seen on phonological STM, where again significant heritability of the deficit was seen. Both impairments were found in SLI, and both were heritable, yet they were only weakly correlated, and genetic analysis suggested that different genes were implicated in the two deficits.

SLI as a Disorder of Multiple Underlying Deficits

As argued in the previous section, various underlying skills are impaired in SLI, but these different deficits have different causes, some genetic and some environmental. Our first reaction to such results was to think that the genetic analysis might help us identify distinct subgroups of SLI, each with a different underlying cause. However, what repeatedly emerged in our studies was that children who had a single area of deficit were less likely to be identified clinically as cases of SLI than were those who had more than one deficit. Thus, although different deficits have different origins and can be dissociated, it seems as though a child has to be impaired in more than one domain in order for language to be seriously impaired. This brings us back to the point made at the start of this article: Language is usually surprisingly robust in the face of adverse developmental circumstances. This suggests that there may be multiple routes to effective language acquisition, and if one route is blocked, another can usually be found. However, if two or more routes are blocked, then language learning will be compromised. Many researchers are still engaged in the quest for a parsimonious single-factor theory of SLI. However, the genetic studies are forcing us to rethink this perspective and to regard SLI as a case in which development is compromised precisely because more than one cognitive process is disrupted (Bishop, 2006). This conceptualisation challenges any notion of SLI as a single syndrome and also suggests that we may need to analyze it in terms of dimensions of impairment instead of looking for discrete subtypes.

Clinical Implications

All too often people assume that genes exert a deterministic effect and that nothing can be done to help a child whose impairment has a constitutional origin. This is a serious misconception. To say that a disorder is highly heritable is to imply that variations in children's genetic makeup are more important than variations in their environmental experiences in determining who has a disorder. However, it says nothing about how the child might respond to a novel intervention that is not usually encountered in the environment. By analogy, consider the case of Huntington's disease, a progressive late-onset degenerative disease that is caused by a dominantly inherited mutation. Mouse models have shown that onset and severity of the motor symptoms can be modified by early-environmental enrichment (Spires & Hannan, 2005). So even in the case of a strongly genetic disorder, environmental modifications can have an effect. And in a disorder such as SLI, in which multiple genetic and environmental risk factors are implicated, there is every reason to suppose that ways of modifying the course of the disorder may be discovered, especially if new genetic knowledge is used to identify children at risk early so that intervention can begin at a young age.

Future Directions

The study of SLI is a field in which interdisciplinary collaboration is vital. It is sometimes assumed that once a disorder is discovered to have a genetic component, the psychologists have no further role to play, and the only task left is for molecular geneticists to isolate the gene responsible. SLI provides a clear counterexample to such reasoning, demonstrating that without theoretically motivated measures of the underlying phenotype, geneticists are unlikely to make progress in unravelling the causes of these complex but common developmental disorders. The task for psychologists is to identify which components of language show significant heritability and, hence, constitute good candidates for genetic analysis, as well as to discover new endophenotypes. Measures of phonological STM and use of grammatical morphology have already been discussed as showing good potential in this regard. A further promising approach would be to use dynamic measures that assess how well children respond to particular kinds of interventions—i.e., measure the extent to which language abilities can be modified, rather than taking a single measure at one point in time (e.g., Peña, Iglesias, & Lidz, 2001).

References

Bishop, D.V.M. (2001). Genetic and environmental risks for specific language impairment in children. *Philosophical Transactions of the Royal Society, Series B, 356,* 369–380.

Bishop, D.V.M. (2002). The role of genes in the etiology of specific language impairment. *Journal of Communication Disorders, 35,* 311–328.

Bishop, D.V.M. (2006). Developmental cognitive genetics: How psychology can inform genetics and vice versa. *Quarterly Journal of Experimental Psychology, 59,* 1153–1168.

Bishop, D.V.M., & Adams, C. (1990). A prospective study of the relationship between specific language impairment, phonological disorders and reading retardation. *Journal of Child Psychology and Psychiatry, 31,* 1027–1050.

Bishop, D.V.M., Adams, C.V., & Norbury, C.F. (2006). Distinct genetic influences on grammar and phonological short-term memory deficits: Evidence from 6-year-old twins. *Genes, Brain and Behavior, 5,* 158–169.

Bishop, D.V.M., & Mogford, K. (Eds.). (1993). *Language development in exceptional circumstances.* Hove: Psychology Press.

Bishop, D.V.M., North, T., & Donlan, C. (1996). Nonword repetition as a behavioural marker for inherited language impairment: Evidence from a twin study. *Journal of Child Psychology and Psychiatry, 37,* 391–403.

Fisher, S.E. (2005). Dissection of molecular mechanisms underlying speech and language disorders. *Applied Psycholinguistics, 26,* 111–128.

Gottesman, I.I., & Gould, T.D. (2003). The endophenotype concept in psychiatry: Etymology and strategic intentions. *American Journal of Psychiatry, 160,* 636–645.

Newbury, D.F., Bishop, D.V.M., & Monaco, A.P. (2005). Genetic influences on language impairment and phonological short-term memory. *Trends in Cognitive Sciences, 9,* 528–534.

Peña, E., Iglesias, A., & Lidz, C.S. (2001). Reducing test bias through dynamic assessment of children's word learning ability. *American Journal of Speech-Language Pathology, 10,* 138–154.

Spires, T.L., & Hannan, A.J. (2005). Nature, nurture and neurology: Gene-environment interactions in neurodegenerative disease. *FEBS Journal, 272,* 2347–2361.

Tomblin, J.B., Records, N.L., Buckwalter, P., Zhang, X., Smith, E., & O'Brien, M. (1997). Prevalence of specific language impairment in kindergarten children. *Journal of Speech and Hearing Research, 40,* 1245–1260.

Vargha-Khadem, F., Gadian, D., Copp, A., & Mishkin, M. (2005). FOXP2 and the neuroanatomy of speech and language. *Nature Reviews Neuroscience, 6,* 131–138.

Address correspondence to Dorothy. V. M. Bishop, Department of Experimental Psychology, University of Oxford, OX1 3UD, United Kingdom; e-mail: dorothy.bishop@psy.ox.ac.uk.

Acknowledgments—The author is supported by a Principal Research Fellowship from the Wellcome Trust.

Treatment and Prevention of Posttraumatic Stress Reactions in Children and Adolescents Exposed to Disasters and Terrorism: What Is the Evidence?

ANNETTE M. LA GRECA AND WENDY K. SILVERMAN

In the United States and abroad, research has documented high levels of posttraumatic stress disorder (PTSD) and post-traumatic stress (PTS) reactions in children and adolescents exposed to catastrophic natural disasters (hurricanes, earthquakes, tsunamis, and floods; e.g., Goenjian et al., 2005; La Greca, Silverman, Vernberg, & Prinstein, 1996; Weems et al., 2007) and terrorist attacks (Hoven et al., 2005; Lengua, Long, Smith, & Meltzoff, 2005; see reviews by Comer & Kendall, 2007; Gurwitch, Sitterle, Young, & Pfefferbaum, 2002). The development of interventions for youths' reactions to natural disasters and acts of terrorism to prevent serious youth adjustment problems is of considerable public health significance (Vernberg, 2002).

This article summarizes existing evidence on the prevention and treatment of PTS reactions in youth exposed to natural disasters and terrorism, with an eye toward highlighting gaps in current knowledge and directions for future research. (For information on the prevalence and course of PTS and other reactions in children following disasters and terrorism, see the American Academy of Child and Adolescent Psychiatry, 1998; Gurwitch et al., 2002; Vogel & Vernberg, 1993; Yule, Udwin, & Bolton, 2002; for studies of risk factors of PTS reactions, see Comer & Kendall, 2007; Silverman & La Greca, 2002.)

Evidence-Based Interventions for PTS Reactions

A useful way to conceptualize postdisaster interventions is whether they were designed for the *immediate* aftermath of the event, the *short-term* recovery and rebuilding phase, or the *long-term* recovery phase (Vernberg, 2002); there has also been recent interest in predisaster efforts to prevent PTS reactions. Treatment goals depend on the time frame and context in which interventions are delivered.

Immediate Postimpact Phase (The Event through the First Few Weeks Postdisaster)

After a devastating natural disaster or act of terrorism, victims' concerns about personal safety and physical needs (such as food and shelter) are paramount (Vogel & Vernberg, 1993). Youth exposed to such events may also experience sudden loss and bereavement (Gurwitch et al., 2002). Psychological interventions provided during this period are *brief and present focused;* their main goal is to *reduce or prevent long-term psychological difficulties* (La Greca, 2008).

Critical Incident Stress Debriefing (CISD)

CISD was designed to relieve trauma-related distress by providing opportunities for victims to express their feelings, to understand that their responses are normal reactions to trauma, and to learn about common disaster reactions in a supportive context (Chemtob, Tomas, Law, & Cremniter, 1997). Mental health workers and disaster responders typically deliver CISD in field settings, such as community shelters.

There is currently no empirical support for CISD's effectiveness (Gibson, 2006; Rose, Bisson, & Wessely, 2003). In the only controlled study of youth that we are aware of, Stallard et al. (2006) compared a single session of CISD to a single-session "neutral discussion" control condition with 158 youth (7–18 years) who survived motor vehicle accidents. Significant improvements in PTS levels and reduction in anxiety and depression symptoms were evident in both the CISD and the control condition. Because both conditions produced improvement, it appears premature to recommend CISD. In addition, although Stallard et al reported no inadvertent negative effects from the intervention, concerns about using CISD include the possibility that recipients may be "retraumatized";

that the intervention may be insufficient to address the multiple, complex stressors resulting from disasters and terrorism; and that it may reduce further help-seeking behaviors because individuals may believe they have received sufficient care (La Greca, 2008; Ruzek et al., 2007).

Psychological First Aid (PFA)

PFA, which can be implemented in field settings such as schools and community crisis centers (Amaya-Jackson & March, 1995), was developed by disaster mental health experts from the National Child Traumatic Stress Network. It is an "evidence-informed" approach that is culturally informed and appropriate for developmental levels across the life span and can be flexibly delivered (Brymer et al., 2008; Vernberg et al., 2008).

PFA's key elements include promoting a sense of safety, "calming," self and community efficacy, connectedness, and hope (Brymer et al., 2008). It provides children with an opportunity to express their feelings through drawings and storytelling, to clarify areas of confusion, and to identify areas of need (Amaya-Jackson & March, 1995). PFA also allows mental health professionals and disaster responders to identify youth who are experiencing severe postdisaster reactions so that these youth may receive further assistance.

PFA appears promising as part of a comprehensive, post-disaster intervention strategy. However, controlled evaluations of PFA are scant (Brymer et al., 2008; Ruzek et al., 2007), probably because of the challenges of conducting postdisaster treatment research. Further, PFA requires trained personnel to administer, and many disaster and terrorism youth victims may not be present in the field settings, such as shelters, where PFA typically is delivered (La Greca, 2008).

Psychoeducational Materials

Relief (such as the American Red Cross and the Federal Emergency Management Agency) and mental health organizations (including the American Psychological Association, National Institute of Mental Health [NIMH], and the American Academy of Child and Adolescent Psychiatry) have developed psychoeducational brochures and fact sheets that provide useful information about children's coping; children's fears, worries, and security concerns; and how to encourage children to resume roles and routines following disasters (Prinstein, La Greca, Vernberg, & Silverman, 1996). Similar to CISD and PFA, however, no evidence is available on these materials' effectiveness, and some sophistication may be needed to adapt the materials to the specific disaster or event. Further, however, useful psychoeducational information alone is unlikely to be sufficient to alleviate severe PTS reactions in youth.

Summary

At present, there is no evidence that psychological interventions delivered in the immediate aftermath of disasters and terrorist events are effective for reducing short or long-term distress (Gibson, 2006; La Greca, 2008). Although PFA and well-designed psychoeducational materials are promising for certain purposes, we still need controlled evaluations of these materials. Moreover, it is unclear whether interventions should be implemented directly with children (as are PFA or CISD) or whether it would be more beneficial to target parents, teachers, or school counselors, who in turn can help children. The latter strategy may be more practical for reaching a large number of youth affected by disasters. On the other

hand, "early detection" for further referral and treatment of youth with severe, acute responses might be as beneficial as universal interventions. We need further investigation of whether and how to deliver services in the aftermath of disasters.

Undoubtedly, the lack of evidence about the effectiveness of postdisaster interventions is directly related to the numerous challenges of conducting controlled research in the aftermath of disasters or terrorist events (such as ethical concerns regarding withholding treatment and difficulties obtaining Institutional Review Board [IRB] approval or funding). Interested readers should review *Methods for Disaster Mental Health Research* (Norris, Galea, Friedman, & Watson, 2006) and consult the Research Education in Disaster Mental Health [REDMH] Website (http://www.redmh.org).

Until then, however, our "best practices" suggestions for this phase would be for caring adults (parents, teachers, and health professionals) to reassure children; to encourage (but not press) them to express their feelings; to provide information and "normalize" disaster reactions; to address their fears, worries, and security concerns as they arise; and to help them resume normal roles and routines. It is also important to help parents and teachers identify acute stress responses.

Short-Term Recovery Phase (First Few Weeks Postdisaster through the 1st Year)

Although most youth will recover during this period, as many as one third report severe or very severe levels of PTS reactions 3 months postdisaster, about 18% report severe or very severe levels 7 months postdisaster, and about 13% report such levels close to 1 year after the disaster event (e.g., La Greca et al., 1996). This highlights the need to expend efforts to reduce or prevent long-term youth psychological difficulties and promote positive adaptation. "High-risk" youth or those with high PTS reactions may require intensive psychological interventions.

To date, no controlled outcome studies are available for the interventions developed for this short-term recovery phase. These interventions typically provide psychoeducation, often in combination with cognitive behavioral therapy (CBT). In one of the few studies, Wolmer, Laor, Dedeoglu, Siev, and Yazgan (2005) conducted a classroom-based "School Reactivation Program" 4–5 months after a major 1999 earthquake in Turkey. In the program, which was led by teachers over a 4-week period, in eight 2-hr meetings ($N = 202$; 9–17 years), PTSD rates were reduced from 32% to 17% among treated youth. At 3-year follow-up, 33% of the treated youth were compared to 220 untreated control youth who reported similar levels of PTS symptoms and disaster exposure. Although PTS symptoms in both groups declined, almost 50% in both groups reported moderate to severe levels of PTS symptoms. More positively, however, teacher ratings of youth adaptive functioning were higher for treated than for untreated youth.

Several "empirically informed" psychoeducational manuals were developed to help youth cope with large-scale disasters, including *The Bushfire and Me: A Story of What Happened to Me and My Family* (Storm, McDermott, & Finlayson, 1994), *Helping Children Prepare for and Cope With Natural Disasters* (La Greca, Vernberg, Silverman, Vogel, & Prinstein, 1994), *After the Storm* (La Greca, Sevin, & Sevin, 2005), and *StArT: Strength*

After Trauma (Saltzman, 2007). Manuals focusing on coping with terrorism include *Healing After Trauma Skills* (Gurwitch & Messenbaugh, 1998) and *Helping America Cope: A Guide to Help Parents and Children Cope With the September 11th Terrorist Attacks* (La Greca, Sevin, & Sevin, 2001). Several intervention manuals, each focusing on specific youth symptom clusters (including PTS), were also developed after the September 11th attacks for "Project Liberty."

Overall, these "evidence-informed" manuals cover strategies for helping children and adolescents "process" the traumatic events in a supportive manner, developing effective coping strategies for dealing with feelings of distress and with ongoing stressors that result from the trauma, maintaining regular roles and routines, increasing social support, and preparing for future events. The manuals also contain "lessons" that teachers, parents, and mental health providers can use with children and provide information to help identify children with severe reactions. The Project Liberty PTSD manuals also provide information on developing trauma-focused narratives and prescribing graded in vivo or imaginal exposure tasks to therapeutically reactivate youth's traumatic disaster memories.

Many of the above materials require Internet connections (for downloads) or substantial funding to print the large number of copies needed after major disasters. The manuals typically require an eighth-grade reading level and may need adaptation to fit new disasters or to be used effectively by different adults (such as parent vs. teacher vs. counselor). Ongoing, open trial investigations for several of the manuals are assessing feasibility, counselor adherence, and preliminary evidence for effectiveness. Such efforts may set the stage for future randomized controlled trials.

Long-Term Recovery Phase (1 Year or More Postdisaster)

Most children recover within 1 year or more of devastating, traumatic events. However, a significant minority experience persistent, chronic stress reactions (Gurwitch et al., 2002; La Greca & Prinstein, 2002; Yule et al., 2002), which may be complicated by secondary stressors (including relocation and loss of family members). Current interventions typically target persistent or chronic youth PTSD reactions.

Cognitive-Behavioral Therapy

Exposure-based CBT is thought to promote habituation by targeting stimulus-response associations and correcting distorted cognitions (see Foa & Rothbaum, 1998), although determining exactly how this works requires further empirical verification. Prolonged exposure involves psychoeducation, breathing retraining, imaginal exposure to the trauma memory, and in vivo exposure to trauma reminders. Despite the scarcity of disaster-related studies, well-controlled studies with sexual abuse victims provide relatively strong evidence that CBT may reduce PTS in youth (e.g., Cohen, Deblinger, Mannarino, & Steer, 2004; Cohen, Mannarino, & Knudsen, 2005; Deblinger, Stauffer, & Steer, 2001), although follow-up data have been reported in only a few studies (e.g., Deblinger, Mannarino, Cohen, & Steer, 2006). A positive feature of this literature is that most of these studies have compared CBT to an active credible control comparison condition (such as client-centered therapy). Importantly, reductions in youth PTS (as well

as in depression and externalizing problem behaviors) have been significantly greater for CBT than for other comparison control conditions.

In the absence of any alternative intervention with supportive empirical evidence for traumatized youth, we recommend that CBT be used with children and adolescents traumatized by disasters and terrorism. Below, we summarize the open trials researchers have conducted in this area.

Multimodality Trauma Treatment

March, Amaya-Jackson, Murray, and Schulte (1998) evaluated an 18-week exposure-based CBT with 17 youth (10–15 years of age; average duration of PTSD was 1.5–2.5 years) who displayed PTSD after a single-stressor trauma (such as car accidents or shootings), including disasters (severe storms and fires). Multimodality trauma treatment focused on (a) habituating conditioned anxiety through narrative exposures, (b) modifying maladaptive trauma-related cognitions through positive self-talk and cognitive restructuring, (c) teaching adaptive coping strategies for disturbing feelings and physiological reactions, and (d) reducing co-occurring symptoms through problem-solving and self-management strategies. Several sessions included imaginal exposures, and in vivo exposures were assigned out of session.

March et al. (1998) used a single-case multiple-baseline design, and their findings revealed significant improvements in clinician-rated PTSD, which were maintained at 6-month follow-up. They also observed improvements in child ratings of depression, anxiety, and anger. Of the 14 treatment completers, 8 (57%) no longer met PTSD criteria at posttreatment and 12 (86%) no longer met criteria at 6-month follow-up. These findings provide initial evidence for the effectiveness of exposure-based CBT, although further randomized controlled studies using larger samples of children are needed.

Brief Trauma-/Grief-Focused Psychotherapy

Goenjian et al. (1997) evaluated a school-based brief trauma-/grief-focused intervention that contained treatment components similar to exposure-based CBT with 64 adolescents (median age = 13.2 years) who experienced a devastating earthquake in Armenia and displayed high levels of PTS and depressive reactions 1.5 years later. Because of limited resources, schools and students were not randomly assigned; 35 youth participated in the treatment and 29 were not treated. The intervention included two individual and four classroom sessions over 3 weeks that addressed reconstructing and reprocessing traumatic experiences and associated thoughts and feelings, identifying trauma reminders and cues and improving tolerance for and reactivity to these reminders and cues, enhancing social support-seeking behaviors, enhancing coping strategies, dealing with grief and bereavement, and identifying missed developmental opportunities and promoting positive development.

Treated adolescents had significantly lower rates of PTSD (28%) than untreated adolescents (69%) at 18 months posttreatment (i.e., 3 years postearthquake). Estimated rates of depression symptoms did not change from pretreatment (46%) to follow-up (46%) for the treated adolescents but increased significantly (from 35% to 75%) for the untreated adolescents. In a second follow-up, 5 years postdisaster (Goenjian et al., 2005), reductions in youth PTS symptoms were 3 times greater for the treated group than for the untreated comparison group. Untreated adolescents also showed significant increases in depression. This nonrandomized trial suggests the importance of intervening with youth in the aftermath of natural disasters because PTS symptoms did not necessarily remit spontaneously.

School-Based Psychosocial Interventions

Chemtob, Nakashima, and Hamada (2002) screened children enrolled in all of the public elementary schools in Kauai, HI (Grades 2–6; $n = 3,864$) for high levels of PTS symptoms 2 years after Hurricane Iniki. The 248 children (6.4%) with high PTSD scores (above the 94th percentile) were randomly assigned to consecutively treated cohorts (i.e., children (6.4%) with high PTSD scores (above the 94th percentile) were randomly assigned to consecutively treated cohorts (i.e., children awaiting treatment served as wait-list controls). Within each cohort, children were randomly assigned to individual or group treatment. Four weekly sessions focused on helping children (a) restore a sense of safety, (b) grieve losses and renew attachments, (c) express disaster-related anger, and (d) achieve closure about the disaster. Treated children reported significant reductions in PTS symptoms and maintained these reductions at 12-month follow-up. Although the group and individual treatment approaches did not differ significantly, more children completed group treatment (95%) than individual treatment (85%).

This study is important because it demonstrates the feasibility of screening a large population of disaster-affected children 2 years postdisaster, as well as the feasibility and efficacy of a brief school-based psychosocial intervention. Future studies would benefit from incorporating measures of clinically significant change and evaluating potential moderators of treatment outcome (Kazdin, 2002).

Eye Movement Desensitization Processing (EMDR)

EMDR aims to reduce distress associated with traumatic memories by engaging clients' attention to an external stimulus (such as by tracking a therapist's finger movements back and forth with one's eye movements) while clients are concurrently focusing on the distressing memories (i.e., engaged in imaginal exposures; Shapiro, 1989). Eye movements are most often used as the external stimulus to which clients are asked to attend, but other stimuli such as hand tapping and auditory stimulation can also be used (Shapiro, 1989). Chemtob, Nakashima, and Carlson (2002) reported the results of EMDR among 32 children (median age = 8.4 years) who were nonresponders at 1-year follow-up of a prior intervention for disaster-related PTS. Using an ABA design plus follow-up, Group 1 was assessed at pretreatment, provided treatment (three weekly sessions), and reassessed at posttreatment. Group 2 consisted of wait-listed children who were assessed at baseline; then, following treatment for Group 1, they were reassessed at pretreatment, provided treatment, and assessed at posttreatment. Both groups were assessed 6 months posttreatment. EMDR involved the identification of distressing memories and images, cognitive restructuring, and inducing sets of eye movements by having the child track the therapist's hand movements back and forth while concentrating on the traumatic memories and images.

On child-rated symptoms of PTS, anxiety, and depression, both the immediate and the delayed treatment groups showed significant declines from pre- to posttreatment that were maintained at 6-month follow-up. Although the study demonstrated positive effects, the design did not include an active comparison control condition. Moreover, because EMDR contains many of the same components as exposure-based CBT, it is possible that CBT elements, rather than eye movements, contributed to the positive effects.

Predisaster Preventive Interventions

Because it is difficult to conduct controlled investigations after unexpected disasters or terrorist attacks, efforts are under way to examine ways of screening children *even before a disaster strikes* to identify those who may be vulnerable to experiencing severe reactions and to develop predisaster "resilience" programs. Along with Claudio Ortiz, and with support from the Terrorism and Disaster Branch of the National Center for Child Traumatic Stress (led by Dr. Pfefferbaum), we have developed and gathered preliminary data on a "Resilience Building Screen" designed to identify children who are at risk for showing impairing, negative reactions to the cues, and signals of disasters prior to personal experience with a hurricane or natural disaster (Silverman, La Greca, & Ortiz, 2004).

The Screen is based on empirical research showing that the most consistent predictors of enduring PTS reactions to hurricanes are (a) aspects of traumatic exposure, (b) lack of a social support network, and (c) psychopathology before the traumatic event (e.g., La Greca, Silverman, & Wasserstein, 1998; Lengua et al., 2005; Weems et al., 2007; for a review, see Silverman & La Greca, 2002). Other predictors, less consistently found in the literature, include children's coping strategies and parental reactions. Items for the Screen map onto each of these predictors or variables. Analyses for this project are ongoing; our primary objective is to develop a screening measure to identify children who might benefit from a predisaster "Resilience Building Training" program. Such a program would focus on targeting and enhancing those variables the Screen shows to be deficient (such as children's coping strategies) so that youth might be better prepared for a disaster. On a related note, we are revising *After the Storm* (La Greca et al., 2005) to help youth in the aftermath of hurricanes; a *Before the Storm* version will include lessons on preparing for storms and coping with hurricane-related stressors (e.g., disruption of normal routines). This program could then be implemented in hurricane-prone areas, and its effectiveness evaluated when a disaster or near-disaster strikes.

Conclusions

Remarkably, few evidence-based interventions are available for children and adolescents exposed to natural disasters and acts of terrorism. The few well-controlled studies have focused on children with persistent PTSD, occurring a year or more after the disaster or event and suggest that exposure-based CBT interventions are promising. We know considerably less about interventions designed for the immediate aftermath of a disaster or during the short-term recovery phase. Until further studies have been conducted, mental health professionals are advised to draw on "evidence-informed" psychoeducational materials and CBT procedures for helping children and adolescents cope with the aftermath of disasters and acts of terrorism.

Although the limited amount of evidence on interventions for children following disasters and acts of terrorism is disheartening, this reflects the challenges of conducting controlled outcome research following such events, especially in their immediate aftermath (La Greca, 2006; La Greca, Silverman, Vernberg, & Roberts, 2002). These challenges include numerous ethical and practical constraints, including ethical concerns regarding withholding treatment and difficulties obtaining IRB approval or funding. Schools, for example, are often in chaos after destructive communitywide disasters and have more pressing priorities than conducting research (La Greca, 2006). Moreover, significant adults in children's lives also are affected by the disaster and may be unaware of children's distress. Nevertheless, continued research is important, and we recommend that interested readers review *Methods for Disaster Mental Health Research* (Norris et al., 2006) and consult the REDMH Web site: http://www.redmh.org.

We emphasize that children and adolescents exposed to disasters and acts of terrorism are likely to need *more than* interventions that focus exclusively on PTSD reactions because their reactions are often complex and multifaceted and may include other problems (such as grief, depression, and anxiety). Additional intervention components (dealing with grief and bereavement, handling anger, and promoting coping) are likely to be important adjuncts to PTSD-oriented interventions. Although further evidence is needed, children and adolescents with complex disaster reactions might profit from CBT treatments that focus on comorbid psychological reactions, in addition to PTSD reactions.

References

Amaya-Jackson, L., & March, J. S. (1995). Posttraumatic stress disorder. In J. S. March (Ed.), *Anxiety disorders in children and adolescents* (pp. 276–300). New York: Guilford.

American Academy of Child and Adolescent Psychiatry. (1998). Practice parameters for the assessment and treatment of children and adolescents with posttraumatic stress disorder. *Journal of the American Academy of Child and Adolescent Psychiatry, 37*(Suppl.), 4S–26S.

Brymer, M. J., Steinberg, A. M., Vernberg, E. M., Layne, C. M., Watson, P. J., Jacobs, A. K., et al. (2008). Acute interventions for children and adolescents exposed to trauma. In E. Foa, T. Keane, M. Friedman, & J. A. Cohen (Eds.), *Effective treatments for PTSD* (2nd ed., pp. 106–116). New York: Guilford.

Chemtob, C. M., Nakashima, J., & Carlson, J. G. (2002). Brief treatment for elementary school children with disaster-related posttraumatic stress disorder: A field study. *Journal of Clinical Psychology, 58,* 99–112.

Chemtob, C. M., Nakashima, J. P., & Hamada, R. S. (2002). Psychosocial intervention for postdisaster trauma symptoms in elementary school children: A controlled community field study. *Archives of Pediatric and Adolescent Medicine, 156,* 211–216.

Chemtob, C. M., Tomas, S., Law, W., & Cremniter, D. (1997). Postdisaster psychosocial intervention: A field study of the impact of debriefing on psychological distress. *American Journal of Psychiatry, 154,* 415–417.

Cohen, J. A., Deblinger, E., Mannarino, A. P., & Steer, R. A. (2004). A multisite randomized controlled study of sexually abused, multiply traumatized children with PTSD: Initial treatment outcome. *Journal of the American Academy of Child and Adolescent Psychiatry, 43,* 393–402.

Cohen, J. A., Mannarino, A. P., & Knudsen, K. (2005). Treating sexually abused children: 1 year follow-up of a randomized controlled trial. *Child Abuse and Neglect, 29,* 135–145.

Comer, J. S., & Kendall, P. C. (2007). Terrorism: The psychological impact on youth. *Clinical Psychology: Science and Practice, 14,* 179–214.

Deblinger, E., Mannarino, A. P., Cohen, J. A., & Steer, R. A. (2006). A follow-up study of a multisite, randomized, controlled trial for children with sexual abuse-related PTSD symptoms. *Journal of the American Academy of Child and Adolescent Psychiatry, 45,* 1474–1484.

Deblinger, E., Stauffer, L., & Steer, R. (2001). Comparative efficacies of supportive and cognitive behavioral group therapies for young children who have been sexually abused and their nonoffending mothers. *Child Maltreatment, 6,* 332–343.

Foa, E. B., & Rothbaum, B. O. (1998). *Treating the trauma of rape: Cognitive-behavioral therapy for PTSD.* New York: Guilford.

Gibson, L. E. (2006). *A review of the published empirical literature regarding early- and later-stage interventions for individuals exposed to traumatic stress.* Research Education Disaster Mental Health. Retrieved September 10, 2007, from http://redmh.org/research/general/treatm.html

Goenjian, A. K., Karayan, I., Pynoos, R. S., Minassian, D., Najarian, L. M., Steinberg, A. M., et al. (1997). Outcome of psychotherapy among early adolescents after trauma. *American Journal of Psychiatry, 154,* 536–542.

Goenjian, A. K., Walling, D., Steinberg, A. M., Karayan, I., Najarian, L. M., & Pynoos, R. (2005). A prospective study of posttraumatic stress and depressive reactions among treated and untreated adolescents 5 years after a catastrophic disaster. *American Journal of Psychiatry, 162,* 2302–2308.

Gurwitch, R. H., & Messenbaugh, A. K. (1998). *Healing after trauma: Skills manual for helping children.* Oklahoma City, OK: Author.

Gurwitch, R. H., Sitterle, K. A., Young, B. H., & Pfefferbaum, B. (2002). The aftermath of terrorism. In A. M. La Greca, W. K. Silverman, E. M. Vernberg, & M. C. Roberts (Eds.), *Helping children cope with disasters and terrorism* (pp. 327–358). Washington, DC: American Psychological Association.

Hoven, C. W., Duarte, C. S., Lucas, C. P., Wu, P., Mandell, D. J., Goodwin, R. D., et al. (2005). Psychopathology among New York City public school children 6 months after September 11. *Archives of General Psychiatry, 62,* 545–552.

Kazdin, A. (2002). A school based psychosocial intervention was effective in children with persistent post-disaster trauma symptoms. *Evidence Based Mental Health, 5,* 76.

La Greca, A. M. (2006). School-based studies of children following disasters. In F. Norris, S. Galesto, D. Reissman, & P. Watson (Eds.), *Methods for disaster mental health research* (pp. 141–157). New York: Guilford.

La Greca, A. M. (2008). Interventions for posttraumatic stress in children and adolescents following natural disasters and acts of terrorism. In M. C. Roberts, D. Elkin, & R. Steele (Eds.), *Handbook of evidence based therapies for children and adolescents* (pp. 137–157). New York: Springer.

La Greca, A. M., & Prinstein, M. J. (2002). Hurricanes and tornadoes. In A. M. La Greca, W. K. Silverman, E. M. Vernberg, & M. C. Roberts (Eds.), *Helping children cope with disasters and terrorism* (pp. 107–138). Washington, DC: American Psychological Association.

La Greca, A. M., Sevin, S., & Sevin, E. (2001). *Helping America cope: A guide for parents and children in the aftermath of the September 11th national disaster.* Miami, FL: Sevendippity. Retrieved September 24, 2007, from http://www.7-dippity.com/index.html

La Greca, A. M., Sevin, S., & Sevin, E. (2005). *After the storm.* Miami, FL: Sevendippity. Retrieved September 24, 2007, from http://www.7-dippity.com/index.html

La Greca, A. M., Silverman, W. K., Vernberg, E. M., & Prinstein, M. (1996). Symptoms of posttraumatic stress after Hurricane Andrew: A prospective study. *Journal of Consulting and Clinical Psychology, 64,* 712–723.

La Greca, A. M., Silverman, W. K., Vernberg, E. M., & Roberts, M. C. (2002). Children and disasters: Future directions for research and public policy. In A. M. La Greca, W. K. Silverman, E. M. Vernberg, & M. C. Roberts (Eds.), *Helping children cope with disasters and terrorism* (pp. 405–423). Washington, DC: American Psychological Association.

La Greca, A. M., Silverman, W. K., & Wasserstein, S. B. (1998). Children's predisaster functioning as a predictor of posttraumatic stress following Hurricane Andrew. *Journal of Consulting and Clinical Psychology, 66,* 883–892.

La Greca, A. M., Vernberg, E. M., Silverman, W. K., Vogel, A., & Prinstein, M. (1994). *Helping children cope with natural disasters: A manual for school personnel.* Miami, FL: Author.

Lengua, L. J., Long, A. C., Smith, K. I., & Meltzoff, A. N. (2005). Preattack symptomatology and temperament as predictors of children's responses to the September 11th terrorist attacks. *Journal of Child Psychology and Psychiatry, 46,* 631–645.

March, J. S., Amaya-Jackson, L., Murray, M. C., & Schulte, A. (1998). Cognitive-behavioral psychotherapy for children and adolescents with posttraumatic stress disorder after a single-incident stressor. *Journal of the American Academy of Child and Adolescent Psychiatry, 37,* 585–593.

Norris, F. H., Galea, S., Friedman, M. J., & Watson, P. J. (Eds.). (2006). *Methods for disaster mental health research.* New York: Guilford.

Prinstein, M. J., La Greca, A. M., Vernberg, E. M., & Silverman, W. K. (1996). Children's coping assistance after a natural disaster. *Journal of Clinical Child Psychology, 25,* 463–475.

Rose, S., Bisson, J., & Wessely, S. (2003). A systematic review of single-session psychological interventions ("debriefing") following trauma. *Psychotherapy and Psychosomatics, 72,* 176–184.

Ruzek, J. I., Brymer, M. J., Jacobs, A. K., Layne, C. M., Vernberg, E. M., & Watson, P. J. (2007). Psychological first aid. *Journal of Mental Health Counseling, 29,* 17–49.

Saltzman, W. (2007). *StArT: Strength after trauma: A modular intervention for children and adolescents affected by hurricanes.* Los Angeles: Author.

Shapiro, F. (1989). Eye movement desensitization: A new treatment for post-traumatic stress disorder. *Journal of Behavior Therapy and Experimental Psychiatry, 20,* 211–217.

Silverman, W. K., & La Greca, A. M. (2002). Children experiencing disasters: Definitions, reactions, and predictors of outcomes. In A. M. La Greca, W. K. Silverman, E. M. Vernberg, & M. C. Roberts (Eds.), *Helping children cope with disasters and terrorism* (pp. 11–34). Washington, DC: American Psychological Association.

Silverman, W. K., La Greca, A. M., & Ortiz C.D. (2004, July). Resilience building in children prior to traumatic exposure: Screening considerations. In R. H. Gurwitch (Chair), *Trauma risk factors and resilience: Making connections.* Symposium presented at the annual meeting of the American Psychological Association, Honolulu, HI.

Stallard, P., Velleman, R., Salter, E., Howse, I., Yule, W., & Taylor, G. (2006). A randomised controlled trial to determine the effectiveness of an early psychological intervention with children involved in road traffic accidents. *Journal of Child Psychology and Psychiatry, 47,* 127–134.

Storm, V., McDermott, B., & Finlayson, D. (1994). *The bushfire and me: A story of what happened to me and my family.* Newtown, Australia: VBD Publications.

Vernberg, E. M. (2002). Intervention approaches following disasters. In A. M. La Greca, W. K. Silverman, E. M. Vernberg, & M. C. Roberts (Eds.), *Helping children cope with disasters and terrorism* (pp. 55–72). Washington, DC: American Psychological Association.

Vernberg, E. M., Steinberg, A. M., Jacobs, A. K., Brymer, M. J., Watson, P. J., Osofsky, J. D., et al. (2008). Innovations in disaster mental health: Psychological first aid. *Professional Psychology: Research and Practice, 39,* 381–388.

Vogel, J., & Vernberg, E. M. (1993). Children's psychological responses to disaster. *Journal of Clinical Child Psychology, 22,* 464–484.

Weems, C., Pina, A. A., Costa, N. M., Watts, S. E., Taylor, L. K., & Cannon, M. F. (2007). Predisaster trait anxiety and negative affect predict posttraumatic stress in youths after Hurricane Katrina. *Journal of Consulting and Clinical Psychology, 75,* 154–159.

Wolmer, L., Laor, N., Dedeoglu, C., Siev, J., & Yazgan, Y. (2005). Teacher mediated intervention after disaster: A controlled three-year follow-up of children's functioning. *Journal of Child Psychology and Psychiatry, 46,* 1161–1168.

Yule, W., Udwin, O., & Bolton, D. (2002). Mass transportation disasters. In A. M. La Greca, W. K. Silverman, E. M. Vernberg, & M. C. Roberts (Eds.), *Helping children cope with disasters and terrorism* (pp. 223–240). Washington, DC: American Psychological Association.

Correspondence concerning this article should be addressed to **ANNETTE M. LA GRECA**, Department of Psychology, University of Miami, PO Box 249229, Coral Gables, FL 33124; e-mail: alagreca@miami.edu.

Test-Your-Knowledge Form

We encourage you to photocopy and use this page as a tool to assess how the articles in *Annual Editions* expand on the information in your textbook. By reflecting on the articles you will gain enhanced text information. You can also access this useful form on a product's book support website at *http://www.mhcls.com*.

NAME: DATE:

_____

TITLE AND NUMBER OF ARTICLE:

_____

BRIEFLY STATE THE MAIN IDEA OF THIS ARTICLE:

_____

LIST THREE IMPORTANT FACTS THAT THE AUTHOR USES TO SUPPORT THE MAIN IDEA:

_____

WHAT INFORMATION OR IDEAS DISCUSSED IN THIS ARTICLE ARE ALSO DISCUSSED IN YOUR TEXTBOOK OR OTHER READINGS THAT YOU HAVE DONE? LIST THE TEXTBOOK CHAPTERS AND PAGE NUMBERS:

_____

LIST ANY EXAMPLES OF BIAS OR FAULTY REASONING THAT YOU FOUND IN THE ARTICLE:

_____

LIST ANY NEW TERMS/CONCEPTS THAT WERE DISCUSSED IN THE ARTICLE, AND WRITE A SHORT DEFINITION:

We Want Your Advice

ANNUAL EDITIONS revisions depend on two major opinion sources: one is our Advisory Board, listed in the front of this volume, which works with us in scanning the thousands of articles published in the public press each year; the other is you—the person actually using the book. Please help us and the users of the next edition by completing the prepaid article rating form on this page and returning it to us. Thank you for your help!

ANNUAL EDITIONS: Child Growth and Development 10/11

ARTICLE RATING FORM

Here is an opportunity for you to have direct input into the next revision of this volume.
We would like you to rate each of the articles listed below, using the following scale:

1. **Excellent: should definitely be retained**
2. **Above average: should probably be retained**
3. **Below average: should probably be deleted**
4. **Poor: should definitely be deleted**

Your ratings will play a vital part in the next revision.
Please mail this prepaid form to us as soon as possible.
Thanks for your help!

RATING	ARTICLE	RATING	ARTICLE
	1. New Calculator Factors Chances for Very Premature Infants		19. The Role of Neurobiological Deficits in Childhood Antisocial Behavior
	2. Success at Last		20. Children of Lesbian and Gay Parents
	3. Infants' Differential Processing of Female and Male Faces		21. Evidence of Infants' Internal Working Models of Attachment
	4. The Other-Race Effect Develops during Infancy		22. Children of Alcoholics
	5. New Advances in Understanding Sensitive Periods in Brain Development		23. Within-Family Differences in Parent–Child Relations across the Life Course
	6. Contributions of Neuroscience to Our Understanding of Cognitive Development		24. Adoption Is a Successful Natural Intervention Enhancing Adopted Children's IQ and School Performance
	7. It's Fun, but Does It Make You Smarter?		25. The Case against Breast-Feeding
	8. Language and Children's Understanding of Mental States		26. Goodbye to Girlhood
	9. Children's Biased Evaluations of Lucky versus Unlucky People and Their Social Groups		27. Trials for Parents Who Chose Faith Over Medicine
	10. Future Thinking in Young Children		28. How Many Fathers Are Best for a Child
	11. When Should a Kid Start Kindergarten?		29. Childhood for Sale
	12. A Neurobiological Perspective on Early Human Deprivation		30. Childhood's End
	13. Children's Capacity to Develop Resiliency		31. How to Win the Weight Battle
	14. Emotions and the Development of Childhood Depression: Bridging the Gap		32. The Epidemic That Wasn't
	15. Children's Social and Moral Reasoning about Exclusion		33. Three Reasons Not to Believe in an Autism Epidemic
	16. A Profile of Bullying at School		34. Getting Back to the Great Outdoors
	17. When Girls and Boys Play: What Research Tells Us		35. What Causes Specific Language Impairment in Children?
	18. Girls Just Want to Be Mean		36. Treatment and Prevention of Posttraumatic Stress Reactions in Children and Adolescents Exposed to Disasters and Terrorism: What Is the Evidence?

BUSINESS REPLY MAIL
FIRST CLASS MAIL PERMIT NO. 551 DUBUQUE IA

POSTAGE WILL BE PAID BY ADDRESSEE

McGraw-Hill Contemporary Learning Series
501 BELL STREET
DUBUQUE, IA 52001

ABOUT YOU

Name

Date

Are you a teacher? ❏ A student? ❏
Your school's name

Department

Address

City

State

Zip

School telephone #

YOUR COMMENTS ARE IMPORTANT TO US!

Please fill in the following information:
For which course did you use this book?

Did you use a text with this ANNUAL EDITION? ❏ yes ❏ no
What was the title of the text?

What are your general reactions to the Annual Editions concept?

Have you read any pertinent articles recently that you think should be included in the next edition? Explain.

Are there any articles that you feel should be replaced in the next edition? Why?

Are there any World Wide Websites that you feel should be included in the next edition? Please annotate.

May we contact you for editorial input? ❏ yes ❏ no
May we quote your comments? ❏ yes ❏ no